T0236779

Lecture Notes in Artificial Intelligence 10333

Subseries of Lecture Notes in Computer Science

More information about this series at http://www.springer.com/series/1244

Henning Christiansen · Hélène Jaudoin
Panagiotis Chountas · Troels Andreasen
Henrik Legind Larsen (Eds.)

Flexible Query Answering Systems

12th International Conference, FQAS 2017
London, UK, June 21–22, 2017
Proceedings

Springer

Editors
Henning Christiansen
Roskilde University
Roskilde
Denmark

Troels Andreasen
Roskilde University
Roskilde
Denmark

Hélène Jaudoin
ENSSAT-IRISA
Lannion Cedex
France

Henrik Legind Larsen
Aalborg University
Esbjerg
Denmark

Panagiotis Chountas
University of Westminster
London
UK

ISSN 0302-9743 ISSN 1611-3349 (electronic)
Lecture Notes in Artificial Intelligence
ISBN 978-3-319-59691-4 ISBN 978-3-319-59692-1 (eBook)
DOI 10.1007/978-3-319-59692-1

Library of Congress Control Number: 2017942986

LNCS Sublibrary: SL7 – Artificial Intelligence

Printed on acid-free paper

This Springer imprint is published by Springer Nature
The registered company is Springer International Publishing AG
The registered company address is: Gewerbestrasse 11, 6330 Cham, Switzerland

Preface

This volume contains the papers presented at FQAS 2017, the 12th International Conference on Flexible Query Answering Systems held during June 21–22, 2017, at University of Westminster, London, UK.

FQAS was organized for the first time in Roskilde, Denmark, in 1994, and has been running since then roughly as a biennial conference, four times in Roskilde; in Warsaw, Poland; Copenhagen, Denmark; Lyon, France; Milan, Italy; Ghent, Belgium; Granada, Spain; and Krakow, Poland. It has developed into the premier conference concerned with the very important issue of providing users of information systems with flexible querying capabilities and with an easy and intuitive access to information. More specifically, the overall theme of the FQAS conferences is the modelling and design of innovative and flexible modalities for accessing information systems. The main objective is to achieve more expressive, informative, cooperative, and productive systems that facilitate retrieval from information repositories such as databases, libraries, heterogeneous archives, and the Web. With these aims, FQAS is a multidisciplinary conference drawing on several research areas, including information retrieval, database management, information filtering, knowledge representation, computational linguistics and natural language processing, artificial intelligence, soft computing, classical and non-classical logics, and human-computer interaction. Papers presented over the years span from basic, foundational research, over methodological and tool-oriented considerations, to descriptions and evaluations of actual systems that represent paradigms of flexible query answering.

The 2017 conference had presentations of 25 original papers – this year a mix of full and a few short papers, ranging over a representative collection of FQAS topics. We want to express our gratitude to the members of the Program Committee and the International Advisory Board, and to everyone who contributed at any level to the organization of FQAS 2017; Krassimir T. Atanassov in particular, who organized two special sessions included in the program. Also special thanks to our invited speakers, Anne Laurent, Jens Lehmann, and Alexandra Poulovassilis, and to our publisher who kindly contributed with a prize for the best paper. We also thank every author who submitted a paper to FQAS 2017 and finally the team of EasyChair, without whose free software the handling of submissions and editing of the proceedings could not have been managed so smoothly. Last but not the least, we thank Alfred Hofmann and Anna Kramer of Springer for their continuous support.

April 2017

Henning Christiansen
Hélène Jaudoin
Panagiotis Chountas
Troels Andreasen
Henrik Legind Larsen

Organization

General Chairs

Panagiotis Chountas	University of Westminster, UK
Henning Christiansen	Roskilde University, Denmark

Program Chairs

Henning Christiansen	Roskilde University, Denmark
Hélène Jaudoin	Université de Rennes 1, IRISA, France

Publicity Chair

Thierry Chaussalet	University of Westminster, UK

Steering Committee

Troels Andreasen	Roskilde University, Denmark
Henning Christiansen	Roskilde University, Denmark
Henrik Legind Larsen	Aalborg University, Denmark

International Advisory Board

Adnan Yazici, Turkey
Amihai Motro, USA
Bruce Croft, USA
Donald Kraft, USA
Gabriella Pasi, Italy
Guy De Tré, Belgium
Henri Prade, France
Janusz Kacprzyk, Poland
Jesús Cardeñosa, Spain
Norbert Fuhr, Germany
Olivier Pivert, France
Roman Slowinski, Poland
Ronald R. Yager, USA
Slawomir Zadrozny, Poland
Zbigniew W. Raś, USA and Poland
Fred Petry, USA
Jørgen Fischer Nilsson, Denmark

Program Committee

Troels Andreasen	Roskilde University, Denmark
Krassimir Atanassov	Centre of Biomedical Engineering, Bulgarian Academy of Sciences, Bulgaria
Elena Baralis	Politecnico di Torino, Italy
Ignacio J. Blanco	University of Granada, Spain
Gloria Bordogna	National Research Council of Italy, CNR, Italy
Antoon Bronselaer	Ghent University, Belgium
Patrice Buche	INRA, France
Henrik Bulskov	Roskilde University, Denmark
Thierry Chaussalet	University of Westminster, UK
Panagiotis Chountas	University of Westminster, UK
Henning Christiansen	Roskilde University, Denmark
Fabio Crestani	University of Lugano (USI), Switzerland
Bruce Croft	University of Massachusetts Amherst, USA
Juan Carlos Cubero	University of Granada, Spain
Ernesto Damiani	University of Milan, Italy
Agnieszka Dardzinska-Glebocka	Bialystok University of Technology, Poland
Bernard De Baets	Ghent University, Belgium
Guy De Tre	Ghent University, Belgium
Didier Dubois	IRIT/RPDMP, France
Sebastien Ferre	Université de Rennes 1, France
Ana Garcia-Serrano	ETSI Informatica, UNED
Allel Hadjali	LIAS/ENSMA, France
Enrique Herrera-Viedma	University of Granada, Spain
Hélène Jaudoin	IRISA-ENSSAT, France
Janusz Kacprzyk	Systems Research Institute, Polish Academy of Sciences, Poland
Etienne Kerre	Ghent University, Belgium
Donald Kraft	Louisiana State University, USA
Rudolf Kruse	University of Magdeburg, Germany
Marzena Kryszkiewicz	Warsaw University of Technology, Poland
Anne Laurent	LIRMM, UM, France
Henrik Legind Larsen	Aalborg University, Denmark
Marie-Jeanne Lesot	LIP6, UPMC, France
Antoni Ligeza	AGH University of Science and Technology, Poland
Nicolas Marin	University of Granada, Spain
Christophe Marsala	Université Pierre et Marie Curie Paris 6, France
Trevor Martin	University of Bristol, UK
Maria J. Martin-Bautista	University of Granada, Spain
Juan Miguel Medina	University of Granada, Spain
Boughanem Mohand	IRIT, Paul Sabatier University of Toulouse, France
Amihai Motro	George Mason University, USA
Grzegorz J. Nalepa	AGH University of Science and Technology, Poland

Jørgen Fischer Nilsson	Technical University of Denmark (DTU), Denmark
Andreas Nürnberger	Otto von Guericke University of Magdeburg, Germany
Jose Angel Olivas	UCLM
Daniel Ortiz-Arroyo	Aalborg University, Denmark
Gabriella Pasi	Università degli Studi di Milano Bicocca, Italy
Fred Petry	Naval Research Lab, USA
Olivier Pivert	IRISA-ENSSAT, France
Olga Pons	University of Granada, Spain
Henri Prade	IRIT, CNRS, France
Giuseppe Psaila	University of Bergamo, Italy
Zbigniew Ras	University of North Carolina, USA
Guillaume Raschia	LINA, University of Nantes, France
Marek Reformat	University of Alberta, USA
Francisco P. Romero	Universidad de Castilla-La Mancha, Spain
Miguel-Angel Sicilia	University of Alcala, Spain
Andrzej Skowron	Warsaw University, Poland
Dominik Slezak	University of Warsaw and Infobright, Poland
Grégory Smits	IRISA/University of Rennes 1, France
Umberto Straccia	ISTI-CNR, Italy
Eulalia Szmidt	Systems Research Institute, Polish Academy of Sciences, Poland
Farouk Toumani	Limos, Blaise Pascal University, Clermont-Ferrand, France
Maria-Amparo Vila	University of Granada, Spain
Adnan Yazici	Middle East Technical University, Turkey
Slawomir Zadrozny	Systems Research Institute, Polish Academy of Sciences, Poland
Wlodek Zadrozny	UNCC
Shuigeng Zhou	Fudan University, China
Krzysztof Zielinski	AGH-UST, Poland

Additional Reviewers

Fatiha Boubekeur
Veselina Bureva
Christoph Doell
Krystian Jobczyk
Chiraz Latiri
Mohsen Mesgarpour
Olympia Roeva
Jose Manuel Soto Hidalgo
Peter Vassilev
Sotir Sotirov

Contents

Knowledge Discovery and Information/Data Retrieval

Intuitionistic Sets

Generalized Net Model

Foundations of Flexible Querying

Abductive Question-Answer System (AQAS) for Classical Propositional Logic

Szymon Chlebowski(✉) and Andrzej Gajda

Department of Logic and Cognitive Science, Institute of Psychology, Adam Mickiewicz University in Poznań, Poznań, Poland
szymon.chlebowski@amu.edu.pl

Abstract. We propose a new approach to modelling abductive reasoning by means of an abductive question-answer system. We introduce the concept of an abductive question which is the starting point of abductive reasoning. The result of applying the question processing procedure is a question, which is simpler than the initial one. AQAS generates abductive hypotheses that fulfil certain criteria in one step, i.e. processes of generation and evaluation of abductive hypotheses are integrated.

Keywords: Logic of questions · Inferential Erotetic Logic · Erotetic calculi · Abduction

1 Introduction

The general schema of abductive reasoning could be described as follows: given the known rule *if H, then A* and an observation of A, infer H [15]. In other words, we can say that products of abductive procedures serve as a filler of the cognitive gap when some puzzling phenomenon is observed [7]. These properties account for the fact that abductive reasoning is used to solve problems in science (e.g. explanation of new observations), real life (e.g. diagnosis in medicine), and also in fiction (e.g. detective Sherlock Holmes) [12,15,16,18,19].

There are abductive procedures designed for Classical Propositional Calculus (e.g. [1]), other propositional logics (e.g. [13]) and first-order logic (e.g. [14], [9]). Different kinds of approaches to the problem use different proof methods for abductive procedures (for example [1] used analytic tableaux, [13] sequent calculi and [14] proof method of adaptive logics).

The aim of this article is to propose a model of abductive reasoning based on logic of questions. We interpret the abductive problem as an abductive question: *what should be added to the knowledge base Γ in order to be able to derive a fact φ?*, where φ is not derivable from Γ. Our proposal is based on a decomposition of the initial question an agent asks himself when he encounters an abductive problem. Therefore Wiśniewski's method of Socratic Proofs (see for example [21]) is being used as a main proof theoretical mechanism. It is a tool developed on the grounds of Wiśniewski's Inferential Erotetic Logic (IEL) (see [22,23]).

H. Christiansen et al. (Eds.): FQAS 2017, LNAI 10333, pp. 3–14, 2017.
DOI: 10.1007/978-3-319-59692-1_1

In general, approaches to the problem of formal specification of the abductive reasoning may differ in many respects and, in our opinion, one of the most interesting features of these procedures pertains to the relation between the generation and evaluation of abductive hypotheses. On the one hand, there are procedures which generate a large set of abductive hypotheses and then select 'good' hypotheses from this set, i.e. hypotheses which fulfil certain criteria [1,10]. On the other hand, one may think of abductive reasoning in such a way that the creation and evaluation of hypotheses are strongly intertwined: only those hypotheses are generated which are permitted given a certain set of criteria. The latter seems to us more natural. In the real-life as well as in scientific reasoning people do not waste time on the creation of hypotheses that may or may not be 'good'. They are interested only in 'good' hypotheses [12].

We consider algorithmic account of abduction with the following ingredients: Classical Propositional Logic as a basic logic and the method of Socratic Proofs [2,11,21] as a proof method.[1] As we mentioned, we exploit the approach where generation and evaluation of the hypotheses is conducted in one step. Our goal here is to introduce a new model of abductive reasoning based on IEL, therefore any detailed comparison concerning efficiency of the abductive procedures with the existing approaches will not take place in this article[2].

2 Question Processing

Since in our model abductive reasoning is triggered by an abductive question, we need some techniques enabling question processing. For that purpose we use some concepts and tools of IEL.

2.1 Language of IEL

We use the language $\mathcal{L}_{\mathsf{CPL}}$ of Classical Propositional Logic defined as usual. The language $\mathcal{L}^{?}_{\vdash\mathsf{CPL}}$ is an object-level language in which our erotetic calculi will

[1] Urbański and Wiśniewski [20] proposed a mechanism which enables to obtain abductive hypotheses in the form of law-like statements. The basis of the mechanism is similar as we use here. However, the two approaches differ when results of the abductive procedures are concerned. What is more, Urbański and Wiśniewski put it explicitly at the beginning of their article that they will not consider problem of the evaluation of abductive hypotheses.

[2] However some remarks should be made at this point. In the well-known *Abductive Logic Programming* (ALP) framework (on the propositional level) it is assumed that the set of abductive hypotheses (the set of abducibles) is known before abductive reasoning is triggered. Then, using integrity constraints and information from the knowledge base it can be figured out which hypotheses are good. Moreover, abductive hypotheses can be only of the form of atomic formulas. In AQAS the set of abductive hypotheses is not known before the initial question is transformed and abductive hypotheses can be literals as well as formulas of the form of implication. We think that the novelty of our approach lays in the fact that the concept of abductive hypothesis is defined in a more general way.

be worded. The meaningful expressions of the language $\mathcal{L}^?_{\vdash\mathsf{CPL}}$ belong to two disjoint sets. The first one consists of *declarative well-formed formulas* (d-wffs for short). The second one is the set of *erotetic well-formed formulas* (e-wffs or simply questions).

To obtain the vocabulary of $\mathcal{L}^?_{\vdash\mathsf{CPL}}$ we add to the vocabulary of $\mathcal{L}_{\mathsf{CPL}}$ the following signs: $\vdash$ (turnstile, intuitively stands for derivability relation in CPL), ? (a question mark for constructing questions of $\mathcal{L}^?_{\vdash\mathsf{CPL}}$) and , (comma), ; (semicolon).

Definition 1. *Let Γ, Δ be finite, non-empty, sequences of formulas of $\mathcal{L}_{\mathsf{CPL}}$. An* atomic declarative formula *of $\mathcal{L}^?_{\vdash\mathsf{CPL}}$ or* sequent *is of the following form:*

$$\Gamma \vdash \Delta$$

Definition 2. *Questions of $\mathcal{L}^?_{\vdash\mathsf{CPL}}$ have the following form:*

$$?(\Phi)$$

where Φ is a finite, non-empty sequence of sequents of $\mathcal{L}^?_{\vdash\mathsf{CPL}}$.

We use commas for separating formulas in sequents and semicolons for separating sequents in sequences. The following expressions are thus questions of $\mathcal{L}^?_{\vdash\mathsf{CPL}}$: $?(\neg(p \rightarrow q), \neg r \vdash r \wedge q)$, $?(p, \neg r \vdash p \vee r\ ;\ q \wedge \neg r \vdash r\ ;\ p \vdash p)$.

The intuitive meaning of a sequent $\Gamma \vdash \Delta$ is given in terms of multiple-conclusion entailment (mc-entailment for short): if all formulas in Γ are true, then at least one formula in Δ is true also (in symbols: $\Gamma \Vdash_{\mathsf{CPL}}$).

However '$\vdash$' is an object level expression of the language $\mathcal{L}^?_{\vdash\mathsf{CPL}}$ that should not be confused with the metalanguage expression '$\vdash_{\mathsf{CPL}}$' which is a syntactical or semantical consequence relation generated by CPL or with the mc-entailment relation '$\Vdash_{\mathsf{CPL}}$'.

If $\Gamma \Vdash_{\mathsf{CPL}} \Delta$ then we say that the sequent $\Gamma \vdash \Delta$ of $\mathcal{L}^?_{\vdash\mathsf{CPL}}$ is *closed*, otherwise it is *open*. If a sequent consists of literals only, it is called an *atomic sequent*. If $\Psi = \langle \phi_1, \ldots, \phi_n \rangle$ and for each i $(1 \leq i \leq n)$, ϕ_i is an atomic sequent, then the question $?(\Psi)$ is called a *minimal question*.

Definition 3 (Abductive question). *An* abductive question *(or* abductive problem*) has the following form:*

$$?(\Psi)$$

where Ψ is a non-empty sequence of sequents such that at least one term of Ψ is an open sequent of $\mathcal{L}^?_{\vdash\mathsf{CPL}}$. If $\Psi = \langle \phi \rangle$ is a one-term sequence, then the question $?(\Psi)$ is called simple. *If ϕ is also an open sequent, then $?(\Psi)$ is an* simple abductive question. *If $\Psi = \langle \phi_1, \ldots, \phi_n \rangle$ and for each i $(1 \leq i \leq n)$, ϕ_i is an atomic sequent, then the question $?(\Psi)$ is called a* minimal abductive question.

Intuitively, given an open sequent $\Gamma \vdash \Delta$, the antecedent Γ represents a knowledge base (such that some formulas/pieces of information can be repeated), which is used by an agent to 'explain' (derive) the data represented by Δ.

Table 1. Rules of $\mathbb{E}^{\mathsf{CPL}}$

$$\frac{?(\Phi; \Gamma, \alpha, \Gamma' \vdash \Delta; \Psi)}{?(\Phi; \Gamma, \alpha_1, \alpha_2, \Gamma' \vdash \Delta; \Psi)} \mathbf{L}_\alpha \qquad \frac{?(\Phi; \Gamma \vdash \Delta, \alpha, \Delta'; \Psi)}{?(\Phi; \Gamma \vdash \Delta, \alpha_1, \Delta'; \Gamma \vdash \Delta, \alpha_2, \Delta'; \Psi)} \mathbf{R}_\alpha$$

$$\frac{?(\Phi; \Gamma, \beta, \Gamma' \vdash \Delta; \Psi)}{?(\Phi; \Gamma, \beta_1, \Gamma' \vdash \Delta; \Gamma, \beta_2, \Gamma' \vdash \Delta; \Psi)} \mathbf{L}_\beta \qquad \frac{?(\Phi; \Gamma \vdash \Delta, \beta, \Delta'; \Psi)}{?(\Phi; \Gamma \vdash \Delta, \beta_1, \beta_2, \Delta'; \Psi)} \mathbf{R}_\beta$$

$$\frac{?(\Phi; \Gamma, \neg\neg A, \Gamma' \vdash \Delta; \Psi)}{?(\Phi; \Gamma, A, \Gamma' \vdash \Delta; \Psi)} \mathbf{L}_{\neg\neg} \qquad \frac{?(\Phi; \Gamma \vdash \Delta, \neg\neg A, \Delta'; \Psi)}{?(\Phi; \Gamma \vdash \Delta, A, \Delta'; \Psi)} \mathbf{R}_{\neg\neg}$$

2.2 Erotetic Rules of Inference

Let $?(\Gamma \vdash \Delta)$ be an abductive question. The formulas which belong to Γ as well as those which belong to Δ may be complex. It seems that abductive problems expressed by syntactically complex abductive questions are not easy to solve. In order to obey the Erotetic Decomposition Principle, the first step in solving an abductive problem (or, to put it differently, in answering an abductive question) is to make this problem 'simpler'. In the formulation of erotetic rules of inference we make use of the α, β-notation[3]. These rules constitute an erotetic calculus for CPL[4]. We denote it by the symbol $\mathbb{E}^{\mathsf{CPL}}$.

A sequent of a premise question distinguished in the scheme of a rule of $\mathbb{E}^{\mathsf{CPL}}$ is called *premise sequent* and sequent(s) distinguished in the conclusion is (are) called a *conclusion sequent(s)* of a given rule. In a similar manner we can define the *premise formulas* and *conclusion formulas* of a given rule (and of a given sequent). Occasionally we will say that a conclusion formula *results from* a premise formula.

Sequences of questions governed by erotetic rules of inference are *Socratic transformations* (Table 1).

Definition 4 (Socratic transformation). *A finite sequence of questions* $\mathbf{s} = \langle s_1, \ldots, s_n \rangle$ *is a* Socratic transformation *(s-transformation) of the question* $?(\Phi)$ *by means of* $\mathbb{E}^{\mathsf{CPL}}$ *iff the following conditions hold:*

1. $s_1 = ?(\Phi)$.
2. s_i *results from* s_{i-1} *(where* $i > 1$*) by an application of a rule of* $\mathbb{E}^{\mathsf{CPL}}$.

An s-transformation $\mathbf{s} = \langle s_1, \ldots, s_n \rangle$ is said to be *complete* iff the last term of $\mathbf{s}$, s_n, is a minimal question. A sequent ϕ is *basic* if ϕ is of one of the following forms: $\Gamma, B, \Gamma' \vdash \Delta, B, \Delta'$ or $\Gamma, B, \Gamma', \neg B, \Gamma'' \vdash \Delta$ or $\Gamma \vdash \Delta, B, \Delta', \neg B, \Delta''$. Naturally, each basic sequent is closed.

[3] α, β-notation was introduced by Smullyan in [17] to simplify metalogical considerations.

[4] A version of this calculus was introduced by Wiśniewski in [21]. In his approach only one formula can occur in the consequent of the sequent.

Definition 5 (Socratic proof). *A Socratic proof (s-proof) of a sequent $\Gamma \vdash \Delta$ in $\mathbb{E}^{\mathsf{CPL}}$ is a finite s-transformation $\mathbf{s}$ of the question $?(\Gamma \vdash \Delta)$, such that each constituent of the last question of $\mathbf{s}$ is a basic sequent.*

Socratic transformation of a question $?(\Gamma \vdash \Delta)$ is *successful* iff there exists a socratic proof of $\Gamma \vdash \Delta$. In the light of Definition 3 there are no successful s-transformations of abductive questions.

3 How to Answer an Abductive Question

To answer an abductive question $?(\Gamma \vdash \Delta)$ we employ the following procedure:

Step 1. Create a complete s-transformation of the question $?(\Gamma \vdash \Delta)$; the last question of this s-transformation is based on a sequence of sequents each of which consists of literals only.

Step 2. Apply some abductive rules (to be introduced later on) to this last question; each rule is *local* in the sense that only one sequent at a time is active in such a rule.

Step 3. Combine the results of the applications of rules using a conjunction; the resulting hypothesis has the form $H = A_1 \wedge \ldots \wedge A_n$, where each A_i $(1 \leq i \leq n)$ is the conclusion of an abductive rule.

There are several criteria of evaluation of abductive hypotheses [1,10]. To implement those criteria we need some auxiliary notions which allow us to illustrate the proposed method. Let $?(\Gamma \vdash \Delta)$ be an abductive question and H — an answer to the initial question. An abductive hypothesis has the following form $H = A_1 \wedge \ldots \wedge A_n$ where A_i $(1 \leq i \leq n)$ is a formula which closes some sequent in the last question of an s-transformation of $?(\Gamma \vdash \Delta)$.

We distinguish the following criteria[5]: 1. *Consistency:* $\Gamma \cup \{H\}$ is consistent. 2. *Significance:* $H \nvdash_{\mathsf{CPL}} \Delta$.

3.1 Abductive Rules

In this section our aim is to design rules for answering abductive questions which produce hypotheses/answers, which are significant and consistent with the knowledge base.

Definition 6 (Partial answer). *Let $Q = ?(\Gamma_1 \vdash \Delta_1, \ldots, \Gamma_n \vdash \Delta_n)$ be an abductive question. Let us further assume that the sequent $\Gamma_i \vdash \Delta_i$ (for some i, where $1 \leq i \leq n$) is open.* Partial answer *for Q is such a formula A that the addition of A to the Γ_i results in $\Gamma_i \vdash \Delta_i$ becoming a closed sequent or a sequent which after transformation to the atomic sequent is also a closed one.*

[5] Similar constraints are also defined in [1, p. 74] (Aliseda describes those two criteria as constituting the *consistent* and the *explanatory* Abductive Explanatory Styles respectively) and as properties of the abduction for Abductive Logic Programming in [5].

Table 2. Examples of abductive rules

$$\frac{?(\Phi\ ;\ \Theta, l, \Theta' \vdash \Theta''\ ;\ \Psi)}{\bar{l}}\ \mathbf{R}^1_{abd} \qquad \frac{?(\Phi\ ;\ \Theta, l, \Theta' \vdash \Theta'', k, \Theta'''\ ;\ \Psi)}{l \rightarrow k}\ \mathbf{R}^2_{abd}$$

Definition 7 (Abductive rule). *Let Q be a minimal abductive question and A be a partial answer for Q. The premise of an* abductive rule *is Q and the conclusion is A.*

In this paper we propose two rules for answering abductive questions Table 2. Note that the premises of abductive rules are questions (minimal abductive questions) and conclusions are declarative formulas. Thus, abductive rules enable a kind of inference between a question and an answer to that question. Note also that abductive rules close an active sequent (a sequent distinguished in the premise of a rule) in a natural way: atomic sequent is closed either by making its antecedent contradictory, or by making some connection between antecedent and consequent.

3.2 Restrictions for Abductive Rules

The proposed rules cannot be applied without some restrictions, if we want to maintain the consistency or significance of generated abductive hypotheses. To state those restrictions precisely we need some auxiliary notions, which are familiar from the work of Hintikka and Fitting (see for example [6]).

Definition 8 (Downward saturated set). *Let Γ be a sequence of formulas of $\mathcal{L}^*_{\mathsf{CPL}}$. By a* downward saturated set *(or* Hintikka set*) corresponding to a sequence Γ we mean a set $\mathfrak{U}_\Gamma$, which fulfils the following conditions:*

(i) if A is a term of Γ, then $A \in \mathfrak{U}_\Gamma$,
(ii) if $\alpha \in \mathfrak{U}_\Gamma$, then $\alpha_1 \in \mathfrak{U}_\Gamma$ and $\alpha_2 \in \mathfrak{U}_\Gamma$,
(iii) if $\beta \in \mathfrak{U}_\Gamma$, then $\beta_1 \in \mathfrak{U}_\Gamma$ or $\beta_2 \in \mathfrak{U}_\Gamma$,
(iv) if $\neg\neg A \in \mathfrak{U}_\Gamma$, then $A \in \mathfrak{U}_\Gamma$.
(v) nothing more belongs to $\mathfrak{U}_\Gamma$ except those formulas which enter $\mathfrak{U}_\Gamma$ on the grounds of conditions (i)–(iv).

A Hintikka set $\mathfrak{U}_\Gamma$ is satisfied under a Boolean valuation v (or is consistent) iff each element of $\mathfrak{U}_\Gamma$ is true under v. A Hintikka set $\mathfrak{U}_\Gamma$ is inconsistent iff for every v, at least one formula in $\mathfrak{U}_\Gamma$ is false under v. If $\mathfrak{U}_\Gamma = \emptyset$, then $\mathfrak{U}_\Gamma$ is satisfied by each Boolean valuation ($\mathfrak{U}_\Gamma$ is valid).

Definition 9 (Consistency property). *By a* consistency property *corresponding to a sequence Γ we mean a finite set $\mathfrak{U}^{\mathsf{c}}_\Gamma = \{\mathfrak{U}^1_\Gamma, \ldots, \mathfrak{U}^n_\Gamma\}$, which contains all Hintikka sets for Γ that do not contain complementary literals.*

Lemma 1. *If a non-empty sequence of formulas Γ is satisfiable, then at least one downward saturated set corresponding to Γ belongs to consistency property of Γ.*

Lemma 2 (Hintikka's Lemma). *For arbitrary Γ, each set belonging to the consistency property of Γ is satisfiable.*

Corollary 1. *A Hintikka set $\mathfrak{U}_\Gamma$ is inconsistent iff for some literal l, $l \in \mathfrak{U}_\Gamma$ and $\bar{l} \in \mathfrak{U}_\Gamma$.*

Definition 10 (Dual downward saturated set). *Let Δ be a sequence of formulas of $\mathcal{L}^*_{\mathsf{CPL}}$. By a* dual downward saturated set *(or* dual Hintikka set*) corresponding to a sequence Δ we mean a set $\mathfrak{W}_\Delta$, which fulfils the following conditions:*

(i) if A is a term of Δ, then $A \in \mathfrak{W}_\Delta$,
(ii) if $\alpha \in \mathfrak{W}_\Delta$, then $\alpha_1 \in \mathfrak{W}_\Delta$ or $\alpha_2 \in \mathfrak{W}_\Delta$,
(iii) if $\beta \in \mathfrak{W}_\Delta$, then $\beta_1 \in \mathfrak{W}_\Delta$ and $\beta_2 \in \mathfrak{W}_\Delta$,
(iv) if $\neg\neg A \in \mathfrak{W}_\Delta$, then $A \in \mathfrak{W}_\Delta$.
(v) nothing more belongs to $\mathfrak{W}_\Delta$ except those formulas which enter $\mathfrak{W}_\Delta$ on the grounds of conditions (i)–(iv).

A dual Hintikka set $\mathfrak{W}_\Delta$ is d-satisfied under a Boolean valuation v iff at least one element of $\mathfrak{W}_\Delta$ is true under v. A dual Hintikka set $\mathfrak{W}_\Delta$ is d-satisfied by each classical valuation ($\mathfrak{W}_\Gamma$ is valid) iff there is no Boolean valuation v such that each formula in $\mathfrak{W}_\Delta$ is false under v. If $\mathfrak{W}_\Delta = \emptyset$, then $\mathfrak{W}_\Delta$ is d-inconsistent.

Corollary 2. *A dual Hintikka set $\mathfrak{W}_\Delta$ is d-satisfied by each classical valuation ($\mathfrak{W}_\Delta$ is d-valid) iff for some l, $l \in \mathfrak{W}_\Delta$ and $\bar{l} \in \mathfrak{W}_\Delta$.*

Definition 11 (Non-validity property). *By a* non-validity property *corresponding to a sequence Δ we mean a finite set $\mathfrak{W}^{nv}_\Delta = \{\mathfrak{W}^1_\Delta, \ldots, \mathfrak{W}^n_\Delta\}$, which contains all dual Hintikka sets for Δ that do not contain complementary literals.*

Lemma 3 (Dual Hintikka's Lemma). *For an arbitrary Δ, each set belonging to the non-validity property of Δ is not d-valid.*

Let us consider the rules from Definition 2 again. Let us focus on rule $\mathbf{R}^1_{abd}$ and let $?(\Gamma \vdash \Delta)$ be the first question of a complete s-transformation which ends with the minimal question of the following form $?(\Phi\ ;\ \Theta, l, \Theta' \vdash \Theta''\ ;\ \Psi)$. We have two kinds of restrictions which guarantee the consistency and significance of abductive hypotheses generated by $\mathbf{R}^1_{abd}$.

Restriction 1 (Consistency restriction on $\boldsymbol{R}^1_{abd}$). *There exists a set $\mathfrak{U}_\Gamma \in \mathfrak{U}^c_\Gamma$ such that $l \notin \mathfrak{U}_\Gamma$.*

Restriction 2 (Significance restriction on $\boldsymbol{R}^1_{abd}$). *There exists a set $\mathfrak{W}_\Delta \in \mathfrak{W}^{nv}_\Delta$ such that $\bar{l} \notin \mathfrak{W}_\Delta$.*

Let us focus on rule $\mathbf{R}^2_{abd}$ and let $?(\Gamma \vdash \Delta)$ be the first question of a complete s-transformation which ends with a minimal question of the following form $?(\Phi \ ; \ \Theta, l, \Theta' \vdash \Theta'' \ ; \ \Psi)$. We have two kinds of restrictions which guarantee the consistency and significance of our abductive hypotheses generated by $\mathbf{R}^2_{abd}$.

Restriction 3 (Consistency restriction on $\boldsymbol{R}^2_{abd}$). *There exists a set $\mathfrak{U}_\Gamma \in \mathfrak{U}^{\mathfrak{c}}_\Gamma$ such that $l \notin \mathfrak{U}_\Gamma$ or $\overline{k} \notin \mathfrak{U}_\Gamma$.*

Restriction 4 (Significance restriction on $\boldsymbol{R}^2_{abd}$). *There exists a set $\mathfrak{W}_\Delta \in \mathfrak{W}^{nv}_\Delta$ such that $\overline{l} \notin \mathfrak{W}_\Delta$ or $k \notin \mathfrak{W}_\Delta$.*

Let $\mathbf{s} = \langle Q_1, \ldots, Q_n \rangle$ be a complete s-transformation of the question $?(\Gamma \vdash A)$, ϕ be an active sequent of an abductive rule, l, k–active literals and $\mathfrak{U}^{\mathfrak{c}}_\Gamma$ the consistency property for Γ. The application of a given rule to ϕ with restriction, with respect to l (or l and k), generates a set of Hintikka sets which are not compatible with a given restriction. Let us call this set $\mathfrak{U}^{\mathfrak{c}-}_\Gamma$. Now we can define a new set $\mathfrak{U}^{\mathfrak{c}+}_\Gamma = \mathfrak{U}^{\mathfrak{c}}_\Gamma \backslash \mathfrak{U}^{\mathfrak{c}-}_\Gamma$, which is a consistency property compatible with a given partial answer. If $\mathfrak{U}^{\mathfrak{c}+}_\Gamma$ results from $\mathfrak{U}^{\mathfrak{c}}_\Gamma$ in the case of an application of rule $\mathbf{R}^1_{abd}$ with an active literal l, then by $\mathfrak{U}^{\mathfrak{c}+\overline{l}}_\Gamma$ we mean the consistency property such that literal $\overline{l}$ is added to each element of $\mathfrak{U}^{\mathfrak{c}+}_\Gamma$. In the case of an application of $\mathbf{R}^2_{abd}$, the consistency property $\mathfrak{U}^{\mathfrak{c}+\overline{l},k}_\Gamma$ is the effect of adding literals $\overline{l}$ and k to each element of $\mathfrak{U}^{\mathfrak{c}+}_\Gamma$.

In a similar manner, we can define the set $\mathfrak{W}^{nv+}_\Delta = \mathfrak{W}^{nv}_\Delta \backslash \mathfrak{W}^{nv-}_\Gamma$ and the set $\mathfrak{W}^{nv+l}_\Gamma$. In the case of an application of $\mathbf{R}^2_{abd}$ things are slightly more complicated. First we have to construct two sets $\mathfrak{W}^{nv+l}_\Delta$ and $\mathfrak{W}^{nv+\overline{k}}_\Delta$, and then the set $\mathfrak{W}^{nv+l,\overline{k}}_\Delta = \mathfrak{W}^{nv+l}_\Delta \cup \mathfrak{W}^{nv+\overline{k}}_\Delta$.

In order to prove a correctness of the procedure we need to modify its second step.

Step2*. Apply some abductive rules to the last question with consistency (significance) restriction; after each application of an abductive rule modify the consistency property (non-validity property) in order to make it compatible with a given partial answer.

In the example at the end of the paper we show in details how the procedure works. Before that we introduce the following lemmas (sometimes without proofs, if they are trivial) and theorems proving our method to be correct.

Lemma 4. *Let $\mathfrak{U}_\Gamma \in \mathfrak{U}^{\mathfrak{c}}_\Gamma$ be a downward saturated set corresponding to some Γ. If a literal $l \notin \mathfrak{U}_\Gamma$, then the set $\mathfrak{U}_\Gamma \cup \{\overline{l}\}$ is consistent.*

Proof. $\mathfrak{U}_\Gamma$ is consistent by definition of the consistency property. Let us assume that $l \notin \mathfrak{U}_\Gamma$. If $\mathfrak{U}_\Gamma \cup \{\overline{l}\}$ is inconsistent then $l \in \mathfrak{U}_\Gamma \cup \{\overline{l}\}$, which contradicts the assumption. □

Lemma 5. *Let $\mathfrak{U}_\Gamma \in \mathfrak{U}^{\mathfrak{c}}_\Gamma$ be a downward saturated set corresponding to some Γ. If $l \notin \mathfrak{U}_\Gamma$ or $\overline{k} \notin \mathfrak{U}_\Gamma$, then the set $\mathfrak{U}_\Gamma \cup \{l \to k\}$ is consistent.*

Theorem 1. *Each abductive hypothesis generated by the procedure, where each abductive rule is applied with a consistency restriction is consistent with the initial knowledge base.*

Proof. The proof follows from Lemmas 4 and 5 and from the construction of $\mathfrak{U}^{c+}_{\Gamma}$. □

Lemma 6. *Let $\mathfrak{W}_{\Delta} \in \mathfrak{W}^{nv}_{\Delta}$ be a dual downward saturated set corresponding to some Δ. If a literal $\bar{l} \notin \mathfrak{W}_{\Delta}$, then the set $\mathfrak{W}_{\Delta} \cup \{l\}$ is not valid.*

Proof. We know that $\mathfrak{W}_{\Delta}$ is not valid, i.e. there exists a valuation v such that each formula in $\mathfrak{W}_{\Delta}$ is false under v. Since $\bar{l} \notin \mathfrak{W}_{\Delta}$ we can assume that $v(l) = 0$. It follows that $\mathfrak{W}_{\Delta}$ is not valid. □

Lemma 7. *Let $\mathfrak{W}_{\Delta} \in \mathfrak{W}^{nv}_{\Delta}$ be a dual downward saturated set corresponding to some Δ. If $\bar{l} \notin \mathfrak{W}_{\Delta}$ or $k \notin \mathfrak{W}_{\Delta}$, then the set $\mathfrak{W}_{\Delta} \cup \{l\}$ is not valid or $\mathfrak{W}_{\Delta} \cup \{\bar{k}\}$ is not valid.*

Lemma 8. $l \nvdash_{\mathsf{CPL}} A_1 \vee \ldots \vee A_n$ *(where each A_i $(1 \leq i \leq n)$ is a literal) if and only if a dual Hintikka set $\mathfrak{W} = \{\bar{l}, A_1, \ldots, A_n\}$ is not valid.*

Proof. $(\rightarrow)$ Assume that $l \nvdash_{\mathsf{CPL}} A_1 \vee \ldots \vee A_n$. There exists a classical valuation v such that $v(l) = 1$ and $v(A_1 \vee \ldots \vee A_n) = 0$. In this case $v(\bar{l}) = 0$ and each formula in $\mathfrak{W}$ is false under v. Therefore $\mathfrak{W}$ is not valid.

$(\leftarrow)$ Assume $\mathfrak{W}$ is not valid. There exists a classical valuation v, such that each formula in $\mathfrak{W}$ is false under v. In this case $v(l) = 1$ and $v(A_1 \vee \ldots \vee A_n) = 0$. Therefore $l \nvdash_{\mathsf{CPL}} A_1 \vee \ldots \vee A_n$. □

Lemma 9. $l \rightarrow k \nvdash_{\mathsf{CPL}} A_1 \vee \ldots \vee A_n$ *(where each A_i $(1 \leq i \leq n)$ is a literal) if and only if a dual Hintikka set $\mathfrak{W} = \{l, A_1, \ldots, A_n\}$ is not valid or $\mathfrak{W} = \{\bar{k}, A_1, \ldots, A_n\}$ is not valid.*

Theorem 2. *Each abductive hypothesis generated by the procedure, where each abductive rule is applied with a significance restriction, is significant.*

Proof. The proof is a consequence of Lemmas 6, 7 and the construction of $\mathfrak{W}^{nv+}_{\Gamma}$. □

Theorem 3. *Each abductive hypothesis generated by the procedure, where each abductive rule is applied with a significance and consistency restriction is significant and consistent.*

Proof. The proof follows from Theorems 1 and 2. □

Let us consider the following example. The knowledge base $\Gamma = \langle p \rightarrow (z \rightarrow q), r \wedge s \rangle$, and $\Delta = \langle r \rightarrow q \rangle$. Therefore the initial question is of the following form: $?(p \rightarrow (z \rightarrow q), r \wedge s \vdash r \rightarrow q)$, and the last question of s-transformation is of the form: $?(\neg p, r, s \vdash \neg r, q \ ; \ \neg z, r, s \vdash \neg r, q \ ; \ q, r, s \vdash \neg r, q)$.

After constructing the s-transformation of our problem we have to calculate Hintikka and dual Hintikka sets. From the knowledge base $\Gamma = \langle p \rightarrow (z \rightarrow q), r \wedge s\rangle$ we can generate the following seven Hintikka sets and the consistency property ($\mathfrak{U}^{c}_{\Gamma} = \{\mathfrak{U}^1_{\Gamma}, \mathfrak{U}^2_{\Gamma}, \mathfrak{U}^3_{\Gamma}, \mathfrak{U}^4_{\Gamma}, \mathfrak{U}^5_{\Gamma}, \mathfrak{U}^6_{\Gamma}, \mathfrak{U}^7_{\Gamma}\}$):

$\mathfrak{U}^1_{\Gamma} = \{p \rightarrow (z \rightarrow q), r \wedge s, r, s, \neg p, z \rightarrow q, \neg z, q\}$
$\mathfrak{U}^2_{\Gamma} = \{p \rightarrow (z \rightarrow q), r \wedge s, r, s, \neg p, z \rightarrow q, \neg z\}$
$\mathfrak{U}^3_{\Gamma} = \{p \rightarrow (z \rightarrow q), r \wedge s, r, s, \neg p, z \rightarrow q, q\}$
$\mathfrak{U}^4_{\Gamma} = \{p \rightarrow (z \rightarrow q), r \wedge s, r, s, \neg p\}$
$\mathfrak{U}^5_{\Gamma} = \{p \rightarrow (z \rightarrow q), r \wedge s, r, s, z \rightarrow q, \neg z, q\}$
$\mathfrak{U}^6_{\Gamma} = \{p \rightarrow (z \rightarrow q), r \wedge s, r, s, z \rightarrow q, \neg z\}$
$\mathfrak{U}^7_{\Gamma} = \{p \rightarrow (z \rightarrow q), r \wedge s, r, s, z \rightarrow q, q\}$

The abductive goal is $\Delta = \langle r \rightarrow q\rangle$ and we can generate the following dual Hintikka set: $\mathfrak{W}^1_{\Delta} = \{r \rightarrow q, \neg r, q\}$ and non-validity property: $\mathfrak{W}^{nv}_{\Delta} = \{\mathfrak{W}^1_{\Delta}\}$

Now, let us consider the set of possible abductive hypotheses generated by the introduced rules. The first open sequent $\neg p, r, s \vdash \neg r, q$ can be closed by formulas which belong to the set $\Sigma_1 \cup \Sigma_2$, where:

1. $\Sigma_1 = \{p, \neg r, \neg s\}$ is the set of formulas generated by means of the application of the rule $\mathbf{R}^1_{abd}$;
2. $\Sigma_2 = \{\neg p \rightarrow \neg r, r \rightarrow \neg r, s \rightarrow \neg r, \neg p \rightarrow q, r \rightarrow q, s \rightarrow q\}$ is the set of formulas generated by means of the application of the rule $\mathbf{R}^2_{abd}$.

The second open sequent $\neg z, r, s \vdash \neg r, q$ can be closed by formulas which belong to the set $\Sigma^*_1 \cup \Sigma^*_2$, where:

1*. $\Sigma^*_1 = \{z, \neg r, \neg s\}$ is the set of formulas generated by means of the application of the rule $\mathbf{R}^1_{abd}$;
2*. $\Sigma^*_2 = \{\neg z \rightarrow \neg r, r \rightarrow \neg r, s \rightarrow \neg r, \neg z \rightarrow q, r \rightarrow q, s \rightarrow q\}$ is the set of formulas generated by means of the application of the rule $\mathbf{R}^2_{abd}$.

An abductive answer to the initial question $?(p \rightarrow (z \rightarrow q), r \wedge s \vdash r \rightarrow q)$ is a conjunction of formulas which close all the open sequents in the minimal abductive question (conjunction of all partial answers). In this particular case the set of all answers has the form:

$$\{A \wedge B \mid A \in \Sigma_i,\ B \in \Sigma^*_i,\ \text{for}\ \ i \in \{1, 2\}\}$$

Note that not all of these answers would be generated, when abductive rules are used along with restrictions. Let us look at some examples of answers. Some of them will be consistent and significant while other will not.

(a) $H = p \wedge z$. In this case rule $\mathbf{R}^1_{abd}$ has been applied to close both open sequents. Formula p closes the first open sequent. Moreover the consistency restriction is fulfilled: there exists a set $\mathfrak{U}^i_{\Gamma} \in \mathfrak{U}^c_{\Gamma}$ such that $\neg p \notin \mathfrak{U}_{\Gamma}$. In fact there are three such sets: $\mathfrak{U}^5_{\Gamma}$, $\mathfrak{U}^6_{\Gamma}$, $\mathfrak{U}^7_{\Gamma}$. Formula z closes the second open sequent. The consistency restriction is also fulfilled in this case, because there exists a set $\mathfrak{U}^i_\Gamma \in \mathfrak{U}^{c+p}_\Gamma$, namely $\mathfrak{U}^{7+p}_\Gamma$, such that $\neg z \notin \mathfrak{U}^{7+p}_\Gamma$. Thus H is consistent with the knowledge base. This hypothesis is also significant. Significance restriction is fulfilled in the case of partial answer p, because there exists a set $\mathfrak{W}^i_\Delta \in \mathfrak{W}^{nv}_\Delta$ such that $p \notin \mathfrak{W}^i_\Delta$, namely $\mathfrak{W}^1_\Delta$. The significance restriction is also fulfilled for the second partial answer z, because $z \notin \mathfrak{W}^{1+p}_\Delta$.

(b) $H = p \wedge (r \rightarrow \neg r)$. This hypothesis is significant because of similar reasons as in the previous example (a). However it is not consistent with the knowledge base due to the fact that for each $\mathfrak{U}^{i+p}_\Gamma \in \mathfrak{U}^{c+p}_\Gamma$, $r \in \mathfrak{U}^{i+p}_\Gamma$, which contradicts consistency restriction on $\mathbf{R}^2_{abd}$.

(c) $H = \neg r$. In this case rule $\mathbf{R}^1_{abd}$ has been applied to close both open sequents. This hypothesis is neither consistent nor significant, because each $\mathfrak{U}^i_\Gamma \in \mathfrak{U}^c_\Gamma$ is such that $r \in \mathfrak{U}_\Gamma$ and each $\mathfrak{W}^i_\Delta \in \mathfrak{W}^{nv}_\Delta$ is such that $\neg r \in \mathfrak{W}^i_\Delta$.

4 Summary and Further Work

In this article we introduced Abductive Question-Answer System for classical propositional logic. We interpret the abductive problem as an abductive question: *what should be added to the knowledge base Γ in order to be able to derive a fact φ?* where φ is not derivable from Γ. Firstly, (possibly) complex initial abductive question is decomposed into a minimal abductive question. Afterwards, partial answers are generated for the minimal abductive question. The abductive hypothesis is obtained by combining all partial answers with conjunction. If partial answers are generated along with restrictions, obtained abductive hypothesis have 'desired' properties i.e., it is consistent with the knowledge base Γ and φ is not obtainable from the abductive hypothesis alone. Therefore, AQAS integrates generation and evaluation of abductive hypotheses.

The knowledge-based systems are better and more often described by means of modal or paraconsistent logics. Therefore, our future work is concerned with the application of the Abductive Question-Answer System for these logics. Our future work will also cover the implementation of the Abductive Question-Answer System in programming language. This will enable us to test the system on huge datasets and compare it with solutions that already exist, such as the one presented by Komosiński [10] or those proposed on the ground of Abductive Logic Programming [5].

Acknowledgements. This work has been supported by the Polish National Science Center, grant no. 2012/04/A/HS1/00715 (first author) and DEC-2013/10/E/HS1/00172 (second author).

References

1. Aliseda, A.: Abductive Reasoning. Logical Investigations into Discovery and Explanation. Springer, Dordrecht (2006). doi:10.1007/1-4020-3907-7
2. Chlebowski, S., Leszczyńska-Jasion, D.: Dual erotetic calculi and the minimal LFI. Studia Logica **103**(6), 1245–1278 (2015). doi:10.1007/s11225-015-9617-0

3. Ciardelli, I., Roelofsen, F.: Inquisitive logic. J. Philos. Log. **40**, 55–94 (2011). doi:10.1007/s10992-010-9142-6
4. Ciardelli, I., Groenendijk, J., Roelofsen, F.: On the semantics and logic of declaratives and interrogatives. Synthese (2013). doi:10.1007/s11229-s013-0352-7
5. Denecker, M., Kakas, A.: Abduction in logic programming. In: Kakas, A.C., Sadri, F. (eds.) Computational Logic: Logic Programming and Beyond. LNCS, vol. 2407, pp. 402–436. Springer, Heidelberg (2002). doi:10.1007/3-540-45628-7_16
6. Fitting, M.: First-Order Logic and Automated Theorem Proving. Springer, New York (1996). doi:10.1007/978-1-4612-2360-3
7. Hintikka, J.: What is abduction? The fundamental problem of contemporary epistemology. In: Inquiry as Inquiry: A Logic of Scientific Discovery, pp. 91–113. Springer, Dordrecht (1999). doi:10.1007/978-94-015-9313-7_4
8. Hintikka, J.: Socratic Epistemology: Explorations of Knowledge-Seeking by Questioning. Cambridge University Press, Cambridge (2007). ISBN: 9780521616515
9. Kakas, A.C., Kowalski, R.A., Toni, F.: Abductive logic programming. J. Log. Comput. **2**(6), 719–770 (1992)
10. Komosiński, M., Kupś, A., Leszczyńska-Jasion, D., Urbański, M.: Identifying efficient abductive hypotheses using multi-criteria dominance relation. ACM Trans. Comput. Log. (TOCL) **15**(4), 28:1–28:20 (2014). doi:10.1145/2629669
11. Leszczyńska-Jasion, D.: Socratic proofs for some normal modal propositional logics. Logique et Analyse **47**(185–188), 259–285 (2004)
12. Magnani, L.: Abductive Cognition. The Epistemological and Eco-cognitive Dimensions of Hypothetical Reasoning. Springer, Dordrecht (2009). doi:10.1007/s10838-011-9146-0
13. Mayer, M.C., Pirri, F.: Propositional abduction in modal logic. Log. J. IGPL **3**(6), 907–919 (1995). doi:10.1093/jigpal/3.6.907
14. Meheus, J., Batens, D.: A formal logic of abductive reasoning. Log. J. IGPL **14**(2), 221–236 (2006). doi:10.1093/jigpal/jzk015
15. Peirce, C.S.: Collected Works. Harvard University Press, Cambridge (1931). Republished in 1958
16. Sintonen, M.: Reasoning to hypotheses: where do questions come? Found. Sci. **9**(3), 249–266 (2004). doi:10.1023/B:FODA.0000042842.55251.c1
17. Smullyan, R.M.: First-Order Logic. Springer, Heidelberg (1968)
18. Thagard, P.: Abductive inference: from philosophical analysis to neural mechanisms. In: Feeney, A., Heit, E. (eds.) Inductive Reasoning: Cognitive, Mathematical, and Neuroscientific Approaches, pp. 226–247. Cambridge University Press, Cambridge (2007). doi:10.1017/CBO9780511619304.010
19. Urbański, M.: Rozumowania abdukcyjne. Wydawnictwo Naukowe UAM, Poznań (2009)
20. Urbański, M., Wiśniewski, A.: On search for law-like statements as abductive hypotheses by socratic transformations. In: Baskent, C. (ed.) Perspectives on Interrogative Models of Inquiry. Developments in Inquiry and Questions, vol. 8, pp. 111–127. Springer, Cham (2016). doi:10.1007/978-3-319-20762-9_7
21. Wiśniewski, A.: Socratic proofs. J. Philos. Log. **33**(3), 299–326 (2004). doi:10.1023/B:LOGI.0000031374.60945.6e
22. Wiśniewski, A.: Questions, Inferences, and Scenarios. Studies in Logic, vol. 46. College Publications, London (2013)
23. Wiśniewski, A.: The Posing of Questions: Logical Foundations of Erotetic Inferences. Kluwer, Dordrecht (1995)

Querying with Vague Quantifiers Using Probabilistic Semantics

Christian G. Fermüller(✉), Matthias Hofer(✉), and Magdalena Ortiz

TU Vienna, Vienna, Austria
{chrisf,hofer}@logic.at

Abstract. Many realistic scenarios call for answers to questions involving vague expressions like *almost all*, *about half*, or *at least about a third*. We present a modular extension of classical first-order queries over relational databases, with *binary, proportional, semi-fuzzy quantifiers* modeling such expressions via random sampling. The extended query language has an intuitive semantics and allows one to pose natural queries with probabilistic answers. This is also demonstrated by experiments with an implementation involving the (geographical) MONDIAL data set.

1 Introduction

In verbal communication one frequently uses expressions like *about half*, *at least about a third*, *at most about a quarter*, *almost all*, etc. Obviously the meaning of these expressions is vague, context dependent and potentially also involves intensional aspects, like considerations about specific expectations of speakers and listeners. Nevertheless such quantifier expressions may be understood as mainly referring to the *proportion* of those domain elements satisfying the range predicate that also satisfy the scope predicate. For example, *Almost all capitals have airports* refers to the proportion of capitals in the domain of discourse (range predicate) that satisfy the scope predicate *'has an airport'*, and claims that this proportion is close to 1. The intrinsic vagueness of quantifier expressions is often a virtue, rather than a problem: it allows us to communicate concisely and effectively without having to compute or even to know the precise proportion in question. This observation motivates the design of formal models of proportionality quantifiers that support efficient and intuitive answers to queries that involve corresponding formal counterparts of relevant natural language expressions.

In this paper we propose to augment a standard first order query language over relational and RDF data with quantifiers that allow one to formulate queries like *Which countries are larger than almost all other countries?* or (Boolean queries) like *Do at least about two thirds of all capitals have more than a million inhabitants?* The vagueness of the corresponding quantifier expressions is modeled by a probabilistic, sampling based semantics, connecting our approach

H. Christiansen et al. (Eds.): FQAS 2017, LNAI 10333, pp. 15–27, 2017.
DOI: 10.1007/978-3-319-59692-1_2

to game based semantics for so-called semi-fuzzy proportionality quantifiers [5,6] as explained below.[1]

Related work. Flexible and approximate query answering has received significant attention in the database community for several decades, and the literature on the subject is vast. Our work has some relation to fuzzy query answering, see [14] and references therein. However, our approach is different in at least two respects: (1) we want to keep the user interface free of references to degrees of truth or of set membership, and (2) we base the semantics of semi-fuzzy quantifiers on sampling, rather than on *ad hoc* truth functions, as usual in fuzzy set based approaches. We are not aware of similar proposals that modularly extend existing query languages with proportional quantifiers only, while keeping crisp both the database and underlying query formalism. Sampling plays an important role on approximate query answering (see, e.g., [2,9]), but in this area, the focus is usually on keeping suitable samples of the data to support the efficient computation of aggregate queries over large data sets, rather than supporting vague quantifiers formalizing natural language expressions. In this light, we think that our specific combination of ideas is original and may be of interest.

The paper is organized as follows. We start by providing basic terminology on (semi-)fuzzy quantifiers in Sect. 2, and we briefly recall the game and sampling based approach to fix their semantics in Sect. 3. Section 4 reviews principles of statistical sampling that are used in the central Sect. 5, which presents our proposal for extending queries with vague proportional quantifiers. In Sect. 6 we illustrate our approach on a concrete use case. Section 7 briefly summarizes our work and presents a few topics for related future research.

2 (Semi-)fuzzy Proportionality Quantifiers

The standard model for vague quantifier expressions in a computational context uses fuzzy logic (see, e.g., [20]). A fuzzy set over a *domain* D is a function $\widetilde{X} : D \to [0,1]$, assigning to each element of D a *membership degree* in the real unit interval. Fuzzy sets are intended to model vague or imprecise predicates, where any given element does not necessarily either determinately satisfy or not satisfy the predicate, but where $\widetilde{X}(d)$ is understood as the *degree of truth* of the assertion that d satisfies the predicate modeled by $\widetilde{X}$. If $\widetilde{X}(d) \in \{0,1\}$ for all $d \in D$, one speaks of a *crisp set* or predicate. Identifying 0 with 'definitely false' and 1 with 'definitely true', crisp predicates clearly correspond to classical (bivalent) predicates and crisp sets turns into (membership functions of) ordinary sets.

[1] Although this is not a main concern in this work, we point out that a sampling based semantics may also be useful to compute quick, approximative answers in face of massive volumes of data. For example it might be useful to quickly obtain a highly, but not perfectly reliable answer to a query like *Have at least about a quarter of all citizens lived abroad at some time?* without having to visit each relevant entry in a huge database containing such data for all citizens.

As already indicated, commonly used (logical) natural language quantifiers involve a range as well as a scope predicate, i.e. they are *binary* in the terminology of, e.g., [4]. This also holds for standard universal and existential quantification: one routinely asserts sentences of the form *All A are B* or *Some A are B*.[2] For crisp predicates, we may express the first sentence in classical logic as $\forall x(A(x) \rightarrow B(x))$ and the second one as $\exists x(A(x) \wedge B(x))$. But note that such a reduction of binary quantification to unary quantification is in general not possible for other binary quantifiers.

Initiated by Zadeh [19], the literature on *fuzzy quantifiers* is large; we refer to the monograph [12] and the more recent survey article [4] for an overview of relevant work. Focusing on binary quantification, a corresponding fuzzy quantifier is given by a *truth function* $v_I(\widetilde{Q}) : \widetilde{A} \times \widetilde{B} \rightarrow [0,1]$ mapping any two fuzzy sets over the domain D into a truth value (*degree of truth*) in $[0,1]$. Here I refers to an interpretation, that assigns a fuzzy set (fuzzy predicate) over D to each monadic predicate symbol. If both, the range predicate $\widetilde{A}$ and the scope predicate $\widetilde{B}$, are crisp, then the quantifier $\widetilde{Q}$ is called *semi-fuzzy*. We identify the domain elements (members of D) with corresponding constants and assume throughout this paper that D is finite. Note that both stipulations are well justified in our database oriented context. This context also motivates the focus on semi-fuzzy quantifiers, since the predicates correspond to the relations of the given dataset, which is assumed to be of the usual relational format. (Indeed, we will not distinguish between a crisp predicate and the corresponding relation of the dataset.) If $v_I(\widetilde{Q})(A, B)$ only depends on the proportion

$$Prop(A, B) =_{df} \frac{|A \cap B|}{|A|}$$

then $\widetilde{Q}$ is a binary *proportional* semi-fuzzy quantifier. This is the type of quantifier models that we want to incorporate into a classical query language.

3 Semantics via Sampling in Giles's Game

As we have seen in the last section, every binary semi-fuzzy proportional quantifier is characterized by a truth function that maps $Prop(A, B)$ into a truth value in $[0,1]$. This triggers the question which of the uncountably many candidates for truth functions are adequate for modeling particular natural language quantifiers like *almost all* or *about half*. Moreover, one may want to embed corresponding formal quantifiers into a standard t-norm based fuzzy logic, following the paradigm of contemporary mathematical fuzzy logic, as represented, e.g., in [3]. To address both challenges, Fermüller and Roschger [5,6] introduced an extension of Giles's game based semantics for Łukasiewicz logic [10,11] that allows one to derive the truth functions for certain families of proportional semi-fuzzy

[2] Unary quantification, as in *All are B* and *Some are B*, can be considered as a special instance of binary quantification, where the range predicate A is suppressed since it is identified with the one satisfied by all elements of the range of discourse.

quantifiers from rules that regulate attacks on and defenses of logically complex formulas. We do not care about the logical connectives of Łukasiewicz logic here, but rather consider queries that feature a single vague quantifier expression applied to crisp range and scope predicates. For monadic quantifiers (where the domain D is identified with the range A and thus $Prop(A, B) = Prop(B)$) one may formulate game rules like the following for a family of semi-fuzzy quantifiers G^k_m, taken from [6]:

- If the proponent **P** asserts $\mathsf{G}^k_m xF(x)$ then her opponent **O** may attack this statement by betting against k random instances of $F(x)$, while **P** bets for m random instances of $F(x)$.

Here, 'random instance' refers to a uniformly random choice of a constant d. By betting for (against) the corresponding instance $F(d)$ a player of the game risks to have to pay one unit of money to the opposing player if the corresponding formula turns out to be false (true) in the given interpretation.[3] By identifying the inverse of the expected loss of money of the proponent of a formula with its degree of truth, one obtains truth functions for corresponding semi-fuzzy quantifiers. In this manner truth functions for G^n_{2n}, for $n \geq 1$, can be extracted from the above rule that amount to reasonable models of the natural language quantifier *at least about a third*, parameterized by a certain measure of 'tolerance'. For querying we will not directly refer to truth functions, but rather make use of the observation that each concrete run of the semantic game yields a (dispersive) classical truth value. This yes/no-reply corresponds to a statistical test using the randomly chosen constants as sample. In this manner standard principles of statistics, as explained in the next section, will lead us to a semantics for queries featuring semi-fuzzy proportionality quantifiers.

4 Principles of Sampling

We briefly review the theoretical basis of our sampling based evaluation methods [13], which we use to specify the semantics of quantifiers in Sect. 5.2.

Let $Y_1, \ldots, Y_s$ be independent and identically distributed Bernoulli random variables, i.e. for each $i \in \{1, \ldots, s\}$ we have $Y_i \in \{0, 1\}$. Then, it is easy to see that $\frac{\sum_{i=1}^{s} Y_i}{s} := \frac{X}{s}$ is a random variable with (scaled) binomial distribution. To evaluate binary vague proportional quantifiers, we need to estimate the proportion of range elements that also fulfill the scope formula. To this end we need to relate three parameters, namely the *sample size* s, the *confidence* $1 - \alpha \in (0, 1)$, and the *precision* of the estimate $\epsilon \in [0, 1]$. This can be expressed as follows [13], where $\mathbb{P}_{s,\rho}$ denotes the probability distribution for a binomial distributed random variables with parameters $s \in \mathbb{N}$ and $\rho \in [0, 1]$:

$$\mathbb{P}_{s,\rho}(\mid \frac{X}{s} - \rho \mid \geq \epsilon) \leq \alpha. \tag{1}$$

[3] Actually the overall game is more involved than indicated here, since whole *multisets* of formulas have to be considered in general, when decomposing formulas into subformulas in accordance with the rules. For details we refer to [7].

The most accurate way to proceed would be to construct confidence regions, using binomial and beta quantiles, which should certainly be performed for real life applications where accuracy matters the most. Another well known and widely used approach, due to its more efficient nature, makes use of the central limit theorem [13], for which we have to assume that the sample size is sufficiently large. Following this way we may calculate:

$$\mathbb{P}_{s,\rho}(|\frac{X}{s}-\rho|<\epsilon)=\mathbb{P}_{s,\rho}(|\frac{X-s\rho}{\sqrt{s\rho(1-\rho)}}|<\epsilon\sqrt{\frac{s}{\rho(1-\rho)}})\approx$$
$$\approx\Phi(\epsilon\sqrt{\frac{s}{\rho(1-\rho)}})-\Phi(-\epsilon\sqrt{\frac{s}{\rho(1-\rho)}})=2\Phi(\epsilon\sqrt{\frac{s}{\rho(1-\rho)}})-1.$$

Since Φ is bijective[4] and $\rho(1-\rho)\leq\frac{1}{4}$, we obtain $s\geq(\frac{\Phi^{-1}(\frac{2-\alpha}{2})}{2\epsilon})^2$.

This last inequality tells us which minimum sample size s we have to use to achieve a certain precision ϵ with confidence $1-\alpha$. To refer to this functional relation of the parameters later, we define $f:[0,1]\times(0,1)\rightarrow\mathbb{N}$ as follows:

$$f(\epsilon,\alpha)=\lceil(\frac{\Phi^{-1}(\frac{2-\alpha}{2})}{2\epsilon})^2\rceil. \tag{2}$$

5 Querying with Semi-fuzzy Quantifiers

In this section, we present our concrete proposal for querying datasets, using a standard query language extended with semi-fuzzy proportional quantifiers.

For ease of presentation, we take a declarative, logic based view of relational databases and queries over them [1]. Databases are defined as finite relational structures over a given signature or *schema*, and we consider first-order logic formulas over the same signature as basic query language. As data values we use constants and integer numbers, and we allow (in)equalities between values (both constants and integers), and comparisons $(<,>,\geq,\neq)$ over integers. This basic setting captures relational algebra expressions (and thus, basic SQL) over relational databases. Moreover, significant fragments of other datamodels and their corresponding query languages can be viewed as special case of FO-queries over relational data as considered here. This applies in particular to the fragment of the SPARQL query language for RDF data [17] considered in Sect. 6

5.1 Relational Databases and FO-Queries

As usual, we denote by $\mathbb{Z}$ the integer numbers, and by $\mathbb{N}$ the positive integers. We define a *(relational) schema* as comprising a set $\mathcal{R}$ of *relation names*, together

[4] As it is the distribution function of standard normally distributed random variables.

with an *arity function* $ar : \mathcal{R} \to \mathbb{N}$, and a function *npos* that maps each R to a (possibly empty) subset of $\{1, \dots, ar(R)\}$ of *numeric positions* of R.[5]

Let a relational schema $(\mathcal{R}, ar, npos)$ be given. Let $\mathbf{U}$ be a set of constants or *data values*, and $\mathbf{V}$ be a countably infinite set of *variables*. A *term* is an object in $\mathbf{U} \cup \mathbb{Z} \cup \mathbf{V}$. *Atoms* take the following forms:

(i) $R(t_1, \dots, t_{ar(R)})$ with $R \in \mathcal{R}$, and the t_i are terms such that $t_i \in \mathbb{Z} \cup \mathbf{V}$ if $i \in npos(R)$, and $t_i \in \mathbf{U} \cup \mathbf{V}$ if $i \notin npos(R)$;
(ii) $t = t'$ and $t \neq t'$ with t, t' terms; and
(iii) $t < t'$, $t > t'$, $t \leq t'$ or $t \geq t'$, for t, t' terms in $\mathbb{Z} \cup \mathbf{V}$.

An atom is called *relational* if it is of the form (i), and *ground* if all its terms are from $\mathbf{U} \cup \mathbb{Z}$. A *database instance* (or simply a *database*) is a *finite* set D of ground relational atoms. The *active domain* of a database D, denoted $ADom(D)$ is the set of constants and numbers from $\mathbf{U} \cup \mathbb{Z}$ that occur in the atoms of D.

Example 1. Consider a schema containing, among others, the following relations:

- unary *country* and *city*, with no numeric positions, that is: $npos(city) = \{\}$ and $npos(country) = \{\}$;
- a binary *city_of* that relates cities and the countries they are located in, also with $npos(city\_of) = \{\}$;
- a binary *cap_of* that relates each capital city with the country it is capital of; again, $npos(cap\_of) = \{\}$;
- a binary *has_pop* with $npos(has\_pop) = \{2\}$, which relates countries and cities, with an integer number denoting its total population;
- a binary *hasGDP_agr* with $npos(hasGDP\_agr) = \{2\}$, which relates countries with an integer number (between 0 and 100) denoting the percentage of its GDP that comes from agriculture.

A database D_1 over this schema may contain, for example, ground atoms:
$country(USA)$, $country(India)$, ... $city(Chicago)$, $city(Beijing)$, ...
$cap\_of(Beijing, China)$, $cap\_of(NewDelhi, India)$, ...
$has\_pop(China, 1385 * 10^6)$, $has\_pop(Beijing, 21.6 * 10^6)$, $has\_pop(Shanghai, 24.3 * 10^6)$ ...

An *FO-query* is a first-order formula $\psi(\boldsymbol{x})$ with free variables $\boldsymbol{x}$, built from atoms in the usual way, using the connectives $\neg$, $\wedge$, $\vee$, and the quantifiers $\exists$ and $\forall$. We refer to these variables as the *answer variables* of ψ. The *arity* of the query is the number of variables in $\boldsymbol{x}$. We call a query *Boolean* if it is 0-ary, that is, it has no free variables.

We note that a database D can be seen as a Herbrand interpretation over the predicates in the schema, and with domain $ADom(D)$. An n-ary FO query over D defines an n-ary relation over $ADom(D)$, which contains precisely the tuples for which the corresponding formula is satisfied, under the usual semantics.

[5] We use a simple definition, compatible with more complex notions of schema, which may assign, e.g., names and domains to attributes, and integrity constraints.

Let D be a database. A *substitution* is a mapping σ from variables in $\mathbf{V}$ to values in $ADom(D)$. We write $\sigma(\boldsymbol{t})$ for the tuple that results from $\boldsymbol{t}$ by substituting each variable x with $\sigma(x)$, and we write $\sigma(\varphi)$ to denote the formula that results from φ by applying the substitution σ to all its atoms. For $x \in \mathbf{V}$, $c \in ADom$, and a substitution σ, we denote by $\sigma\{x \mapsto c\}$ the substitution σ' that has $\sigma'(x) = c$, and $\sigma'(y) = \sigma(y)$ for all remaining variables in the domain of σ. Abusing notation, we may disregard order in tuples and treat them as sets.

The *satisfaction* in D of a formula ψ w.r.t. σ, in symbols $D \models_\sigma \psi$, is defined inductively in the natural way:

- For relational atoms, $D \models_\sigma R(\boldsymbol{t})$ if $R(\sigma(\boldsymbol{t})) \in D$.
- For the other atoms, $D \models_\sigma t \circledcirc t'$ if $\sigma(t) \circledcirc \sigma(t')$, where each binary predicate $\circledcirc \in \{=, \neq, \geq \ldots\}$ is interpreted as usual.
- $D \models_\sigma \psi_1 \wedge \psi_2$ if $D \models_\sigma \psi_1$ and $D \models_\sigma \psi_2$.
- $D \models_\sigma \psi_1 \vee \psi_2$ if $D \models_\sigma \psi_1$ or $D \models_\sigma \psi_2$.
- $D \models_\sigma \neg\psi$ if $D \not\models_\sigma \psi$.
- $D \models_\sigma \exists x\ \psi$ if for some $c \in ADom(D)$, we have $D \models_{\sigma\{x \mapsto c\}} \psi$.
- $D \models_\sigma \forall x\ \psi$ if for each $c \in ADom(D)$, we have $D \models_{\sigma\{x \mapsto c\}} \psi$.

Let $\psi(\boldsymbol{x})$ be a query with answer variables $\boldsymbol{x} = (x_1, \cdots, x_n)$, and let $\boldsymbol{c} = c_1, \cdots, c_n$ be a tuple of values from $\mathbf{U} \cup \mathbb{Z}$ of the same arity. Then we say that $\boldsymbol{c}$ *is an answer to* ψ *over* D if $D \models_\sigma \psi$ for the substitution σ with $x_i = c_i$ for each $1 \leq i \leq n$. In this case, we may write $D \models \psi(\boldsymbol{c})$.

Note that for ψ a Boolean query, there are two possibilities: if $D \models \psi$, then the empty tuple is an answer to ψ. In this case, we may say that ψ is *true* in D, or that its answer in D is *yes*. In the other case, if $D \not\models \psi$, then the empty tuple is *not* an answer to ψ: we say that ψ is *false* or that its answer is *no*.

Example 2. The following are simple examples of FO-queries over our example schema; ψ_1 is a Boolean query, while ψ_2 is unary and ψ_3 is binary.

ψ_1: Is there a country with a population of more than one billion people?
ψ_2: Which countries have a city with higher population than its capital?
ψ_3: Which are the countries, and their capitals, such that no other city in the country has more inhabitants?

$$\begin{aligned}
\psi_1 &:= \exists x, y(\mathit{country}(x) \wedge \mathit{has_pop}(x, y) \wedge (y > 1000 * 10^6)) \\
\psi_2(x) &:= \exists y_1, y_2, z_1, z_2(\mathit{country}(x) \wedge \mathit{cap_of}(y_1, x) \wedge \mathit{city_of}(y_2, x) \wedge \\
&\qquad \wedge \mathit{has_pop}(y_1, z_1) \wedge \mathit{has_pop}(y_2, z_2) \wedge (z_1 < z_2)) \\
\psi_3(x, y) &:= \exists z(\mathit{country}(x) \wedge \mathit{cap_of}(y, x) \wedge \mathit{has_pop}(y, z) \wedge \\
&\qquad \forall y_1, z_1((\mathit{city_of}(y_1, x) \wedge \mathit{has_pop}(y_1, z_1)) \rightarrow (z_1 \leq z)))
\end{aligned}$$

We note that $D_1 \models \psi_1$, that is, its answer is *yes*, since the substitution $\sigma(x) =$ *China*, $\sigma(y) = 1385 * 10^6$ makes the formula true. We can also observe that the answers to ψ_2 contain *China*, and that (*Beijing*, *China*) is *not* an answer to ψ_3.

5.2 Extending FO-Queries with Proportional Quantifiers

Assume $m \in \mathbb{N}$, and let $n, k \in \{0, \ldots, m\}$ with $n \neq 0$. We consider the following *proportional quantifiers*:

$Q^{[\approx \frac{k}{n}]}$ about k/n $\quad$ $Q^{[\gtrsim \frac{k}{n}]}$ at least about k/n $\quad$ $Q^{[\lesssim \frac{k}{n}]}$ at most about k/n

If $k = n$, then we may read both $Q^{[\approx \frac{k}{n}]}$ and $Q^{[\gtrsim \frac{k}{n}]}$ as *almost all*, and simply write $Q^{[\approx 1]}$. If $k = 0$, then we may read $Q^{[\approx \frac{k}{n}]}$ and $Q^{[\lesssim \frac{k}{n}]}$ as *almost none* and write $Q^{[\approx 0]}$. Note that each value of m determines a family of proportional quantifiers. Throughout the paper we assume $m = 4$, but any number can be used.[6] Now we define our query language, which extends FO-queries with these quantifiers:

Definition 1 (Queries). *A* query *is an expression* $q(\boldsymbol{y})$ *of the form*

$$\widetilde{Q}x(R(x, \boldsymbol{y}'), \psi(x, \boldsymbol{y}))$$

where $\boldsymbol{y}' \subseteq \boldsymbol{y}$*, and:*

- $\widetilde{Q}$ *is any of the proportional quantifiers defined above,*
- $R(x, \boldsymbol{y}')$ *is a relational atom using the variables in* $\{x\} \cup \boldsymbol{y}'$*, and whose additional terms are from* $\mathbf{U} \cup \mathbb{Z}$*, and*
- $\psi(x, \boldsymbol{y})$ *is an FO-query with answer variables* $\{x\} \cup \boldsymbol{y}$*.*

The answer variables *of* q *are* $\boldsymbol{y}$*, and its* arity *is the number of variables in* $\boldsymbol{y}$*.*

Example 3. To illustrate our language, we consider the following queries:

q_1: Do at least about three quarters of all countries make at most 20% of their GDP in agriculture?
q_2: Do about half of all cities have more than 200000 inhabitants?
q_3: Which countries have a capital which has more inhabitants than about half of all other capitals in the world?
q_4: Which countries have a capital that has more inhabitants than almost all other cities of that country?

The first two are Boolean queries, the other two are unary. Queries q_3 and q_4 are very similar, but they differ on the range predicate: it is unary in q_3 and binary in q_4. In our syntax, they look as follows:

$$\begin{aligned}
q_1 &:= Q^{[\gtrsim \frac{3}{4}]}x(\mathit{country}(x), \exists y(\mathit{hasGDP_agr}(x, y) \wedge (y \leq 20))) \\
q_2 &:= Q^{[\approx \frac{1}{2}]}x(\mathit{city}(x), \exists y(\mathit{has_pop}(x, y) \wedge (y > 200000))) \\
q_3(y) &:= Q^{[\approx \frac{1}{2}]}x(\mathit{capital}(x), \exists z, z', w(\mathit{cap_of}(y, w) \wedge \mathit{has_pop}(w, z) \wedge \\
&\qquad \wedge \mathit{has_pop}(x, z') \rightarrow (z > z'))) \\
q_4(y) &:= Q^{[\approx 1]}x(\mathit{city_of}(x, y), \exists z, z', w(\mathit{cap_of}(y, w) \wedge \mathit{has_pop}(w, z) \wedge \\
&\qquad \wedge \mathit{has_pop}(x, z') \rightarrow (z > z')))
\end{aligned}$$

[6] We remark that very large values of m do not usually occur in natural language.

We note that $D_1 \models q_1$, that is, its answer is *yes*, since the substitution $\sigma(x) = China$, $\sigma(y) = 1385 * 10^6$ makes the formula true. We can also observe that the answers to q_2 contain *China*, and that (*Beijing*, *China*) is *not* an answer to q_3.

Now we define the semantics of our query language. As we have anticipated, it is based on *sampling*, according to the principles discussed in Sect. 4. We assume that values in the interval $[0, 1]$ are given for the confidence $1 - \alpha \in (0, 1)$ and precision ϵ. These values then determine a minimal sample size $s = f(\epsilon, \alpha)$ as in Eq. 2. Then, for testing whether a given tuple of variables $\mathbf{c} = c_1, \cdots, c_n$ of values from $\mathbf{U} \cup \mathbb{Z}$ is an answer to a query $\widetilde{Q}x(R(x, \boldsymbol{y}'), \psi(x, \boldsymbol{y}))$, we take a sufficiently large random sample of objects x that satisfy $R(x, \mathbf{c}')$ (where $\mathbf{c}'$ is the restriction of $\mathbf{c}$ to the positions from $\boldsymbol{y}$ that occur in $\boldsymbol{y}'$), and verify whether the proportion of those for which $\psi(x, \mathbf{c})$ holds are within the desired range. Note that, since the sample is random, for the same tuple $\mathbf{c}$, we may get different proportions, and hence a different value, if we repeat the query evaluation. This is natural, since our semantics of the proportional quantifiers defines a probability function over the possible answer tuples. As we will illustrate in the next section, the answers retrieved in this way are reliable, even for modest sample sizes.

Definition 2 (Semantics). *Let D be a database, let $R(x, \mathbf{c}')$ be a relational atom and $\psi(x, \mathbf{c})$ be a FO-query, such that x is the only free variable in both. Let $S \subseteq ADom(D)$ with $S \neq \emptyset$. We define*

$$Prop_D(S, \psi(x, \mathbf{c})) = \frac{|\{c \in S \mid D \models_{\{x \mapsto c\}} \psi(x, \mathbf{c})\}|}{|S|}$$

Now we let σ be a substitution from $\mathbf{V}$ to $ADom(D)$, and let $D_R = \{c \in ADom(D) \mid R(c, \sigma(y')) \in D\}$. We define the semantics of queries as follows:

- $D \models_{\sigma,S,\epsilon} Q^{[\approx\frac{k}{n}]}x(R(x, \boldsymbol{y}'), \psi(x, \boldsymbol{y}))$ *if* $S \subseteq D_R$ *and* $Prop_D(S, \sigma(\psi(x, \boldsymbol{y}))) \in [\frac{k}{n} - \epsilon, \frac{k}{n} + \epsilon]$.
- $D \models_{\sigma,S,\epsilon} Q^{[\gtrsim\frac{k}{n}]}x(R(x, \boldsymbol{y}'), \psi(x, \boldsymbol{y}))$ *if* $S \subseteq D_R$ *and* $Prop_D(S, \sigma(\psi(x, \boldsymbol{y}))) \in [\frac{k}{n} - \epsilon, 1]$.
- $D \models_{\sigma,S,\epsilon} Q^{[\lesssim\frac{k}{n}]}x(R(x, \boldsymbol{y}'), \psi(x, \boldsymbol{y}))$ *if* $S \subseteq D_R$ *and* $Prop_D(S, \sigma(\psi(x, \boldsymbol{y}))) \in [0, \frac{k}{n} + \epsilon]$.

Let ϵ and α in the interval $[0, 1]$ be given. A tuple $\mathbf{c} = c_1, \cdots, c_n$ of values from $\mathbf{U} \cup \mathbb{Z}$ of the same arity as $\boldsymbol{y}$ is called a sampled answer to ψ over D (with precision ϵ and confidence $1 - \alpha$) *if $D \models_{\sigma,S,\epsilon} Q^{[\lesssim\frac{k}{n}]}x(R(x, \boldsymbol{y}'), \psi(x, \boldsymbol{y}))$, where σ is the substitution with $x_i = c_i$ for each $1 \leq i \leq n$, and $S \subseteq ADom(D)$ is a random sample (with replacement) of size $|S| \geq f(\epsilon, \alpha)$ as described in Sect. 4. In this case, we may write $D \models_{\epsilon,\alpha} \psi(\mathbf{c})$.*

6 Proof-of-Concept: Querying the MONDIAL Database

For illustrating the proposed approach on real life data, we chose the MONDIAL database[7]. It is a dataset containing geographical data, that relies on open web data, such as the CIA factbook, Wikipedia, and atlases. The last major revision took place in 2015. Like most open web data, the database is not complete, and data may be somewhat imprecise. However, this is not of major concern here.

We evaluated the queries in Example 3. (In fact, the schema and queries of our running example are based on MONDIAL). We used the RDF version of MONDIAL locally and posed standard SPARQL queries, using the Java extension Apache Jena. This, together with random sampling on the list of query results, suffices to simulate the evaluation of queries in our language efficiently. In contrast to other fuzzy querying approaches, like the ones of Bosc and Pivert [18] we here rely on strictly classical data, and focus on a probabilistic evaluation of them. Our goal was to test how the sampling based evaluation performs for particular sample queries. Obviously, if the amount of sampled data increases, then the difference between the evaluation times for full and partial answers, respectively, increases as well. However, for the present example, the MONDIAL database (16.4 MB), they are still in a similar range. Some of our observations are captured in Figs. 1 and 2, which show how the sample size correlates with the calculated proportions, using only a single iteration per size. Figure 1 shows the results for the queries q_1–q_3, and Fig. 2 for particular instances of the answer variable y in query q_4. From those results one can straightforwardly evaluate the answers to the natural language queries. Taking the first one, which asks whether the proportion in question is at least about 75 %, the results show that, for almost all samples sizes, this is the case with (high) confidence $1 - \alpha = 0.95$. Similar results hold for the other queries. (Note that in Fig. 2 just a small range

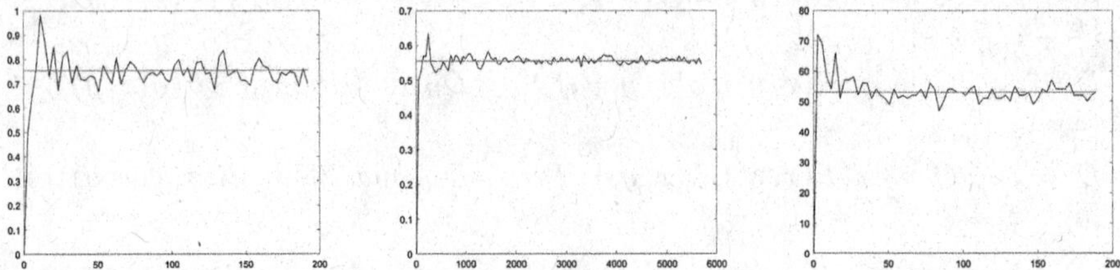

Fig. 1. Left: query q_1; middle: query q_2; right: query q_3. The x-axis always represents possible sample sizes, i.e. the number of domain elements that fulfill the respective range predicate. For the left and the middle picture, the y-axis stands for the proportion of these range objects that also fulfill the scope predicate, while for the right picture it displays the sizes of answer sets. The blue graph shows the achieved results for one sample of the sizes from the x-axis. The red graph displays the correct proportions, or answer set size respectively. (Color figure online)

[7] MONDIAL database. (Last accessed January 30th, 2017). Retrieved from: https://www.dbis.informatik.uni-goettingen.de/Mondial/.

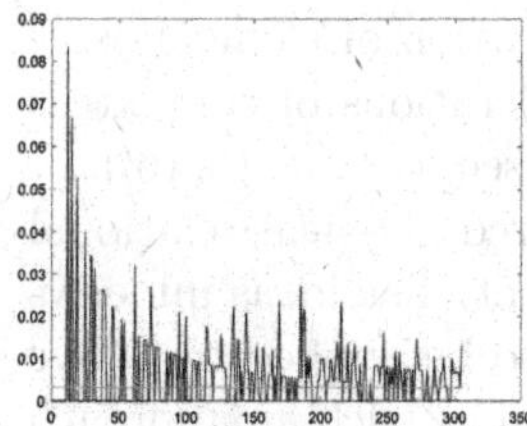
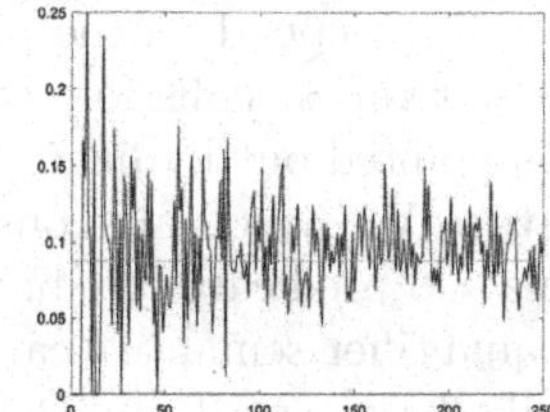
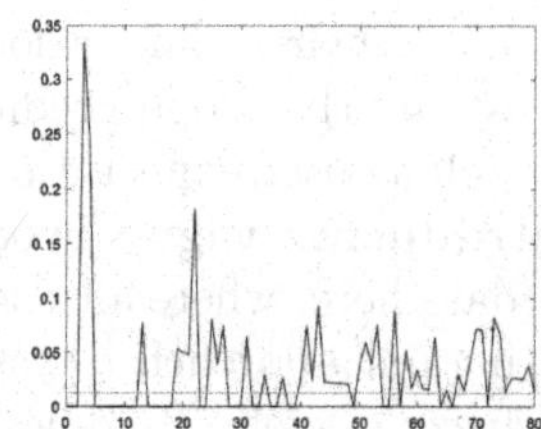

Fig. 2. Query q_4, for: left: y = China; middle: y = USA; right: y = India. The x-axis always represents possible sample sizes, i.e. the number of domain elements that fulfill the respective range predicate. The y-axis stands for the proportion of these range objects that also fulfill the scope predicate. The blue graph shows the achieved results for sample sizes from the x-axis. The red graph displays the correct proportions. (Color figure online)

of proportions is displayed). Finally, we emphasize that the graphs show the proportions obtained for *one* random sample of each size. But the blue line (sampled results) converges quickly to the red line (correct proportion) if we increase the number of iterations.

7 Conclusions and Outlook

We have presented an extension of a classical first order query language over relational data with quantifiers that model vague natural language quantifiers like *about half*, *almost all*, *at least about a third*, and *at most about a quarter*.

The proposed semantics of these quantifiers is inspired by an extension of Giles's semantic game [10] for Łukasiewicz logic to semi-fuzzy proportional quantifiers that makes use of random selection of witnessing constants [5,6]. In the context of Giles game, fuzzy truth functions for these quantifiers are extracted by identifying expected values resulting from sampling based games with degrees of truth. Similarly, our queries trigger a sampling mechanism to return probabilistic answers; i.e. answers that might differ upon repetition, but that conform to the specified meaning of the quantifier expressions with high probability, given particular levels of confidence and precision. We have specified this semantics in a manner that directly extends standard classical FO-queries and thus fits well into the usual frameworks for querying relational and RDF data. As a proof-of-concept we applied the proposed machinery to the RDF version of the MONDIAL database, illustrating that our approach yields promising results that encourage further investigations.

We conclude by briefly commenting on some further challenges, possible extensions, and additional use cases.

Other vague quantifier expressions: The quantifier expressions selected in Sect. 5.2 are only specific examples, illustrating a general principle, but many other interesting natural language quantifiers could be considered. A particular challenge arises for modeling the often used expressions *many* and *few*, since their meaning does not just depend on the proportion of elements satisfying the scope predicate, but rather calls for considerations of context as well as user expectations, as pointed out by linguists (see, e.g., [8,15,16]).

Introducing vague predicates: We have only considered classical relational data here, where all relations and predicates are bi-valent. The ideas underlying our approach to vague quantifier semantics can also be applied to derive fuzzy models of predicates like *large*, *small*, etc. Developing such an approach and comparing it with existing fuzzy databases might be useful.

Computational gains: Sampling may not only be viewed as a tool for modeling vagueness, but is also a well known approach to obtain more efficient, approximate answers in face of huge volumes of data [2]. Our current prototype implementation is not intended to illustrate such computational gains, but this is clearly an interesting topic for further research.

Data summarization: While we have focused on querying here, we finally want to point out that our approach to modeling vague quantifiers may be even more useful for data summarization. It seems natural to offer sentences like *About half of the provincial capitals have airports* and *Almost all countries have ethnic minorities* summaries instead of precise statistical data, in particular if the later are marred by spurious precision.

Acknowledgements. This work was supported by the Austrian Science Fund (FWF) projects I1897-N25 and W1255-N23.

References

1. Abiteboul, S., Hull, R., Vianu, V.: Foundations of Databases: The Logical Level. Addison-Wesley Longman Publishing Co. Inc., Boston (1995)
2. Agarwal, S., Mozafari, B., Panda, A., Milner, H., Madden, S., Stoica, I.: BlinkDB: queries with bounded errors and bounded response times on very large data. In Proceedings of the 8th ACM European Conference on Computer Systems, pp. 29–42. ACM (2013)
3. Cintula, P., Fermüller, C.G., Hájek, P., Noguera, C. (eds.): Handbook of Mathematical Fuzzy Logic (in three volumes). College Publications (2011/2015)
4. Delgado, M., Ruiz, M., Sánchez, D., Vila, M.: Fuzzy quantification: a state of the art. Fuzzy Sets Syst. **242**, 1–30 (2014)
5. Fermüller, C.G., Roschger, C.: Randomized game semantics for semi-fuzzy quantifiers. In: Greco, S., Bouchon-Meunier, B., Coletti, G., Fedrizzi, M., Matarazzo, B., Yager, R.R. (eds.) IPMU 2012. CCIS, vol. 300, pp. 632–641. Springer, Heidelberg (2012). doi:10.1007/978-3-642-31724-8_66
6. Fermüller, C., Roschger, C.: Randomized game semantics for semi-fuzzy quantifiers. Log. J. IGPL **22**(3), 413–439 (2014)
7. Fermüller, C.G.: Semantic games for fuzzy logics. In: Cintula, P., Fermüller, C.G., Noguera, C. (eds.) Handbook of Mathematical Fuzzy Logic, vol. 3, pp. 969–1028. College Publications, London (2015)
8. Fernando, T., Kamp, H.: Expecting many. In: Semantics and Linguistic Theory, vol. 6, pp. 53–68 (1996)

9. Gibbons, P.B., Matias, Y.: New sampling-based summary statistics for improving approximate query answers. In: ACM SIGMOD Record, vol. 27, pp. 331–342. ACM (1998)
10. Giles, R.: A non-classical logic for physics. Studia Logica **33**(4), 397–415 (1974)
11. Giles, R.: Semantics for fuzzy reasoning. Int. J. Man Mach. Stud. **17**(4), 401–415 (1982)
12. Glöckner, I.: Fuzzy Quantifiers: A Computational Theory. Studies in Fuzziness and Soft Computing, vol. 193. Springer, Heidelberg (2006)
13. Grimmett, G., Welsh, D.: Probability: An Introduction. Oxford University Press, New York (2014)
14. Kacprzyk, J., Zadrożny, S., De Tré, G.: Fuzziness in database management systems: half a century of developments and future prospects. Fuzzy Sets Syst. **281**, 300–307 (2015)
15. Lappin, S.: An intensional parametric semantics for vague quantifiers. Linguist. Philos. **23**(6), 599–620 (2000)
16. Partee, B.: Many quantifiers. In: Proceedings of ESCOL, vol. 5, pp. 383–402 (1988)
17. Pérez, J., Arenas, M., Gutierrez, C.: Semantics and complexity of SPARQL. ACM Trans. Database Syst. (TODS) **34**(3), 16 (2009)
18. Pivert, O., Bosc, P.: Fuzzy Preference Queries to Relational Databases. World Scientific, Singapore (2012)
19. Zadeh, L.: A computational approach to fuzzy quantifiers in natural languages. Comput. Math. Appl. **9**(1), 149–184 (1983)
20. Zadeh, L.: Fuzzy logic. IEEE Comput. **21**(4), 83–93 (1988)

Towards Analogy-Based Decision - A Proposal

Richard Billingsley[2], Henri Prade[1,2(✉)], Gilles Richard[1], and Mary-Anne Williams[2]

[1] IRIT, CNRS and Toulouse University, Toulouse, France
{prade,richard}@irit.fr

[2] QCIS, University of Technology Sydney, Sydney, Australia
Richard.Billingsley@uts.edu.au, Mary-Anne@themagiclab.org

Abstract. This short paper outlines an analogy-based decision method. It takes advantage of analogical proportions between situations, i.e., a is to b as c is to d, for proposing plausibly good decisions that may be appropriate for a new situation at hand. It goes beyond case-based decision where the idea of graded similarity may hide some small but crucial differences between situations. The method relies on triples of known cases rather than on individual cases for making a prediction on the appropriateness of a potential decision, or for proposing a way of adapting a decision according to situations. The approach may be of interest in a variety of problems ranging from flexible querying systems to cooperative artificial agents.

1 Introduction

Making decision on a daily basis often relies on past experience [1], rather than being an explicit utility-maximization business based on the knowledge of a utility function. This observation has led decision theorists to propose an axiomatic modeling of case-based decision, relying on a repository of cases already experienced, where expected utility is replaced by a weighted average of the utilities of the results of this decision in various situations that are *similar* to the current situation, the sum being weighted in terms of this similarity [7].

A qualitative counterpart to case-based decision has been proposed [2,3]. Thus an optimistic (resp. pessimistic) decision criterion implements the idea that a decision is all the better as it led to a good decision in at least one (resp. all) situation(s) similar to the current situation, where the decision was made. Since both goodness and similarity are matters of degree, these two decision criteria estimate respectively to what extent the intersection of two fuzzy sets is not empty and to what extent a fuzzy set is included in another one.

While the idea of case-based decision is intuitively attractive, it may be difficult to implement it due to the difficulty of eliciting meaningful similarity relations between situations. Indeed, two situations may be quite similar in many respects and still have one crucial difference, in such a way that for a considered decision, we may obtain a good result in one case and a bad one in the other. Such a remark calls for an analysis in terms of analogical proportions. Analogical

H. Christiansen et al. (Eds.): FQAS 2017, LNAI 10333, pp. 28–35, 2017.
DOI: 10.1007/978-3-319-59692-1_3

proportions are statements of the form a is to b as c is to d, which compare a pair (a, b) with a pair (c, d) in terms of the similarities and of the differences between the elements of each pair [11].

In the following, we outline an approach to analogy-based decision where we take advantage of a repository of past experiences in terms of analogical proportions, suggesting the benefits that may be expected from such a view. We first provide a short background on case-based decision, and then on analogical proportions, before presenting the approach. The structural resemblances between case-based decision and flexible querying have been already discussed [4]; this leads to conjecture some applications of analogy-based decision to flexible querying. We also advocate the interest of analogy-based decision for artificial agents that have to cooperate with humans on the basis of past interactions.

2 Case-Based Decision

In case-based decision, we are supposed to have at our disposal a repository $\boldsymbol{R}$ of experienced decisions under the form of cases $c_i = (s_i, \delta_i, r_i), i \in [1, n]$. Case c_i means that decision $\delta_i \in \mathcal{D}$ ($\mathcal{D}$ is the set of potential decisions), applied in situation $s_i \in \mathcal{S}$ ($\mathcal{S}$ is the set of considered situations), has led to result $r_i \in \mathcal{R}$; it is assumed that r_i is uniquely determined by s_i and δ_i. Consider a new situation s_0, which may not be in $\mathcal{S}$, for which we have to take a decision δ_0. Let S be a similarity measure defined on $\mathcal{S} \times \mathcal{S}$ that associates each pair (s_i, s_j) of situations with a positive real number $S(s_i, s_j) \in [0, 1]$.

Classical expected utility is then changed [7], for a candidate decision δ into

$$U(\delta) \triangleq \frac{\Sigma_{(s_i,\delta,r_i)\in \boldsymbol{R}\ s.t.\ \delta_i=\delta}\ S(s_0, s_i) \cdot u(r_i)}{\Sigma_{(s_i,\delta_i,r_i)\in \boldsymbol{R}\ s.t.\ \delta_i=\delta}\ S(s_0, s_i)},$$

where u is a utility function, here supposed to be valued in $[0, 1]$. Note that the value of u needs to be known only for the cases in the repository. Decision is made by choosing $\delta \in \mathcal{D}$ such that it maximizes $U(\delta)$.

A pessimistic and an optimistic qualitative counterparts [2] are given by

$$U_*(\delta) \triangleq \min_{(s_i,\delta_i,r_i)\in \boldsymbol{R}\ s.t.\ \delta_i=\delta} S(s_0, s_i) \rightarrow u(r_i) \text{ and}$$
$$U^*(\delta) \triangleq \max_{(s_i,\delta_i,r_i)\in \boldsymbol{R}\ s.t.\ \delta_i=\delta} \min(S(s_0, s_i), u(r_i)).$$

$U_*(\delta)$ expresses that decision δ is all the better as the fuzzy set of results associated with situations similar to s_0 where decision δ was experienced is included in the fuzzy set of good results. When $x \rightarrow y = \max(1 - x, y)$, $U_*(\delta) = 1$ only if the result obtained with decision δ in any known situation somewhat similar to s_0 was fully satisfactory. $U^*(\delta)$ expresses that a decision δ is all the better as it was already successfully experienced in a situation similar to s_0. See [3] for postulate-based justifications. The very pessimistic and optimistic nature of criteria U_* and U^* may be softened by introducing fuzzy quantifiers; for example, one might already be satisfied if a decision was a good choice in *most* similar cases, thus allowing for a few exceptions [4]. Note that these criteria may lead to prefer a rarely experienced decision that always led to good results (if any), rather to choose a decision with more feedbacks, but some bad ones. However, it may be desirable to avoid an accumulation effect if the same decision is chosen routinely for the same, frequently occurring, situation and thus is stored several times in the repertory of cases. In fact, what is addressed here is the possible variability of the output of a decision made in more or less similar situations rather than its possible non deterministic nature when repeatedly applied in (apparently) the same situation.

A situation s is usually described by means of several features, i.e., $s = (s^1, ..., s^m)$. Then the evaluation of the similarity between two situations s and $s' = (s'^1, ..., s'^m)$ amounts to estimating the similarity for each feature k according to a similarity relation S^k, and to combine these partial similarities using some aggregation operator agg, namely $S(s, s') = agg_{k=1,...,m} S^k(s^k, s'^k)$. A classical choice for agg is the conjunction operator min, which retains the smallest similarity value as the global evaluation. But one may also think, for instance, of using some weighted aggregation if all the features have not the same importance. See [4,5] for more details, references to generalizations to incompletely specified cases, or with discounting of untypical cases, and applications to flexible querying including examples (and counter-examples)-based querying[1].

3 Analogy: Brief Review

Analogical proportions provide another way to compare situations. Analogical proportions are statements of the form a is to b as c is to d. Let us assume that the four items a, b, c, d are represented by sets of binary features belonging to a universe U (i.e., an item is then viewed as the subset of the binary features in U that it satisfies). Then, the dissimilarity between a and b can be appreciated in terms of $a \cap \overline{b}$ and/or $\overline{a} \cap b$, where $\overline{a}$ denotes the complement of a in U. Indeed $a \cap \overline{b}$ (resp. $\overline{a} \cap b$) is the subset of properties possessed by a (resp. b) and not by b (resp. a). The similarity is estimated by means of $a \cap b$ (the subset of properties possessed by both a and b) and/or of $\overline{a} \cap \overline{b}$ (the subset of properties that both a and b do not possess). Then, an analogical proportion between subsets is formally defined [9] as a conjunction of equalities:

$$a \cap \overline{b} = c \cap \overline{d} \text{ and } \overline{a} \cap b = \overline{c} \cap d$$

This expresses that "a differs from b as c differs from d" and that "b differs from a as d differs from c". It can be viewed as the expression of a co-variation.

It has an easy counterpart in Boolean logic, here denoted $a : b :: c : d$, where a, b, c, d now denote simple Boolean variables. In this logical setting, "are equated to" translates into "are equivalent to" ($\equiv$), $\overline{a}$ is now the negation of a, and $\cap$ is changed into a conjunction ($\wedge$), and we get the logical condition expressing that 4 Boolean variables make an analogical proportion:

$$a : b :: c : d \triangleq (a \wedge \overline{b} \equiv c \wedge \overline{d}) \wedge (\overline{a} \wedge b \equiv \overline{c} \wedge d)$$

[1] An item is all the more a solution as it resembles to some example(s) in all important aspects, and is dissimilar from all counter-examples in some important aspect(s).

It is logically equivalent to the following condition that expresses that the pairs made by the extremes and the means, namely (a, d) and (b, c), are (positively and negatively) similar [9]. This could be used as a definition as well:

$$a : b :: c : d \triangleq (a \wedge d \equiv b \wedge c) \wedge (\overline{a} \wedge \overline{d} \equiv \overline{b} \wedge \overline{c}).$$

An analogical proportion is then a Boolean formula. $a : b :: c : d$ takes the truth value "1" only for the 6 following patterns for *abcd*: $1111, 0000, 1100, 0011, 1010, 0101$. For the 10 other lines of its truth table, it is false (i.e., equal to 0).

A worth noticing property, beyond reflexivity ($a : b :: a : b$), symmetry ($a : b :: c : d \Rightarrow c : d :: a : b$), and central permutation ($a : b :: c : d \Rightarrow a : c :: b : d$) is the fact that the analogical proportion remains true for the negation of the Boolean variables [11]. It expresses that the result does not depend on a positive or a negative encoding of the features describing the situations:

$$a : b :: c : d \Rightarrow \overline{a} : \overline{b} :: \overline{c} : \overline{d} \text{ (code independency).}$$

Moreover, analogical proportions satisfy a unique solution property, which means that, 3 Boolean values a, b, c being given, when we have to find a fourth one x such that $a : b :: c : x$ holds true, we have either no solution (as in the cases of $011x$ or $100x$), or a unique one (as, e.g., in the case of $110x$). More formally, the analogical equation $a : b :: c : x$ is solvable iff $((a \equiv b) \vee (a \equiv c)) = 1$. In that case, the unique solution x is $a \equiv (b \equiv c)$ [9]. The following example provides an illustration with nominal values, where the Boolean patterns are replaced by patterns of the forms XXYY, XYXY, and XXXX. Note that the 4th line (i.e., the description of `Queen`) can be calculated from the 3 first lines by solving here three analogical equations in terms of nominal values. This validates that "a man is to a king as a woman is to a queen".

	Sex	Position	Human
Man	*M*	*ordinary*	*yes*
King	*M*	*power*	*yes*
Woman	*F*	*ordinary*	*yes*
Queen	*F*	*power*	*yes*

The basic idea underlying the analogical proportion-based inference is as follows: if there is a proportion that holds between p components of four vectors, then this proportion may hold for the last remaining components as well. This inference principle [12] can be formally stated as below:

$$\frac{\forall i \in \{1, ..., p\}, \quad a_i : b_i :: c_i : d_i \text{ holds}}{\forall j \in \{p+1, ..., n\}, \quad a_j : b_j :: c_j : d_j \text{ holds}}$$

This is a generalized form of analogical reasoning, where we transfer knowledge from some components of our vectors to their remaining components, tacitly assuming that the values of the p first components determine the values of the others. Then analogical reasoning amounts to finding completely informed triples suitable for inferring the missing value(s) of an incompletely informed item. In case of the existence of several possible triples leading to possibly distinct plausible conclusions, a voting procedure may be used, as in case-based reasoning where the inference is based on a collection of single cases (i.e., the nearest neighbors) rather than on a collection of triples. We may now move from case-based decision to analogical-proportion based decision.

4 Analogy-Based Decision

Let us consider a generic scenario where a decision δ was experienced in two different situations sit_1 and sit_2 in the presence or not of special circumstances, leading to *good* or *bad* results respectively depending on the absence or on the presence of these special circumstances. Suppose we have in our repository the first three lines of the following table (cases a, b, c), while we wonder if we should consider applying decision δ or not in sit_2 when no special circumstances are present (case d). The analogical inference leads here to the prediction that the result should be *good*.

Case	Situation	Special circumstances	Decision	Result
a	sit_1	*yes*	δ	*bad*
b	sit_1	*no*	δ	*good*
c	sit_2	*yes*	δ	*bad*
d	sit_2	*no*	$\boldsymbol{\delta}$	***good***

Further comments are in order here.

- First, note that if we apply a case-based decision view, case d might be found quite similar to case c, since they are identical on all the features used for describing situation sit_2, and differs only on the maybe unique feature describing the so-called "special circumstances"; this would lead to favor the idea that decision δ in case d would also lead to a *bad* result as in case c.
- However, a more careful examination of cases a, b, c may lead to an opposite conclusion. Indeed it is natural to implicitly assume here that the possibly many features gathered here under the labels "situation" and "special circumstances" are enough for describing the cases and for determining the quality of the result of decisions applied to the cases. Thus, the fact that in sit_1, the quality of the result of decision δ is *bad* (resp. *good*) is explained by the presence (resp. absence) of "special circumstances". Then the analogical inference enforces here that we should have the same behavior in sit_2.
- But, note that nothing forbids to also have in the repository a pair of cases pertaining to another situation, say sit_3, which is a counter-example to this behavior, namely one may have the two cases $a' = (sit_3, yes, \delta, good)$ and $c' = (sit_3, no, \delta, good)$ that states in sit_3 the "special circumstances" feature

has no influence when δ is applied; then from cases a', c, c', observing that $(sit_3, yes, \delta) : (sit_2, yes, \delta) :: (sit_3, no, \delta) : (sit_2, no, \delta)$, one concludes by analogical inference that the result of decision δ in case d is then *bad*. This would mean here that it is the situation itself that determines if the result is good or bad.

- Thus different triples may lead to different predictions for the case d under consideration. Thus, one may associate each potential decision δ with the multiset $\mathcal{E}(\delta)$ of the evaluations expected for its result in the current case. For instance, $\mathcal{E}(\delta) = \{good, good, bad\}$, or more generally in case of a non binary evaluation, e.g., $\mathcal{E}(\delta) = \{very\ good, good, good, bad, very\ bad\}$. The difficulty is then to compare multisets of different sizes, e.g.,$\{good\}$ and $\{good, good, bad\}$. Indeed what is better? To choose a rarely experienced decision that is always associated with a good prediction? Or to choose a decision with many good predictions, but some bad ones? Then, several ways of handling these multiple evaluations are possible:
  - a simple majority vote for summarizing the evaluation of each candidate decision δ_i;
  - a more sophisticated weighted sum; for instance, in the above example, sit_2 may be much closer to sit_1 than to sit_3 (in terms of Hamming distance), which leads to somewhat discount the evaluation *bad* and consider that we are closer to *good*.

Generally speaking, this approach can be split in two steps:

step 1: For each candidate decision δ, one first looks for triples (a, b, c) of available cases pertaining to δ whose utilities $u(a), u(b), u(c)$ are known, such that the utility equation $u(a) : u(b) :: u(c) : x$ is solvable (an analogical proportion that holds involves one or two distinct utilities). This task which reduces the space of candidate triples can be performed offline.

step 2: When one wonders what to do in a case $d = (d_1, \ldots, d_p)$, one looks for candidate triples $a = (a_1, \ldots, a_p), b = (b_1, \ldots, b_p)$ and $c = (c_1, \ldots, c_p)$ such that analogical proportions hold component-wise for the feature values, i.e., the proportion holds on all features (if they are all regarded as relevant), or at least on a maximum number of features (analogical inference tolerates irrelevant features, but then requiring that the proportion holds on all features would diminish the number of triples available). Then, the solution of the utility equation $u(a) : u(b) :: u(c) : x$ for any such triple (a, b, c) is a possible value of the utility $u(d)$ of the result of the application of δ in case d.

This approach extends from the Boolean features case to nominal and numerical features, since the definition of analogical proportion can be extended to these cases [5,6].

5 Adaptive Decision with Analogy

Rather than analogically predicting the evaluation of the output of a potential decision in a new situation, one may suppose that we start with a repertory of recommended actions in a variety of circumstances, and then one may also think of trying to take advantage of the creative capabilities of analogy for adapting a decision to the new situation. Indeed, from three patterns, say, e.g., 00, 01, 10, by solving equations $0 : 0 :: 1 : x$ and $0 : 1 :: 0 : y$, one may obtain a fourth pattern, here 11, which is new.

This may be useful when the final decision has diverse options. Such as *Serve a tea* with or without sugar, with or without milk. Let us consider this example to illustrate the idea. As stored in the table below, in situation sit_1 with contraindication ($c\ i$), it is recommended to serve tea only, in situation sit_1 with no $c\ i$, tea with sugar, while in situation sit_2 with $c\ i$ one serves tea with milk. What to do in situation sit_2 with no $c\ i$? Common sense suggests tea with sugar and milk, maybe. It is what analogical proportion equations says: indeed $\delta : \delta :: \delta : x$, $0 : 1 :: 0 : y$ and $0 : 0 :: 1 : z$ yield $xyz = \delta 11$ as in the table below.

Case	Situation	Contraindication	Decision	Option 1	Option 2
a	sit_1	*yes*	δ	0	0
b	sit_1	*no*	δ	1	0
c	sit_2	*yes*	δ	0	1
d	sit_2	*no*	$\boldsymbol{\delta}$	**1**	**1**

We have only outlined how to adapt a decision, viewed as a compound act, depending on circumstances, by means of an analogical proportion-based reasoning. Further investigations are needed for developing the idea.

6 Some Potential Uses

The approach has been presented in general decision terms, and may be applied to different problems. We suggest here two examples of potential uses we may think of.

In querying systems it is important to try to avoid empty sets of answers. Replacing *good* (resp. *bad*) by *non empty set* (resp. *empty set*) in the kind of generic example of the Sect. 4, one may predict when a query may lead to an empty set of answers based on the results of past queries that are not too far from the query under consideration (i.e. differing on few points on which the risk of empty set of answers is sensitive). Then one may also identify the special circumstances that favor empty sets of answers.

Robots must learn utilities from sparse feedback. If the context of the situations is to be considered when learning preferences then the parameter set may be far larger than the training set resulting in over-fitting. The ability to make generalizations between alternative preferences allows the robot to learn more from less data. Just as linear regression does not need the power set of alternatives to learn corresponding weights, the ability for a robot to learn relationships in the data leads to an acceleration of the learning process with fewer mistakes. It also enables small but crucial situational differences in circumstance to be more quickly identified which may otherwise be hard to untangle.

7 Concluding Remarks

This short paper only intends to suggest the potentialities of analogical proportion-based decision. In that respect it is preliminary and much remains to be done for its effective use in practice. Moreover, the proposed approach belongs to a general trend of research that amounts to reasoning with data [10]. Another benefit of this approach relies in its explanation capabilities, i.e., that the robot will be able to explain what it is doing and why. Besides, interestingly enough, the use of quaternary relation where the variation (or the dissimilarity) from a to b is greater (or smaller) than the variation from c to d, rather than being equal to as in analogical proportion, has been also recently introduced in deep learning [8]. This might lead to fruitful developments.

References

1. Amgoud, L., D'Inverno, M., Osman, N., Prade, H., Sierra, C.: Experiences, a forgotten component of epistemic states. In: Ossowski, S., Toni, F., Vouros, G. (eds.) Proceedings of the 1st International Conference on Agreement Technologies (AT'), Dubrovnik, 15–16 October, CEUR Workshop Proceedings, vol. 918, pp. 220–230 (2012)
2. Dubois, D., Esteva, F., Garcia, P., Godo, L., López de Màntaras, R., Prade, H.: Fuzzy set modelling in cased-based reasoning. Int. J. Intell. Syst. **13**(4), 345–373 (1998)
3. Dubois, D., Godo, L., Prade, H., Zapico, A.: On the possibilistic decision model: from decision under uncertainty to case-based decision. Int. J. Uncertain. Fuzziness Knowl. Based Syst. **7**(6), 631–670 (1999)
4. Dubois, D., Hüllermeier, E., Prade, H.: Fuzzy methods for case-based recommendation and decision support. J. Intell. Inf. Syst. **27**, 95–115 (2006)
5. Dubois, D., Prade, H., Richard, G.: Case-based and analogical reasoning. In: Festschrift for Ramon Lopez de Mantaras' 60 years' birthday, pp. 59–77 (2012)
6. Dubois, D., Prade, H., Richard, G.: Multiple-valued extensions of analogical proportions. Fuzzy Sets Syst. **292**, 193–202 (2016)
7. Gilboa, I., Schmeidler, D.: Case-based decision theory. Q. J. Econ. **110**, 605–639 (1995)
8. Law, M.T., Thome, N., Cord, M.: Quadruplet-wise image similarity learning. In: Proceedings of the IEEE International Conference on Computer Vision (ICCV), Sydney, 1–8 December, pp. 249–256 (2013)
9. Miclet, L., Prade, H.: Handling analogical proportions in classical logic and fuzzy logics settings. In: Sossai, C., Chemello, G. (eds.) ECSQARU 2009. LNCS (LNAI), vol. 5590, pp. 638–650. Springer, Heidelberg (2009). doi:10.1007/978-3-642-02906-6_55
10. Prade, H.: Reasoning with data - a new challenge for AI? In: Schockaert, S., Senellart, P. (eds.) SUM 2016. LNCS (LNAI), vol. 9858, pp. 274–288. Springer, Cham (2016). doi:10.1007/978-3-319-45856-4_19
11. Prade, H., Richard, G.: From analogical proportion to logical proportions. Logica Universalis **7**(4), 441–505 (2013)
12. Stroppa, N., Yvon, F.: Analogical learning and formal proportions: definitions and methodological issues. Technical report ENST D-2005-004, Paris, June 2005

Flexible Query Answering with the powerset-AI Operator and Star-Based Ranking

Lena Wiese(✉)

Institute of Computer Science, University of Göttingen,
Goldschmidtstraße 7, 37077 Göttingen, Germany
lena.wiese@uni-goettingen.de

Abstract. Query generalization is one option to implement flexible query answering. In this paper, we introduce a generalization operator (called powerset-AI) that extends conventional Anti-Instantiation (AI). We analyze structural modifications imposed by the generalization to obtain syntactic similarity measures (based on the star feature) that rank generalized queries with regard to their closeness to the original query.

1 Introduction

Flexible query answering supports users in the search for data in databases or information systems. Users might be unaware of the exact structure of the data and hence an exact formulation of the query conditions is often difficult. However, when using a conventional database system it tries to exactly answer the user query. In case the database system is not able to find an exactly matching answer, the query *fails* and the database system returns an empty answer. This is undesirable for the user, because he has to find alternative ways to express his query in order to receive some information. *Flexible* query answering systems offer intelligent procedures to revise user queries and are able to return answers that are related to the user's original query intent. However, one problem of flexible query answering is *overabundance* of related answers: too many answers are returned that might even be irrelevant for the user.

In this paper, we focus on query generalization of logical queries with the Anti-Instantiation (AI) operator. We extend the basic AI operator used in prior work by defining a novel *powerset-AI* operator. Queries resulting from powerset-AI retain more equality conditions than the conventional AI operator. To address the overabundance problem, we propose a ranking based on the amount of equality conditions retained. In this way, the higher-ranked queries can be answered by the database system with priority while the lower-ranked ones are assumed to be less important for the user. In this paper we make the following contributions:

- We extend the conventional AI operator by introducing our novel powerset-AI operator that allows to obtain a greater set of syntactically and semantically distinct generalized queries than conventional AI.

H. Christiansen et al. (Eds.): FQAS 2017, LNAI 10333, pp. 36–48, 2017.
DOI: 10.1007/978-3-319-59692-1_4

- We apply the star feature (counting equality conditions between query conjuncts) of the original query and a generalized query to obtain a value for the closeness of the generalized formula to the original formula.

After surveying related work in Sect. 2, we introduce theoretical background in Sect. 3 and present the powerset-AI operator in Sect. 4. Syntactic similarity of queries is analyzed in Sects. 6 and 7 concludes the paper.

2 Related Work

The CoopQA system [1,2] applies three generalization operators to a conjunctive query (which – among others – can already be found in the seminal paper of Michalski [3]): **Dropping Condition** (*DC*) removes one conjunct from a query; **Anti-Instantiation** (*AI*) replaces a constant (or a variable occurring at least twice) in Q with a new variable y; **Goal Replacement** (*GR*) takes a rule from Σ, finds a substitution θ that maps the rule's body to some conjuncts in the query and replaces these conjuncts by the head (with θ applied).

The operators *DC*, *AI* and *GR* have been applied to obtain neighborhood proposals [4] or related answers guided by explanations [5] in multi-agent communication. Other approaches propose some form of semantic query generalization where terms a generalized according to their meaning; these methods can be combined with generalization operators, including ranked data tables [6], fuzzy logic [7], taxonomies [8] or clustering [9]. More generally, the term "cooperative database system" was for example used in [10] for a system called "CoBase" that relies on several type abstraction hierarchies (TAH) to relax queries and hence to return a wider range of answers. In a similar manner, Halder and Cortesi [11] employ abstraction of domains and define optimality of answers with respect to some user-defined relevancy constraints. The approach by Pivert et al. using fuzzy sets [12] analyzes cooperative query answering based on semantic proximity. Other related systems are Flex [13], Carmin [14] and Ishmael [15] that introduce and analyze dedicated generalization operators.

Hurtado et al. [16] relax RDF queries based on an ontology. Similarly, [17] introduce the two operators APPROX and RELAX in the query language SPARQL. [18] improve upon existing work of RDF relaxation by finding related answers without generating all relaxed queries. Query relaxation has also been investigated for XML queries. For example, [19] analyze expressiveness of generalization operators for (a fragment of) XPath queries. Similarly, [20] apply structural generalization of XML queries; the authors also provide a recent survey of related work on approximate XML query answering.

3 Background

In this paper we focus on flexible query answering for conjunctive queries. Throughout this article we assume a logical language $\mathscr{L}$ consisting of a finite set of predicate symbols (for example denoted *Ill*, *Treat* or P), a possibly infinite set *dom* of constant symbols (for example denoted Mary or a), and an infinite set of variables (for example denoted x or y). A term is either a constant or a variable. The capital letter X denotes a vector of variables; if the order of variables in X does not matter, we identify X with the set of its variables and apply set operators – for example we write $y \in X$. We use the standard logical connectors conjunction $\wedge$, disjunction $\vee$, negation $\neg$ and material implication $\rightarrow$ and universal $\forall$ as well as existential $\exists$ quantifiers. An atom is a formula consisting of a single predicate symbol; a literal is an atom (a "positive literal") or a negation of an atom (a "negative literal"); a ground formula is one without variables; the existential (universal) closure of a formula ϕ is written as $\exists\phi$ ($\forall\phi$) and denotes the closed formula where all free variables are bound the respective quantifier.

Table 1. Health records

Ill	PatientID	Diagnoses
	Pete	Cough
	Mary	Flu
	Mary	Bronchitis
	Lisa	Asthma
	Lisa	Cough
	Tom	Cough

Treat	PatientID	Prescription
	Pete	Antitussive
	Mary	Inhalation
	Lisa	Inhalation
	Tom	Antitussive
	Tom	Throat Lozenge

A query formula Q is a conjunction of literals with some variables X occurring freely (that is, not bound by variables); that is, $Q(X) = L_{i_1} \wedge \ldots \wedge L_{i_n}$. By abuse of notation, we will also write $L_{ij} \in Q$ when L_{ij} is a conjunct in formula Q. A query $Q(X)$ is sent to a knowledge base Σ (a set of logical formulas) and then evaluated in Σ by a function *ans* that returns a set of answers containing instantiations of the free variables (in other words, a set of formulas that are logically implied by Σ); as we focus on the generalization of queries, we assume the *ans* function and an appropriate notion of logical truth given. A special case of a knowledge base can be a relational database with database tables; as for example in [21] we apply a closed world assumption that makes all information not contained in the database false. As already established in [22] we apply a notion of generalization based on a consequence operator $\models$ as follows.

Definition 1 (Deductive generalization wrt. knowledge base [22]**).** *Let Σ be a knowledge base, $\phi(X)$ be a formula with a tuple X of free variables, and $\psi(X, Y)$ be a formula with an additional tuple Y of free variables disjoint from X. The formula $\psi(X, Y)$ is a* deductive generalization *of $\phi(X)$, if it holds in Σ that the less general ϕ implies the more general ψ where for the free variables X (the ones that occur in ϕ and possibly in ψ) the universal closure and for free variables Y (the ones that occur in ψ only) the existential closure is taken:*

$$\Sigma \models \forall X \exists Y (\phi(X) \rightarrow \psi(X, Y))$$

The three operators Dropping Condition (DC), Anti-Instantiation (AI) and Goal Replacement (GR) used in [2] satisfy the definition of deductive generalization (Definition 1), provided the consequence operator ($\models$) satisfies some reasonable properties. For example, the semantic consequence $\models$ should be implemented by syntactic entailment that satisfies *generalized modus ponens* (for GR), *conjunction elimination* (for DC) and *existential introduction* (for AI).

Example 1. As a running example, we consider a hospital information system that stores illnesses and treatments of patients (see Table 1). The example query $Q(x_1, x_2, x_3) = \mathit{Ill}(x_1, \mathit{Flu}) \wedge \mathit{Ill}(x_1, \mathit{Cough})$ asks for all the patients x_1 that suffer from both flu and cough. This query fails with the given database tables as there is no patient with both flu and cough. However, the querying user might instead be interested in the patient called Mary who is ill with both flu and bronchitis. Query generalization (and in particular Anti-Instantiation) will enable a flexible query answering system to find this informative answer.

4 The powerset-AI Operator

Conventional Anti-Instantiation chooses one occurrence of a term (that is, a constant or variable) of a query and introduces a new variable y for. In this way the conditions of the query are relaxed. In particular, AI covers these cases:

- turning constants into variables: $P(a)$ is converted to $P(y)$ (see [3])
- breaking joins: $P(x) \wedge S(x)$ is converted to $P(x) \wedge S(y)$ (introduced in [22])

For each constant a all occurrences must be anti-instantiated; the same applies to variables x – however, with the exception that if x only occurs twice, one occurrence of x need not be anti-instantiated due to equivalence. Operator 1 lists the steps of conventional AI.

Operator 1. Anti-instantiation (AI)

Input: Query $Q(X) = L_1 \wedge \ldots \wedge L_n$ of length n
Output: Generalized query $Q^{gen}(X, Y)$ with Y containing one new variable y
1: From $Q(X)$ choose a term t such that t is

- either a variable occurring in $Q(X)$ at least twice
- or a constant

2: Choose one literal L_j where t occurs
3: Let L'_j be the literal with one occurrence of t replaced with y
4: **return** $Q^{gen}(X, Y) = L_1 \wedge \ldots \wedge L_{j-1} \wedge L'_j \wedge L_{j+1} \wedge \ldots \wedge L_n$

Example 2. For $Q(x_1) = \mathit{Ill}(x_1, \mathit{Flu}) \wedge \mathit{Ill}(x_1, \mathit{Cough})$ an example generalization with AI is $Q^{AI}(x_1, y) = \mathit{Ill}(x_1, \mathit{Flu}) \wedge \mathit{Ill}(x_1, y)$. It results in an non-empty (and hence informative) answer: $\mathit{Ill}(\mathit{Mary}, \mathit{Flu}) \wedge \mathit{Ill}(\mathit{Mary}, \mathit{Bronchitis})$.

The conventional AI operator only replaces a single occurrence of a term. We now introduce a novel AI operator that replaces several occurrences of a term at once. In doing so, different equality conditions can be retained – a property that is impossible with the conventional AI operator. We call the operator *powerset-AI* because first the powerset of all equality conditions is computed and then an element of this powerset (that is, a subset of equalities) is chosen for anti-instantiation. We first provide an example showing limits of conventional AI.

Example 3. Suppose a user is interested in four (possibly different) patients being treated with an inhalation. The user hence submits the query

$$Q'(x_1,x_2,x_3) = \mathit{Treat}(x_1,\mathit{Inhalation}) \wedge \mathit{Treat}(x_2,\mathit{Inhalation}) \\ \wedge \mathit{Treat}(x_3,\mathit{Inhalation}) \wedge \mathit{Treat}(x_4,\mathit{Inhalation}).$$

Demanding that the x_i are pairwise distinct ($x_i \neq x_j$ for $i,j \in \{1,\dots,4\}$), the database cannot find an answer to this query and hence the query fails. Conventional Anti-Instantiation can replace only a single occurrence of *Inhalation* by a new variable y_1; for example

$$Q'_1(x_1,x_2,x_3,y_1) = \mathit{Treat}(x_1,y_1) \wedge \mathit{Treat}(x_2,\mathit{Inhalation}) \\ \wedge \mathit{Treat}(x_3,\mathit{Inhalation}) \wedge \mathit{Treat}(x_4,\mathit{Inhalation})$$

Again demanding that the x_i are pairwise distinct, the query Q_1 is still failing. A second application of conventional Anti-Instantiation can replace another occurrence of *Inhalation* by a new variable y_2; for example

$$Q'_2(x_1,x_2,x_3,y_1,y_2) = \mathit{Treat}(x_1,y_1) \wedge \mathit{Treat}(x_2,y_2) \\ \wedge \mathit{Treat}(x_3,\mathit{Inhalation}) \wedge \mathit{Treat}(x_4,\mathit{Inhalation})$$

In this case an answer can be found; however, no equality between y_1 and y_2 is expressed. For example, one answer for our table is $\mathit{Treat}(\mathit{Pete},\mathit{Antitussive}) \wedge \mathit{Treat}(\mathit{Tom},\mathit{Throat\ Lozenge}) \wedge \mathit{Treat}(\mathit{Mary},\mathit{Inhalation}) \wedge \mathit{Treat}(\mathit{Lisa},\mathit{Inhalation})$.

The powerset-AI operator we propose keeps the equality condition by replacing several occurrences of a term with the same new variable.

Example 4. Continuing the above example, we can simultaneously replace the first two occurrences of *Inhalation* with the same new variable y:

$$Q'_3(x_1,x_2,x_3,y) = \mathit{Treat}(x_1,y) \wedge \mathit{Treat}(x_2,y) \\ \wedge \mathit{Treat}(x_3,\mathit{Inhalation}) \wedge \mathit{Treat}(x_4,\mathit{Inhalation})$$

In this way the equality condition between the first and second occurrence is retained. With this query we can retrieve the answer $\mathit{Treat}(\mathit{Pete},\mathit{Antitussive}) \wedge \mathit{Treat}(\mathit{Tom},\mathit{Antitussive}) \wedge \mathit{Treat}(\mathit{Mary},\mathit{Inhalation}) \wedge \mathit{Treat}(\mathit{Lisa},\mathit{Inhalation})$ without retrieving any less relevant answers as in the previous example.

We now formalize the approach of powerset-AI. First we need the notion of occurrences of a term t.

Definition 2 (Occurrences of a term). *If a term t occurs k times in a query then the set of occurrences in the (left-to-right) order of appearance in the query is defined as* $\mathcal{O}_t = \{t.1, \ldots, t.k\}$.

For the set of occurrences $\mathcal{O}_t$ the powerset $\rho(\mathcal{O}_t)$ contains all $2^{|\mathcal{O}_t|}$ subsets. When anti-instantiating a *constant*, all non-empty subsets of $\rho(\mathcal{O}_t)$ can be chosen leading to semantically different generalized queries. In other words, we consider the sets $\mathcal{P}_t = \{\mathcal{S} \in \rho(\mathcal{O}_t) \mid 1 \leq |\mathcal{S}| \leq |\mathcal{O}_t|\}$ for anti-instantiation with a new variable y.

When anti-instantiating a *variable* with at least two occurrences, the situation is different. For such variables it suffices to consider only the sets of occurrences of size up to half of the total amount of occurrences. More formally, we consider $\mathcal{P}_t = \{\mathcal{S} \in \rho(\mathcal{O}_t) \mid 1 \leq |\mathcal{S}| \leq \lfloor\frac{|\mathcal{O}_t|}{2}\rfloor\}$ for anti-instantiation with a new variable y. The reason for this is that all anti-instantiations considering larger sets of occurrences (that is, sets $\{\mathcal{S} \in \rho(\mathcal{O}_t) \mid \lceil\frac{|\mathcal{O}_t|}{2}\rceil \leq |\mathcal{S}| \leq |\mathcal{O}_t|\}$) lead to queries that are equivalent (more precisely, identical up to variable renaming) to one considering one set from $\mathcal{P}_t$. Operator 2 lists the steps of powerset-AI.

Operator 2. powerset Anti-instantiation (powerset-AI)

Input: Query $Q(X) = L_1 \wedge \ldots \wedge L_n$ of length n
Output: Generalized query $Q^{gen}(X,Y)$ with Y containing one new variable y

From $Q(X)$ choose a term t such that t is
- either a variable occurring in $Q(X)$ at least twice
- or a constant

Let $\mathcal{O}_t$ be the set of all occurrences of t and $\rho(\mathcal{O}_t)$ the powerset
If t is a constant, compute the set $\mathcal{P}_t = \{\mathcal{S} \in \rho(\mathcal{O}_t) \mid 1 \leq |\mathcal{S}| \leq |\mathcal{O}_t|\}$
If t is a variable, compute the set $\mathcal{P}_t = \{\mathcal{S} \in \rho(\mathcal{O}_t) \mid 1 \leq |\mathcal{S}| \leq \left\lfloor\frac{|\mathcal{O}_t|}{2}\right\rfloor\}$
Choose one set $\mathcal{S} \in \mathcal{P}_t$ of occurrences
Let $L_{i_1}, \ldots, L_{i_m}$ denote the literals of $Q(X)$ containing the occurrences in $\mathcal{S}$
Let $L'_{i_1}, \ldots, L'_{i_m}$ denote the literals with each occurrence of t in $\mathcal{S}$ replaced with the new variable y
Let $L_{i_{m+1}}, \ldots, L_{i_n}$ denote the literals of $Q(X)$ apart from $L_{i_1}, \ldots, L_{i_m}$
return $Q^{gen}(X,Y) = L'_{i_1} \wedge \ldots \wedge L'_{i_m} \wedge L_{i_{m+1}} \wedge \ldots \wedge L_{i_n}$

Example 5. Similar to the above example, we can replace occurrences of a variable contained in the original query with the same new variable y. Suppose a user is interested in a patient x with four specified diseases. The user hence submits the query

$$Q''(x) = \mathit{Ill}(x, \mathit{Flu}) \wedge \mathit{Ill}(x, \mathit{Bronchitis}) \wedge \mathit{Ill}(x, \mathit{Asthma}) \wedge \mathit{Ill}(x, \mathit{Cough})$$

Replacing three occurrences of x by y leads to a query equivalent to one obtained by replacing one occurrence of x by y:

$$Q''_1(x, y) = \mathit{Ill}(x, \mathit{Flu}) \wedge \mathit{Ill}(y, \mathit{Bronchitis}) \wedge \mathit{Ill}(y, \mathit{Asthma}) \wedge \mathit{Ill}(y, \mathit{Cough})$$

is identical to

$$Q''_2(x, y) = \mathit{Ill}(y, \mathit{Flu}) \wedge \mathit{Ill}(x, \mathit{Bronchitis}) \wedge \mathit{Ill}(x, \mathit{Asthma}) \wedge \mathit{Ill}(x, \mathit{Cough})$$

only with the roles of x and y reversed. Moreover, a query that replaces two occurrences of x by y, e.g.

$$Q''_3(x, y) = \mathit{Ill}(x, \mathit{Flu}) \wedge \mathit{Ill}(x, \mathit{Bronchitis}) \wedge \mathit{Ill}(y, \mathit{Asthma}) \wedge \mathit{Ill}(y, \mathit{Cough})$$

leads to a non-failing query and the answer $\mathit{Ill}(\mathit{Mary}, \mathit{Flu}) \wedge \mathit{Ill}(\mathit{Mary}, \mathit{Bronchitis}) \wedge \mathit{Ill}(\mathit{Lisa}, \mathit{Asthma}) \wedge \mathit{Ill}(\mathit{Lisa}, \mathit{Cough})$ can be returned to the user.

We now show that the powerset-AI operator complies with Definition 1 independent of any specific knowledge base Σ.

Proposition 1. *powerset-AI is a deductive generalization operator.*

Proof. As in Operator 2, let $L_{i_1} \wedge \ldots \wedge L_{i_m}$ be the subquery containing occurrences of term t. Let $L'_{i_1} \wedge \ldots \wedge L'_{i_m}$ be the subquery with the occurrences of term t replaced by y. It holds that $\models \forall X \exists y\, (L_{i_1} \wedge \ldots \wedge L_{i_m} \rightarrow L'_{i_1} \wedge \ldots \wedge L'_{i_m})$. The same applies to the whole query: $\models \forall X \exists y\, (Q(X) \rightarrow Q^{gen}(X, Y))$.

Note that by choosing different sets S in a powerset-AI step a set of different output queries $Q^{gen}(X, Y)$ can be produced. Moreover, multiple powerset-AI steps can be executed in sequence by choosing a different t for each step. The question we want to analyze next is how to obtain a ranking on all these output queries based on their structural differences.

5 The Star Feature and Similarities

Features are properties that can be attributed to objects; in our case objects are queries. The similarity of two objects can then be determined by evaluating (for example, counting) the feature commonalities and differences. Here we focus on the so-called star feature. We borrow the definition of a star of a chosen literal from [23]. The star contains all predicate symbols of other literals that share a term with the chosen literal. In this way, the star can express connections between different literals. In particular, two occurrences of the same variable (inside different literals) correspond to a join condition of an equality join; and using the same constants corresponds to a join followed by a selection with the constant as the specific value required for the join attribute. Hence, losing one such shared variable or constant in a generalization corresponds to "breaking joins" (see [22]) which should be penalized with a lower similarity. Moreover, losing a literal with many connections is worse than losing a literal with few connections to other literals. The star is the appropriate feature for this: stars of other literals are less affected by breaking a join with a literal with less connections. More formally, we denote $Terms(L_i, Q)$ the set of terms (that is, constants and variables) of literal L_i in a conjunctive query Q; moreover, let $Pred(Q)$ be the set of predicate symbols occurring in Q. For a given literal we use the following definition of its star (cf. [23]) resulting in a multiset of predicate symbols:

Definition 3. (Star of a literal [23]). *For a literal L_i in a given query Q we define the* star *of L_i to be a multiset of predicate symbols as follows*

$$\begin{aligned} Star(L_i, Q) = \{P \mid\ & \textit{there is a literal } L_j \in Q, i \neq j, \\ & \textit{such that } L_j = P(t_1, \ldots t_k) \textit{ and} \\ & Terms(L_j, Q) \cap Terms(L_i, Q) \neq \emptyset\} \subseteq Pred(Q) \end{aligned}$$

We compare the star feature of literals in the original query Q and a query Q^{gen} (which is obtained by one or more applications of the powerset-AI operator). We see that for each literal L_i of the original query Q the amount of connections to other literals is always greater or equal to the amount of connections of the corresponding literal L'_i in the anti-instantiated query. Hence, $Star(L'_i, Q^{gen}) \subseteq Star(L_i, Q)$.

Example 6. We compare the star of the first literal of

$$\begin{aligned} Q'(x_1, x_2, x_3) = & \ Treat(x_1,\ Inhalation) \wedge Treat\ (x_2,\ Inhalation) \\ & \wedge Treat\ (x_3,\ Inhalation) \wedge Treat\ (x_4,\ Inhalation) \end{aligned}$$

to the stars of its generalizations in the queries

$$\begin{aligned} Q'_1(x_1, x_2, x_3, y_1) &= Treat(x_1, y_1) \wedge Treat(x_2,\ Inhalation) \\ &\quad \wedge Treat(x_3,\ Inhalation) \wedge Treat(x_4,\ Inhalation) \\ Q'_2(x_1, x_2, x_3, y_1, y_2) &= Treat(x_1, y_1) \wedge Treat(x_2, y_2) \\ &\quad \wedge Treat(x_3,\ Inhalation) \wedge Treat(x_4,\ Inhalation) \\ Q'_3(x_1, x_2, x_3, y) &= Treat(x_1, y) \wedge Treat(x_2, y) \\ &\quad \wedge Treat(x_3,\ Inhalation) \wedge Treat(x_4,\ Inhalation) \end{aligned}$$

We obtain $Star(Treat(x_1, Inhalation), Q') = \{Treat, Treat, Treat\}$ for the original query, $Star(Treat(x_1, y_1), Q'_1) = \emptyset$, $Star(Treat(x_1, y_1), Q'_2) = \emptyset$, as well as $Star(Treat(x_1, y), Q'_3) = \{Treat\}$.

One way to judge the relation of two objects is determining a similarity between them.

Definition 4 (Similarity Measure). *For a set of objects $\mathcal{O}$, a function sim : $\mathcal{O} \times \mathcal{O} \rightarrow \mathbb{R}$ is called a similarity on $\mathcal{O}$, if for all $a, b \in \mathcal{O}$ it holds that*

1. ***(Non-negativity)*** $sim(a, b) \geq 0$
2. ***(Maximality)*** $sim(a, a) \geq sim(a, b)$

Based on feature sets of two objects a and b, similarity between these two objects can be calculated by means of different similarity measures. That is, if A is a feature set of a and B is the corresponding feature set of b, then $A \cap B$ is the set of their common features, $A \setminus B$ is the set of features that are only attributed to A, and $B \setminus A$ is the set of features that are only attributed to B. In Tversky's seminal paper [24], a function f is applied to each set such that it is mapped to a numerical value. Typically the cardinality function is used. We will also follow this approach in this paper. That is, we obtain the cardinalities of each set: $\mathfrak{l} = |A \cap B|$, $\mathfrak{m} = |A \setminus B|$, and $\mathfrak{n} = |B \setminus A|$ and use them as input to specific similarity measures. In this paper, we focus on the ratio model (in particular, one of its special cases called Jaccard index).

Definition 5 (Tversky's Ratio Model [24], Jaccard Index). *A similarity measure sim between two objects a and b can be represented by the ratio of features common to both a and b and the joint features of a and b using a non-negative scale f and two non-negative scalars α and β:*

$$sim_T(a, b) = \frac{f(A \cap B)}{f(A \cap B) + \alpha \cdot f(A \setminus B) + \beta \cdot f(B \setminus A)}$$

The Jaccard index *is a special form of the ratio model where* $\alpha = \beta = 1$ *and* f *is the cardinality* $|\cdot|$*:*

$$sim_{jacc}(a, b) = \frac{|A \cap B|}{|A \cap B| + |A \setminus B| + |B \setminus A|} = \frac{|A \cap B|}{|A \cup B|} = \frac{\mathfrak{l}}{\mathfrak{l} + \mathfrak{m} + \mathfrak{n}}$$

The Jaccard index satisfies the property of monotonicity (see [24]): whenever a formula has more features in common with one formula than with another formula and they differ on less features, then the similarity between the first two is higher than the similarity between the first and the last.

Definition 6 (Monotonicity [24]). *For three objects a, b and c, if* $A \cap B \supseteq A \cap C$, $A \setminus B \subseteq A \setminus C$, *and* $B \setminus A \subseteq C \setminus A$, *then* $sim(a, b) \geq sim(a, c)$. *When the inclusions are proper, the inequality is strict.*

6 Similarity for powerset-AI

Based on the star feature, we want to calculate the similarity between the original query Q and a query Q^{gen} (which is obtained by one or more applications of the powerset-AI operator). We calculate the Jaccard index for the feature sets by taking the cardinalities of their commonalities and differences: if A is a feature set of Q and B is the corresponding feature set of Q^{gen}, then $A \cap B$ is the set of their common features, $A \setminus B$ is the set of features that are lost during generalization, and $B \setminus A$ is the set of features that have been added during generalization.

Note that the star feature is a multiset and we define the operators $\cup$, $\cap$ and $\setminus$ to be multiset operations. To obtain similarity $sim(Q, Q^{gen})$ between the original query Q and a query Q^{gen} we proceed as follows:

- For each literal L_i in Q and the corresponding L'_i in Q^{gen} compute the star features $A = Star(L_i, Q)$ and $B = Star(L'_i, Q^{gen})$.
- Compute the literal similarities $sim_{jacc}(L_i, L'_i)$ for each such pair of literals.
- Compute the average by summing all literal similarities and dividing by the total amount n of literals in the query.

Example 7. We compute the stars of all literals of

$$Q'(x_1, x_2, x_3) = Treat(x_1, Inhalation) \wedge Treat(x_2, Inhalation) \\ \wedge Treat(x_3, Inhalation) \wedge Treat(x_4, Inhalation)$$

and the stars of its generalizations in the query

$$Q'_1(x_1, x_2, x_3, y_1) = Treat(x_1, y_1) \wedge Treat(x_2, Inhalation) \\ \wedge Treat(x_3, Inhalation) \wedge Treat(x_4, Inhalation)$$

to compute the literal similarities. We obtain for all literal pairs $sim_{jacc}(L_1, L'_1) = 0$, $sim_{jacc}(L_2, L'_2) = \frac{2}{3}$, $sim_{jacc}(L_3, L'_3) = \frac{2}{3}$, $sim_{jacc}(L_4, L'_4) = \frac{2}{3}$. By summing all literal similarities and dividing by 4 (the total amount of literals), we obtain the query similarity $sim(Q', Q'_1) = 0.5$ Similarly, for the query

$$Q'_2(x_1, x_2, x_3, y_1, y_2) = Treat(x_1, y_1) \wedge Treat(x_2, y_2) \\ \wedge Treat(x_3, Inhalation) \wedge Treat(x_4, Inhalation)$$

we obtain $sim_{jacc}(L_1, L'_1) = 0$, $sim_{jacc}(L_2, L'_2) = 0$, $sim_{jacc}(L_3, L'_3) = \frac{1}{3}$, and $sim_{jacc}(L_4, L'_4) = \frac{1}{3}$. By summing all literal similarities and dividing by 4 (the total amount of literals), we obtain the query similarity $sim(Q', Q'_2) = \frac{1}{6}$. Lastly, for

$$Q'_3(x_1, x_2, x_3, y) = Treat(x_1, y) \wedge Treat(x_2, y) \\ \wedge Treat(x_3, Inhalation) \wedge Treat(x_4, Inhalation)$$

we obtain $sim_{jacc}(L_1, L'_1) = \frac{1}{3}$, $sim_{jacc}(L_2, L'_2) = \frac{1}{3}$, $sim_{jacc}(L_3, L'_3) = \frac{1}{3}$, and $sim_{jacc}(L_4, L'_4) = \frac{1}{3}$. By summing all literal similarities and dividing by 4 (the total amount of literals), we obtain the query similarity $sim(Q', Q'_3) = \frac{1}{3}$.

In the example we see that the query Q'_3 where two occurrences of *Inhalation* are replaced by one new variable y is ranked better than the query Q'_2 where the same occurrences are replaced by two new variables y_1 and y_2. We now formally show this fact when replacing multiple occurrences.

Theorem 1. *Let Q be the original query containing term t. Let $\mathcal{S} \in \rho(\mathcal{O}_t)$ be the set of occurrences of t chosen for powerset-AI. Let $Q^{gen}(x, y)$ be a query obtained by anti-instantiating occurrences $\mathcal{S}$ of the term t with one new variable y. Let $Q^{AI}(x, y_1, \ldots, y_{|\mathcal{S}|})$ be a query obtained by anti-instantiating the same occurrences of term t with $|\mathcal{S}|$ new variables $y_1, \ldots, y_{|\mathcal{S}|}$. Then it holds that $sim_{jacc}(Q, Q^{AI}(x, y_1, \ldots, y_{|\mathcal{S}|})) \leq sim_{jacc}(Q, Q^{gen}(x, y))$.*

Proof. As in Operator 2, let $L_{i_1},\ldots,L_{i_m}$ be the literals containing occurrences of term t that are replaced (Case 1). Let $L_{i_{m+1}},\ldots,L_{i_n}$ be the literals unaffected by anti-instantiation (Case 2). We analyze the stars of the literals in these cases:

- Case 1: Let $L'_{i_1},\ldots,L'_{i_m}$ be the literals in $Q^{gen}(x,y)$ with the occurrences of term t replaced by y. Let $L''_{i_1},\ldots,L''_{i_m}$ be the literals in $Q^{AI}(x,y_1,\ldots,y_{|S|})$ with the occurrences of term t replaced by $y_1,\ldots,y_{|S|}$. It holds that for $A = \mathit{Star}(L_{i_j},Q)$ and $B = \mathit{Star}(L'_{i_j},Q^{gen})$ and $C = \mathit{Star}(L''_{i_j},Q^{AI})$ (where $j = 1,\ldots,m$) both A and B definitely contain predicate symbols of literals in $L_{i_1},\ldots,L_{i_m}$: In Q, a literal L_{i_j} has connections to all other such literals based on t, while in $Q^{gen}(x,y)$ these connections are based on y. C does not necessarily contain them; however, if it contains such a predicate symbol then only due to some other term different from t and y; in this case also A and B necessarily contain this predicate symbol, too.
- Case 2: The literals $L_{i_{m+1}},\ldots,L_{i_n}$ occur unmodified in both $Q^{gen}(x,y)$ and $Q^{AI}(x,y_1,\ldots,y_{|S|})$, too. When comparing $A = \mathit{Star}(L_{i_j},Q)$ and $B = \mathit{Star}(L_{i_j},Q^{gen})$ and $C = \mathit{Star}(L_{i_j},Q^{AI})$ (where $j = m+1,\ldots,n$), A, B and C are identical if L_{i_j} does not contain t. If L_{i_j} contains t, then A contains all predicate symbols of literals $L_{i_1},\ldots,L_{i_m}$ due to connections based on t; in contrast, B and C are identical: they are both reduced by the predicate symbols of literals $L_{i_1},\ldots,L_{i_m}$ (as long as no other occurrence of t remains in one such literal).

In both cases it follows that $A\cap B \supseteq A\cap C$, $A\setminus B \subseteq A\setminus C$, and $B\setminus A \subseteq C\setminus A$. Due to these facts we can apply the notion of monotonicity according to Definition 6 and the theorem follows.

Hence we conclude that the star feature is an appropriate measure to rank different queries obtained by applying several generalization steps (in particular, powerset-AI) to the same original query.

7 Discussion and Conclusion

We introduced powerset-AI as a novel generalization operator that replaces terms in a given query to obtain relaxed queries that provide related information. In order to restrict query answering to the most relevant queries (and hence avoid overabundance of answers), we proposed a ranking of these relaxed queries based on the star feature. Future work will investigate the application of powerset-AI in combination with other generalization operators (like GR and DC) and their joint behavior as in [2]. Ongoing work covers efficient computation of query relaxation with powerset-AI which includes duplicate checking and computing answers without generating all queries as in [18].

References

1. Bakhtyar, M., Dang, N., Inoue, K., Wiese, L.: Implementing inductive concept learning for cooperative query answering. In: Spiliopoulou, M., Schmidt-Thieme, L., Janning, R. (eds.) Data Analysis, Machine Learning and Knowledge Discovery. SCDAKO, pp. 127–134. Springer, Cham (2014). doi:10.1007/978-3-319-01595-8_14
2. Inoue, K., Wiese, L.: Generalizing conjunctive queries for informative answers. In: Christiansen, H., Tré, G., Yazici, A., Zadrozny, S., Andreasen, T., Larsen, H.L. (eds.) FQAS 2011. LNCS, vol. 7022, pp. 1–12. Springer, Heidelberg (2011). doi:10.1007/978-3-642-24764-4_1
3. Michalski, R.S.: A theory and methodology of inductive learning. Artif. Intell. **20**(2), 111–161 (1983)
4. Sakama, C., Inoue, K.: Negotiation by abduction and relaxation. In: International Joint Conference on Autonomous Agents and Multiagent Systems (AAMAS), IFAAMAS, pp. 1010–1025 (2007)
5. Sá, S., Alcântara, J.: Abduction-based search for cooperative answers. In: Leite, J., Torroni, P., Ågotnes, T., Boella, G., Torre, L. (eds.) CLIMA 2011. LNCS, vol. 6814, pp. 208–224. Springer, Heidelberg (2011). doi:10.1007/978-3-642-22359-4_15
6. Urbanova, L., Vychodil, V., Wiese, L.: Applications of ordinal ranks to flexible query answering. In: Hüllermeier, E., Link, S., Fober, T., Seeger, B. (eds.) SUM 2012. LNCS, vol. 7520, pp. 16–29. Springer, Heidelberg (2012). doi:10.1007/978-3-642-33362-0_2
7. Belohlavek, R., Vychodil, V.: A logic of graded attributes. Arch. Math. Logic **54**(7–8), 785–802 (2015)
8. Wiese, L.: Taxonomy-based fragmentation for anti-instantiation in distributed databases. In: Proceedings of the 2013 IEEE/ACM 6th International Conference on Utility and Cloud Computing International Workshop on Intelligent Techniques and Architectures for Autonomic Clouds (ITAAC13), pp. 363–368. IEEE Computer Society (2013)
9. Wiese, L.: Clustering-based fragmentation and data replication for flexible query answering in distributed databases. J. Cloud Comput. **3**(1), 18 (2014)
10. Chu, W.W., Yang, H., Chiang, K., Minock, M., Chow, G., Larson, C.: CoBase: a scalable and extensible cooperative information system. JIIS **6**(2/3), 223–259 (1996)
11. Halder, R., Cortesi, A.: Cooperative query answering by abstract interpretation. In: Černá, I., Gyimóthy, T., Hromkovič, J., Jefferey, K., Královič, R., Vukolić, M., Wolf, S. (eds.) SOFSEM 2011. LNCS, vol. 6543, pp. 284–296. Springer, Heidelberg (2011). doi:10.1007/978-3-642-18381-2_24
12. Pivert, O., Jaudoin, H., Brando, C., Hadjali, A.: A method based on query caching and predicate substitution for the treatment of failing database queries. In: Bichindaritz, I., Montani, S. (eds.) ICCBR 2010. LNCS, vol. 6176, pp. 436–450. Springer, Heidelberg (2010). doi:10.1007/978-3-642-14274-1_32
13. Motro, A.: Flex: a tolerant and cooperative user interface to databases. IEEE Trans. Knowl. Data Eng. **2**(2), 231–246 (1990)
14. Godfrey, P., Minker, J., Novik, L.: An architecture for a cooperative database system. In: Litwin, W., Risch, T. (eds.) ADB 1994. LNCS, vol. 819, pp. 3–24. Springer, Heidelberg (1994). doi:10.1007/3-540-58183-9_35
15. Godfrey, P.: Minimization in cooperative response to failing database queries. IJCS **6**(2), 95–149 (1997)

16. Hurtado, C.A., Poulovassilis, A., Wood, P.T.: Query relaxation in RDF. In: Spaccapietra, S. (ed.) Journal on Data Semantics X. LNCS, vol. 4900, pp. 31–61. Springer, Heidelberg (2008). doi:10.1007/978-3-540-77688-8_2
17. Selmer, P., Poulovassilis, A., Wood, P.T.: Implementing flexible operators for regular path queries. In: Proceedings of the Workshops of the EDBT/ICDT 2015 Joint Conference (EDBT/ICDT), CEUR Workshop Proceedings, vol. 1330, pp. 149–156 (2015)
18. Hermann, A., Ferré, S., Ducassé, M.: An interactive guidance process supporting consistent updates of RDFS graphs. In: Teije, A., Völker, J., Handschuh, S., Stuckenschmidt, H., d'Acquin, M., Nikolov, A., Aussenac-Gilles, N., Hernandez, N. (eds.) EKAW 2012. LNCS, vol. 7603, pp. 185–199. Springer, Heidelberg (2012). doi:10.1007/978-3-642-33876-2_18
19. Fazzinga, B., Flesca, S., Furfaro, F.: On the expressiveness of generalization rules for XPath query relaxation. In: ACM International Conference on Proceedings Series Fourteenth Int'l Database Engineering and Applications Symposium (IDEAS), pp. 157–168. ACM(2010)
20. Liu, J., Yan, D.: Answering approximate queries over XML data. IEEE Trans. Fuzzy Syst. **24**(2), 288–305 (2016)
21. Biskup, J., Wiese, L.: A sound and complete model-generation procedure for consistent and confidentiality-preserving databases. Theoret. Comput. Sci. **412**(31), 4044–4072 (2011)
22. Gaasterland, T., Godfrey, P., Minker, J.: Relaxation as a platform for cooperative answering. JIIS **1**(3/4), 293–321 (1992)
23. Ferilli, S., Basile, T.M.A., Biba, M., Mauro, N.D., Esposito, F.: A general similarity framework for horn clause logic. Fundam. Informaticae **90**(1–2), 43–66 (2009)
24. Tversky, A.: Features of similarity. Psychol. Rev. **84**(4), 327–352 (1977)

Recommendation and Ranking

On the Need for Explicit Confidence Assessments of Flexible Query Answers

Guy De Tré(✉), Robin De Mol, and Antoon Bronselaer

Department of Telecommunications and Information Processing, Ghent University, St.-Pietersnieuwstraat 41, 9000 Ghent, Belgium
{Guy.DeTre,Robin.DeMol,Antoon.Bronselaer}@UGent.be

Abstract. Flexible query answering systems aim to exploit data collections in a richer way than traditional systems can do. In approaches where flexible criteria are used to reflect user preferences, expressing query satisfaction becomes a matter of degree. Nowadays, it becomes more and more common that data originating from different sources and different data providers are involved in the processing of a single query. Also, data sets can be very large such that not all data within a database or data store can be trusted to the same extent and consequently the results in a query answer can neither be trusted to the same extent. For this reason, data quality assessment becomes an important aspect of query processing. In this paper we discuss the need for explicit data quality assessments of query results. Indeed, To correctly inform users, it is in our opinion essential to communicate not only the satisfaction degrees in a query answer, but also the confidence about these satisfaction degrees as can be derived from data quality assessment. As illustration, we propose a hierarchical approach for query processing and data quality assessment, supporting the computation of as well a satisfaction degree, as its associated confidence degree for each element of the query result. Providing confidence information adds an extra dimension to query processing and leads to more soundly query answers.

Keywords: Fuzzy criterion evaluation · Big data · Data quality handling

1 Introduction

With ever increasing data volumes, database systems face new challenges. An important characteristics of 'Big' data is veracity. Veracity refers to the trust one has in the data that are being used. Our aim with this paper is to contribute to the development of novel techniques for the proper handling of veracity problems. More specifically, we depart from the fact that not all data are of the same quality in large data collections. This is especially the case if data result from data integration, are provided by (volunteered) users, are collected from social media, do not serve the same purposes, or have a different precision.

H. Christiansen et al. (Eds.): FQAS 2017, LNAI 10333, pp. 51–58, 2017.
DOI: 10.1007/978-3-319-59692-1_5

As an illustrative example consider a database with geological data, describing sediment samples and built to establish the substrate composition of the seabed for the purpose of sustainable resource management. Such a database has been built in the project Transnational and Integrated Long-term Marine Exploitation Strategies (TILES) [7]. Seabed samples are taken by various parties for different purposes. For example, construction companies collect samples for stability studies, the government collects samples for the purpose environmental monitoring, while extracting companies might collect samples for resource-quality assessment. Each party can voluntary share data with the others. Different sample data are of different quality. The varying confidence in sample quality propagates to a varying confidence in query results: query satisfaction degrees computed during query processing can neither be trusted to the same extent.

In this paper we describe how confidence in computed satisfaction degrees can be estimated and properly handled. The proposed solution consists of a novel technique that assesses data quality and computes an additional confidence degree for each computed satisfaction degree. In this way, users are provided with extra information needed to end up with best solutions. The data quality of each data item used in query evaluation is characterized by a number of elementary aspects. For example, elementary quality aspects of sample descriptions include the sampling method and sampling date. These elementary data quality aspects are evaluated and their evaluation results are aggregated to an overall confidence degree. This aggregation takes into account how the query results are computed, such that an overall confidence degree reflects the confidence in the query result.

The paper is organized as follows. In Sect. 2 we give some preliminaries on relational databases and 'fuzzy' querying of regular databases. In Sect. 3 we respectively deal with the specification of elementary aspects of data quality assessment, the evaluation of elementary quality aspects and the aggregation of quality aspects. An illustrative example is presented in Sect. 4. Finally, in Sect. 5 we provide some conclusions of this work.

2 Preliminaries

In this paper, conventional relational databases are considered. A relational database consists of a collection of relations comprising of attributes (columns) and tuples (rows) [1]. Each relation R can be represented by a table and is defined by a relation schema

$$R(A_1 : T_1, \ldots, A_n : T_n)$$

where the $A_i : T_i$'s are the attributes of R, each consisting of a name A_i and an associated data type T_i. This data type, among others, determines the domain dom_{T_i} consisting of the allowed values for the attribute. Each tuple

$$t_i(A_1 : v_1, \ldots, A_n : v_n)$$

with $v_i \in dom_{T_i}$, $1 \leq i \leq n$ represents a particular entity of the (real) world modelled by the given relation.

Relational database systems support the SQL query language, which among others, offers users facilities to formulate Boolean selection criteria that express what they are looking for. However, adequately translating the user's needs and preferences into a representative Boolean expression is often considered to be too restrictive because Boolean conditions either evaluate to true or false and do not allow for any flexibility regarding partial criterion satisfaction. Soft computing techniques help developing fuzzy approaches for flexible querying that solve these limitations [5]. An overview of basic works can be found in [8].

The essence of 'fuzzy' querying techniques is that they allow to express user preferences with respect to query conditions using linguistic terms which are modelled by fuzzy sets. The basic kind of preferences considered are those which are expressed *inside* an elementary query condition that is defined on a single attribute $A : T$. Hereby, fuzzy sets are used to express in a gradual way that some values of the domain dom_T are more desirable to the user than others. During query processing, basically all relevant database tuples t are evaluated to determine whether they satisfy the user's preferences (to a certain extent) or not. Hereby, each elementary query criterion c_i, $i = 1, \ldots, m$ of the query is evaluated, resulting in an elementary satisfaction degree $\gamma_{c_i}(t)$ which is usually modelled by a real number of the unit interval $[0, 1]$ (where $\gamma_{c_i}(t) = 1$ represents that the tuple t fully satisfies the criterion and $\gamma_{c_i}(t) = 0$ denotes no satisfaction).

Next, the elementary satisfaction degrees are aggregated to compute the overall satisfaction degree $\gamma(t)$ of the tuple. In its simplest form, the aggregation of satisfaction degrees is determined by the fuzzy logical connectives conjunction, disjunction and negation which are respectively defined as follows:

$$\gamma_{c_1 \wedge c_2}(t) = i(\gamma_{c_1}(t), \gamma_{c_2}(t)) \tag{1}$$

$$\gamma_{c_1 \vee c_2}(t) = u(\gamma_{c_1}(t), \gamma_{c_2}(t)) \tag{2}$$

$$\gamma_{\neg c}(t) = 1 - \gamma_c(t) \tag{3}$$

where i and u resp. denote a t-norm and its corresponding t-conorm.

In a more complex approach, users are allowed to express their preferences related to the relative importance of the elementary conditions in a query, hereby indicating that the satisfaction of some query conditions is more desirable than the satisfaction of others. Such preferences are usually denoted by associating a relative weight w_i ($\in [0, 1]$) to each elementary criterion c_i, $i = 1, \ldots, m$ of the query.

The impact of a weight can be computed by first matching the condition as if there is no weight and then second modifying the resulting matching degree in accordance with the weight. A modification function that strengthens the match of more important conditions and weakens the match of less important conditions is used for this purpose. As described in [5], some of the most practical interpretations of weights can be formalised in a universal scheme. Namely, let us assume that query condition c is a conjunction of weighted elementary query conditions c_i (for a disjunction a similar scheme has been offered). Then the matching degree $\gamma_{c_i^*}(t)$ of an elementary condition c_i with associated implicative importance weight w_i is computed by

$$\gamma_{c_i^*}(t) = (w_i \Rightarrow \gamma_{c_i}(t)) \tag{4}$$

where $\Rightarrow$ denotes a fuzzy implication connective. The overall matching degree of the whole query composed of the conjunction of conditions c_i is calculated using a standard t-norm operator. Other uses and interpretations of weights have been presented [8].

3 Data Quality Handling

The illustrative example in the introduction and many other applications reveal that there is a need for facilities to properly handle data quality in databases.

Most research on data quality assessment has been done in the area of Semantic Web as trust management is an important part of its architecture [6]. Pioneering work in the area of data warehouses has been presented in [3,4]. Herewith, data quality is assessed by means of a linguistic scale and evidence theory is used to estimate the overall reliability of the used data. The approach handles conflicting information by using a merging strategy, which is based on maximal coherent subsets (MCS). Overall reliability scores can be used to order the data and MCS gives insight on how an overall reliability score has been obtained. Query answers can also be enriched with reliability scores, which provides the users with extra information.

Data quality assessment has also been addressed in conventional relational databases [2]. Basically, a database is enriched with quality relations which contain data for data quality assessment and regular relations are extended with foreign key attributes to refer to related data quality assessment data. Selection criteria on quality relations can be included in a query to put extra constraints on data quality characteristics. As a consequence, data quality evaluations and evaluations of other user preferences are mixed and no extra information on data quality is provided to the user.

In this paper we propose to extend 'fuzzy' querying on conventional relational databases in such a way that a separate confidence assessment for each tuple in a query result is computed based on the quality assessments of the data that are used to produce the query result. Such an approach is relevant for many applications like TILES where one cannot afford it to discard data that are of lower quality because else there will not be enough data left. Instead of putting extra quality constraints on the data, a separate assessment of the confidence in each result is computed an provided to the user. The user can use this extra information to better interpret the results.

In the remainder of this section, we introduce an approach where satisfaction degrees of 'fuzzy' queries are enriched with confidence degrees. For a given database tuple, these degrees respectively express to what extent the tuple satisfies a 'fuzzy' query and to what extent one can be confident about this satisfaction.

3.1 Data Quality Assessment

In this stage of our research it is assumed that the database schema contains extra attributes and/or relations that are used to denote data quality. We call these attributes elementary data quality attributes. For every conventional attribute in the database, one or more elementary data quality attributes can be provided. For example consider a relation that contains information about sediment composition and water depth at a location (x, y, z), as given in Table 1. The attributes P_{clay}, P_{c_sand}, P_{m_sand} and P_{f_sand} respectively denote the probability (percentage) for clay, coarse sand, medium sand and fine sand at that location. The attributes *s_method* and *s_year* are elementary quality attributes that respectively denote which sampling method has been used and on which year the sample was taken. The attribute *w_depth* contains information about the water depth at the location, whereas *m_year* is an elementary quality attribute indicating on which year the water depth was measured.

Table 1. An example of a relation 'geology' that contains elementary quality attributes

Location	P_{clay}	P_{c_sand}	P_{m_sand}	P_{f_sand}	*s_method*	*s_year*	*w_depth*	*m_year*
*P*1	0%	50%	50%	0%	m_1	1993	54 m	2016
*P*2	0%	45%	25%	30%	m_1	1980	32 m	2012
*P*4	50%	45%	5%	0%	m_3	2016	41 m	2016

Data for elementary data quality attributes can originate from meta data, e.g. sampling method and sampling date in Table 1, or can be the result of a data audit process.

3.2 Evaluation of Elementary Quality Aspects

Elementary data quality attributes can be queried like conventional attributes. This implies that the 'fuzzy' querying techniques described in the preliminary section can be applied to them.

The innovative aspect proposed in this paper is that we advocate to make an explicit distinction between criteria on conventional attributes and criteria on data quality attributes. The elementary criteria c_i, $i = 1, \ldots, m$ on conventional attributes are evaluated and their evaluation with the data that are related to a given tuple t results in an elementary satisfaction degree $\gamma_{c_i}(t)$. The criteria c_i^Q, $i = 1, \ldots, p$ on elementary data quality attributes are also evaluated and their evaluation with the data that are related to a given tuple t results in an elementary confidence degree $\gamma^Q_{c_i^Q}(t)$.

Elementary satisfaction degrees will be aggregated to an overall satisfaction degree $\gamma(t)$ and elementary confidence degrees will be aggregated independently to an overall confidence degree $\gamma^Q(t)$. Considered together, $\gamma(t)$ and $\gamma^Q(t)$ respectively express to what extent tuple t satisfies the criteria imposed by the query and to what extent one can be confident about this overall satisfaction degree.

By making an explicit distinction between criteria on conventional attributes and criteria on data quality attributes, one can keep control over and be more adequately informed about the quality of the data involved in the query processing and hence also about the confidence each tuple of a query result.

3.3 Aggregation of Quality Aspects

Consider a database tuple t and a 'fuzzy' database query with weighted elementary selection criteria c_i, $i = 1, \ldots, m$. The impact of each weight is modelled by a 'fuzzy' implication connective as presented in Eq. (4). Furthermore, consider that the associated criteria on data quality attributes for the attributes in these elementary selection criteria are c_i^Q, $i = 1, \ldots, p$. For each elementary selection criterion c_i, $i = 1, \ldots, m$ we then have one of the following situations:

1. **One elementary data quality criterion c^Q is specified for c_i.** In this case c^Q is evaluated with t and $\gamma_{c^Q}^Q(t)$ becomes the confidence score for c_i, i.e. $\gamma_{c_i}^Q(t) = \gamma_{c^Q}^Q(t)$.
2. **Multiple elementary data quality criteria c_j^Q, $j = 1, \ldots, k$ are specified for c_i.** In such a case, all c_j^Q, $j = 1, \ldots, k$ are evaluated with t and the resulting confidence scores $\gamma_{c_j^Q}^Q(t)$, $j = 1, \ldots, k$ are aggregated. Up to now we use a simple t-norm operator i as aggregator. Using the minimum t-norm, the confidence score for c_i is $\gamma_{c_i}^Q(t) = \min_j(\gamma_{c_j^Q}^Q(t))$.
3. **No elementary data quality criteria are specified for c_i.** In this case, the user has to assign an ad hoc confidence score to c_i. If the data to evaluate c_i are considered to be adequate enough, an ad hoc confidence score of $\gamma_{c_i}^Q(t) = 1$ can be assigned to c_i. Otherwise another value $0 \leq v < 1$ can be chosen.

The overall confidence degree $\gamma^Q(t)$ for the database query is then computed by aggregating the confidence scores $\gamma_{c_i}^Q(t)$ of its elementary selection criteria c_i, $i = 1, \ldots, m$. As aggregator, a weighted sum can be used as follows.

$$\gamma^Q(t) = \frac{w_1'}{\sum_{i=1}^m w_i'}\gamma_{c_1}^Q(t) + \cdots + \frac{w_m'}{\sum_{i=1}^m w_i'}\gamma_{c_m}^Q(t) \tag{5}$$

where $w_i' = d_{max}(t) - |\gamma(t) - \gamma_{c_i}(t)|$ and $d_{max}(t) = \max_i(\gamma_{c_i}(t)) - \min_i(\gamma_{c_i}(t))$.

With Eq. (5) it is reflected that the impact of a satisfaction degree $\gamma_{c_i}(t)$ on the computation of the overall satisfaction degree $\gamma(t)$ determines the impact of its associated confidence degree $\gamma_{c_i}^Q(t)$ on the computation of the overall confidence degree $\gamma^Q(t)$. This impact is estimated by the difference $|\gamma(t) - \gamma_{c_i}(t)|$. The smaller this difference, the larger the impact. Hence a weight $w_i' = d_{max}(t) - |\gamma(t) - \gamma_{c_i}(t)|$ can be considered for each $\gamma_{c_i}^Q(t)$, where $d_{max}(t)$ is the largest possible difference between an input and the outcome of the aggregation of the satisfaction degrees. The property of internality, which states that the output of an aggregator is bound by the minimum and maximum of its inputs, holds for standard aggregation in 'fuzzy' weighted querying that is based on the operators given in Eqs. (1)–(4). Hence, $d_{max} = \max_i(\gamma_{c_i}(t)) - \min_i(\gamma_{c_i}(t))$. A weighted average aggregator is used to normalize the results.

4 Illustrative Example

Consider the 'fuzzy' query: 'Find locations with a *reasonable* probability for coarse sand which are at a *workable* water depth for ships of type A', imposed on the relation presented in Table 1. Assume that we have 'fuzzy' criteria for the probability of coarse sand (i.e., a fuzzy set with membership function $c_1 = \mu_{reasonable}$) and water depth (i.e., a fuzzy set with membership function $c_2 = \mu_{workable}$). Moreover we have elementary quality criteria for the sampling method, sampling date and depth measurement date. These criteria are respectively defined by fuzzy sets with membership functions $c_1^Q = \mu_{trusted\_method}$, $c_2^Q = \mu_{recent\_sampling\_year}$ and $c_3^Q = \mu_{recent\_measurement\_year}$.

Assume that evaluating these criteria with the data in Table 1 yields the elementary satisfaction degrees and confidence degrees presented in Table 2.

Table 2. Evaluation of elementary query criteria and elementary data quality criteria

Location	$\gamma(c_1)(t)$	$\gamma(c_2)(t)$	$\gamma^Q(c_1^Q)(t)$	$\gamma^Q(c_2^Q)(t)$	$\gamma^Q(c_3^Q)(t)$
*P*1	$c_1(50\%) = 0.8$	$c_2(54\,\text{m}) = 0.5$	$c_1^Q(m_1) = 0.5$	$c_2^Q(1993) = 0.5$	$c_3^Q(2016) = 1$
*P*2	$c_1(45\%) = 0.6$	$c_2(32\,\text{m}) = 0.9$	$c_1^Q(m_1) = 0.5$	$c_2^Q(1980) = 0.2$	$c_3^Q(2012) = 0.6$
*P*4	$c_1(45\%) = 0.6$	$c_2(41\,\text{m}) = 0.7$	$c_1^Q(m_3) = 1$	$c_2^Q(2016) = 1$	$c_3^Q(2016) = 1$

Aggregation yields the query results presented in Table 3. The interpretation of these results is as follows. Location *P*1 satisfies the query to an extent 0.5, whereas locations *P*2 and *P*4 satisfy it to an extent 0.6. The satisfaction degree for location *P*1 is due to the criterion on the water depth, for which the confidence in data quality is 1, hence the full confidence in the result *P*1. The satisfaction degrees for locations *P*2 and *P*4 are both due to the criterion on coarse sand. The confidence in the data for this criterion is 0.2 for *P*2 and 1 for *P*4, hence the confidence of 0.2 and 1 for the results *P*2 and *P*4.

Table 3. Aggregation of elementary query criteria and elementary data quality criteria

Location	$\gamma(t) = \min(\gamma(c_1)(t), \gamma(c_2)(t))$	$\gamma^Q(t)$
*P*1	0.5	1
*P*2	0.6	0.2
*P*4	0.6	1

Both locations *P*2 and *P*4 equally satisfy the query, but lower confidence in the query results makes location *P*2 less attractive. Location *P*1 satisfies the query slightly less, but this satisfaction is obtained with data with higher confidence.

5 Conclusions

In this paper, we discussed and advocated the need for explicit data quality assessment in database and information management systems. Giving the users explicit feedback on the confidence in query results is useful, especially in case of very large data sets with varying data quality. The presented research is also relevant in view of studying the veracity problem in 'big' data. A novel, initial technique for data quality assessment in 'fuzzy' database querying has been presented. At the core of this technique is the explicit distinction between query criteria on conventional attributes and criteria on data quality attributes.

More research is definitely required. Among the research topics we identify are: the development of a better data quality assessment framework, the handling of uncertain data, advanced aggregation techniques and the incorporation in a query language like SQL.

References

1. Codd, E.F.: A relational model of data for large shared data banks. Commun. ACM **13**(6), 377–387 (1970)
2. de F. Mendes Sampaio, S., Dong, C., Sampaio, P.: DQ^{2}S - a framework for data quality-aware information management. Expert Syst. Appl. **42**, 8304–8326 (2015)
3. Destercke, S., Buche, P., Charnomordic, B.: Data reliability assessment in a data warehouse opened on the web. In: Christiansen, H., Tré, G., Yazici, A., Zadrozny, S., Andreasen, T., Larsen, H.L. (eds.) FQAS 2011. LNCS, vol. 7022, pp. 174–185. Springer, Heidelberg (2011). doi:10.1007/978-3-642-24764-4_16
4. Destercke, S., Buche, P., Charnomordic, B.: Evaluating data reliability: an evidential answer with application to a web-enabled data warehouse. IEEE Trans. Knowl. Data Eng. **25**(1), 92–105 (2013)
5. Dubois, D., Prade, H.: Using Fuzzy Sets in Flexible Querying: Why and How? Flexible Query Answering Systems. Kluwer Academic Publishers, Dordrecht (1997)
6. Richardson, M., Agrawal, R., Domingos, P.: Trust management for the semantic web. In: Fensel, D., Sycara, K., Mylopoulos, J. (eds.) ISWC 2003. LNCS, vol. 2870, pp. 351–368. Springer, Heidelberg (2003). doi:10.1007/978-3-540-39718-2_23
7. Van Lancker, V., Francken, F., Kint, L., Terseleer, N., Van den Eynde, D., De Mol, L., De Tré, G., De Mol, R., Missiaen, T., Chademenos, V., Bakker, M., Maljers, D., Stafleu, J., van Heteren, S.: Building a 4D voxel-based decision support system for a sustainable management of marine geological resources. In: Diviacco, P., Leadbetter, A., Glaves, H. (eds.) Oceanographic and Marine Cross-Domain Data Management for Sustainable Development, pp. 224–252. IGI Global, Hershey (2017)
8. Zadrozny, S., Tré, G., Caluwe, R., Kacprzyk, J.: An overview of fuzzy approaches to flexible database querying. In: Handbook of Research on Fuzzy Information Processing in Databases, pp. 34–54. IGI Global, Hershey (2008)

Meeting and Joining Theme Models in Vector Spaces for Information Retrieval

Emanuele Di Buccio and Massimo Melucci(✉)

University of Padua, Padua, Italy
{emanuele.dibuccio,massimo.melucci}@unipd.it

Abstract. The upper bounds of Information Retrieval (IR) effectiveness could be improved if new frameworks were investigated beyond traditional retrieval models. Vector spaces and their untraditional operators – meet and join – are a step in this direction. On the other hand, users might express complex information needs. Complex information needs may take the form of themes, which cannot be effortlessly expressed using plain natural language queries. Therefore, new theoretical structures and operators should be designed for allowing users to express themes.

This paper illustrates how meet and join of vector spaces can rank documents by a relevance measure. Meet and join act on themes modeled as vector subspaces; for example, meet intersects two planes while join builds a plane from two lines. Since an operator applies to a pair of themes and results in another theme operators and theme models replace the traditional retrieval models. The experimental results show that this approach can compete with – it can retrieve relevant documents missed by – traditional retrieval models.

1 Introduction

Information Retrieval (IR) is the complex of models, languages and techniques aimed to retrieve all and only the documents relevant to a user's information needs. When searching for information, end users express their information needs through behaviour (e.g. click-through activity) and queries (e.g. natural language phrases). However complex, the combination of queries, operators and behaviour in conventional IR basically exploits the logic that documents are elements of *sets* weighted according to functions of query terms, operators and behaviour features.

In this paper, we consider users such as journalists and scholars who are expert in their own application domain and may be willing to utilize operators for building complex queries and searching by *themes* rather than queries. While the logic of sets can be utilized for standard search, to the contrary, in this paper, we investigate the hypothesis that a document collection can be searched by themes using the logic of *vector spaces.* Moreover, we argue that themes should not – actually cannot – be combined by traditional set operators but rather by vector space operators – meet and join.

H. Christiansen et al. (Eds.): FQAS 2017, LNAI 10333, pp. 59–70, 2017.
DOI: 10.1007/978-3-319-59692-1_6

A user may meet and join subspaces in the context of vector spaces, instead of intersecting and complementing subsets. Although meet and join are well known operators of quantum theory, however, we do not argue that documents and queries are quantum objects like subatomic particles. Instead, we are investigating whether the retrieval process involving expert users may exhibit some quantum-*like* behaviour.

The intuitions in using meet and join in IR are that, in order to significantly improve retrieval effectiveness, users need a radically different approach to searching a document collection beyond the classical mechanics of an IR system; for example, the distributive law of intersection and union does not remain valid for subspaces equipped with meet and join. The lack of distributive properties gives a further one degree of freedom in building new information need representations.

While the relevant work is briefly surveyed in Sect. 2, the theme model is illustrated in Sect. 3. Then, Sect. 4 explains meet and join, both theoretically and algorithmically. The first experimental investigation of meet and join is reported in Sect. 5. Finally, some future works are suggested in Sect. 6.

2 Related Work

The research on

- algorithms for extracting complex descriptors, e.g. set of (possibly related) terms, on
- models for exploiting such descriptors for document ranking and on
- approaches for interacting with those descriptors

are all relevant to this paper. Automatic Query Expansion (AQE) is the standard approach to supporting the end user during the interaction with the retrieval system. A number of techniques that obtain a better description of the user's information need have been experimented [1]. In this paper, we compare a new language based on vector spaces – theme model and the operators thereof – with traditional ad-hoc retrieval and Pseudo Relevance Feedback (PRF).

Latent Semantic Analysis (LSA) was proposed to extract descriptors able to capture word and document relationships within one single model [2]. Following LSA, Latent Dirichlet Allocation (LDA) aims at automatically discovering the main "themes" in a document corpus. A corpus is usually modelled as a probability distribution over a shared set of topics, these topics in turn are probability distributions over words, and each word in a document is assumed to be generated by one of these topics [3]. This paper focusses on the geometry provided by vector spaces, yet is also linked to topic models, since a probability distribution over documents or features can always be defined in a vector space, the latter being a core concept of the quantum mechanical framework applied to IR [4–6].

We implement a vector-based language in a way different from the approaches described in [7,8] where term dependencies are investigated or in [9,10] where meet and join are not explicitly modeled and implemented. Our contribution is the possibility that the user may explicitly add meet and join to the query, thus directly assessing the impact of the operators on retrieval results.

This paper also provides an effective language to implement the principle of poly-representation [11], which aims to generate and exploit the cognitive overlap between different representations of documents to estimate an accurate representation of the usefulness of the document. Documents that lie in the same representations are assumed to be relevant to a user's information need. Poly-representation was not developed in a mathematical framework encompassing it completely and precisely for some years until it was described within the quantum mechanical framework which may describe various aspects of document representation: fusion of document content representations; temporal aspects and dynamic changes; document structure and layout; and the relationships between these aspects according to [12].

Efforts that aim to implement query languages equipped with operators over vector spaces were made and resulted in Quantum Query Language (QQL) [13]. For example, `SELECT * FROM t WHERE x='b' OR x='c'` can be modelled as the sum $\mathbf{P}_{bc} = \mathbf{P}_b + \mathbf{P}_c$ of the projectors corresponding to the subspaces spanned by b and c and then computing $\boldsymbol{\phi}'\mathbf{P}_{bc}\boldsymbol{\phi}$. In [14] the combination of the dual approaches reported in [12,13] is mentioned but not addressed. Our proposal differs in that meet and join are directly added to the user's queries and are not hidden in SQL queries.

3 The Theme Model

In the following, we use the following main vector notations: $\boldsymbol{t}$ refers to term, $\boldsymbol{\tau}$ refers to theme, and $\boldsymbol{\phi}$ refers to document.

Consider the features extracted from a collection of documents; for example, a word is an example of textual feature, the gray level of a pixel or a codeword of an image is an example of visual feature, and a chroma-based descriptor for content-based music representation is an example of audio feature. Despite differences, the features extracted from a collection of multimedia documents can co-exist together in the same vector space provided that each feature is represented by a canonical basis vector.

Consider a finite vector space over the real field and k distinct features; k is also the dimension of the vector space. Therefore, the canonical basis vector of the i-th feature has k elements, the i-th element is 1 and the other elements are zeros; for example, when $k = 3$ the canonical basis vectors are $(1,0,0)$, $(0,1,0)$ and $(0,0,1)$.

The features can be combined together to build terms. Given k coefficients $a_i \in \mathbb{R}, i = 1,\ldots,k$ and the k feature vectors $\boldsymbol{w}_i \in \mathbb{R}^k, i = 1,\ldots,k$, a term vector is defined as

$$\boldsymbol{t} = a_1\boldsymbol{w}_1 + \cdots + a_k\boldsymbol{w}_k \qquad a_i \in \mathbb{R}$$

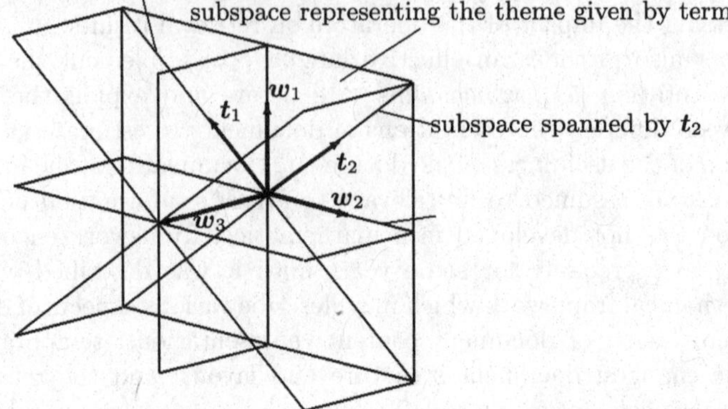

Fig. 1. A pictorial representation of features, terms and themes. Three feature vectors $\boldsymbol{w}_1, \boldsymbol{w}_2, \boldsymbol{w}_3$ span a tri-dimensional vector space. Each term vector $\boldsymbol{t}$ can be spanned by any subset of feature vectors; for example, $\boldsymbol{t}_1 = a_1\boldsymbol{w}_1 + a_2\boldsymbol{w}_2$ for some a_1, a_2. A theme can be represented by a subspace spanned by term vectors or feature vectors; for example, $\boldsymbol{t}_1$ and $\boldsymbol{t}_2$ span a bi-dimensional subspace representing a theme and including all vectors $\boldsymbol{\tau} = b_1\boldsymbol{t}_1 + b_2\boldsymbol{t}_2$.

For example, consider two textual features, say "information" and "retrieval", then "information retrieval" is a term represented by

$$\text{information retrieval} = a_{\text{information}}\text{information} + a_{\text{retrieval}}\text{retrieval}$$

Given m term vectors $\boldsymbol{t}_1, \ldots, \boldsymbol{t}_m, m \leq k$, a *theme* is represented by the subspace of all vectors

$$\boldsymbol{\tau} = b_1\boldsymbol{t}_1 + \cdots + b_m\boldsymbol{t}_m \qquad b_i \in \mathbb{R}$$

Note that, a term is the simplest form of theme and can be combined with other terms to further define more complex themes; for example, a theme can be represented by a one-dimensional subspace (i.e. a ray) in the k-dimensional space as follows; if $\boldsymbol{t}$ represents a term, we have that $\boldsymbol{\tau} = b\boldsymbol{t}$ spans a one-dimensional subspace (i.e. a ray) and represents a theme. A theme can also be represented by a bi-dimensional subspace (i.e. a plane) in the k-dimensional space as follows; if $\boldsymbol{t}_1, \boldsymbol{t}_2$ are term vectors, we have that $b_1\boldsymbol{t}_1 + b_2\boldsymbol{t}_2$ spans a bi-dimensional subspace (i.e. a plane) representing a theme.

In sum, both features and terms are represented by vectors spanning a one-dimensional subspace (i.e. a ray), but term vectors are linear combinations of feature vectors where coefficients measure the role of features. Themes are represented by multi-dimensional subspaces and are spanned by one or more term vectors; for example, themes can be planes when defined by two term vectors, cubes when defined by three term vectors and in general they are hyperplanes. Thus, a term is a theme because a term vector is a one-dimensional subspace; it follows that a feature is also a theme. The conceptual relationships between features, terms and themes are depicted in Fig. 1.

The ranking rule utilised to measure the degree to which a document is about a theme relies on the theory of abstract vector spaces. To measure this degree, a representation of a document in a vector space and a representation of a theme in the same space are necessary. A document is represented by a vector

$$\boldsymbol{\phi} = (c_1, \ldots, c_m)' \qquad c_i \in \mathbb{R}$$

such that c_i is the measure of the degree to which the document that is represented by the vector is about term i. A ranking rule is then the squared projection of $\boldsymbol{\phi}$ on the subspace spanned by a set of m term vectors [4,15].

Consider that a m-dimensional subspace is spanned by $\boldsymbol{t}_1, \ldots, \boldsymbol{t}_m$, which is a basis. However, the basis should be an orthogonal set – not only independent – because orthogonality allows us not to compute term correlations when the degree to which a document is about a theme has to be computed. To this end, an orthogonal basis of the *same* subspace can be obtained through rotation of the $\boldsymbol{t}$'s. Let $\{\boldsymbol{v}_1, \ldots, \boldsymbol{v}_m\}$ be such an orthogonal basis. The measure of the degree to which a document is about a theme represented by the subspace spanned by this basis is the size of the projection of the document vector on the theme subspace, that is

$$\mathrm{tr}[(\boldsymbol{v}_1\boldsymbol{v}_1' + \cdots \boldsymbol{v}_m\boldsymbol{v}_m')\boldsymbol{\phi}\,\boldsymbol{\phi}'] \tag{1}$$

where $\boldsymbol{v}\,\boldsymbol{v}'$ is the projector of the one-dimensional subspace spanned by $\boldsymbol{v}$ and tr is the trace operator. After a few passages, the following measure is obtained [16]:

$$|\boldsymbol{v}_1'\boldsymbol{\phi}|^2 + \cdots + |\boldsymbol{v}_m'\boldsymbol{\phi}|^2 \tag{2}$$

4 Meet and Join Operators

Themes can be created through operators applied to other themes defined on a vector space. In this paper, we utilise two operators called *meet* and *join*. Thus, the subspaces that represents a theme can meet or join the subspace of another theme and the result of this meet is a subspace that represents another theme. In particular:

- The meet of two one-dimensional themes τ_1 and τ_2 can be defined by $\tau = \tau_1 \vee \tau_2$. It can be represented by the subspace of vectors $\boldsymbol{\tau} = b_1\boldsymbol{\tau}_1 + b_2\boldsymbol{\tau}_2$, which is therefore displayed as one plane; see Fig. 2(a). Note that the meet is the smallest subspace containing both subspaces.
- The join of two bi-dimensional themes τ_3 and τ_4 can be defined by $\tau_5 = \tau_3 \wedge \tau_4$, which is therefore displayed as one ray, i.e. the intersection between the subspace spanned by τ_3 and the subspace spanned by τ_4; see Fig. 2(b). Note that the join is the largest subspace contained by both subspaces.

The definition of meet and join requires algorithms for computing an effective representation of the subspaces stemming from these operators. To this end, we consider:

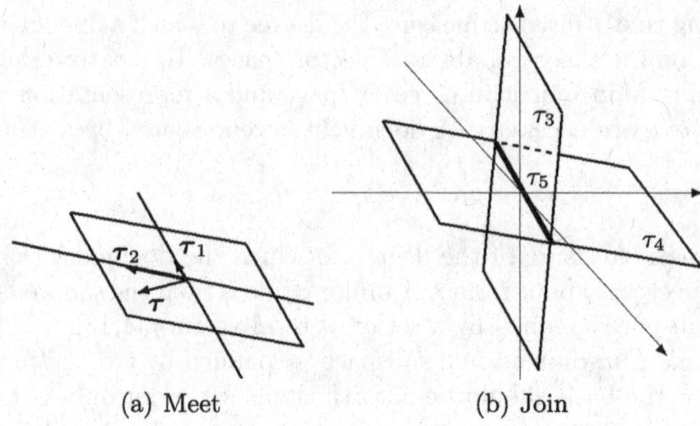

Fig. 2. Meet and join

1. the meet of two one-dimensional themes and
2. the join of two bi-dimensional themes.

The "meet" algorithm for two one-dimensional themes τ_1, τ_2 consists of rotating the theme vectors $\boldsymbol{\tau}_1, \boldsymbol{\tau}_2$ to obtain $\boldsymbol{u}_1, \boldsymbol{u}_2$ as depicted in Fig. 3(a). The "join" algorithm for two bi-dimensional themes consists of (i) the algorithm of the meet for obtaining the representation of each bi-dimensional subspace and (ii) the algorithm for calculating the solution of the linear system

$$c_1 \boldsymbol{u}_1 + c_2 \boldsymbol{u}_2 = c_3 \boldsymbol{u}_3 + c_4 \boldsymbol{u}_4$$

where $\{\boldsymbol{u}_1, \boldsymbol{u}_2\}$ is the basis of one bi-dimensional subspace and $\{\boldsymbol{u}_3, \boldsymbol{u}_4\}$ is the basis of the other bi-dimensional subspace as described by Fig. 3(b).

The theme model violates the distributive law of meet and join [17]. Although the violation of a property might seem a negative feature of a theory, it is on the contrary a potential of the theme model since it allows a user who is interacting with a retrieval system to experiment many more expressions of his information need. If, on the one hand, an expression like $(A \wedge B) \vee (A \wedge C)$ would be equivalent to $A \wedge (B \vee C)$ using the tradition Boolean logic an expression like $(\boldsymbol{t}_1 \wedge \boldsymbol{t}_2) \vee (\boldsymbol{t}_1 \wedge \boldsymbol{t}_3)$ is, on the other hand, not equivalent to $\boldsymbol{t}_1 \wedge (\boldsymbol{t}_2 \vee \boldsymbol{t}_3)$ using the theme model and the meet and join operators thereof.

5 Experiments

The experiments aimed to measure the performance of the theme model and of the Quantum Theme Language (QTL) operators thereof (i.e. meet and join). Since the main focus of our work is on modelling themes and operators, we have assumed that a feature is a word, thus leaving applications to other media for future investigations.

The experiments were performed using the disks 4 and 5 of the TIPSTER test collection of Text Retrieval Conference (TREC) and 150 topics from topic

```
meet(t_1, t_2)
normalize so that |t't|^2 = 1
a_2 ← t_1't_2
b_2 ← √(1 − a_2^2)
u_1 ← t_1
u_2 ← (t_2 − a_2 t_1)/b_2
return u_1, u_2
```

(a) The meet algorithm

```
join(t_1, t_2, t_3, t_4)
u_1, u_2 ← meet(t_1, t_2)
u_3, u_4 ← meet(t_3, t_4)
A ← (u_1, u_2, −u_3)
b ← u_4
Q, R ← QR(A)
q_b ← Q'b
x ← solution of Rx = q_b
v ← x_1 u_1 + x_2 u_2
return v
```

(b) The join algorithm

Fig. 3. (a): To compute the meet, an orthogonal basis of the subspace spanned by $\boldsymbol{t}_1, \boldsymbol{t}_2$ is computed by rotation. It can be checked that $\boldsymbol{u}_1'\boldsymbol{u}_2 = \boldsymbol{t}_1'\boldsymbol{u}_2 = (\boldsymbol{t}_1'\boldsymbol{t}_2 - a_2\boldsymbol{t}_1'\boldsymbol{t}_1)/b_2 = (a_2 - a_2)/b_2 = 0$ and that $\boldsymbol{u}_2'\boldsymbol{u}_2 = 1$. (b): To compute the join, one orthogonal basis is computed for each bi-dimensional subspace using the meet algorithm. Then, the QR decomposition is computed for the matrix given by $\boldsymbol{u}_1, \boldsymbol{u}_2, -\boldsymbol{u}_3$. Finally, the one-dimensional subspace that is the intersection between the two bi-dimensional subspaces is the solution of the linear system $\mathbf{R}x = \mathbf{Q}\boldsymbol{t}_4$ and can be expressed by the basis of one subspace out of the intersected subspaces.

n. 301 to topic n. 450. The document words were stemmed and stopwords were removed. For each topic, the title was used as query and the documents were ranked by cover density ranking algorithm [18] which is based on proximity and cooccurrence and it is thus suitable for very short queries. The list of 1000 top ranked retrieved documents was the baseline.

Given n, the n top-ranked documents were utilised to select terms as follows. For each query term, the terms occurring in the 11-word window centered around the query term were selected from each document. Given f, the terms with frequency equal to or greater than f in the n top ranked documents were selected. Finally, we utilised k terms as follows:

- Pseudo Relevance Feedback (PRF): The terms expanded the original query.
- Quantum Theme Language (QTL): Given m, k, n we built a $k \times n$ matrix $\mathbf{X}$ and then Non-negative Matrix Factorization (NMF) was performed [19] as follows:

$$\mathbf{X} = \mathbf{W}\mathbf{H} \qquad \mathbf{W} \in \mathbb{R}^{k \times m} \qquad \mathbf{H} \in \mathbb{R}^{m \times n} \tag{3}$$

  where $\mathbf{W}$ is a matrix of m column vectors of $\mathbb{R}^k$ and $\mathbf{H}$ is a matrix of n coefficient column vectors of $\mathbb{R}^m$. The theme vectors were obtained rescaling $\mathbf{W}$ as follows:

$$(\boldsymbol{t}_0 \ \cdots \ \boldsymbol{t}_{m-1}) = \mathbf{W}\mathrm{diag}(\mathbf{H}\mathbf{1})$$

  where $\mathbf{1}$ is the vector of n 1's and "diag" transforms a vector into a diagonal matrix. Each element i of each column vector of $\mathbf{W}$ was multiplied by the sum of the coefficients of row i of $\mathbf{H}$; as h_{jl} measures the contribution of column j of $\mathbf{W}$ to document vector l (i.e. column l of $\mathbf{X}$), this multiplication amplifies element i of each column vector of $\mathbf{W}$ by the total contribution of term i to the themes. The experiments reported in this section were performed using $m = 4$ as follows:

- First, the projectors of the unidimensional subspaces spanned by $\boldsymbol{t}_0$, $\boldsymbol{t}_1$, $\boldsymbol{t}_2$, $\boldsymbol{t}_3$ re-ranked the retrieved document vectors using (1). As the subspaces were unidimensional, a projector of the subspace spanned by $\boldsymbol{t}$ is $\boldsymbol{t}\boldsymbol{t}'$.
- Then, we tested the projectors of the bi-dimensional subspaces spanned by $\boldsymbol{t}_0 \vee \boldsymbol{t}_1, \boldsymbol{t}_0 \vee \boldsymbol{t}_2, \boldsymbol{t}_0 \vee \boldsymbol{t}_3, \boldsymbol{t}_1 \vee \boldsymbol{t}_2, \boldsymbol{t}_1 \vee \boldsymbol{t}_3, \boldsymbol{t}_2 \vee \boldsymbol{t}_3$; such a projector was $\boldsymbol{u}_1\boldsymbol{u}_1' + \boldsymbol{u}_2\boldsymbol{u}_2'$ where the $\boldsymbol{u}$'s are returned by meet.
- Finally, we tested the projectors of the unidimensional subspaces spanned by each of the following expressions: $(\boldsymbol{t}_0 \vee \boldsymbol{t}_1) \wedge (\boldsymbol{t}_2 \vee \boldsymbol{t}_3), (\boldsymbol{t}_0 \vee \boldsymbol{t}_2) \wedge (\boldsymbol{t}_1 \vee \boldsymbol{t}_3), (\boldsymbol{t}_0 \vee \boldsymbol{t}_3) \wedge (\boldsymbol{t}_1 \vee \boldsymbol{t}_2)$.

Two performance measures were utilised in the experiments. One measure of performance is the well-known Normalized Discounted Cumulative Gain (NDCG) [20]:

$$\text{NDCG}(B) = \frac{\sum_{i \in B} \frac{\text{rel}_i}{\log_2 i+1}}{\text{NDCG}(\text{ideal}\, B)}$$

where B is a list of retrieved documents, rel_i is the relevance grade of document ranked at i and $\text{NDCG}(\text{ideal}\, B)$ is the maximum NDCG. In particular, the additional quantity of relevant documents retrieved other than the relevant documents of the baseline list was measured since what can be added by QTL or PRF to the baseline list was of interest. To this end, we defined the other measure of performance called differential Normalized Discounted Cumulative Gain (dNDCG) as

$$\text{dNDCG}(A, B) = \text{NDCG}(A \backslash B)$$

where A is another list of retrieved documents. dNDCG is thus the NDCG computed for all and only the top-ranked documents – twenty documents in the experiments of this paper – retrieved in A but not retrieved in B; if A is the list of documents retrieved by PRF or QTL and B is the baseline list of documents, $A \backslash B$ contains the newly relevant documents ranked among the twenty newly top ranked documents; in this way, dNDCG can measure the increment of performance caused by an increment of recall and an increment of precision.

The results are reported in Table 1. In general, all the methods perform at the same level of effectiveness as shown by NDCG although the NDCG values of PRF are a little below the baseline values; this outcome is consistent with the results reported in the literature on PRF and other automatic query expansion methods which are not based on explicit relevance assessments [21].

dNDCG measured the degree to which the unidimensional projectors obtained from the $\boldsymbol{t}$'s and $\boldsymbol{\tau}'s$ causes the retrieval of new relevant documents that are not retrieved by the baseline in about half of the cases. This proportion

Table 1. The experimental results were obtained for $n = 5, 10, 20$ and $f = 1, 10, 20$. The rows where two method names are separated by slash report dNDCG values, the other rows report NDCG values. The rows that include a slash report the comparison between the method on the left of the slash and the method on the right of the slash; these rows are labeled by (dNDCG) and report the increment of effectiveness when using the method on the left of the slash. The values labeled by * or ** are statistically significant with $p < 0.05$ or $p < 0.01$, respectively, according to Student's t-test. When an dNDCG value is compared with that of PRF (e.g. τ_0/PRF (dNDCG)), the one-sample t-test was calculated and the dNDCG value of the method on the left of the slash was compared with zero.

	$n = 5$			$n = 10$			$n = 20$		
	$f = 1$	$f = 10$	$f = 20$	$f = 1$	$f = 10$	$f = 20$	$f = 1$	$f = 10$	$f = 20$
Baseline	0.561	0.546	0.543	0.561	0.549	0.546	0.561	0.548	0.547
PRF	0.522	0.514	0.515	0.519	0.514	0.518	0.518	0.514	0.518
PRF/Baseline	0.082	0.056	0.045	0.077	0.049	0.042	0.081	0.043	0.036
τ_0	0.514	0.510	0.516	0.510	0.510	0.516	0.511	0.508	0.514
τ_0/Baseline	0.091	0.072*	0.063*	0.086	0.070*	0.058*	0.094*	0.071**	0.061**
τ_0/PRF	0.031**	0.044**	0.041**	0.026**	0.047**	0.039**	0.035**	0.053**	0.042**
τ_1	0.516	0.510	0.514	0.512	0.510	0.517	0.512	0.507	0.513
τ_1/Baseline	0.096*	0.071	0.065**	0.090	0.062	0.056*	0.095	0.059	0.051
τ_1/PRF	0.031**	0.039**	0.046**	0.034**	0.042**	0.039**	0.037**	0.044**	0.040**
τ_2	0.513	0.507	0.511	0.511	0.513	0.515	0.512	0.508	0.514
τ_2/Baseline	0.090	0.066	0.051	0.095**	0.081**	0.060*	0.089	0.067**	0.050
τ_2/PRF	0.031**	0.040**	0.032**	0.030**	0.046**	0.035**	0.034**	0.050**	0.035**
τ_3	0.514	0.510	0.513	0.511	0.506	0.516	0.511	0.506	0.514
τ_3/Baseline	0.093	0.072*	0.063*	0.088	0.067*	0.049	0.096*	0.068**	0.050
τ_3/PRF	0.030**	0.042**	0.041**	0.025**	0.041**	0.033**	0.033**	0.047**	0.032**
$\tau_0 \vee \tau_1$	0.521	0.511	0.515	0.515	0.513	0.516	0.516	0.507	0.517
$\tau_0 \vee \tau_1$/Baseline	0.082	0.067	0.050	0.072	0.054	0.050	0.079	0.053	0.057*
$\tau_0 \vee \tau_1$/PRF	0.021**	0.036**	0.032**	0.023**	0.040**	0.034**	0.022**	0.032**	0.044**
$\tau_0 \vee \tau_2$	0.520	0.508	0.513	0.516	0.512	0.518	0.515	0.510	0.518
$\tau_0 \vee \tau_2$/Baseline	0.081	0.064	0.050	0.085	0.066	0.056	0.082	0.068*	0.054
$\tau_0 \vee \tau_2$/PRF	0.024**	0.032**	0.033**	0.032**	0.030**	0.036**	0.021**	0.050**	0.042**
$\tau_0 \vee \tau_3$	0.520	0.512	0.515	0.515	0.510	0.517	0.515	0.508	0.514
$\tau_0 \vee \tau_3$/Baseline	0.077	0.074*	0.055	0.075	0.066	0.046	0.085	0.055	0.049
$\tau_0 \vee \tau_3$/PRF	0.025**	0.047**	0.032**	0.022**	0.044**	0.032**	0.016**	0.037**	0.030**
$\tau_1 \vee \tau_2$	0.518	0.510	0.512	0.517	0.511	0.516	0.514	0.510	0.517
$\tau_1 \vee \tau_2$/Baseline	0.082	0.065	0.057	0.095**	0.059	0.061*	0.075	0.055	0.048
$\tau_1 \vee \tau_2$/PRF	0.020**	0.039**	0.033**	0.026**	0.038**	0.037**	0.019**	0.038**	0.032**
$\tau_1 \vee \tau_3$	0.519	0.511	0.514	0.517	0.511	0.517	0.516	0.509	0.515
$\tau_1 \vee \tau_3$/Baseline	0.077	0.074	0.055	0.078	0.050	0.054	0.090	0.062	0.048
$\tau_1 \vee \tau_3$/PRF	0.012**	0.042**	0.030**	0.024**	0.028**	0.042**	0.019**	0.047**	0.032**
$\tau_2 \vee \tau_3$	0.519	0.510	0.512	0.517	0.510	0.520	0.514	0.508	0.515
$\tau_2 \vee \tau_3$/Baseline	0.084	0.057	0.054	0.082	0.064*	0.059	0.083	0.058	0.053*
$\tau_2 \vee \tau_3$/PRF	0.025**	0.028**	0.029**	0.022**	0.036**	0.043**	0.018**	0.044**	0.031**
$\tau_0 \vee \tau_1 \wedge \tau_2 \vee \tau_3$	0.523	0.515	0.516	0.520	0.513	0.520	0.517	0.514	0.514
$\tau_0 \vee \tau_1 \wedge \tau_2 \vee \tau_3$/Baseline	0.077	0.059	0.053	0.075	0.045	0.045	0.072	0.045	0.042

(*continued*)

Table 1. (*continued*)

	$n=5$			$n=10$			$n=20$		
	$f=1$	$f=10$	$f=20$	$f=1$	$f=10$	$f=20$	$f=1$	$f=10$	$f=20$
$\tau_0 \vee \tau_1 \wedge \tau_2 \vee \tau_3$/PRF	0.023**	0.044**	0.022**	0.034**	0.022**	0.026**	0.024**	0.040**	0.018**
$\tau_0 \vee \tau_2 \wedge \tau_1 \vee \tau_3$	0.521	0.509	0.512	0.519	0.511	0.521	0.515	0.513	0.519
$\tau_0 \vee \tau_2 \wedge \tau_1 \vee \tau_3$/Baseline	0.082	0.060	0.039	0.078	0.047	0.056*	0.068	0.055*	0.043
$\tau_0 \vee \tau_2 \wedge \tau_1 \vee \tau_3$/PRF	0.032**	0.031**	0.019**	0.028**	0.026**	0.024**	0.030**	0.038**	0.014**
$\tau_1 \vee \tau_2 \wedge \tau_0 \vee \tau_3$	0.522	0.514	0.514	0.519	0.513	0.517	0.518	0.512	0.521
$\tau_1 \vee \tau_2 \wedge \tau_0 \vee \tau_3$/Baseline	0.086	0.060	0.042	0.088*	0.056	0.045	0.072	0.047	0.045
$\tau_1 \vee \tau_2 \wedge \tau_0 \vee \tau_3$/PRF	0.029**	0.043**	0.022**	0.030**	0.039**	0.024**	0.032**	0.037**	0.022**

is reduced when the themes are combined using meet and join, however, dNDCG still suggests that some new relevant documents may anyway be retrieved and ranked within the twenty top ranked documents, the latter being a positive event for the user, although the values may appear low. The values of dNDCG are always significantly different from zero when a QTL method is compared with PRF, thus suggesting that such a method can retrieve a significant amount of new relevant documents other than those retrieved by PRF.

6 Future Work

The experimental results show that the theme model and the join and meet operators can compete with, and can retrieve relevant documents that cannot be retrieved by effective PRF methods. The increments of retrieval performance due to the relevant documents retrieved by meet and join did not result from random variations and were on the contrary significant variations. We aim to investigate the potential of this approach to a greater extent.

To this end, some experiments are underway using the subtopics of the TREC 2010 Web Track Test Collection as themes.[1] Instead of implementing themes using index terms, we will implement themes using subtopics, which may be viewed as aspects of the main topic. The experiments will simulate a scenario more interactive than the scenario simulated in this paper. A user will submit a query (i.e. the main topic) and the retrieval system will extract a set of pertinent themes. The effectiveness of the ranked list obtained by the representation based only on the query terms, on all the distinct terms associated to the extracted themes, or on themes through meet and join will finally be measured.

Further experiments will be carried out on the Dynamic Domain Track Test Collections. The goal of the Dynamic Domain Track is to "support research

[1] http://trec.nist.gov/data/web/10/wt2010-topics.xml.

in dynamic, exploratory search of complex information domains"[2]. The task is highly interactive and the interaction with the user is simulated through the Jig, that returns explicit judgments on the top five retrieved documents, along with relevant passages in those documents. We will investigate the use of relevant passages as source to implement themes.

Acknowledgements. This paper is part of a project that has received funding from the European Union's Horizon 2020 research and innovation programme under the Marie Skłodowska-Curie grant agreement No 721321.

References

1. Carpineto, C., Romano, G.: A survey of automatic query expansion in information retrieval. ACM Comput. Surv. **44**(1), 1–50 (2012)
2. Deerwester, S., Dumais, S., Furnas, G., Landauer, T., Harshman, R.: Indexing by latent semantic analysis. J. Am. Soc. Inf. Sci. **41**(6), 391–407 (1990)
3. Blei, D.M., Ng, A.Y., Jordan, M.I.: Latent Dirichlet allocation. J. Mach. Learn. Res. **3**, 993–1022 (2003)
4. Van Rijsbergen, C.J.: The Geometry of Information Retrieval. Cambridge University Press, UK (2004)
5. Melucci, M., van Rijsbergen, C.J.: Quantum Mechanics and Information Retrieval, pp. 125–155. Springer, Berlin (2011)
6. Melucci, M.: Introduction to Information Retrieval and Quantum Mechanics. Springer, Heidelberg (2015)
7. Sordoni, A., Nie, J.Y., Bengio, Y.: Modeling term dependencies with quantum language models for IR. In: Proceedings of SIGIR, pp. 653–662 (2013)
8. Sordoni, A., He, J., Nie, J.Y.: Modeling latent topic interactions using quantum interference for information retrieval. In: Proceedings of CIKM, pp. 1197–1200 (2013)
9. Piwowarski, B., Frommholz, I., Lalmas, M., van Rijsbergen, C.J.: What can quantum theory bring to information retrieval. In: Proceedings of CIKM, pp. 59–68. ACM (2010)
10. Caputo, A., Piwowarski, B., Lalmas, M.: A query algebra for quantum information retrieval. In: Proceedings of the IIR Workshop (2011)
11. Ingwersen, P.: Information Retrieval Interaction. Taylor Graham Publishing, London (1992)
12. Frommholz, I., Larsen, B., Piwowarski, B., Lalmas, M., Ingwersen, P., van Rijsbergen, K.: Supporting polyrepresentation in a quantum-inspired geometrical retrieval framework. In: Proceedings of IIiX, pp. 115–124 (2010)
13. Schmitt, I.: QQL: a DB&IR query language. VLDB J. **17**(1), 39–56 (2008)
14. Zellhöfer, D., Frommholz, I., Schmitt, I., Lalmas, M., Rijsbergen, K.: Towards quantum-based DB+IR processing based on the principle of polyrepresentation. In: Clough, P., Foley, C., Gurrin, C., Jones, G.J.F., Kraaij, W., Lee, H., Mudoch, V. (eds.) ECIR 2011. LNCS, vol. 6611, pp. 729–732. Springer, Heidelberg (2011). doi:10.1007/978-3-642-20161-5_81
15. Melucci, M.: A basis for information retrieval in context. ACM Trans. Inf. Syst. **26**(3), 1–41 (2008)

[2] http://trec-dd.org.

16. Halmos, P.: Finite-Dimensional Vector Spaces. Undergraduate Texts in Mathematics. Springer, New York (1987)
17. Di Buccio, E., Melucci, M.: Two operators to define and manipulate themes of a document collection. In: Proceedings of ICTIR (2015)
18. Clarke, C.L., Cormack, G.V., Tudhope, E.A.: Relevance ranking for one to three term queries. Inf. Process. Manage. **36**, 291–311 (2000)
19. Lee, D.D., Seung, H.S.: Learning the parts of objects by non-negative matrix factorization. Nature **401**, 788–791 (1999)
20. Jarvëlin, K., Kekäläinen, J.: Cumulated gain-based evaluation of IR techniques. ACM Trans. Inf. Syst. **20**(4), 422–446 (2002)
21. Harman, D., Buckley, C.: Overview of the reliable information access workshop. Inf. Retr. **12**, 615–641 (2009)

A Typicality-Based Recommendation Approach Leveraging Demographic Data

Aurélien Moreau[(✉)], Olivier Pivert, and Grégory Smits

Irisa – University of Rennes 1, Technopole Anticipa,
22305 Lannion Cedex, France
{aurelien.moreau,olivier.pivert,gregory.smits}@irisa.fr

Abstract. In this paper, we introduce a new recommendation approach leveraging demographic data. Items are associated with the audience who liked them, and we consider similarity based on audiences. More precisely, recommendations are computed on the basis of the (fuzzy) typical demographic properties (age, sex, occupation, etc.) of the audience associated with every item. Experiments on the MovieLens dataset show that our approach can find predictions that other tested state-of-the-art systems cannot.

Keywords: Recommender systems · Demographics · Typicality · Fuzzy logic

1 Introduction

E-commerce applications thrive on getting users to buy anything and everything. Displaying recommendations everywhere has now become normal, they present users with items predicted as relevant or interesting to them. These items should satisfy a few properties, such as being new to the user (as opposed to recommending items too similar to some already owned by the user). Recommender systems do not require large amounts of data to provide users with suggestions: only a few rated items or some demographics are enough. Recommendations are computed by predicting a user's interest in items they have not used or bought yet. If the prediction score is high, then the item may be recommended. Predictions are ranked to fit the scale of the system, which could be a 1–5 star scale for instance.

Our objective is to extend previous work with typicality [12] to demographic data (e.g. age, occupation) in recommender systems. Demographics are a valuable source of information and we believe that in many domains (e.g. movies, music, literature) they can be used to suggest items to users. The concept of typicality has been studied in the fields of both cognitive psychology [9] and fuzzy logic [17]. In this work we will focus on the definition presented by Zadeh in [18].

Here is an example of the approach presented in [12]: let us consider a user interested in actors querying the database who wishes to find actors similar to

H. Christiansen et al. (Eds.): FQAS 2017, LNAI 10333, pp. 71–83, 2017.
DOI: 10.1007/978-3-319-59692-1_7

one in the result. Similarity may be based on values or/and on relations: we shall consider similarity based on relations between entities. In this cinematographic context, "similar" may have different meanings, such as working with the same directors, starring with the same co-actors, or playing in movies of the same genres. An actor such as Tom Cruise will have a set of typical directors, a set of typical co-actors, a set of typical genres and so on. To compute the similarity between Tom Cruise and other actors, we compute the set of typical elements of the other actors in the database and compare them to those of Tom Cruise. For instance if $T_{\text{Tom Cruise}} = \{0.4/\text{Cameron Crowe}, 0.3/\text{Steven Spielberg}, 0.2/\text{Christopher McQuarrie}, ...\}$ is the set of typical directors with which Tom Cruise is associated, then actors with a similar set of typical directors will be considered similar to Tom Cuise.

The key idea of our approach is to figure out the typical properties attached to each movie and find similarities with other movies based on these typical demographic properties. With our demographic approach, let us consider a user who likes *Terminator* and *Tron*. Let us assume that these movies are usually liked by young men in college. This frequent association between movies and demographics can be measured with a typicality degree: young and male are two typical properties of the audience of these two movies. The recommendation process may leverage these typicality links to provide the user (who is not necessarily a young man) with other movies appreciated by young men.

In this work, we consider two visions to leverage demographic data with collaborative filtering and typicality in a movie context:

- compute for all movies the demographic multisets representative of the users who liked them, compare them all with a similarity measure and provide users with movies similar to the ones they liked based on this notion of similarity;
- compute the sets of typical movies liked by users with the same profile elements as the current user.

In other words, recommendations may be computed based on the user's profile or the user's ratings. We treat the new user problem with their demographic data.

This paper is structured as follows: in Sect. 2 we will position our approach with respect to the existing literature. In Sect. 3 we will introduce how we use typicality with demographic data in recommender systems. Then we will detail how explanations are provided in Sect. 4. The results of our experiments with the first approach are detailed in Sect. 5 and we will conclude in Sect. 6.

2 Related Work

Classical recommender systems (RS) include content-based (CB), collaborative filtering systems (CF) and hybrid systems (HS). Others include demographic, knowledge-based (constraint-based and case-based) and community-based systems [13]. More generally it all comes down to predicting whether or not the user will be interested in an item, and to which degree. Several metrics presented in Sect. 5 help compare recommenders.

CF RS provide predictions based on the ratings of users. No additional data—whether about items or users—are required, which makes these approaches very popular. Some of these approaches consider neighborhoods: sets of users or items similar to the one for which a prediction is made. There are two subclasses of neighborhood-based CF RS: user-based CF and item-based CF. User-based CF RS consider the ratings of similar users on the same item to predict scores. Item-based CF RS consider the ratings of similar items by the same user to predict scores. The prediction score is the aggregation of the similarity scores between the user's profile and the neighborhood's users profiles. To improve these approaches, the rating behavior of the user is taken into account—whether or not the user usually rates items higher or lower than other people. CF RS also have issues with cold start (both new user and new item problems).

The use of typicality in CF RS has already been investigated in [2]. The authors propose to start by creating item groups, in which items are fuzzily affected to by a clustering method—meaning that items may belong to several groups to different degrees. Then for each item group a corresponding user group is created, and populated with users who liked the movies in these item groups. Users are more or less typical in user groups, depending on their appreciation of the movies in the item groups associated. The affectation of users in user groups is done by a fuzzy clustering algorithm, meaning that users belong to a group to a certain degree $\in [0, 1]$. Recommendations for a given user are computed based on the ratings of other users in the given user's neighborhood. A neighborhood selects users with close typicality degrees in the different user groups—aggregated and compared with classical distance measures. Our approach also uses typicality to find similar users, however our use of typicality is different from theirs insofar as we look for items typically associated with groups of people based on their demographic characteristics.

Approaches based on demographic data are popular in marketing papers, but there has not been much research from the RS community on the topic of pure demographic RS according to [13]. They are often used to improve CF methods by restricting the neighborhood based on the user's characteristics [14]. Our use of demographic data is different as we look for the similarities in the audience who liked the movies. Krulwich leveraged demographics in [6] with LifeStyle Finder to create clusters of people. His approach focuses on acquiring large amounts of personal data through dialog. We do not use so many different data types nor do we use clustering in our approach. Pazzani described the needs of CB, CF and demographic recommenders to provide users with good recommendations [11]. He notes that the effort made to obtain demographic data is reflected with the quality of this information, hinting at the large amounts of information used by [6]. In his experiment, the demographic recommendations do not perform as well as CB and CF recommendations. Demographics can also help with the cold start problem, by using stereotypes to recommend items to new users who have not rated any item yet. We present one such approach based on typicality in Subsect. 3.2. However in some contexts such as tourist attractions [15] demographic RS have had mitigated results. Users are not always inclined to share their personal data, even though these can sometimes be deduced from their own ratings and the personal data of some other users as reported in [16].

3 Typicality-Based Collaborative Filtering

In our movie context, we consider two visions to typicality-based collaborative filtering applied to demographic data. We view demographics as statistical characteristics of human populations. To this end, we consider movies "liked" by users (*i.e.* the movies they gave 4 or 5 stars):

- link to a movie the sets of profession, age, and other characteristics of people who typically liked it; based on the movies liked by the current user, recommendations can be processed by comparing the typical fuzzy sets associated with these movies with those of other movies in the database. The current user's profile is not used in this approach, only the movies s/he liked;
- for each element of the user's profile, a fuzzy set of typical movies liked by users with this profile element is computed. The movies liked by the current user are not considered.

Each approach is first formalized and then illustrated with a detailed example. A hybrid approach mixing the above two is outlined at the end of this section.

3.1 Using the Current User's Favorite Items

This approach consists of several steps, the first two can be done offline, and the last one on the fly to provide recommendations to users. These steps are:

1. compute for each item the sets of typical demographic features of the users who liked them;
2. compare all items, based on these fuzzy sets of typical features;
3. look for the most similar items to those liked by the current user.

Step 1: Computing the Fuzzy Sets of Typical Features. For each item m and for each demographic characteristic c (*e.g.* age, occupation, etc.) we compute the multi-set $E_c(m)$ representing the profile of the users who liked them (we assume liking is the same as giving 4 or 5 stars on a 5-star rating scale).

$$E_c(m) = \{(k/x) \mid x \text{ a modality of } c \text{ and } \\ k \text{ the number of users having the characteristic } x \text{ and who liked } m\}.$$

In order to assess the extent to which x is a typical value in E, two cases have to be taken into account: that where a metric—on which a similarity relation can be based—over the considered domain is available, and that where such a metric is not available and strict equality must be used. Details on how to compute typicality based on similarity can be found in [12]. In any case, starting from a multiset E, the objective is to obtain a fuzzy set T such that for all x, $\mu_T(x)$ expresses the extent to which x is typical in E. In the absence of any similarity measure, one solution is to consider the frequency of x in E and take

$$\mu_T(x) = \frac{k}{n}, \tag{1}$$

where k is the number of copies of x in E and n is the cardinality of E. Based on the multi-set $E_c(m)$, the fuzzy set $T_c(m)$ of typical values is computed.

$$\begin{aligned} T_c(m) = \{(\mu_T(x)/x) \mid\ & x \text{ a modality of } c \text{ and} \\ & \mu_T(x) \text{ the frequency-based typicality of } x \text{ in } E_c(m)\}. \end{aligned}$$

Step 2: Comparing Multisets. Several interpretations of the condition E_1 *matches* E_2—where E_1 and E_2 are two regular multisets of attribute values associated with two different items—can be thought of. The problem comes down to assessing the equality of two fuzzy sets, and many measures have been proposed for doing so, see *e.g.* [1,10]. One may for instance test the equality of the two fuzzy sets T_1 and T_2 of (more or less) typical elements in E_1 and E_2 respectively, for example by means of the Jaccard index:

$$\mu_{matches}(E_1, E_2) = \frac{\sum_{x \in U} \min(\mu_{T_1}(x), \mu_{T_2}(x))}{\sum_{x \in U} \max(\mu_{T_1}(x), \mu_{T_2}(x))}, \tag{2}$$

where U denotes the underlying domain of E_1 and E_2, or by means of a measure such as:

$$\mu_{matches}(E_1, E_2) = \inf_{x \in U} 1 - |\mu_{T_1}(x) - \mu_{T_2}(x)|. \tag{3}$$

A square matrix S of size $|movies|$ is created, with each cell $s_{i,j}$ populated with the similarity degree between movies m_i and m_j. This similarity degree is computed by aggregating the matching degrees between the typical fuzzy sets of all pairs of items. We use the Jaccard index as the matching measure, and the minimum as the aggregation operator.

$$s_{i,j} = \min_c(\mu_{matches}(T_c(m_i), T_c(m_j))) \tag{4}$$

Remark 1. Some features may be considered more important than others, and an aggregation operator such as the weighted average or the weighted minimum [3] can then be used instead of the minimum.

Step 3: Browsing the Similarity Matrix. To predict the rating of a user u for an item m_i, denoted by p_{u,m_i} we simply look for the highest similarity value in the matrix S between m_i and the items that user u liked:

$$p_{u,m_i} = \max_j(s_{i,j} \in S \mid m_j \text{ liked by } u). \tag{5}$$

It is worth noticing that instead of the maximum aggregation operator, others such as the weighted mean or the kth highest degree (which corresponds to a quantifier of the form "at least k") can be considered. The idea is to be as faithful to the demographic profiles as possible, leading to the utilization of less conventional aggregation operators than the max. An ordered list of recommendations is generated from S.

Example 1. Let us consider a user who liked the movies *Star Wars IV* and *Tron.*

Step 1. consists in computing the fuzzy sets of demographic data representing the users who liked these movies. As such, we get for the *age* characteristic the following multisets ([18–24] refers to people aged 18–24):

E_{age}(Star Wars IV) = {67/[−18], 378/[18–24], 813/[25–34], 442/[35–44], 162/[45–49], 147/[50–55], 87/[56+]}

E_{age}(Tron) = {9/[−18], 92/[18–24], 154/[25–34], 51/[35–44], 22/[45–49], 23/[50–55], 8/[56+]}

Based on these multisets, the associated fuzzy sets of typical demographic values are then computed:

T_{age}(SW IV) = {0.03/[−18], 0.18/[18–24], 0.39/[25–34], 0.21/[35–44], 0.08/[45–49], 0.07/[50–55], 0.04/[56+]}

T_{age}(Tron) = {0.03/[−18], 0.26/[18–24], 0.43/[25–34], 0.14/[35–44], 0.06/[45–49], 0.06/[50–55], 0.2/[56+]}

Let us recall that these fuzzy sets of typical values are computed offline for all movies in the database. Then for **Step 2** they are compared in order to compute the similarity matrix S. As such, we will compare *Star Wars IV* to all other movies in the database, such as *Star Wars V*. We will use the Jaccard index between their fuzzy sets of typical values, for all profile features considered. Then we will aggregate these matching degrees. Assuming that we have

T_{age}(SW V) = {0.03/[−18], 0.21/[18–24], 0.4/[25–34], 0.19/[35–44], 0.07/[45–49], 0.06/[50–55], 0.4/[56+]},

then we get $\mu_{matches}(T_{age}(\text{SW IV}), T_{age}(\text{SW V})) = 0.923$.

For other characteristics such as *occupation* and *gender* we consider $\mu_{matches}(T_{occ}(\text{SW IV}), T_{occ}(\text{SW V})) = 0.929$ and $\mu_{matches}(T_{gender}(\text{SW IV}), T_{gender}(\text{SW V})) = 0.925$.

As a result, $s_{\text{SW IV,SW V}} = \min(0.923, 0.929, 0.995) = 0.923$. This process is repeated for all unordered pairs of movies.

Once the similarity matrix S has been completed, we look for the movies the most similar to those liked by the current user, *i.e.* movies with the highest degrees in S in the columns of the movies *Star Wars IV* and *Tron.*◇

3.2 Using the Current User's Demographic Data

Typicality may also be used to define a method to compute recommendations based on the audience who typically liked some items. This method starts with computing the favorite items of users based on each profile feature value (*e.g.* for the age feature, we compute a set of favorite items for users [−18], another for users [18–24], etc.). Afterwards, we aggregate the sets of favorite items to fit to the list of profile characteristics of a user.

Computing Items Typically Liked by People Based on One Characteristic. For each profile characteristic $c \in C$ of the current user $u_{current}$, select the other users U with the same profile element. For each such user $u \in U$, compute the fuzzy multi-set of items $E_c(u)$ each user liked with elements of the form r/m where r is the rating (divided by 5 to fit the [0, 1] scale, which gives values such as 0.2, 0.4, 0.4, 0.8 and 1) given by user u to item m.

Then compute the multiset sum $E_c(U)$ from the different $E_c(u)$ with $u \in U$ by writing each element in the form $(r_{avg}, nb)/m$, where r_{avg} is the average rating of users in U for the item m, and nb the number of users who rated it.

Finally compute $T_c(U)$ from $E_c(U)$, $T_c(U)$ being the typical set of items representing the users U. In $T_c(U)$ each element is of the form μ/m, where μ is the min between r_{avg} and $nb/card(E_c(U))$ in $E_c(U)$ for m, cf Example 2 below.

Aggregating Typical Sets of Items. For all characteristics $c \in C$, we aggregate the multisets $T_c(U)$ with an intersection (using the T-norm min for instance) to get the items typically liked by people based on all criteria, resulting in $T_C(U)$. Items need to be in every $T_c(U)$ fuzzy set to appear in $T_C(U)$. Should no item satisfy this condition, another aggregation operator (such as the mean) should be considered instead of the intersection.

Final step: return the elements with the highest typicality degree in $T_C(U)$.

Example 2. Let us consider the users described in Table 1, and start looking for recommendations for *Sophie.* Based on her age, *Sophie* is similar to *Melanie* and *Aaron.* Based on her occupation, *Sophie* is similar to *Hiroki.* Based on her location, *Sophie* is similar to *Alice* and *Nolan.* Based on her gender, *Sophie* is identical to *Melanie* and *Alice* (the dataset we use only features two genders). To assess the extent to how similar users are, degrees of similarity—computed by the means of similarity relations, such as identity for the gender, a metric distance for the age and location and a semantic distance for the occupation—should be considered. In this example we consider a crisp vision of similarity for the sake of clarity.

The known ratings associated with the users in Table 1 are presented in Table 2. Considering the *age* characteristic, we look for the favorite movies of both *Melanie* and *Aaron.* By dividing their ratings by 5, we get:

E_{age}(Melanie) = {0.4/T, 0.8/HP3} and E_{age}(Aaron) = {0.6/T, 0.6/HP4}. Then we aggregate these sets and get:

$E_{age}(U) = \{(0.5, 2)/\text{T}, (0.8, 1)/\text{HP3}, (0.6, 1)/\text{HP4}\}$.

Table 1. User profile examples

Name	Gender	Age	Occupation	Area
Sophie	F	25	Grad Student	Denmark
Hiroki	M	16	Pupil	Japan
Aaron	M	32	Engineer	Canada
Melanie	F	29	Sales Exec	Spain
Alice	F	43	Educator	Germany
Nolan	M	34	Lawyer	Netherlands

Table 2. User ratings examples

	Sophie	Hiroki	Aaron	Melanie	Alice	Nolan
Da Vinci Code (DVC)	?				4	
Harry Potter 2 (HP2)	?	4				3
Harry Potter 3 (HP3)	?			4		5
Harry Potter 4 (HP4)	?	1	3			4
Star Wars IV (SW IV)	?				2	4
Terminator (T)	?	4	3	2	3	

Remark 2. To compute average marks we only consider the ratings given by users and divide by the number of users having rated the movie, leading to an average of 0.8 for the movie *Harry Potter 3*.

The typical set of movies obtained is:

$T_{age}(U) = \{min(0.5, 1)/\text{T}, min(0.8, 0.5)/\text{HP3}, min(0.6, 0.5)/\text{HP4}\}$

$T_{age}(U) = \{0.5/\text{T}, 0.5/\text{HP3}, 0.5/\text{HP4}\}$.

Now, assuming that for the other characteristics we get:

$T_{area}(U) = \{0.6/\text{SW IV}, 0.5/\text{T}, 0.5/\text{DVC}, 0.3/\text{HP2}, 0.5/\text{HP3}, 0.4/\text{HP4}\}$ and

$T_{occupation}(U) = \{0.5/\text{T}, 0.4/\text{HP2}, 0.2/\text{HP4}\}$.

By aggregating these three sets, we finally get:

$T_C(U) = \{0.5/\text{T}, 0.2/\text{HP4}\}$.◇

In both approaches, it is possible to consider domain-dependent filters to reduce the number of items to consider. In this case, in order to reduce the number of movies to consider and alleviate computational costs, we suggest limiting the search to one movie genre in particular, meaning letting users specify which movie genre they are interested in.

The two approaches can be combined naively by computing the two separately and then intersecting the results (the first one uses similarity matching degrees between a set of movies liked by the user and other movies, and the second one uses typicality degrees of movies associated with a set of users). They can be seen as complementary as the first one requires more data to work, while the second one can handle the new user problem, simply using the user's demographic data. We intend to combine the two approaches by using the second one with new users, for so long as they do not have enough ratings. Once they have rated at least k items, we only use the first approach. However due to lack of space we only report results from the first approach.

4 Explanations

Explanations to recommendations increase the trust of users in the system [8] and satisfy their curiosity when facing unexpected recommendations, provided that they do not invade their privacy [5]. Demographic explanations may be considered as "awkward" since people may feel uncomfortable receiving recommendations seemingly based on stereotypes. Two forms of demographic explanations are considered here, based on:

- the movies associated with those liked by the user (Subsect. 3.1), leading to explanations such as "X-Men *was recommended to you because you liked movies such as* Harry Potter *and* LOTR, *and all of these movies have the same typical audience who liked them;"*
- the user's own characteristics in the case of the new user problem (Subsect. 3.2), leading to explanations such as "X-Men *was recommended to you because this movie is typically liked by* young men in college *such as yourself."*

As the similarity score is based on the minimum between the matching degrees for all profile characteristics, and the occupation characteristic often turns up in the matrix, providing more detailed explanations—than "have a similar audience"—for the first approach may be difficult. Indeed, the occupation characteristic has the highest number of modality values (21 in the 1M MovieLens dataset) so it may be misguiding to present a modality actually explaining the recommendation if it is so only by a small degree.

5 Experiments

In this section we evaluated our approach presented in Subsect. 3.1 (henceforth referred to as *Demo*). We seek to determine how it fares against state-of-the-art recommenders on several metrics defined below. We experimented with the 1M MovieLens[1] dataset which contains some demographic information about users, such as their age, occupation, gender and zip code. The 1 M dataset (1,000,209 ratings) contains 3,883 movies partially rated by 6,040 users. The sparsity of the dataset is $1 - \frac{1{,}000{,}209}{3{,}883 * 6{,}040} = 0,957$. The dataset is split into a training set R_{train} and a test set R_{test} with ratios 80% and 20% respectively. These sets are subsets randomly extracted from the 1M dataset.

Following the Demo algorithm, a prediction score between 0 and 1 is given for each movie for each user based on some of their ratings. This score is then

[1] http://grouplens.org/datasets/movielens/.

transformed into a rating on the 1–5 star scale. To this end, we considered the following mapping:

$$\text{prediction} = 4 * \text{score} + 1.$$

We evaluated Demo and compared it to other standard approaches such as user-user collaborative filtering (UU CF), item-item collaborative filtering (II CF), personalized mean [7] (PM) and matrix factorization [4] (MF). To the best of our knowledge, given the low interest of the RS community for demographic RS, there is no baseline to evaluate recommendations based on demographic data. We used the following metrics: mean average error (MAE), root mean square error (RMSE), precision, recall, F-measure, and coverage. For a given user u and item i, we have a hidden reference rating r_{ui}, and we compute a prediction p_{ui}.

The MAE and RMSE are popular metrics for evaluating the difference between the predicted ratings and the actual ratings.

$$\text{MAE} = \frac{1}{|R_{test}|} \sum_{r_{ui} \in R_{test}} (|r_{ui} - p_{ui}|) \qquad \text{RMSE} = \sqrt{\frac{1}{|R_{test}|} \sum_{r_{ui} \in R_{test}} (r_{ui} - p_{ui})^2}$$

The precision, recall, F-measure and coverage enable offline evaluation of recommender systems. They are computed based on the classification of ratings according to Table 3.

Table 3. Classification of a recommendation

	Recommended ($p \geqslant 4$)	Not recommended ($p < 4$)
Liked (rated 4+)	True Positive (tp)	False Negative (fn)
Not liked (rated 3-)	False Positive (ft)	True Negative (tn)

$$\text{Precision} = \frac{\#\text{tp}}{\#\text{tp} + \#\text{fp}} \qquad \text{Recall} = \frac{\#\text{tp}}{\#\text{tp} + \#\text{fn}}$$

$$\text{F-measure} = \frac{2 * \text{precision} * \text{recall}}{\text{precision} + \text{recall}} \qquad \text{Coverage} = \frac{\#\text{distinct items recommended}}{\#\text{distinct items in the database}}$$

We present a comparison of our approach with other approaches in Table 4. Our method is not as effective as the others in terms of MAE and RMSE: indeed, many predictions (over 50%) fall in the 4 stars category, somewhat showing signs of leniency of our approach. This is highlighted with the precision scores. However, the recall is much higher with our approach, and the resulting F-measure is also higher than that of all other tested approaches.

Table 4. Experiment results

Algorithm	MAE	RMSE	Precision	Recall	F-measure	Coverage
Demo	0.85	1.09	0.65	0.81	0.72	0.35
UU CF	0.72	0.89	0.83	0.53	0.65	0.61
II CF	0.69	0.85	0.87	0.50	0.63	0.63
MF	0.70	0.86	0.86	0.48	0.62	0.67
PM	0.73	0.89	0.85	0.41	0.56	0.52

We also compare the correct predictions of all evaluated systems together in Table 5. As it turns out, our approach can correctly predict around 14% of the ratings that another approach would not. Assuming we would fuse all other approaches and always acquire the best prediction possible from all of them, our approach can still provide as many as up to 5.9% good predictions that the others combined cannot. Typicality-based CF leveraging demographic data offers another way to compare items, and so is a good complementary approach that would deserve to be fused with other methods.

Table 5. Comparison of recommendation results: proportions of correct predictions found by Algorithm 1 and not found by Algorithm 2

		Algorithm 2				
		Demo	UU CF	II CF	MF	PM
Algorithm 1	Demo	0	0.13	0.13	0.15	0.14
	UU CF	0.21	0	0.09	0.13	0.10
	II CF	0.22	0.11	0	0.12	0.10
	MF	0.24	0.14	0.01	0	0.14
	PM	0.19	0.08	0.07	0.11	0

Example 3. Let us we present a few recommendations obtained by our system that other tested systems could not provide.

- User 5811 was recommended *William Shakespeare's Romeo and Juliet (1996)* because he liked movies such as *Welcome to the Dollhouse (1995)*, *Cruel Intentions (1999)*, and *Great Muppet Caper, The (1981)*, which all have very similar audiences.
- User 1051 was recommended *Ghostbusters (1984)* because she liked movies such as *Silence of the Lambs, The (1991)*, *Saving Private Ryan (1998)*, and *Indiana Jones and the Last Crusade (1989)*, which all have very similar audiences.
- User 4022 was recommended *Star Wars: Episode IV - A New Hope (1977)* because he liked movies such as *Raiders of the Lost Ark (1981)*, *Back to the Future (1985)*, and *Saving Private Ryan (1998)*, which all have very similar audiences. ◇

A reason why classical CF approaches do not recommend these movies can be simply that they have not been rated by any user who has a rating behavior sufficiently similar to the current user's. Our approach recommends items based purely on the demographics of the audience who liked movies. This is an advantage when considering users that may have an unusual rating pattern and who may have difficulty getting good recommendations from user-based CF systems.

6 Conclusion

In this paper we have presented an approach leveraging the demographics of users rating movies. The approach itself can be extended to any context, provided that some demographic data are available. While some results are not satisfactory, others prove that the approach has a few perks: predicting ratings that other state of the art systems cannot, and having a rather good F-measure.

Perspectives include creating a hybrid recommender system to take advantage of the approach presented here with other approaches from the state of the art. We also intend to further distinguish ratings—no longer consider the dual approach "liked/not liked"—and integrate the similarity degrees—presented as "crisp" in Example 2—to better compare users.

Acknowledgments. This work has been partially funded by the French DGE (Direction Générale des Entreprises) under the project ODIN (Open Data INtelligence).

References

1. Bouchon-Meunier, B., Coletti, G., Lesot, M.-J., Rifqi, M.: Towards a conscious choice of a fuzzy similarity measure: a qualitative point of view. In: Hüllermeier, E., Kruse, R., Hoffmann, F. (eds.) IPMU 2010. LNCS (LNAI), vol. 6178, pp. 1–10. Springer, Heidelberg (2010). doi:10.1007/978-3-642-14049-5_1
2. Cai, Y., Leung, H.F., Li, Q., Min, H., Tang, J., Li, J.: Typicality-based collaborative filtering recommendation. IEEE Trans. Knowl. Data Eng. **26**(3), 766–779 (2014)
3. Dubois, D., Prade, H.: Weighted minimum and maximum operations in fuzzy set theory. Inf. Sci. **39**, 205–210 (1986)
4. Funk, S.: Netflix update: try this at home (2006). http://sifter.org/~simon/journal/20061211.html
5. Jeckmans, A.J.P., Beye, M., Erkin, Z., Hartel, P., Lagendijk, R.L., Tang, Q.: Privacy in recommender systems. In: Ramzan, N., van Zwol, R., Lee, J.-S., Clüver, K., Hua, X.-S. (eds.) Social Media Retrieval, pp. 263–281. Springer, London (2013)
6. Krulwich, B.: LIFESTYLE FINDER: intelligent user profiling using large-scale demographic data. AI Mag. **18**(2), 37 (1997)
7. Lemire, D., Maclachlan, A.: Slope one predictors for online rating-based collaborative filtering. In: Proceedings of the 2005 SIAM International Conference on Data Mining, SDM 2005, pp. 471–475 (2005)
8. Mcsherry, D.: Explanation in recommender systems. Artif. Intell. Rev. **24**(2), 179–197 (2005)
9. Osherson, D., Smith, E.E.: On typicality and vagueness. Cognition **64**(2), 189–206 (1997)

10. Pappis, C., Karacapilidis, N.: A comparative assessment of measures of similarity of fuzzy values. Fuzzy Sets Syst. **56**(2), 171–174 (1993)
11. Pazzani, M.J.: A framework for collaborative, content-based and demographic filtering. Artif. Intell. Rev. **13**(5–6), 393–408 (1999)
12. Pivert, O., Smits, G., Jaun, H.: Finding similar objects in relational databases - an association-based fuzzy approach. In: Flexible Query Answering Systems - 10th International Conference, FQAS 2013, Proceedings, pp. 425–436 (2013)
13. Ricci, F., Rokach, L., Shapira, B. (eds.): Recommender Systems Handbook, 2nd edn. Springer, Boston (2015)
14. Vozalis, M.G., Margaritis, K.G.: Using SVD and demographic data for the enhancement of generalized Collaborative Filtering. Inf. Sci. **177**(15), 3017–3037 (2007)
15. Wang, Y., Chan, S.C.F., Ngai, G.: Applicability of demographic recommender system to tourist attractions: a case study on TripAdvisor. In: Proceeding of WI-IAT 2012, pp. 97–101 (2012)
16. Weinsberg, U., Bhagat, S., Ioannidis, S., Taft, N.: BlurMe: inferring and obfuscating user gender based on ratings. In: Proceedings of the 6th ACM Conference on Recommender Systems - RecSys 2012, pp. 195–202 (2012)
17. Yager, R.R.: A note on a fuzzy measure of typicality. Int. J. Intell. Syst. **12**(3), 233–249 (1997)
18. Zadeh, L.: A computational theory of dispositions. Int. J. Intell. Syst. **2**, 39–63 (1987)

MRRA: A New Approach for Movie Rating Recommendation

Chiraz Trabelsi[1(✉)] and Gabriella Pasi[2]

[1] Faculté des Sciences de Tunis, LIPAH-LR 11ES14, Université de Tunis El Manar, 2092 Tunis, Tunisia
chiraz.trabelsi@fst.rnu.tn

[2] DISCo Viale Sarca, Università degli Studi di Milano-Bicocca, 336 - Edificio U14, 20126 Milano, Italy
pasi@disco.unimib.it

Abstract. Nowadays, Movie constitutes a predominant form of entertainment in human life. Most video websites such as YouTube and a number of social networks allow users to freely assign a rate to watched or bought videos or movies. In this paper, we introduce a new movie rating recommendation approach, called MRRA, based on the exploitation of the Hidden Markov Model (HMM). Specifically, we extend the HMM to include user's rating profiles, formally represented as triadic concepts. Triadic concepts are exploited for providing important hidden correlations between rates, movies and users. Carried out experiments using a benchmark movie dataset revealed that the proposed movie rating recommendation approach outperforms conventional techniques.

Keywords: User's rating profile model · Triadic analysis · Rate recommendation · Hidden Markov Model

1 Context and Motivations

The ability of recommender systems to generate direct connections between users and items that represent matches in interests and preferences makes them an important tool for alleviating information overload for Web users. They are becoming increasingly important in the success of electronic commerce, and being used in most video websites such as YouTube and Hulu and a number of social networks allow users rate on videos or movies. In a general way, a recommendation system constructs items' profiles, and users' profiles based on their previous recorded behaviour. Thereafter it makes a prediction on the given rating by a certain user on a certain item which he/she has not yet evaluated. Based on the prediction, the system makes recommendations. Various techniques for recommendation generation have been proposed and widely deployed in commercial environments, among which collaborative filtering (CF) methods still represents the most commonly adopted technique in crafting academic and commercial [1,5,9] recommender systems. Its basic idea refers to making recommendations

H. Christiansen et al. (Eds.): FQAS 2017, LNAI 10333, pp. 84–95, 2017.
DOI: 10.1007/978-3-319-59692-1_8

based upon ratings that users have assigned to products. Ratings can either be explicit, *i.e.*, by having the user state his opinion about a given product, or implicit, when the mere act of purchasing or mentioning of an item counts as an expression of appreciation. While implicit ratings are generally more facile to collect, their usage implies adding noise to the collected information.

The information domain for a collaborative filtering system consists of users which have expressed preferences for various items. A preference expressed by a user for an item is called a rating and is frequently represented as a (User, Item, Rating) triple. These ratings can take many forms, depending on the system in question. Some systems use real- or integer-valued rating scales such as 0–5 stars, while others use binary or ternary (like/dislike) scales. CF algorithms involve then matching the ratings of a current user for items, *e.g.*, movies or books, with those of similar users in order to produce recommendations for items not yet rated or seen by an active user. Pearson Correlation and Vector Similarity [8] are two most common measures for finding the user similarities. Later several researchers have proposed different other measures for calculating user similarities. Weighted average of the most similar users' ratings for the test items are output as the predicted rating. There are several algorithms that use probabilistic graphical models for solving the task of rating prediction [6,17]. Matrix factorization algorithms have also been widely popular. These algorithms model both the user and items as vectors in a low dimensional feature space. Representation of the user and items in the joint feature space is then used to compute the predicted ratings [4].

Regarding those aforementioned approaches, we introduce in this paper a new approach, called MRRA[1], for movie rating recommendation. MRRA is based on the use of the Hidden Markov Model (HMM). In fact, contrary to existing approaches dedicated to movie rate recommendation, neither a given user nor the co-occurrences of movies or rates values are handled for rate recommendation. We only consider the movie, *i.e.,* a movie to be rated, as input and by matching the movie to its corresponding context according to HMM states [14], we estimate a rate value candidate, that represents the most probable user's rating profile. In fact, HMMs have been successfully applied in many prediction field especially for users' web search query prediction [3,7]. Therefore, in this paper, we introduce a novel Hidden Markov Model (HMM) based approach, to handle two main challenges addressing movie rate recommendation problem: (*i*) Using the three-dimensional structure of the movie rating database for identifying and representing users' rating profiles; and (*ii*) Exploiting users' rating profiles for predicting users' next rate value which could/should be applied by the users to a particular movie.

From the moment that the usage of rates values assigned by users sharing similar interests tends to converge to a shared behavior [10], then we firstly propose, to define a user rating profile as an implicit shared conceptualization formally sketched by a triadic concept. Indeed, triadic concepts allow grouping semantically related movies that take into account the users' rating behavior.

[1] MRRA is the acronym of Movie Rating Recommendation Approach.

Therefore, instead of using matrix based models or co-occurrence techniques, we use an algorithm, called TRICONS [16], to mine users' rating profiles from a movie database. Moreover, on the contrary of the previous approaches which consider a 2-dimensional pair relations, missing by the way a part of the total interaction between the three dimensions, *i.e.*, user, rate and resource, we introduce a unified framework to concurrently model the three dimensions handled by a HMM [14]. Indeed, we propose to exploit the HMMs prediction capabilities [3,7] to model the whole rating process as a sequence of (auto)-transitions between states. Hence, each rating profile, represented as triadic concept, can be defined as a state of the HMM, and the rate value and evaluated movies as observations generated by the state.

The remainder of the paper is organized as follows. In Sect. 2, we introduce our approach for Movie Rating Recommendation consisting of two phases: the model-building phase (Sect. 2.1) and the exploitation phase (Sect. 2.2). The experimental study of our approach is illustrated in Sect. 3. Section 4 concludes this paper.

2 MRRA for Movie Rating Recommendation

In this section, we present our recommendation approach, called *MRRA*, which aims to effectively assigning the right rate value to a particular movie. *MRRA* is able to generate recommendations in constant time and performs a triadic concept analysis to mine users' rating profiles. The triadic concepts can be used as an access structure for providing important hidden correlations between rates, movies and users. In order to achieve theses goals, the proposed *MRRA* approach performs two main phases: the model-building phase and the exploitation phase.

2.1 The Model-Building Phase

MRRA starts by learning users' rating behavior by identifying users' rating profiles behind the assigned rates. Considered as a tripartite graph of users, ratings and movies, the users' movies rates assignments can be, formally, represented as a triadic context [12].

The model-building phase performs concurrently by retrieving user's movies sequences from a given movie database, *e.g.*, an example of a collection of users' movies rates assignments $\mathcal{S}^{\nabla}$ with $\mathcal{U} = \{u_1, u_2, u_3, u_4\}$, $\mathcal{M} = \{m_1, m_2, m_3, m_4, m_5\}$ and $\mathcal{R} = \{r_1, r_2, r_3\}$. Each triple from $\mathcal{S}^{\nabla}$ represents a triadic relationship between a user belonging to $\mathcal{U}$, a rate from $\mathcal{R}$ and a movie belonging to $\mathcal{M}$, and mining users' rating profiles. The results of these previously steps, are then used for the HMM training. Each step in the building phase is described below.

Step 1: User's Movies Ratings Extraction: This step aims to determine for each user u_i the sequences SR_i of his similarly rated movies. It proceeds by firstly collect users' assignments S_i defined as follows:

Table 1. An example of users' ratings assignments.

$S_1{:=}\ \{\{m_{1,1}, m_{1,2}, m_{1,3}\}, r_{1,1}\}; \{\{m_{1,4}\}, r_{1,2}\}$
$S_2{:=}\ \{\{m_{2,3}, m_{2,4}\}, r_{2,3}\}$
$S_3{:=}\ \{\{m_{3,2}, m_{3,3}\}, r_{3,4}\}; \{\{m_{3,4}, m_{3,5}\}, r_{3,6}\}$

$$S_i := \{\{\text{User movies } m_{S_i,p}\}, r_{S_i,j}\}.$$

with $r_{S_i,j}{:=}$ The rate value j assigned by the user u_i in the post S_i, $m_{S_i,p}{:=}$ The p ordered movie rated in S_i.

Table 1 reports an example of users' ratings assignments. For example, the user assignments S_2, highlights that the user u_2 has assigned the rate value $r_{2,3}$ to the two movies $m_{2,3}$ and $m_{2,4}$. Once the users ratings assignments are collected, we generate user's movies sequences by keeping, for each user, the sequences of movies related to his assignments and discard useless information. An example of user's movies sequences associated to Table 1 is given in the following: SL_1: $((m_{1,1}, m_{1,2}, m_{1,3}); (m_{1,1}, m_{1,4}))$, SL_2: $(m_{2,3}, m_{2,4})$, SL_3: $((m_{3,2}, m_{3,3}); (m_{3,4}, m_{3,5}))$ where SL_i, describes movies rating sequences of the user u_i.

Step 2: Users' Rating Profiles Mining: The second step of the model-building phase step is to mine the users' rating profiles, formally represented by triadic concepts. Let us firstly recall in the following the main definition related to a triadic concept [11] that will be used in the remainder.

Definition 1 (TRIADIC CONCEPT). *A triadic concept (tri-concept for short) of a collection of users' movies rates assignments* $\mathcal{S}{:=}\ (\mathcal{U}, \mathcal{R}, \mathcal{M}, \mathcal{G})$ *is a triple* $(\mathcal{U}_1, \mathcal{R}_1, \mathcal{M}_1)$ *with* $\mathcal{U}_1 \subseteq \mathcal{U}$, $\mathcal{R}_1 \subseteq \mathcal{R}$, *and* $\mathcal{M}_1 \subseteq \mathcal{M}$ *with* $\mathcal{U} \times \mathcal{R} \times M \subseteq \mathcal{G}$ *such that the triple* $(\mathcal{U}_1, \mathcal{R}_1, M_1)$ *is maximal.*

Consequently, a rating profile can be formally represented, in $\mathcal{S} = (\mathcal{U}, \mathcal{R}, \mathcal{M}, \mathcal{G})$, as a triadic concept $\mathcal{RP} = (U', R', M')$ where $U' \subseteq \mathcal{U}$, $R' \subseteq \mathcal{R}$, and $M' \subseteq \mathcal{M}$ with $U' \times R' \times M' \subseteq \mathcal{G}$. The users' rating profiles are therefore obtained by invoking the TRICONS algorithm [16] on the collection $\mathcal{S}$. Roughly speaking, the rating profile $RP_1 = \{(u_1, u_2, u_3), (m_1, m_2), (r_4)\}$ highlights that the community of users (u_1, u_2, u_3) share the same rating behaviour on the movies (m_1, m_2) assigned by r_4.

Given the users' movies sequences and the users' rating profiles, previously extracted, *MRRA* proceeds in the next step with the HMM training.

Step 3: HMM Training Sequences Extraction: During this last step of the model-building phase, *MRRA* trains the HMM. Actually, in a HMM, there are two types of states: the observable states and the hidden ones [14]. Thereby, we define users' movies sequences as the observable states in the HMM, whereas the hidden states are modeled by the users' rating profiles.

Hence, given the set of hidden states $St = \{st_1, \ldots, st_{ns}\}$, we denote the set of distinct rates values as $\mathcal{R} = \{r_1, \ldots, r_{nr}\}$, the set of movies $\mathcal{M} = \{m_1, \ldots, m_{nm}\}$

and the set of users $\mathcal{U} = \{u_1, \ldots, u_{nu}\}$, where ns is the number of states of the model, nr is the total number of rates, nm is the total number of movies, nu is the number of users, and SL_i is a state sequence. Our HMM denoted $\lambda = (A, B, B', \pi)$, is a probabilistic model defined as follows:

- $\pi = [\ldots \pi_i \ldots]$, the initial state probability, where $\pi_i = \mathrm{P}(st_i)$ is the probability that a state st_i occurs as the first element of a state sequence SL_i.
- $B = [\ldots b_j(r) \ldots]$, the rate emission probability distribution, where $b_j(r) = \mathrm{P}(r \mid st_j)$, denotes the probability that a user, currently at a state st_j, assigned a rate r.
- $B' = [\ldots b_k(m) \ldots]$, the movie emission probability distribution, where $b_k(m) = \mathrm{P}(m \mid st_k)$, denotes the probability that a user, currently at a state st_j, rates the movie m.
- $A = [\ldots a_{ij} \ldots]$, the transition probability, where $a_{ij} = \mathrm{P}(st_j \mid st_i)$ represents the transition probability from a state st_i to another one st_j.

Once the HMM is formalized, we proceed with learning its parameters (A, B, B', π). This is done by computing the four sets of the HMM parameters: the initial state probabilities $\{\mathrm{P}(st_i)\}$, the rate emission probabilities $\{\mathrm{P}(r \mid st_j)\}$, the movie emission probabilities $\{\mathrm{P}(m \mid st_k)\}$, and the transition probabilities $\{\mathrm{P}(st_j \mid st_i)\}$. Hence, inspired from [3], we compute these sets as follows:

1. $\pi_i = \mathrm{P}(st_i) = \frac{|\varphi(st_j)|}{|SL_c|}$ with:
   - $SL_c = \cup_{i \in 1,\ldots,t}\{E_i\}$ = total set of candidate states sequences to which could be matched a sequence of movies, where E_i denotes the set of candidate states that could match a movie from a given sequence of movies.
   - $\varphi(st_j)$ = set of states sequences in SL_c starting from st_j.
2. $b_j(r) = \mathrm{P}(r \mid st_j) = \frac{\sum_{m \in \mathcal{M}_j} Count(m,r)}{\sum_{r \in \mathcal{R}_j} \sum_{m \in \mathcal{M}_j} Count(m,r)}$.
3. $b_k(m) = \mathrm{P}(m \mid st_k) = \frac{\sum_{r \in \mathcal{R}_k} Count(m,r)}{\sum_{r \in \mathcal{R}_k} \sum_{m \in \mathcal{M}_k} Count(m,r)}$, where $Count(m, r)$ = number of times the movie m is assigned the rate r in the collection.
4. $a_{i,j} = \mathrm{P}(st_j \mid s_i) = \frac{CS(st_i, st_j)}{NC}$ with:
   - NC = the number of occurrences of st_j in SL_c.
   - $CS(st_i, st_j)$ = the number of times the state st_i is followed by the state st_j in SL_c.

2.2 The Exploitation Phase

The exploitation phase aims to identifying the movie's context and then predict the next rate which would/could be used by an active user according to the next HMM state. Actually, during the rating process of a movie m, two consecutive stages are considered: (*i*) Matching the current movie m to its related context according to HMM states; and then (*ii*) Predicting the next HMM state which represents the most similar rating profile. The prediction process proceeds by identifying the most likely HMM state, *i.e.*, rating profile, st_{MS} to which m

could better belong. This is done by computing, for each HMM state, the value of the quantity $Mat_i = \pi_i \times b_i(m)$, where π_i is the initial probability of the state st_i and $b_i(m)$ is the emission probability of m at st_i. Therefore, the state with the highest value, *i.e.*, st_{MS}, of Mat_i will define the context of m. Once the context is found, the rate, with the highest probability, belonging to the rating profile represented by the state st_{MS} is recommended. The prediction of a similar user's rating profile is then performed, by looking for the next state $s_{Next\mathtt{MS}}$ of st_{MS}. This is obtained by calculating the index value $Next\mathtt{MS}$ as follows: $Next\mathtt{MS} = argmax_j\{a_{\{MS,j\}}\}$, where st_j is a successor of st_{MS} in the HMM. Hence, the state $s_{Next\mathtt{MS}}$ represents the most probably rating profile that could match the user behaviour in rating the movie m.

Table 2. An example of a HMM states.

$st_1 = \{\{m_1, m_2, m_3\}, \{r_4\}, \{u_1, u_2, u_3, u_4\}\}$
$st_2 = \{\{m_4, m_3\}, \{r_2\}, \{u_3, u_6\}\}$
$st_3 = \{\{m_4, m_7\}, \{r_1\}, \{u_4, u_7\}\}$
$st_4 = \{\{m_5, m_6\}, \{r_1\}, \{u_4, u_5, u_6\}\}$
$st_5 = \{\{m_8, m_9\}, \{r_3\}, \{u_5, u_6\}\}$

Illustrative Example: Consider a HMM with five states described in Table 2, *i.e.*, $\{st_1, st_2, st_3, st_4, st_5\}$, where each state denotes a user rating profile, *i.e.*, RP_1, RP_2, RP_3, RP_4 and RP_5, extracted by the algorithm TRICONS from a sample taken from the MovieLens dataset (*cf.*, Sect. 3).

Each rating profile is represented by a triplet, *i.e.*, the set of all movies similarly rated by a set of users. The corresponding transition matrix A, and the distributions of the different probabilities of observation (of movies and rates) are obtained by calculating probabilities as described in Sect. 2. Suppose that the generated HMM with five states $\{st_1, st_2, st_3, st_4, st_5\}$ has a transition probability matrix as follows:

$$A = \begin{pmatrix} 0.4 & 0.6 & 0.0 & 0.0 & 0.0 \\ 0.2 & 0.5 & 0.3 & 0.0 & 0.0 \\ 0.0 & 0.0 & 0.3 & 0.2 & 0.5 \\ 0.0 & 0.0 & 0.0 & 0.3 & 0.7 \\ 0.0 & 0.0 & 0.0 & 0.6 & 0.4 \end{pmatrix}$$

And let us assume that $\pi = \begin{pmatrix} 0.2 & 0.2 & 0.2 & 0.2 & 0.2 \end{pmatrix}$. Hence, considering the rating represented by the state st_1, for example, to predict the rate of the movie $m8$, the prediction process starts with finding the context of the movie $m8$ by looking for the most likely HMM state to which the movie $m8$ could better belong. This is obtained by computing for each of the five states, the quantity $Mat_i = \pi_i \times b_i(m8)$ including:

$Mat_1 = \pi_1 \times b_1(m8) = 0$;
$Mat_2 = Mat_3 = Mat_4 = 0$ and
$Mat_5 = \pi_5 \times b_5(m8) = 0.2 \times 0.4 = \mathbf{0.08}$. Consequently, st_5 is the state which has the highest probability to represent the users' rating profile for the resource $m8$. Thus the candidate rate value $r3$ is recommended. Furthermore, possible states transitions from st_5 are either st_4 or st_5. Thus, the corresponding candidate rate to be assigned to the potential next movie, after the $m8$'s movie, are computed by the following formula, $argmax_j\{a_{5,j} \times b_j(m)\}$ with $j \in \{4, 5\}$, *i.e.*, possible state transition from st_5 and m is a movie belonging to the rating profile represented by st_4 or st_5 states.

3 Experiments

In this section we report results of the experimental evaluation of our proposed approach. We describe the data set used, the baselines description, as well as performance measures we consider appropriate for the task of predicting the rating given a user u and a movie m.

3.1 Dataset Description

We conducted experiments on a benchmark dataset: the MovieLens 100 K[2]. MovieLens 100 K is a movie rating dataset consisting of 100,000 ratings (1–5) from 943 users on 1682 movies, and each user has rated at least 20 movies.

3.2 Baselines Description

To confirm the validity of our results, we compare them with the results obtained using three recommendation approaches. We describe in the following the specific setting used to run them.

Item-Based K Nearest Neighbor Algorithm (IB-KNN) [15]. In order to determine the rating of User u on Movie m, we find other movies that are similar to Movie m, and based on User u's ratings on those similar movies we infer his rating on Movie m. Thus, the implemented IB-KNN algorithm performs the following generic pattern:

- Compute the similarity of movie a and movie b. As in [15], we use the adjusted cosine similarity between Movie a and b:

$$sim(a,b) = \frac{\sum_{u \in U(a) \cap U(b)} (r_{a,u} - \bar{r}_u)(r_{b,u} - \bar{r}_u)}{\sqrt{\sum_{u \in U(a) \cap U(b)} (r_{a,u} - \bar{r}_u)^2 \sum_{u \in U(a) \cap U(b)} (r_{b,u} - \bar{r}_u)^2}} \quad (1)$$

  where $r_{a,u}$ is User u's rating on Movie a, $\bar{r}_u$ is User u's average rating, $U(a)$ is the set of users that have rated Movie a and $U(a) \cap U(b)$ is the set of users that have rated both Movie a and b.

[2] http://grouplens.org/datasets/movielens/.

- Select a set of K most similar movies to the target movie and generate a predicted value of user u's rating. Hence, KNN finds the nearest K neighbors of each movie under the above defined similarity function.
- Generate a predicted value $P_{m,u}$ of user u's rating by using the weighted means as follows:

$$P_{m,u} = \frac{\sum_{u \in N_u^K(m)} sim(m,j) r_{j,u}}{\sum_{u \in N_u^K(m)} |sim(m,j)|} \tag{2}$$

where $N_u^K(m) = \{j$: j belongs to the K most similar movies to Movie m and User u has rated $j\}$, and $sim(m,j)$ is the adjusted cosine similarity defined in (1), $r_{j,u}$ represent the existent ratings of User u on Movie j.

Content Based Filtering (CBF) [13]. In CBF approaches, the recommended movies are those having similar features to the ones that the user have already rates. Hence, the implemented CBF, variants pursue the following generic algorithm:

- Compute features similarities $Sim(m, x_i)$ between the candidate movie m and all the other movies x_i based on their sets of features $\boldsymbol{f_i} = \{f_{i,1}, \dots, f_{i,n}\}$, *i.e.*, genre, subject matter, actors and director.
- Select S_m, the set of the k most similar movies to the candidate movie m.
- Generate a predicted value $P_{m,u}$ based on the ratings assigned by the user u to movies in S_m (c.f. Eqs. 1 and 2).

The User-Centred Collaborative Filtering Approach (UC-CF) [9]. UC-CF is based on the assumption that users with similar preferences will rate movies similarly. Thus, the implemented variants of UC-CF proceeds as following:

- Compute $Sim(u_a, u_i) = Sim(\boldsymbol{r_a}, \boldsymbol{r_i})$, the similarities between the active user u_a and all the other users u_i based on their common ratings $\boldsymbol{r_a}$ and $\boldsymbol{r_i}$ assigned to the same movies.
- Select S_{ua}, the set of the k most similar users to the active user u_a.
- Estimate $\bar{r}_{ac}$ using the Mean rating estimator on the set of ratings assigned by S_{ua} to the movie m_c. The Mean rating estimator is implemented for the recommendation algorithms in order to estimate the rating r_{ac} that the active user u_a would assign to a candidate movie m_c. Let N be the number of existing ratings $r_{i,j}$ such as $u_i \in S_{ua}$ and $m_i \in S_{mc}$. The mean estimator is as follows:

$$\hat{r}_{ac} = \frac{1}{N} \sum_{u_i \in S_{ua}} \sum_{m_i \in S_{mc}} r_{i,j}$$

3.3 Effectiveness Evaluation

We used a supervised learning process to assess the performances of our $MRRA$ approach vs. those of IB-KNN, CBF and UC-CF on the MovieLens dataset as our training and testing set. Specifically, we randomly selected 60 rated movies to use as training set, and 40 as a test set. The training set is used to estimate the model while the test set is used for the evaluation. Hence, the main task of our approach is to predict for each user's movie, picked from the test dataset, its related rate. In order to analyze the accuracy of our approach we adopted the common Information Retrieval evaluation measures, namely Recall and Precision that produces scores ranging from 0 to 1 (100%) [2]. Therefore, if we suppose that for a user rate value r, the set of movies actually assigned by the value r is $\mathcal{R}_m$, *i.e.*, as the ground truth, and the set of the predicted rates values is T_r, then the measures of *recall* and *precision* are given as follows: $Recall = \frac{|\{\mathcal{R}_m\} \bigcap \{\mathcal{T}_r\}|}{|\{\mathcal{T}_r\}|}$, $Precision = \frac{|\{\mathcal{R}_m\} \bigcap \{\mathcal{T}_r\}|}{|\{\mathcal{R}_m\}|}$. We report in the following results averaged over all movies from the test set. Ten-fold cross evaluation method was used while the number of nearest neighbors was fixed at 20.

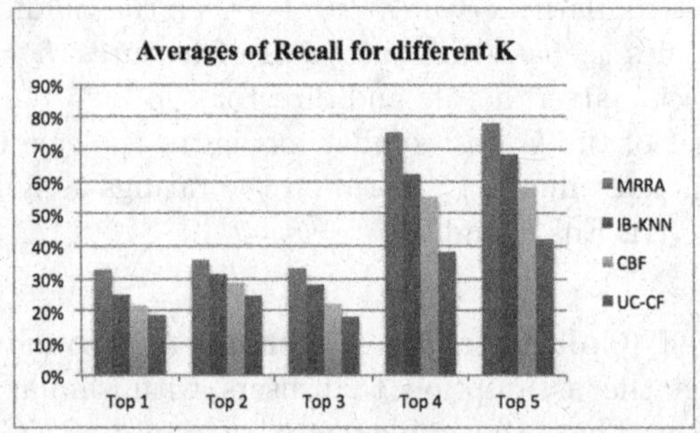

Fig. 1. Averages of recall on the MovieLens dataset.

Figure 1, depicts averages of *recall* for different values of K, *i.e.*, the number of predicted rates values, ranging from 1 to 5. Thus, according to the sketched histograms, we can point out that our approach sharply outperforms those of IB-KNN, CBF and UC-CF. In fact, the *Recall* values of the three baselines are significantly lower than those achieved by our approach. Furthermore, the average *Recall* of $MRRA$ achieves high percentage for higher value of K. Indeed, for $K = 5$, the average *Recall* is equal to 78.16%, showing an increase of 45.44% compared to the average *Recall* for $K = 1$. In this case, for a higher value of K, *i.e.*, $K = 5$, by matching the current movie with its corresponding context, our approach can produce almost all of the ratings that are likely to be assigned by the user on the current movie.

Besides, according to Fig. 2, the percentage of *Precision* of our approach outperforms the two baselines over the MovieLens dataset. Indeed, our approach achieves the best results when we choose the value of K around 5. In fact, for

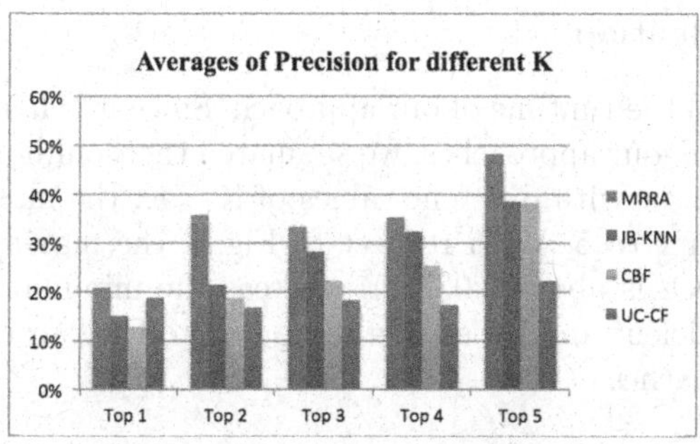

Fig. 2. Averages of precision on the MovieLens dataset.

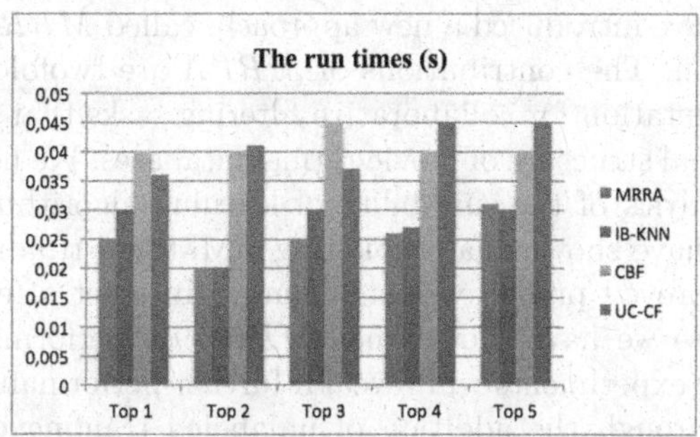

Fig. 3. The run times (s) of MRRA with different values of K vs. those of IB-KNN CBF and UC-CF on the MovieLens dataset

$K = 5$, the mean precision, is equal to 48.16%. Whereas, for $K = 1$, it has an average of 20.72% showing a drop of the rating prediction accuracy around 40% *vs.* an exceeding about 16% against the IB-KNN baseline. It should be pointed out that the performances of UC-CF approach are the lowest. This is because the user-based data appear to be sparser. Indeed, it is very unlikely that a movie has only been rated by 1 or 2 users, and highly possible that a user only rates 1 or 2 movies. Interestingly enough, these results highlight that our approach can better improve rate prediction accuracy, and thus rate recommendation, even for a high number of movies. Moreover, our approach achieves a good coverage, since it produces predictions for 76% of rates assigned to movies contained in the test dataset. Our approach successfully captures the relationship between users, movies and the rates values. From the result, we can see that our approach can generate better performance than those of three well known approaches. It can reach a highest Recall at certain K and this is greatly due to the highly independence of our approach on the characteristic of the dataset. Since no pre-processing stage is made on the data before performing the different phases.

3.4 Online Evaluation

We present in Fig. 3 the runtime of our approach. Since it is hard to measure the exact runtime of the four approaches, we simulated their online execution among the MovieLens dataset with different values of K, *i.e.*, the number of predicted rates, ranging from 1 to 5. With respect to Fig. 3, the maximum value of run time of our approach is about $0.031(s)$, whereas the minimum value is around $0.02(s)$ which is efficient and satisfiable compared to the run times achieved by the baselines approaches.

4 Conclusion

In this paper, we have introduced a new approach, called $MRRA$, for movie rating recommendation. The contributions of $MRRA$ are twofold. First, we have presented a representation for collaborative filtering tasks that allows the use of the three dimensional structure of movie rating databases. We hope that this will lead to further analysis of the suitability of learning algorithms on such databases. Second, we have shown that exploiting HMM and triadic concept analysis can lead to improved predictive performance. In a set of experiments with MovieLens database we have shown that $MRRA$ outperforms three baselines approaches. Future experiments will reveal if further performance improvements can be achieved through the addition of unlabeled training data. We believe that additional knowledge about the similarity of users and items can be gained through the analysis of textual descriptions of movies. Our long-term goal of this work is to combine $MRRA$ approach and content-based filtering techniques. Similarity between users could then be influenced by similarity between features of rated movies. We also plan to address the challenges of the big data era, the efficiency of developing recommender system approaches must be improved.

References

1. Adomavicius, G., Tuzhilin, A.: Toward the next generation of recommender systems: a survey of the state-of-the-art and possible extensions. IEEE Trans. Knowl. Data Eng. **17**, 734–749 (2005)
2. Baeza-Yates, R., Berthier, R.N.: Modern Information Retrieval. Addison-Wesley Longman Publishing Co., Inc., Boston (1999)
3. Cao, H., Jiang, D., Pei, J., Chen, E., Li, H.: Towards context-aware search by learning a very large variable length hidden Markov model from search logs. In: Proceedings of the 18th International World Wide Web Conference, pp. 191–200, Spain (2009)
4. Desarkar, M.S., Saxena, R., Sarkar, S.: Preference relation based matrix factorization for recommender systems. In: Masthoff, J., Mobasher, B., Desmarais, M.C., Nkambou, R. (eds.) UMAP 2012. LNCS, vol. 7379, pp. 63–75. Springer, Heidelberg (2012). doi:10.1007/978-3-642-31454-4_6
5. Deshpande, M., Karypis, G.: A survey of collaborative filtering techniques. ACM Trans. Inf. Syst. **22**(1), 143–177 (2004)

6. Harvey., M., Carman., M.J., Ruthven., I., Crestani., F.: Bayesian latent variable models for collaborative item rating prediction. In: Proceedings of 20th ACM International Conference on Information and knowledge Management, pp. 699–708. ACM (2011)
7. He, Q., Jiang, D., Liao, Z., Hoi, S.C.H., Chang, K., Lim, E., Li, H.: Web query recommendation via sequential query prediction. In: Proceedings of the IEEE International Conference on Data Engineering, pp. 1443–1454. IEEE, USA (2009)
8. Herlocker, J., Konstan, J.A., Riedl, J.: An empirical analysis of design choices in neighborhood-based collaborative filtering algorithms. Inf. Retr. **5**(4), 287–310 (2002)
9. Herlocker, L., Konstan, A., Borchers, A., Riedl, J.: An algorithmic framework for performing collaborative filtering. In: Proceedings of the 22nd Annual International ACM SIGIR Conference on Research and Development in Information Retrieval, Theoretical Models, pp. 230–237. ACM (1999)
10. Hotho, A.: Data mining on folksonomies. In: Armano, G., de Gemmis, M., Semeraro, G., Vargiu, E. (eds.) Intelligent Information Access. Studies in Computational Intelligence, vol. 301, pp. 57–82. Springer, Heidelberg (2010)
11. Jäschke, R., Hotho, A., Schmitz, C., Ganter, B., Stumme, G.: Discovering shared conceptualizations in folksonomies. Web Semant. **6**, 38–53 (2008)
12. Lehmann, F., Wille, R.: A triadic approach to formal concept analysis. In: Ellis, G., Levinson, R., Rich, W., Sowa, J.F. (eds.) ICCS-ConceptStruct 1995. LNCS, vol. 954, pp. 32–43. Springer, Heidelberg (1995). doi:10.1007/3-540-60161-9_27
13. Pazzani, M.J.: A framework for collaborative, content-based and demographic filtering. Artif. Intell. Rev. **13**(5), 393–408 (1999)
14. Rabiner, L.: A tutorial on hidden Markov models and selected applications inspeech recognition. IEEE **77**(2), 257–286 (1989)
15. Sarwar, B., Karypis, G., Konstan, J., Riedl, J.: Item-based collaborative filtering recommendation algorithms. In: Proceedings of 10th International Conference on World Wide Web, pp. 285–295. ACM (2001)
16. Trabelsi, C., Jelassi, N., Ben Yahia, S.: Scalable mining of frequent tri-concepts from folksonomies. In: Tan, P.-N., Chawla, S., Ho, C.K., Bailey, J. (eds.) PAKDD 2012. LNCS, vol. 7302, pp. 231–242. Springer, Heidelberg (2012). doi:10.1007/978-3-642-30220-6_20
17. Yoo, J., Choi, S.: Bayesian matrix co-factorization: variational algorithm and cramér-rao bound. In: Gunopulos, D., Hofmann, T., Malerba, D., Vazirgiannis, M. (eds.) ECML PKDD 2011. LNCS, vol. 6913, pp. 537–552. Springer, Heidelberg (2011). doi:10.1007/978-3-642-23808-6_35

Technologies for Flexible Representations and Querying

New Variants of Hash-Division Algorithm for Tolerant and Stratified Division

Noussaiba Benadjmi(✉) and Khaled Walid Hidouci

Ecole Nationale Supérieure en Informatique(ESI),
BP 270, 160290 Oued-smar, Algiers, Algeria
{an_benadjimi,hidouci}@esi.dz

Abstract. Works done in the context of the relational division for DBMS led to several approaches. Among which, the Hash-Division algorithm proved its superiority compared to the other approaches in the most of the cases. Nowadays, current trends of division are been oriented towards flexible queries and those involving preferences. However, the emphasis was always on proposing new operators which provide more flexibility and tolerance than the classical division operator. The performance aspect has not been adequately addressed. The proposed approaches in the literature suffer from a lack of performance, especially in a large volume of data. In this paper, we attempt to address this problem. Our idea consists in exploiting the advantages offered by the classical Hash-Division algorithm to propose new variants tailored for the flexible context. We paid a special attention to the improvement of some extended tolerant operators. Furthermore, we introduce a parallel implementation of our proposed techniques. Experimental results show the efficiency of our proposition. We obtained a very satisfactory improvement in processing time (the gain exceeds a ratio of 20 in the majority of cases) in both sequential and parallel implementation.

Keywords: Relational division · Preferences · Tolerant division · Stratified division · Hash-division algorithm

1 Introduction

Relational division is an interesting type of queries. They are very useful to many applications, especially in business intelligence applications (on-line analytic processing OLAP, data mining ...), and in recommendation systems. In relational algebra, the division is the most complex operator. That's why several researchers focus on their implementation, algorithms and optimisation [1].

1.1 The Division Operator

Relational division is used when an element that satisfies a whole set of requirements is sought for. In relational algebra, the division of relation *r(X, Y)*, called ***"dividend"***; by relation *s(Y)*, called ***"divisor"***; is a new relation q(X) that

H. Christiansen et al. (Eds.): FQAS 2017, LNAI 10333, pp. 99–111, 2017.
DOI: 10.1007/978-3-319-59692-1_9

includes some parts of projection(r,X) satisfying the following condition: x is in q(X) iff x is in Project (r,X) and for **all** y in s(Y), r(X,Y) contain <x,y> [2]. More formally, the relational division is characterised by the formula (1):

$$Div(r, s, X, Y) = \{x \in projection(r, X) \mid \forall a, (a \in s) \Rightarrow (\langle x, a\rangle \in r)\} \quad (1)$$

To illustrate the division operator, we use the example sketched in Fig. 1, representing data from a department of a university [2]. In the figure above, Bob is the only resulting quotient because he is the unique student who is not missing any of the courses of the divisor.

enrollment (Dividend)

student_id	*course_id*
Bob	Theory
Alice	Compilers
Chris	Theory
Chris	Graphics
Alice	Theory
Bob	Graphics
Chris	Compilers
Bob	Databases
Bob	Compilers

÷ *course* (Divisor)

course_id
Databases
Theory
Compilers

= *result* (Quotient)

student_id
Bob

Fig. 1. Division operation representing the query: ***"Which students have taken all Courses?".***

1.2 Related Works and Current Trends

Division operator has not a specific expression in SQL, because relational algebra does not directly support the quantifier "all" [1]. That's why, in literature, several studies have been focused on how to efficiently implement division [2], including those surveyed in [3] for the relational model, and [1] for the object-oriented model.

However, the approach proposed and detailed in [3], called ***Hash-Division***, has proven to be an effective algorithm. Hash-Division is based especially, as indicated by its name, on the *hashing mechanism.* The experimental results illustrated in the same paper demonstrate that the hash-division, in most cases, is far better than the traditional algorithms in processing time.

On the other hand, the relational division often provides an empty answer. This is a widely studied problem in the last two decades [4]. Flexible division (tolerant division and division dealing with users preferences), is the most desirable technique to solve this problem and improve the DBMS answers quality, especially in the context of recommendation systems [5]. Flexible division consists in the weakening of the universal quantifier all used in the traditional operator. In the literature, many research works, including [6,7] have suggested new operators for the relational division, which are tailored for the flexible context.

Similarly, there are many papers on preferences over simple queries such as the selection operator, most of them are surveyed in [8]. However, there are only few works on preferences over the division, on crisp and fuzzy databases [9].

1.3 Motivations and Main Contributions in This Paper

Researches done for the tolerant division, in literature, has concentrated on improving the quality of systems answer, by introducing new operators that deal with flexible division. Hence, an important, but largely overlooked aspect in these researches, is the performance issue. In fact, all the proposed approaches suffer from a lack of performance. Indeed, these approaches are mainly based on the nested loop algorithm. Experimental results have shown that the response-time is far from being acceptable and deteriorates significantly as data size increases. Even for recent research, queries evaluations are performed with a reduced size of data (dividend and divisor). This does not fit reality, especially with the advent of the Big Data, and analysis treatments on extra-large databases.

In this paper, we attempt to address the previous problem. To the best of our knowledge, processing flexible division, using Hash-Division is not yet investigated. Thus, the main purpose of our work is to improve the performance of the flexible division operator. Hereafter we summarise our contributions:

- Investigate performance enhancement of the flexible division essentially for very large volumes of data.
- Extend the Hash-Division algorithm to the following approaches:
    - Exception-based tolerant division.
    - Division with ordinal layered preferences (Stratified division).
- Propose a new efficient processing to better discriminate and rank the results.
- Examinate the feasibility of the parallel implementation for the extended approaches.

1.4 Outline of the Paper

The remainder of this paper is organised as follows. In Sect. 2, we present the classical Hash-Division algorithm. Section 3 gives an overview of the flexible division, their categories and their semantics. In Sect. 4, our contribution is presented with analytics and discussion of the experimental results obtained. Finally, Sect. 5 concludes the paper and suggests directions for future work.

2 Review of Hash-Division Algorithm

In this section, we give a brief description of the hash-division algorithm ***"HD"*** (see [3] for further detail). It uses two hash tables, one for the divisor and the other for the quotient. Thanks to these two structures, both dividend and divisor tables are scanned exactly once, that makes the division operator faster. Hash-Division algorithm is proceeding in three stages:

Stage 01- Building the hash-divisor table: Here, we insert all divisor tuples into hash buckets in the hash-divisor table. Each entry is stored together with an integer called **divisor number *"Num_div"***. "Num_div" is initialized to zero, and incremented whenever a new insertion in the hash-divisor table has occurred.

Stage 02- Building the hash-quotient table: For each dividend row that corresponds to one of the divisor tuples, we insert a quotient candidate into hash buckets in the hash-quotient table. Together with each inserted candidate, a bitmap is kept with one bit for each divisor. Each bit set to 1, indicate that the candidate is associated with the divisor corresponding to the bit position.

Stage 03- Finding result in the hash-quotient table: In this last stage, during the scan of the constructed hash-quotient table, we select all quotient candidates whose bitmaps contain only ones as valid quotients.

3 Review of Flexible Division

Tolerant (or flexible) division was essentially proposed in order to avoid the empty result, which may occur mostly whenever we use **"for all"** quantifier [4,7]. There are a plethora of suggestions, in literature, showing that original relational division can be extended to different types of flexible queries. In this paper, we are interested in the flexible division over crisp databases exclusively. So, the approaches of flexible division being focused in our work are the following:

1. Exception-based tolerant division.
2. Flexible division over a stratified divisor (involving layered preferences).

3.1 Exception-Based Tolerant Division

In this category, the principle is to weak the universal quantifier all to the fuzzy quantifier almost all. Hence, for this **Gradual Division**, a maximum number of exceptions is allowed to be ignored (some elements, in the divisor set, are allowed to be not associated with the quotient) [9,10]. Satisfaction-level *(SL)* of a quotient is measured by the formula (2). A threshold is required for accepted quotients.

$$SL = \frac{Number\ of\ divisors\ associated\ with\ the\ quotient\ candidate}{total\ number\ of\ divisors} \tag{2}$$

3.2 Division Involving Layered Preferences

In the previous category, neither discrimination nor order is involved between the elements inside the divisor. However, in this category, depending on the users preferences, the divisor set is subdivided into layers S_i; $i = 1..n$. Each layer has a degree of importance, thereby an order between layers is guaranteed $S_1 > S_2 > ... > S_n$. Elements into the same layer have equal importances. The layers are linked with the connectors **"and if possible"**, **"or else"**, or **"and-or"**. Three queries (lets be Q1, Q2 and Q3) are defined (see [11,12] for further detail):

- ***Conjunctive queries (Q1):*** we search to find the best elements associated with S_1 **and if possible** S_2 **and if possible ... and if possible** S_n. Hence, a quotient x must be associated with all values in S_1, and it is more preferred as it is connected with all values from S_1 to S_p and p is high (ideally n).
- ***Disjunctive queries (Q2):*** the purpose is to find the best elements associated with all values in S_1 **or else** S_2 **or else ... or else** S_n. S_1 is no longer mandatory. An element is more preferred as it is connected with all values of S_k and k is small (ideally 1).
- ***Full discrimination-based queries (Q3):*** we aim to find the best elements associated with all values in S_1 **and-or** S_2 **and-or ... and-or** S_n. The idea is to consider all layers for which a fully satisfaction occurs. An element is more preferred as it is associated with multiple layers highly important.

4 Our Proposed Approaches

Different contributions have been achieved for the flexible division. Nevertheless, the concerns were always on how to propose an efficient operator that supports flexible context, and to theoretically demonstrate it. So, the performance issue was not dealt with, whereas it is clearly a critical metric in information systems today, especially with the advent of big data and analysis processing on extra-large databases.

In the next section, we will address the tolerant and the stratified division, mentioned in Sect. 3, from a performance point of view. More specifically, we will present several proposing methods to improve the processing time of the flexible division relying on classic Hash-division like algorithm. Moreover, we propose new techniques to better discriminate quotients with no additional cost. Hence our approaches have the merit to be an efficient processing of the flexible division, in both processing time and answers quality.

4.1 Extend the Hash-Division for Gradual Tolerant Division (G-H-D)

In order to apply the classic hash-division approach on the gradual tolerant division, we have made some adaptations for the basic algorithm (described in Sect. 2). These adaptations are made in the second and the third stage. The first stage remains unchanged. In the second stage, we kept with each quotient-candidate a counter of ones ($bit = 1$) in its bitmap. We called this counter ***Nb_ones***. The latter is incremented at each bit switching (0 *to* 1) in the bitmap. Hereafter is a pseudo-code of this stage with our proposed adaptations:

Algorithm 1. Building of the hash-quotient table for G-H-D.

```
for each tuple t in the dividend table do
    Compute the hash bucket Hdiv on the divisor attributes of the tuple t;
    if the divisor value is contained in the bucket Hdiv of the hash-divisor table
    then
        rank ← num_div of the matching divisor tuple;
        Compute the hash bucket Hqot on the quotient attributes of the tuple t;
        if the candidate (quotient value) is contained in the hash-quotient table at
            the hash bucket Hqot then
            if the rank^th bit in the bitmap of the candidate is set to 0 then
                Switch this bit to 1;
                Nb_ones← Nb_ones +1; /*Increment the number of ones*/
            end if
        else{/*quotient candidate does not yet exist*/}
            Insert a new quotient candidate into the hash-quotient table at the
                bucket Hqot, with a bitmap where all bits are set to zero except
                the num_div^th bit;
            Nb_ones ← 1;   /*Initialize the number of ones to 1*/
        end if
    end if
end for
```

In the tolerant division, quotients haven't the same satisfaction level. Hence, the final stage must discriminate these quotients. To this end, we have, radically, changed the third stage of the basic approach (Sect. 2). To sort the accepted quotients, according to their satisfaction levels, we propose an efficient technique which involves no additional cost. We use an index table to improve the sorting phase. During the scan of the final hash-quotient table, we proceed as follows:

- Each accepted candidate, whose satisfaction level is greater than the predefined threshold, is stored in a bucket of index $\mathbf{class}_d$ ($class_0 > class_1 > ... > class_{max\_exception}$), where $\boldsymbol{d}$ is the number of zeros (**Nb_zeros**) in the candidate bitmap, representing the number of the missing divisors (Nb_zeros = total number of divisors − Nb_ones); and ***max_exception*** is the maximum number of exceptions allowed. The latter, chosen by the user, represent the threshold.
- Candidates having zeros superior to *max_exception*, are rejected.

K-top Answers. Introducing tolerance into the queries mostly returns an overabundant answer, especially for the very large sized dividend. Therefore, ***k-top answer selection*** is paramount (k is chosen by the user) [13]. However, in the classic approaches, *k-top* answers selection requires an additional sorting phase which can be expensive for a big number of results. Whereas, in our approach, no sort is needed. To select the *k-top* answers, we just have to browse through the index table, constructed in the third stage, from the highest satisfaction level quotients to the lowest ones; until k quotients are found. Thus, no additional costs will be incurred.

Implementation and Experimental Results. Hereafter, we consider, in all our implementations, four sizes of the dividend relation: **3.10**^{4}, **5.10**^{5}, **3.10**^{6} and **5.10**^{8} tuples[1] with a divisor of different cardinality (resp. **10, 20, 50, 100** tuples). We run all experiments on a machine with an ***Intel i5 CPU*** and ***8 Gb RAM***.

Figure 2 shows the run-times of our approach *G-H-D*, comparing with the nested loop algorithm presented in [9,10]. We notice that our own performs much faster than the classic one for the four sizes. So, the run-time is improved by several orders of magnitude (a factor of **241** in the case of 5.10^{8} dividend tuples).

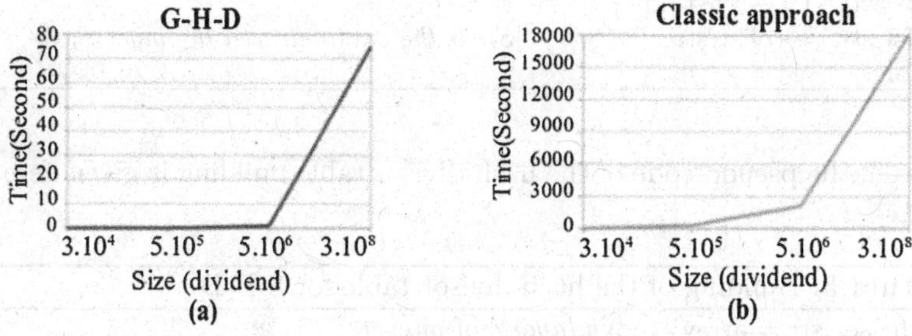

Fig. 2. Algorithm performance of G-H-D and Classic approach.

4.2 Extend Hash-Division for Stratified Division (S-H-D)

Here, for the stratified division involving layered preference, we have made some changes in both data structure and proceeding of our basic hash-division.

Stage 01: In the three variants of stratified division (Q1, Q2 and Q3), the first stage (*Construction of the Hash-divisor table*) is the same. As in the classic approach, we store all divisor tuples in a hash table (see Sect. 2). Each divisor, belonging to the layer S_i, is stored into the hash-divisor table together with two integers:

- ***offst_strt:*** number of divisor tuples in all previous layers S_j $j < i$. This number indicates the offset of the layer inside the bitmap. Bits corresponding to divisors in S_i are located, in the bitmap, between *offset(*S_i*)* and *offset(*S_{i+1}*)*.
- ***num_div_strt:*** the divisor number (*rank*), of the tuple, in its layer.

The data structure of a divisor in the hash-divisor table is shown in Fig. 3.

divisor_value	num_div_strt	offst_strt

Fig. 3. Data structure of a hash-divisor tuple.

[1] In the literature, up to now, the largest dividend used never exceed 30000 tuples.

Hence, for each layer S_i, we first calculate its ***offst_strt***. Then, we keep for each one, its own divisors counter. All counter are initialized to 0. Whenever we insert a new divisor, of the layer S_i, into the hash-divisor table, the divisors counter of S_i will be incremented. The pseudo-code used is as follows:

Algorithm 2. Calculation of the offset of the layers for G-H-AD.

```
offst_str = array [ 1: Nb_layers ] of integer;
offst_str_i← 0;
for i← 1 to Nb_layers do
    offst_str [ i ] ← offst_str_i;
    offst_str_i ← offst_str_i + |Si|; /*|Si| is the cardinality of the layer Si */
end for
```

As well, the pseudo-code of the hash-divisor table building is given hereafter:

Algorithm 3. Building of the hash-divisor table for S-H-D.

```
num_divisor_str = array [1 : Nb_layers] of integer;
initialize all cells of num_divisor_str to zero;
for each tuple in the divisor relation do
    compute its hash bucket (Hdiv) in the hash-divisor table;
    Si ← layer number of the current divisor;
    divisor.offst_strt ← offst_str [Si]; /*assign the layer offset to the current divi-
        sor*/
    divisor.num_div_strt ← num_divisor_str [Si];
    num_divisor_str[Si] + +;
    insert the divisor tuple into the corresponding hash bucket;
end for
```

Stage 02: In the 2nd stage, we proceed as in the classic hash-division (Sect. 2). The only difference is how to update the bitmap. Hence, if a divisor is associated to a quotient candidate, we set the bit to 1 whose position, in the bitmap, is equal to ***"offst_strt+num_div"***, stored with the matching divisor. The data structure of the bitmap is shown in Fig. 4.

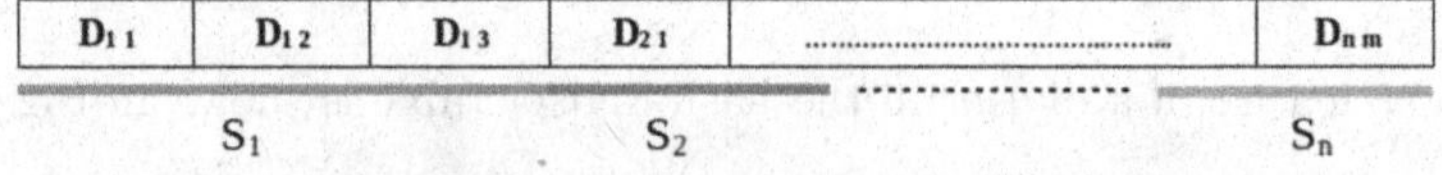

Fig. 4. Data structure for the bitmap for S-H-D.

Stage 03: Here, we have to compute the satisfaction level for each quotient candidate, in order to classify them thereafter. Hence, for the three queries (Q1, Q2 and Q3), we describe how to calculate these satisfaction levels. Moreover, we propose a fast mechanism to better discriminate the accepted candidates. Again, our sorting technique involves no additional cost and maintains the quality of answers.

Conjunctive Queries (Q1): We search to find the best k elements associated with S_1 **and if possible** S_2 **... and if possible** S_n (see Subsect. 3.2). Therefore, we proceed as follows:

- Candidates having zeros in the first layer, in their bitmaps, are immediately rejected.
- We check, in ascending order of layers, if the layer S_i contains only ones in the bitmap. If yes, we pass to the next layer. Otherwise, the candidate is labelled by $\{$***i, Nb_ones_i***$\}$ where:
  - **i,** $i \geq 2$ **:** index of the first layer not fully satisfied.
  - **Nb_ones_i,** $0 \leq Nb\_ones\_i \leq |S_i|$: number of ones in the layer of index i. This number is used to discriminate candidates having equal labels i. It is worth noticing that in the classic approach presented in [11,12] this discrimination does not occur. Thus, candidates having $|\boldsymbol{S}_i| - \boldsymbol{1}$ ones, in S_i, and candidates with **no ones**; will be ranked with a similar satisfaction-level. This we avoid in our technique, thanks to the label *Nb_ones_i*.
- If the layer S_i is the last one, label i takes the value of the S_n index (last layer), and *Nb_ones_i* takes the value of its cardinality ($|S_n|$).

To sort the accepted quotients, depending on their satisfaction levels, we use an index table, as in G-H-D. Its size is "***n (total number of divisors)*** – $|\boldsymbol{S}_1| + \boldsymbol{1}$". Candidate labelled with $\{i, Nb\_ones\_i\}$ are stored into the bucket whose index is equal to "***n*** – ***(offst_strt*** $(\boldsymbol{S}_i)$ + ***Nb_ones_i)***". Thereby, final quotients will be, automatically, sorted in decreasing order according to their satisfaction levels. The cell whose index is 0, points the most preferred quotients.

Disjunctive Queries (Q2): In the case of Q2, S_1 is no longer an obligation. The first check (whether S_1 is fully satisfied) is no longer present. Therefore, we proceed as follows:

- Starting by the first layer, we check if S_i contains only ones. If not, we pass to the next layer. Otherwise, the candidate is labelled by $\{$***i, Nb_zeros_ip***$\}$:
  - **i,** $i \geq 1$: the first layer fully satisfied.
  - **Nb_zeros_ip,** $1 \leq Nb\_zeros\_ip \leq |S_{i-1}|$: number of zeros in the previous layer S_{i-1} (the last layer that contains zeros). As for Q1, this number is used to better discriminate candidates having equal labels i.
- Whenever S_i is the first layer, we assign to i the value **1** and **0** to *Nb_zeros_ip*.

As in Q1, we store the accepted quotients in an index table whose size is "$\boldsymbol{n} - |S_n| + \boldsymbol{1}$". Candidate with label $\{i, Nb\_zeros\_ip\}$ are stored into the bucket of index equal to "***offst_strt*** $(\boldsymbol{S}_{i-1})$ + ***Nb_zeros_ip***". Idem, final quotients will be sorted in decreasing order according to their satisfaction levels.

Full Discrimination-Based Queries (Q3): Here we have to consider all layers that are fully satisfied. Candidates are labelled by a procedure identical to that used in Q2. Nevertheless, accepted quotients would not be totally sorted. Hence, for each bucket in the index table, depending on the *k-top* value, we sort the candidates depending on their satisfaction levels using a traditional sorting algorithm.

Experimentations: To examine the performance of our proposed approaches for stratified division, we make experimental comparisons between ours own and the classic approaches implemented in [11,12]. Queries Q1, Q2 and Q3 are evaluated over a dividend relation having the four sizes previously mentioned (3.10^4, 5.10^5, 3.10^6 and 5.10^8 tuples). The divisor relation has the cardinalities: 10, 20, 50 and 100 uniformly distributed over five layers. Figure 5 illustrates the results obtained.

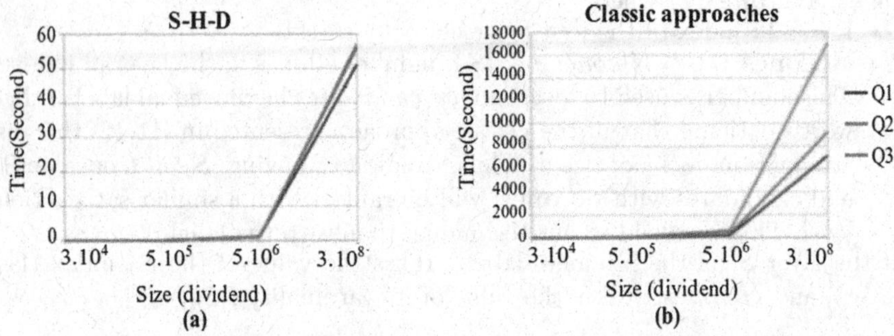

Fig. 5. Algorithm performance of S-H-D and the classic approach.

Analysis of the curves above leads to the following notices:

- Hash-division approach for the three queries (Q1, Q2 and Q3) proves its efficiency in run-time, compared to the classical one, especially for the overly large-sized dividend. The gain on time in this case was ***extremely high***: for the size 5.10^5 in Q1, the improvement was from **12,5** to **0,085** seconds; and for the size 5.10^8 in Q2, the improvement was from **9213** to **56** s.
- In the classic approach, the cost of queries Q1 and Q2 are relatively close. This is done thanks to the stop criteria used. However, Q3 is more expensive as it has to examine all layers. Whereas, for our own, all three queries involve, roughly, the same cost. Hence, it is totally independent on how to introduce preferences. This makes our approaches very beneficial.

4.3 Parallel Implementation

Our objective behind the parallel experiments is to demonstrate the parallelism feasibility of the proposed approaches (**G-H-D** and **S-H-D**). Parallel implementation is realized thanks to the **PVM** framework (**Parallel Virtual Machine**), on machines based on an ***Intel i5 CPU*** and ***8 Gb RAM***. Experimentations were performed over 2, 4 and 6 nodes. The parallelism strategy is as follows:

- The hash-divisor table is created only once on a single node called ***master***.
- The master sends the hash-divisor table created to the other nodes.
- The dividend table is uniformly partitioned (*horizontally*) between all nodes.
- Each node builds its own hash-quotient table.
- The master collects the sub-tables, of the hash-quotient, constructed in the nodes. Then, it merges all of them in one global table to select valid quotients. The pseudo-code of this last step, is given hereafter:

Algorithm 4. Parallel implementation of S-H-D.

```
for each sub-hash-quotient table received from the slave nodes do
    for each quotient-candidate in the sub-hash-quotient table do
        Compute the hash bucket (Hqot) over the quotient value of the candidate;
        if the candidate (quotient value) is contained in the hash-quotient table,
            constructed in the master, at the bucket Hqot then
            Update the candidate bitmap through performing a binary OR) operation
                between the two bitmaps (the bitmap in the master and that's in the
                node);
        else
            Insert a new candidate into the hash-quotient table of the master at the
                bucket Hqot, with a bitmap equal to that's present in the candidate
                received from the node;
        end if
    end for
end for
```

Hereafter, we restrict to describe the empirical results of Q1. Hence, Fig. 6 illustrates the speed-up behaviour of the parallel hash-division of Q1.

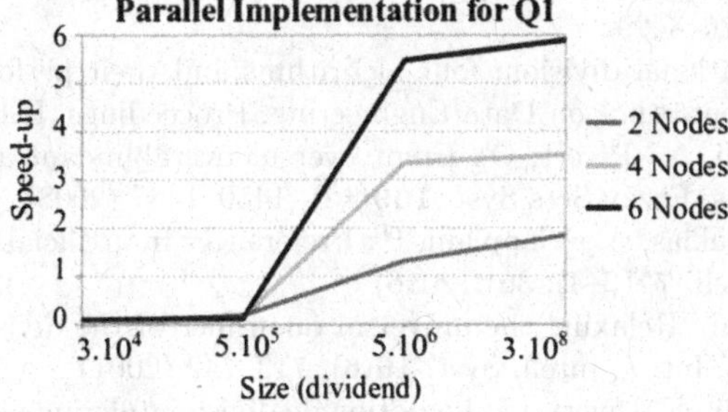

Fig. 6. Speed-up for parallel S-H-D algorithm of type Q1.

Although the parallelism of our approach involved an additional cost, but still negligible, for a relatively small size of the dividend (3.10^4 and 5.10^5), it comes very close to linear speed-up in the case of large dividend (3.10^6 and 5.10^8). Thus, experiments show that our approaches are more optimal when processing tolerant and stratified division over a parallel framework. Our approach is proved to be more efficient than some recent research, using highly-parallel new techniques, namely MapReduce framework [14].

5 Conclusion and Perspectives

We have presented in this paper two new variants **(G-H-D and S-H-D)** of the basic Hash Division algorithm for computing some tolerant division operators (Quantitative tolerant division and Tolerant division involving layered preferences). We have conducted some experiments, particularly for large-sized relations, and compare execution time with the original approaches (nested loop algorithms) proposed for the tolerant division operators studied. We presented also a parallel approach of the new variants of hash-division algorithm for tolerant division. This parallel approach have a near-linear speed-up, especially for large tables. As expected, the performance obtained, both for sequential and parallel versions, are very interesting. We have been able to improve the response time of some queries by several orders of magnitude. This opens up many perspectives in some data analysis using universal quantification and handling preferences over very large volumes of both usual and fuzzy data.

References

1. Habib, W.M., Mokhtar, H.M., El-Sharkawi, M.: Processing universal quantification queries using mapreduce. In: International Conference on Big Data and Smart Computing (BIGCOMP). IEEE (2014)
2. Rantzau, R., Shapiro, L., Mitschang, B., Wang, Q.: Universal quantification in relational databases: a classification of data and algorithms. In: Jensen, C.S., Šaltenis, S., Jeffery, K.G., Pokorny, J., Bertino, E., Böhn, K., Jarke, M. (eds.) EDBT 2002. LNCS, vol. 2287, pp. 445–463. Springer, Heidelberg (2002). doi:10.1007/3-540-45876-X_29
3. Graefe, G.: Relational division: four algorithms and their performance. In: Fifth International Conference on Data Engineering, Proceedings. IEEE (1989)
4. Bosc, P., Hadjali, A., Pivert, O.: Empty versus overabundant answers to flexible relational queries. Fuzzy Sets Syst. **159**(12), 1450–1467 (2008)
5. Pigozzi, G., Tsoukiàs, A., Viappiani, P.: Preferences in artificial intelligence. Ann. Math. Artif. Intell. **77**(3–4), 361 (2016)
6. Galindo, J., et al.: Relaxing the universal quantifier of the division in fuzzy relational databases. Int. J. Intell. Syst. **16**(6), 713–742 (2001)
7. Bosc, P., HadjAli, A., Pivert, O.: La notion de division tolèrante et son intèrêt pour remédier aux réponses vides. Ingénierie des systèmes d'information **13**(5), 131–154 (2008)
8. Kacprzyk, J., Zadrony, S., De Tre, G.: Fuzziness in database management systems: half a century of developments and future prospects. Fuzzy Sets Syst. **281**, 300–307 (2015)

9. Bosc, P., Pivert, O., Rocacher, D.: About quotient and division of crisp and fuzzy relations. J. Intell. Inform. Syst. **29**(2), 185–210 (2007)
10. Bosc, P., Pivert, O., Rocacher, D.: A propos de la sémantique de divers opérateurs de division de relations. In: INFORSID (2006)
11. Bosc, P., Pivert, O., Soufflet, O.: On three classes of division queries involving ordinal preferences. J. Intell. Inform. Syst. **37**(3), 315–331 (2011)
12. Bosc, P., Pivert, O.: On some uses of a stratified divisor in an ordinal framework. In: Kacprzyk, J., Petry, F.E., Yazici, A. (eds.) Uncertainty Approaches for Spatial Data Modeling and Processing. SCI, vol. 271, pp. 133–154. Springer, Heidelberg (2010)
13. Wu, Y., Liu, G., Liu, Y.: Multi-user preferences based top-k query processing algorithm. In: Tenth International Conference on Computational Intelligence and Security (CIS). IEEE (2014)
14. Habib, W.M., Mokhtar, H.M., El-Sharkawi, M.: A new approach for scholars matching using universal quantifier queries. In: IEEE World Congress on Services (SERVICES). IEEE (2015)

Coverage Degree-Based Fuzzy Topological Relationships for Fuzzy Regions

Anderson Chaves Carniel[1(✉)] and Markus Schneider[2]

[1] Department of Computer Science, University of São Paulo, São Carlos, SP 13566-590, Brazil
accarniel@gmail.com

[2] Department of Computer and Information Science and Engineering, University of Florida, Gainesville, FL 32611, USA
mschneid@cise.ufl.edu

Abstract. Geographical Information Systems and spatial database systems are well able to handle *crisp spatial objects*, i.e., objects in space whose location, extent, shape, and boundary are precisely known. However, this does not hold for *fuzzy spatial objects* characterized by vague boundaries and/or interiors. In the same way as fuzzy spatial objects are vague, the topological relationships (e.g., *overlap*, *inside*) between them are vague too. In this conceptual paper, we propose a novel model to formally define *fuzzy topological relationships* for fuzzy regions. For their definition we consider the numeric measure of *coverage degree* and map it to *linguistic terms* that can be embedded into spatial queries.

1 Introduction

Spatial database systems and Geographical Information Systems (GIS) enable the data management and analysis, respectively, of *crisp spatial objects* that are characterized by an exact location and a precisely defined extent, shape, and boundary in space. Examples are land properties with their cadastral boundaries and countries with their political boundaries. *Spatial data types* for crisp points, lines, and regions have been introduced for their representation, together with geometric operations such as topological relationships (e.g., overlap), geometric set operations (e.g., intersection), and numerical operations (e.g., area).

But increasingly, geoscientists are interested in modeling spatial phenomena characterized by the feature of *spatial fuzziness*. It captures the inherent property of many spatial objects in reality that have inexact locations, vague boundaries, and blurred interiors, and hence cannot be adequately represented by crisp spatial objects. Examples are air polluted areas, temperature zones, and habitats of species. In the geoscience and GIS domains, fuzzy set theory has become a popular tool for modeling such *fuzzy spatial objects*. The central idea is to relax the strict decision of belonging (value 1) or non-belonging (value 0) of a point to

Anderson Chaves Carniel: This author has been supported by the following Brazilian research agencies: FAPESP, CAPES, and CNPq.

H. Christiansen et al. (Eds.): FQAS 2017, LNAI 10333, pp. 112–123, 2017.
DOI: 10.1007/978-3-319-59692-1_10

an object. Instead, partial and multiple membership is allowed and expressed by a membership value in the interval $[0, 1]$. A number of fuzzy spatial operations has been defined like fuzzy geometric set operations (e.g., fuzzy geometric union) and fuzzy numerical operations (e.g., fuzzy area).

While topological relationships have been largely explored on crisp spatial objects, this is not the case for fuzzy spatial objects. This paper pursues two main objectives. The first objective is to propose a novel model to formally define *fuzzy topological relationships for fuzzy regions.* For each such relationship, spatial fuzziness is expressed by two fuzzy regions as input and by a fuzzy value in the interval $[0, 1]$ as output. Such a fuzzy value measures to which extent two fuzzy regions are topologically related, e.g., how much two fuzzy regions overlap. For this, different measures are conceivable. In this paper, we focus on the *coverage degree* of two fuzzy regions as the proportion between their overlapping area measure and their total area measure, or their distance and the maximum distance of their universe.

The second objective is to transform the non-intuitive and quantitative fuzzy topological relationship values in the interval $[0, 1]$ into intuitive, qualitatively equivalent terms that have meaning for the user and can be used as crisp Boolean predicates in a spatial query language. We propose to use adequate qualitative linguistic descriptions of nuances of topological relationships as appropriate interpretations of these fuzzy values. We achieve this by leveraging *linguistic values* like *small*, *medium*, and *large* to interpret coverage degrees. The linguistic values are deployed to characterize our *linguistic variables area* and *distance.* We assume that linguistic values are either predefined or user-defined. A query is then, e.g., "Find all fuzzy regions whose overlapping area is *large.*"

The overall goal to which this paper contributes is to provide a conceptual, abstract framework of fuzzy spatial data types and fuzzy topological relationships that can serve as a specification for their later implementation. Hence, aspects of implementation are not considered here (see Sect. 8).

This paper is organized as follows. Section 2 surveys related work. Section 3 briefly summarizes well known crisp spatial concepts. Section 4 introduces some needed concepts from fuzzy set theory. Section 5 provides a formal definition of a *fuzzy spatial data type* named *fregion* for fuzzy regions. Section 6 introduces our new concept of fuzzy topological relationships for fuzzy regions based on the coverage degree measure. Section 7 shows how to transform fuzzy topological relationships into Boolean predicates by linguistic terms, and use these predicates in spatial queries. Section 8 concludes the paper and presents future work.

2 Related Work

The available approaches to modeling fuzzy topological relationships for fuzzy regions can be distinguished regarding three criteria: (i) the range from which a value is returned by a relationship, (ii) the support of linguistic values, and (iii) the support of the concept of coverage degree.

Regarding the first criterion, the approaches differ in the range from which a value is returned by a fuzzy topological relationship. The approach in [5] is based on a three-valued logic with the truth values *true*, *false*, and *maybe*. They subdivide a fuzzy region into the *core* containing all points with membership value 1, the *exterior* including all points with membership value 0, and the vague *boundary* comprising the aggregation of all points with a membership value in the interval $]0,1[$. The small and fixed number of truth values limits the expressiveness of corresponding fuzzy topological relationships. On the other hand, the approaches in [1,2,6,7,12,13] allow that a fuzzy topological relationship returns any value of the interval $[0,1]$, and thus offers a larger flexibility to model real-world phenomena and their fuzzy topological relationships.

Regarding the second criterion, the approaches differ in the support provided for linguistic values in spatial queries. Linguistic values enable a user to express the degree of truth of a fuzzy topological relationship in terms of a qualitative term. For instance, we can distinguish when an overlapping area between two fuzzy regions is *huge* or *small*, including possible intermediary levels, such as *medium* and *large*. The terms *small*, *medium*, *large*, and *huge* are examples of linguistic values. Several approaches [1,5,7] provide support for them.

Regarding the third criterion, only a few approaches employ the concept of coverage degree. Coverage degrees allow a user to analyze the relationship between two fuzzy regions on the basis of the proportion of their overlapping area measure and their total area measure, or their distance and the maximum distance of their universe respectively. For instance, the coverage measure for the relationship *overlap* between two fuzzy regions returns the ratio of their overlapping area and their total area. Thus, we are able to find out whether the overlapping area of two fuzzy regions is *large*. Coverage degrees have been used in [1] only for the relationship *overlap*, and in [7] only for the relationship *inside*.

As a conclusion, none of the aforementioned approaches satisfies all four criteria. Our model, a precursor version of which is briefly sketched in [4], focuses on the coverage degree perspective, returns values in $[0,1]$, and transforms them into intuitive and qualitative linguistic terms that have significance for users.

3 Applied Crisp Spatial Concepts

Applied crisp spatial concepts are presented, e.g., in [11]. We make use of the well known crisp spatial data type *region* whose values may consist of multiple components possibly with holes. Further, we assume the operations $\otimes$, $\oplus$, and $\ominus$ for the geometric intersection, union, and difference of two crisp region objects, respectively. We also deploy the clustered topological relationships $meet_c$ and $disjoint_c$ [11]. These clustered relationships merge similar basic *meet* and *disjoint* relationships, respectively, into a single relationship. We also employ the two metric operations *area* to compute the area of a crisp region object and *dist* to determine the minimum distance between two crisp spatial objects.

4 Applied Concepts from Fuzzy Set Theory

Fuzzy set theory [14] permits that an element has partial membership in a (fuzzy) set and that it has different *membership degrees* in different (fuzzy) sets. Let X

be the universe. Then the function $\mu_{\tilde{A}} : X \to [0,1]$ is called the *membership function* of the *fuzzy set* $\tilde{A} = \{(x, \mu_{\tilde{A}}(x)) \mid x \in X\}$.

Fuzzy set operations generalize Boolean set operations. Let $\tilde{A}$ and $\tilde{B}$ be fuzzy sets in X. We employ the following fuzzy set operations. The *fuzzy bounded difference* of $\tilde{A}$ and $\tilde{B}$, which corresponds to the set difference on crisp sets, is defined as $\tilde{A} \dot{-} \tilde{B} = \{(x, \mu_{\tilde{A} \dot{-} \tilde{B}}(x)) \mid x \in X \wedge \mu_{\tilde{A} \dot{-} \tilde{B}}(x) = \max(0, \mu_{\tilde{A}}(x) - \mu_{\tilde{B}}(x))\}$. The *fuzzy symmetric difference* of $\tilde{A}$ and $\tilde{B}$, which corresponds to the symmetric difference on crisp sets, is defined as $\tilde{A} \Delta \tilde{B} = \{(x, \mu_{\tilde{A}\Delta\tilde{B}}(x)) \mid x \in X \wedge \mu_{\tilde{A}\Delta\tilde{B}}(x) = |\mu_{\tilde{A}}(x) - \mu_{\tilde{B}}(x)|\}$. *Fuzzy set containment* of $\tilde{A}$ in $\tilde{B}$ is defined as $\tilde{A} \subseteq \tilde{B} \Leftrightarrow \forall x \in X : \mu_{\tilde{A}}(x) \leq \mu_{\tilde{B}}(x)$. Proper fuzzy set containment and fuzzy set equality are defined correspondingly. Two often needed operations named *support* and *core* map fuzzy sets to crisp sets. The *support* of a fuzzy set is a crisp set composed of the elements with membership degree greater than 0, i.e., $supp(\tilde{A}) = \{x \in X | \mu_{\tilde{A}}(x) > 0\}$. The *core* of a fuzzy set is a crisp set that comprises the elements with membership degree 1, i.e., $core(\tilde{A}) = \{x \in X | \mu_{\tilde{A}}(x) = 1\}$.

5 Fuzzy Regions

Intuitively, a fuzzy region object has a similar areal geometry as a crisp region object [9] but it may have a vague boundary and/or a vague interior. That is, each of its points is associated with a membership degree indicating to which extent a point belongs to the region object, and the membership function is required to model a smooth change of membership degrees. Formally, a fuzzy point set $\tilde{A}$ in the plane has a membership function $\mu_{\tilde{A}} : \mathbb{R}^2 \to [0,1]$. Regularity avoids that $\tilde{A}$ has geometric anomalies like isolated or dangling line and point features as well as missing lines and points in the form of cuts and punctures (see an example in Fig. 1a) [9]. Let *cl* be a *closure* operator that removes cuts and punctures by appropriately adding points. Let *int* be an *interior* operator that eliminates dangling point and line features. $\tilde{A}$ is called a *regular open fuzzy set* if, and only if, $\tilde{A} = int(cl(\tilde{A}))$. $\tilde{A}$ is called a *regular closed fuzzy set* if, and only if, $\tilde{A} = cl(int(\tilde{A}))$. A regular open set may consist of several disconnected components and that each component may have holes. Applications show that the frontier of a fuzzy region can be completely fuzzy, or completely crisp, or partially crisp and fuzzy. For that purpose, we define the *frontier* of a fuzzy region $\tilde{A}$ as $frontier(\tilde{A}) = \{((x,y), \mu_{\tilde{A}}(x,y)) \mid (x,y) \in supp(\tilde{A}) - supp(int(\tilde{A}))\}$. In other words, the frontier of a fuzzy set $\tilde{A}$ collects all single fuzzy points of $\tilde{A}$ that are not interior points (Fig. 1c). It forms a fuzzy line object, which has the same geometric format as a crisp line [11] but with a membership function associated with special properties discussed in [9].

We are now able to define the fuzzy spatial data type *fregion* as

$$
\begin{aligned}
fregion = \{\tilde{R} \subseteq \mathbb{R}^2 \times]0,1] \mid \\
&\text{(i) } int(cl(\tilde{R})) \subseteq \tilde{R} \subseteq cl(int(\tilde{R})) \\
&\text{(ii) } frontier(\tilde{R}) \subseteq frontier(cl(int(\tilde{R}))) \\
&\text{(iii) } frontier(\tilde{R}) \in fline \\
&\text{(iv) } \mu_{\tilde{R}} \text{ is a (piecewise) continuous function}\}
\end{aligned}
$$

Condition (i) defines the "possible range" of the point set of $\tilde{R}$ between its regular open fuzzy set and its regular closed fuzzy set. In particular, it ensures that the interior of $\tilde{R}$ is free of geometric anomalies. Condition (ii) supports the concept of "partial frontier". One extreme is that $\tilde{R}$ has no frontier ($\mathit{frontier}(\tilde{R}) = \varnothing$). The other extreme is that $\tilde{R}$ has a "complete" frontier ($\mathit{frontier}(\tilde{R}) = \mathit{frontier}(\mathit{cl}(\mathit{int}(\tilde{R})))$). If, in the latter case, all membership values are equal to 1, we can even represent a crisp frontier. Condition (iii) requires that the frontier of $\tilde{R}$ is a fuzzy line object. This allows disconnected frontier parts and prohibits parts that are single fuzzy points. Condition (iv) requires a smooth distribution of membership values with possible exceptions. Figure 1b shows an example of an *fregion* object.

The concept of *fuzzy boundary* (Fig. 1d) helps us distinguish meeting and overlapping situations. Let $\tilde{R} \in \mathit{fregion}$. We define the *fuzzy boundary* $\partial\tilde{R}$ of $\tilde{R}$ as the union of the crisp boundary of the core of $\tilde{R}$, denoted by $\partial_c\tilde{R} = \{(p, 1) \in \tilde{R} \,|\, p \in \partial(\mathit{core}(\tilde{R}))\}$, and the fuzzy non-core part of $\tilde{R}$, denoted by $\partial_f\tilde{R} = \{(p, \mu_{\tilde{R}}(p)) \in \tilde{R} \,|\, 0 < \mu_{\tilde{R}}(p) < 1\}$. That is, $\partial\tilde{R} = \partial_c\tilde{R} \cup \partial_f\tilde{R}$, and $\partial_c\tilde{R} \in \mathit{fline}$ with membership degree 1 for all its points, and $\partial_f\tilde{R} \in \mathit{fregion}$.

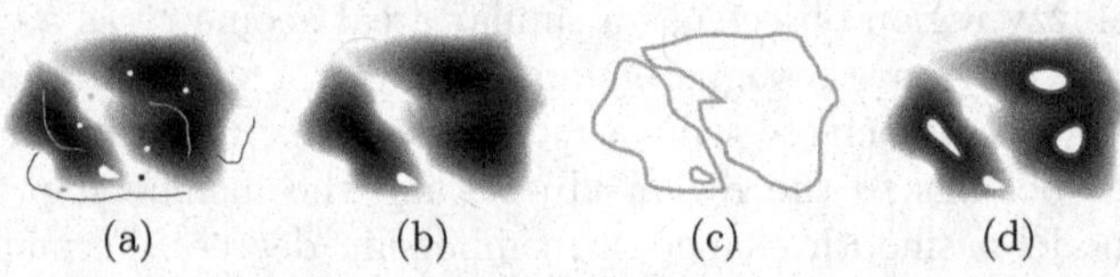

Fig. 1. An invalid fuzzy region with (white) punctures and cuts (a), a valid fuzzy region (*fregion*) object (b), its frontier (c), and its fuzzy boundary (d). Darker areas indicate higher membership degrees than lighter areas.

Two metric operations on fuzzy regions are deployed for the definition of our fuzzy topological relationships. The operation *farea* determines the fuzzy area as the volume under the membership function of an *fregion* object and returns a real value. The operation *fdist* computes the minimum distance of two *fregion* objects. These operations are formally defined in [8] and in [6], respectively. Further, as for crisp spatial objects, we assume the operations $\otimes$, $\oplus$, and $\ominus$ for the geometric intersection, union, and difference of two fuzzy region objects [9].

6 Fuzzy Topological Relationships

While a Boolean relationship performs a strict binary truth valuation and either yields 0 (false) or 1 (true), a fuzzy relationship returns a real value from the interval $[0, 1]$ that is interpreted as the degree of truth. Therefore, a *fuzzy topological relationship* determines the extent to which a relative position (like overlapping or disjointedness) between two fuzzy spatial objects holds. In the following subsections, we introduce a new approach that formally defines the set

$FTR = \{foverlap, fmeet, fdisjoint, fequal, finside, fcontains\}$ of six fuzzy topological relationships on the basis of the concept of *coverage degree*. Note that other concepts can be taken as a basis of such a definition, e.g., membership degrees [3]. In the first subsection, we summarize our main design considerations.

6.1 Design Considerations

We propose a novel approach to fuzzy topological relationships which enables the simultaneous fulfillment of all criteria from Sect. 2 that require (i) the interval $[0, 1]$ as the range of fuzzy topological relationships, (ii) a support of linguistic terms, and (iii) a support of the concept of coverage degree.

Especially the use of coverage degrees offers a new perspective of fuzzy topological relationships to users. Our coverage degree-based fuzzy topological relationships incorporate the ratio of the intersecting area of two fuzzy region objects to their total area as well as the ratio of their minimum distance to the maximum distance in their common universe of discourse. Each relationship $R \in FTR$ is defined as a function $R : fregion \times fregion \to [0, 1]$ to determine the coverage degree for which R holds. In Sect. 7, we will show how coverage degrees can be mapped to Boolean predicates in order to be deployed in spatial queries.

In the following subsections, we formally define the fuzzy topological relationships $R \in FTR$. For each relationship we specify when it yields 0 or a value of the interval $]0, 1]$. In Fig. 2 we present several spatial configurations of two fuzzy region objects to illustrate the fuzzy topological relationships. Figure 2 together with the relationship definitions also shows that *different* fuzzy topological relationships can yield possibly *different* values in the interval $]0, 1]$ for the *same* spatial configuration and are therefore *not* mutually exclusive (in contrast to the crisp case). This behavior corresponds to the classical fuzzy idea. Further, when a fuzzy topological relationship yields 1, none of the other fuzzy relationships can yield 1 too. This behavior corresponds to the classical crisp topological relationships and avoids inconsistencies of the applicability of the relationships since only one relationship may yield 1 for the same configuration.

6.2 Fuzzy Overlap

The fuzzy topological relationship *foverlap* determines the area coverage degree of two fuzzy region objects $\tilde{A}$ and $\tilde{B}$. Two conditions must alternatively hold so that $\tilde{A}$ and $\tilde{B}$ do definitely not overlap, i.e., $foverlap(\tilde{A}, \tilde{B}) = 0$ holds. The first condition is that there is no geometric intersection of the supports of $\tilde{A}$ and $\tilde{B}$, i.e., they are disjoint or meet in a crisp point object and/or a crisp line object (Fig. 2a). The second condition relates to a fuzzy set containment situation between $\tilde{A}$ and $\tilde{B}$ where $\tilde{A}$ is contained in $\tilde{B}$, or $\tilde{B}$ is contained in $\tilde{A}$, or $\tilde{A}$ and $\tilde{B}$ are equal (Fig. 2e). Note that a set containment requirement between the supports of $\tilde{A}$ and $\tilde{B}$ is too weak a condition. For example, if $supp(\tilde{A}) \subseteq supp(\tilde{B})$ and $\tilde{A} \not\subseteq \tilde{B}$ holds, this means that there are points that have a higher membership value in $\tilde{A}$ than in $\tilde{B}$. This represents a fuzzy overlap situation. The remaining case is that $foverlap(\tilde{A}, \tilde{B}) \in]0, 1[$ holds. We compute the ratio of the fuzzy area

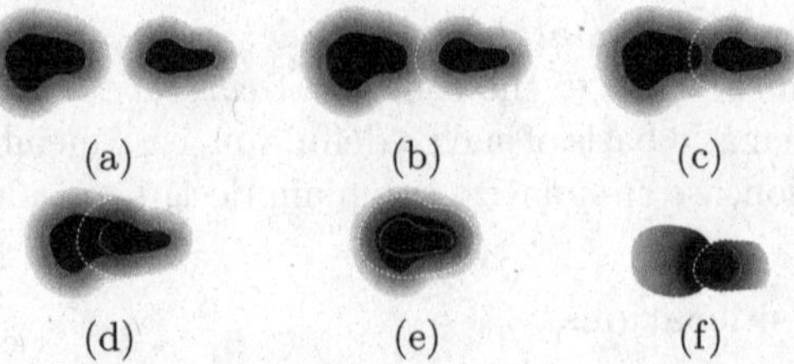

Fig. 2. Different spatial configurations of two fuzzy region objects (one fuzzy region object has its core and frontier highlighted with white lines) for explaining the different fuzzy topological relationships.

of their intersection with the fuzzy area of their union. Figures 2b, c, d, and f show fuzzy overlap situations that return a value in $]0, 1[$ for *foverlap*. The value of *foverlap* in Fig. 2b is smaller than the values of *foverlap* in the other situations since Fig. 2b shows a smaller overlapping area.

We are now able to provide a formal definition for the fuzzy topological relationship *foverlap*. Let $\tilde{A}, \tilde{B} \in fregion$. Then

$$foverlap(\tilde{A}, \tilde{B}) = \begin{cases} 0 & \text{if } disjoint_c(supp(\tilde{A}), supp(\tilde{B})) \vee \\ & \quad meet_c(supp(\tilde{A}), supp(\tilde{B})) \vee \\ & \quad \tilde{B} \subseteq \tilde{A} \vee \tilde{A} \subseteq \tilde{B} \\ \frac{farea(\tilde{A} \otimes \tilde{B})}{farea(\tilde{A} \oplus \tilde{B})} & \text{otherwise} \end{cases}$$

We are able to obtain two important properties from this definition. First, the relationship *foverlap* is symmetric, i.e., $foverlap(\tilde{A}, \tilde{B}) = foverlap(\tilde{B}, \tilde{A})$. This property is guaranteed by the usage of symmetric operators, such the crisp relationships, fuzzy set containment operations, and the fuzzy area. Second, always $foverlap(\tilde{A}, \tilde{B}) \in [0, 1[$ holds. If $foverlap(\tilde{A}, \tilde{B})$ could return the value 1, this would mean that $\tilde{A}$ and $\tilde{B}$ were equal. However, in this situation, $foverlap(\tilde{A}, \tilde{B})$ would return 0 as defined in the first case of the *foverlap* definition.

6.3 Fuzzy Meet

The fuzzy topological relationship *fmeet* determines the area coverage degree of the fuzzy boundaries (Sect. 5) of two fuzzy region objects $\tilde{A}$ and $\tilde{B}$. This is different from the fuzzy overlap case since *fmeet* also considers the intersection of the cores of two fuzzy regions.

Two conditions must alternatively hold so that $\tilde{A}$ and $\tilde{B}$ do definitely not meet, i.e., $fmeet(\tilde{A}, \tilde{B}) = 0$ holds. The first condition is that their cores are not disjoint and do not meet, i.e., their interiors intersect (Figs. 2d and f). The second condition is that $foverlap(\tilde{A}, \tilde{B}) = 0$ holds, i.e., either there is no geometric intersection between their supports or there is a fuzzy set containment situation (Figs. 2a and e). The remaining case is that $fmeet(\tilde{A}, \tilde{B}) \in]0, 1[$ holds. The value for *fmeet* is calculated by using the proportion of the intersection and the union of the fuzzy areas of the fuzzy boundaries of both fuzzy regions in the meeting case. Figures 2b and c show two fuzzy meeting situations that return a value in $]0,1[$ for *fmeet*. The value of *fmeet* in Fig. 2b is smaller than the value of *fmeet* in Fig. 2c since Fig. 2b shows a smaller intersecting boundary area.

We are now able to provide a formal definition of the fuzzy topological relationship *fmeet*. Let $\tilde{A}, \tilde{B} \in fregion$. Then

$$fmeet(\tilde{A},\tilde{B}) = \begin{cases} 0 & \text{if } \neg(disjoint_c(core(\tilde{A}), core(\tilde{B})) \vee \\ & \quad meet_c(core(\tilde{A}), core(\tilde{B}))) \vee \\ & \quad foverlap(\tilde{A},\tilde{B}) = 0 \\ \frac{farea(\partial_f \tilde{A} \otimes \partial_f \tilde{B})}{farea(\partial_f \tilde{A} \oplus \partial_f \tilde{B})} & \text{otherwise} \end{cases}$$

Similarly to *foverlap*, we are able to show that the relationship *fmeet* is symmetric, i.e., $fmeet(\tilde{A},\tilde{B}) = fmeet(\tilde{B},\tilde{A})$, and that always $fmeet(\tilde{A},\tilde{B}) \in [0,1[$ holds. The key difference between *fmeet* and *foverlap* is that the coverage degree of a meeting situation considers only the boundary intersection and thus $fmeet(\tilde{A},\tilde{B}) \leq foverlap(\tilde{A},\tilde{B})$ holds.

6.4 Fuzzy Disjoint

The fuzzy topological relationship *fdisjoint* determines the distance coverage degree of two fuzzy region objects $\tilde{A}$ and $\tilde{B}$. We compute the ratio of the fuzzy distance between $\tilde{A}$ and $\tilde{B}$ with the largest distance in a selected rectangular universe of discourse U in which $\tilde{A}$ and $\tilde{B}$ are located. If U_{ll} is the lower left point and U_{ru} is the right upper point of U, then the largest distance in U is the distance between U_{ll} and U_{ru}. The ratio depends on the extent of U, i.e., the smaller (larger) U is, the larger (smaller) the ratio is. Two possible situations may occur in order to A and B be definitely not disjoint, i.e., $fdisjoint(\tilde{A},\tilde{B}) = 0$ holds. First, it will return 0 when all the points of the overlapping area have a membership degree equal to 1 since the fuzzy distance will be 0 (Fig. 2f). Second, it also will return 0 when there is a fuzzy set containment situation between $\tilde{A}$ and $\tilde{B}$ (Fig. 2e). Otherwise, $fdisjoint(\tilde{A},\tilde{B}) \in]0,1[$ holds. Figures 2a to d depict fuzzy disjoint situations that return a value in $]0,1[$ for *fdisjoint*. The value of *fdisjoint* in Fig. 2a is greater than the values of *fdisjoint* in the other situations since Fig. 2a shows a greater distance between the fuzzy region objects.

We are now able to provide a formal definition of the fuzzy topological relationship *fdisjoint*. Let $\tilde{A}, \tilde{B} \in fregion$. Then

$$fdisjoint(\tilde{A},\tilde{B}) = \frac{fdist(\tilde{A},\tilde{B})}{dist(U_{ll},U_{ru})}$$

We are able to obtain two important properties from this definition. First, as expected, the relationship *fdisjoint* is symmetric, i.e., $fdisjoint(\tilde{A},\tilde{B}) = fdisjoint(\tilde{B},\tilde{A})$ since it employs distance operators. Second, always $fdisjoint \in [0,1[$ holds. If *fdisjoint* could return 1, this would mean that $\tilde{A}$ and $\tilde{B}$ degenerated into the points U_{ll} and U_{ru}; but, they are fuzzy regions.

6.5 Fuzzy Equal

The fuzzy topological relationship *fequal* determines the area coverage degree of the equality situation of the intersecting area of two fuzzy region objects $\tilde{A}$ and $\tilde{B}$. If there is no geometric intersection of the support of $\tilde{A}$ and $\tilde{B}$, then $\tilde{A}$ and $\tilde{B}$ are definitely not equal, i.e., $fequal(\tilde{A}, \tilde{B}) = 0$ holds. Figure 2a depicts this situation. The remaining case is that $fequal(\tilde{A}, \tilde{B}) \in]0, 1]$ holds. We first check how unequal both fuzzy regions are with respect to their intersection area. For this, we leverage a modified fuzzy symmetric difference operator $\Delta_\otimes$ that for a point $p \in \mathbb{R}^2$ yields 0 if $\mu_{\tilde{A}}(p) = 0$ or $\mu_{\tilde{B}}(p) = 0$ holds, and $\mu_{\tilde{A}\Delta\tilde{B}}(p)$ otherwise. Then, we compute the complement of the ratio of the modified fuzzy symmetric difference with the area of the support of their fuzzy intersection. Figures 2b to e depict fuzzy equal situations that return a value in $]0, 1[$ for *fequal*. On the other hand, Fig. 2f shows a fuzzy equal situation that returns 1 for *fequal* since all the points of both fuzzy region objects have the same membership degree in their intersecting area.

We are now able to provide a formal definition of the fuzzy topological relationship *fequal*. Let $\tilde{A}, \tilde{B} \in fregion$. Then

$$fequal(\tilde{A}, \tilde{B}) = \begin{cases} 0 & \text{if } disjoint_c(supp(\tilde{A}), supp(\tilde{B})) \\ & \quad \vee\ meet_c(supp(\tilde{A}), supp(\tilde{B})) \\ 1 - \frac{farea(\tilde{A}\Delta_\otimes\tilde{B})}{area(supp(\tilde{A}\otimes\tilde{B}))} & \text{otherwise} \end{cases}$$

Similarly to the other relationships, the relationship *fequal* is symmetric, i.e., $fequal(\tilde{A}, \tilde{B}) = fequal(\tilde{B}, \tilde{A})$ holds since it employs operators that are symmetric. Further, as expected, this relationship is also reflexive, i.e., $fequal(\tilde{A}, \tilde{A}) = 1$ holds since the intersection area corresponds to $\tilde{A}$, consequently the numerator of the fraction in the definition yields 0, and finally *fequal* yields 1.

6.6 Fuzzy Inside and Fuzzy Contains

The fuzzy topological relationship *finside* computes the degree of containment of the first fuzzy region in the second fuzzy region with respect to their intersection area. Two conditions must alternatively hold so that $\tilde{A}$ is definitely not inside $\tilde{B}$, i.e., $finside(\tilde{A}, \tilde{B}) = 0$ holds. Either all the points of both fuzzy region objects have the same membership degree in their intersecting area (Fig. 2f), or there is no geometric intersection between their supports (Fig. 2a).

The remaining case is that $finside(\tilde{A}, \tilde{B}) \in]0, 1]$ holds. We compute the non-containment degree of $\tilde{A}$ in $\tilde{B}$ by considering the intersection area with a modified fuzzy bounded difference operator $\dot{-}_\otimes$ that yields 0 for a point $p \in \mathbb{R}^2$ if $\mu_{\tilde{A}}(p) = 0$ or $\mu_{\tilde{B}}(p) = 0$ holds, and $\mu_{\tilde{A}\dot{-}\tilde{B}}(p)$ otherwise. Then we compute the complement of the ratio of the modified fuzzy bounded difference with the area of the support of their fuzzy intersection. The relationship returns 1 if the membership degrees of all points of the first fuzzy region object are smaller than the membership degrees of the corresponding points of the second fuzzy region object (Fig. 2e). Otherwise, it returns a value in the interval $]0, 1[$ (Figs. 2b to 2d).

We are now able to provide a formal definition of the fuzzy topological relationship *finside*. Let $\tilde{A}, \tilde{B} \in \mathit{fregion}$. Then

$$\mathit{finside}(\tilde{A},\tilde{B}) = \begin{cases} 0 & \text{if } \mathit{fequal}(\tilde{A},\tilde{B}) = 1 \vee \\ & \quad \mathit{disjoint}_c(\mathit{supp}(\tilde{A}), \mathit{supp}(\tilde{B})) \\ & \quad \vee\ \mathit{meet}_c(\mathit{supp}(\tilde{A}), \mathit{supp}(\tilde{B})) \\ 1 - \frac{\mathit{farea}(\tilde{A} \dot{-}_{\otimes} \tilde{B})}{\mathit{area}(\mathit{supp}(\tilde{A} \otimes \tilde{B}))} & \text{otherwise} \end{cases}$$

Differently from the other relationships, the relationship *finside* is not symmetric, i.e., $\mathit{finside}(\tilde{A},\tilde{B}) \neq \mathit{finside}(\tilde{B},\tilde{A})$ since the order of the operands plays a major role in the computation of this relationship.

The fuzzy topological relationship *fcontains* is the converse of the fuzzy topological relationship *finside*, i.e., $\mathit{fcontains}(\tilde{A},\tilde{B}) = \mathit{finside}(\tilde{B},\tilde{A})$.

7 Querying with Fuzzy Topological Relationships

A fuzzy topological relationship R_{cd} is not suitable as a user concept since it, firstly, returns a value in the interval $[0,1]$ that is non-intuitive for users and, secondly, cannot be used in a spatial query language as a crisp Boolean predicate. In order to make the fuzzy relationships usable in spatial queries, we map a coverage degree in $[0,1]$ to a *linguistic value*.

We use the notion of a *trapezoidal fuzzy set* to map fuzzy topological relationship values to high-level concepts. Let $a, b, c, d \in \mathbb{R}$ with $a \leq b \leq c \leq d$. Then a trapezoidal fuzzy set $\tilde{T}$ is defined as a tuple (a,b,c,d) if its membership function is given by (1) $\mu_{\tilde{T}}(x) = 0$ for $x \leq a$ and $x \geq d$, (2) $\mu_{\tilde{T}}(x) = 1$ for $b \leq x \leq c$, (3) $\mu_{\tilde{T}}$ increases linearly for $a \leq x \leq b$, and (4) $\mu_{\tilde{T}}$ decreases linearly for $c \leq x \leq d$. Applying this concept, we use adequate qualitative linguistic descriptions of nuances of topological relationships as appropriate interpretations of the fuzzy topological relationship values in the interval $[0,1]$ to create a classification of these values. Each qualitative linguistic description is represented by a trapezoidal fuzzy set of the form (a,b,c,d). We assume that the qualitative linguistic descriptions are either predefined or user-defined. For instance, we could define a classification for coverage degrees with the five linguistic values *tiny* = (0, 0, 0.07, 0.09), *small* = (0.07, 0.09, 0.35, 0.45), *medium* = (0.35, 0.45, 0.65, 0.75), *large* = (0.65, 0.75, 0.87, 0.92), and *huge* = (0.87, 0.92, 1, 1).

The combination of linguistic values with (quantitative) fuzzy relationships leads to *qualitative fuzzy topological relationships*, which are supposed to be Boolean predicates. For instance, the result of a fuzzy overlap between two fuzzy regions $\tilde{A}$ and $\tilde{B}$ can be expressed by the Boolean term "the overlapping area of $\tilde{A}$ and $\tilde{B}$ is *large*". This Boolean term represents a qualitative fuzzy topological relationship and has *true* or *false* as possible return values.

In order to embed a qualitative fuzzy topological relationship into spatial queries, we introduce a Boolean function for each fuzzy relationship R. This is achieved by overloading each R by a corresponding qualitative relationship $R : \mathit{fregion} \times \mathit{fregion} \times \Lambda \rightarrow \mathit{bool}$. For instance, in order to check the Boolean term "the statement 'the length of distance between $\tilde{A}$ and $\tilde{B}$ is *tiny*' is *true*", we make use of the Boolean predicate $fdisjoint(\tilde{A}, \tilde{B}, tiny)$ that yields either *true* or *false*. It evaluates whether the coverage degree returned by $fdisjoint(\tilde{A}, \tilde{B})$ matches the interpretation (i.e., fuzzy number) of the linguistic term *tiny*.

All these definitions enable the embedding of qualitative fuzzy topological relationships into SQL queries. We give some examples below by using an ecological application about endangered species, hunting areas, and air polluted areas from emissions of coal-fired power plants and industrial parks. They are represented by the relational table schemas *species*, *hunting*, and *pollution* respectively. Each table has an attribute *geo* representing their areas as fuzzy regions.

The first query asks for the names of each endangered species whose overlapping areas between their habitats with air pollution areas or with hunting areas are *large*.

```
SELECT S.name
FROM   species S, hunting H, pollution P
WHERE  foverlap(S.geo, H.geo, large) OR foverlap(S.geo, P.geo, large)
```

The following query returns the names of pairs of species whose shared fuzzy boundary area is *small* and thus indicates that they are possibly meeting.

```
SELECT S.name, F.name
FROM   species S, species F
WHERE  S.id <> F.id AND fmeet(S.geo, F.geo, small)
```

The final query returns the names of species whose habitat inside a polluted area is *huge*.

```
SELECT S.name
FROM species S, pollution P
WHERE finside(S.geo, P.geo, huge)
```

8 Conclusions and Future Work

This paper provides a new approach to modeling fuzzy topological relationships for fuzzy regions by transforming low-level quantitative measures to high-level fuzzy modifiers and linguistic values that are comprehensible to users. Each such relationship makes use of a coverage degree-based fuzzy topological predicate. The main advantages of our approach are that (i) the interval $[0, 1]$ is used as the range of fuzzy topological predicates to increase expressiveness, (ii) the concept of coverage degree is introduced, (iii) support of linguistic values is provided, and (iv) coverage degrees can be mapped to apt Boolean topological predicates and thus be embedded into spatial queries.

Future work will deal with a number of topics. Due to space limitations, it has been impossible in this paper to evaluate and validate our model by means of case studies, experiments, and human subject testing. A further research issue refers to the extension and generalization of the concepts for fuzzy topological relationships to all combinations of the fuzzy spatial data types for fuzzy points, fuzzy lines, and fuzzy regions. Finally, a topic beyond the scope of this paper is the implementation of all fuzzy topological relationships and their mappings to Boolean topological predicates. Our goal is (i) to perform the implementation in the context of the *Spatial Plateau Algebra* [10], which provides a general concept for the implementation of fuzzy spatial data types, and (ii) to enable the embedding of all implemented components into database systems like PostGIS.

References

1. Bjørke, J.T.: Topological relations between fuzzy regions: derivation of verbal terms. Fuzzy Sets Syst. **141**(3), 449–467 (2004)
2. Bloch, I.: Fuzzy spatial relationships for image processing and interpretation: a review. Image Vis. Comput. **23**(2), 89–110 (2005)
3. Carniel, A.C., Schneider, M.: A conceptual model of fuzzy topological relationships for fuzzy regions. In: IEEE International Conference on Fuzzy Systems, pp. 2271–2278 (2016)
4. Carniel, A.C., Schneider, M., Ciferri, R.R., Ciferri, C.D.A.: Modeling fuzzy topological predicates for fuzzy regions. In: ACM SIGSPATIAL International Conference on Advances in Geographic Information Systems, pp. 529–532 (2014)
5. Clementini, E., Di Felice, P.: Approximate topological relations. Int. J. Approximate Reasoning **16**(2), 173–204 (1997)
6. Dilo, A.: Representation of and reasoning with vagueness in spatial information: a system for handling vague objects. Ph.D. thesis, International Institute for Geo-information Science & Earth Observation (2006)
7. Jifa, G., Tiejun, C.: Topological relation analysis between high-order fuzzy regions based on fuzzy logic. J. Intell. Fuzzy Syst. Appl. Eng. Technol. **26**(4), 2057–2071 (2014)
8. Schneider, M.: Metric operations on fuzzy spatial objects in databases. In: ACM Symposium on Advances in Geographic Information Systems, pp. 21–26 (2000)
9. Schneider, M.: Fuzzy spatial data types for spatial uncertainty management in databases. In: Galindo, J. (ed.) Handbook of Research on Fuzzy Information Processing in Databases, pp. 490–515. IGI Global (2008)
10. Schneider, M.: Spatial Plateau Algebra for implementing fuzzy spatial objects in databases and GIS: Spatial Plateau data types and operations. Appl. Soft Comput. **16**(3), 148–170 (2014)
11. Schneider, M., Behr, T.: Topological relationships between complex spatial objects. ACM Trans. Database Syst. **31**(1), 39–81 (2006)
12. Schockaert, S., De Cock, M., Kerre, E.E.: Spatial reasoning in a fuzzy region connection calculus. Artif. Intell. **173**(2), 258–298 (2009)
13. Verstraete, J.: Deriving topological concepts for fuzzy regions: from properties to definitions. Control Cybern. **41**(1), 7:113–7:144 (2012)
14. Zadeh, L.A.: Fuzzy sets. Inf. Control **8**, 338–353 (1965)

Plug-and-Play Queries for Temporal Data Sockets

Curtis E. Dyreson[1(✉)] and Sourav S. Bhowmick[2]

[1] Department of Computer Science,
Utah State University, Logan, USA
Curtis.Dyreson@usu.edu

[2] School of Computer Engineering,
Nanyang Technological University, Singapore, Singapore
assourav@ntu.edu.sg

Abstract. Plug-and-play queries are portable, reliable, and easier to code. When a plug-and-play query is plugged into a data socket, the socket transforms the data to the shape needed by the query. If data is annotated with metadata, the semantics of the metadata potentially impacts the transformation. In this paper we describe how to account for the metadata in a transformation. We focus on temporal metadata and show how a transformation can preserve temporal semantics. We also show how the transformation can be driven by the metadata, for instance, the temporal metadata could be used to create data versions.

1 Introduction

A *plug-and-play* query is akin to a plug-and-play device which can be plugged into any kind of socket and used. Plug-and-play queries have a specification of what kind of data they need in order to be evaluated. A *data socket* for a plug-and-play query uses this specification to *transform data* to what is needed for the query to evaluate. Hence, a query writer can code a plug-and-play query for a simple, easy-to-understand schema, plug the query into a data socket, and rely on the socket to automatically adapt the data to the schema needed by the query. The data socket can inform the user whether the transformation is possible or the data is insufficient for producing a reliable answer, and can give precise information about what the data lacks. The benefits of plug-and-play queries are that they are *portable*, you can take a plug-and-play query to any data source and evaluate it, more *reliable*, the query checks the data environment to determine if it can be safely and correctly evaluated, and *easier to code* for complex data since a query writer can write the query with respect to a simple view of the data, abstracting away the data's real complexity.

We previously researched plug-and-play queries for hierarchical data sockets [5–10,27]. Hierarchies are a popular way to model data. In the 1960s influential DBMSs, such as IBM's IMS [21], managed hierarchical data. The rise of XML in the 90s led to a renewed interest in hierarchichal models, *c.f.,* [15], which continues today with research in JSON, *c.f.,* [19,26] and "nested" data,

H. Christiansen et al. (Eds.): FQAS 2017, LNAI 10333, pp. 124–136, 2017.
DOI: 10.1007/978-3-319-59692-1_11

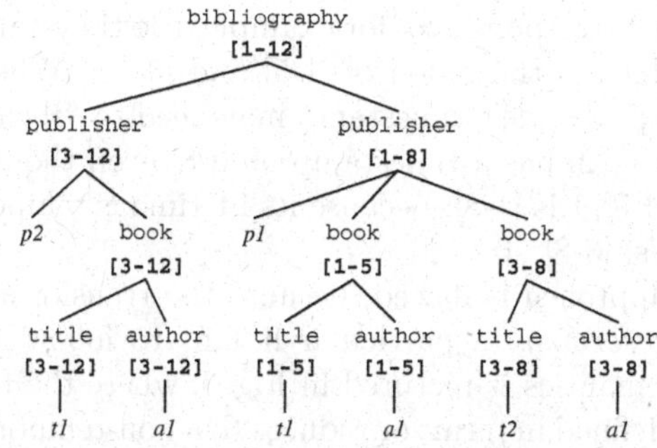

Fig. 1. Books within publishers

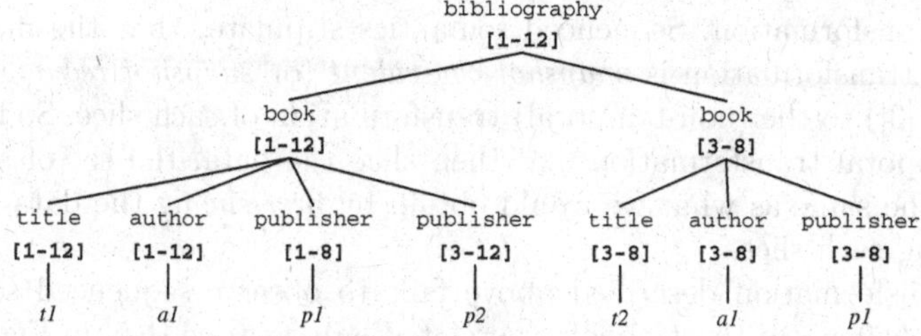

Fig. 2. An incorrect temporal transformation

c.f., [22]. In this paper we extend our previous research to cover temporal, hierarchical plug-and-play queries and data sockets. Data sits in a milieu of descriptive and proscriptive metadata. Examples include a schema, character sets, privacy annotations, and security restrictions. We focus in this paper on temporal data, which is data annotated with time metadata. To plug a query into a temporal data socket, the time metadata together with the data should be adapted to what the temporal query needs. For a socket to correctly transform such data, the transformation must ensure that the semantics of the annotating metadata is observed, in particular *sequenced semantics* for temporal metadata [25].

Consider the following example. A common way to represent temporal hierarchical data is as a tree in which each node has a timestamp [11,12,14]. Figure 1 shows a temporal version of some publisher data where the timestamp (shown below an element) indicates the database lifetime of the node, *i.e.*, the *transaction time* [16]. For instance, the timestamp for publisher *p1* in Fig. 1 indicates that data about *p1* was inserted at time 1 and is current until time 8. Suppose we want to transform the data so that books are above publishers in the hierarchy. A possible strategy is to first transform the timestamp-stripped source tree (using, for example, our transformation language XMorph [10]) and then compute the timestamp for each node in the target. The resulting tree is shown in Fig. 2. Computing the timestamps for the target is straightforward. The timestamp of a node in the target is the union of the timestamps of all the nodes in the source it corresponds to; for example, the timestamp of the *t1* book in Fig. 2 is [1-12], which is the union of [1-5] and [3-12]. When constrained by its parent's timestamp, a node's timestamp may need to "shrink." For example, the *p1* publisher in Fig. 2. has a timestamp of [3-8] even though the timestamp of its counterpart in Fig. 1 is [1-8], because its lifetime is temporally constrained by that of its parent's, [3-8] [4].

But this simple approach is flawed, because the transformation is **not** *temporal information-preserving*, in particular it fails to follow sequenced semantics [2]. Sequenced semantics is pictured in Fig. 3, where the temporal transformation semantics is defined in terms or reduces to a non-temporal transformation semantics. A temporal hierarchy can be thought of as a sequence of snapshots. Each snapshot is the *slice* of temporal data current at an instant. Individually, each snapshot can be transformed by a previously defined and well-known non-temporal transformation. Sequenced semantics stipulates that the meaning of a temporal transformation is *snapshot-equivalent* (or *snapshot reducible* [24] or *S-reducible* [3]) to the (non-temporal) transformation of each slice. So if we perform a temporal transformation and then slice the data, the set of snapshots should be the same as what we would obtain by first slicing the data and then transforming each slice.

The transformation described above fails to observe sequenced semantics. The *p1* publisher and the *t1* book are related only at time [1-5] in Fig. 1 but in Fig. 2 we can see they are related at time [1-8]. A transformation that observes sequenced semantics should relate them at time [1-5] exactly, not including time [6-8]. The timestamps introduce additional semantic constraints that need to be properly taken care of to ensure that the transformation is (temporal) information-preserving.

Our motivating example illustrates that when hierarchical data is annotated with metadata, special techniques are needed to ensure the preservation of the metadata's semantics in a transformation. The metadata can also *explicitly influence the transformation.* Consider for example a transformation that produces "versions" of the data, where a version is defined as a change in the children of a node. Different transformations will induce different versions; so the versions must be constructed dynamically.

This paper makes the following contributions.

- We describe a reversible, temporal transformation technique for data sockets and show how to detect information loss in the transformation, *i.e.*, to determine whether sequenced semantics is preserved.
- We show how the time metadata can drive a transformation.
- We describe how our technique extends to other kinds of metadata.

2 Background: Review of Plug-and-Play Queries

We previously investigated plug-and-play queries for hierarchical data. We introduced the concept of a *query guard*, which turns an ordinary query into a plug-and-play query [7]. A query guard is a lightweight reusable specification of the

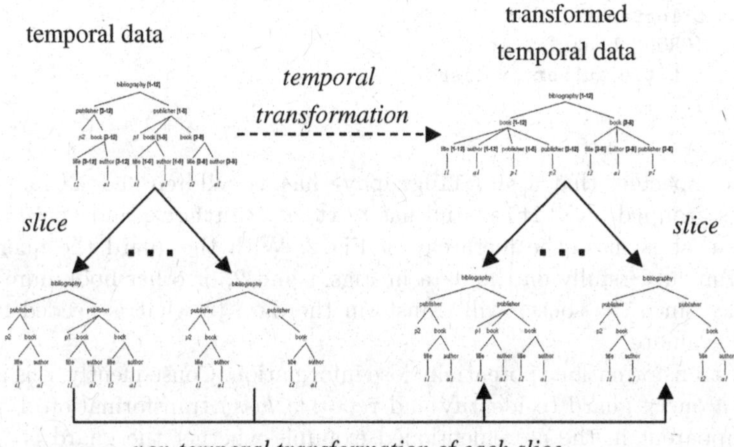

Fig. 3. Sequenced semantics

hierarchy that a query needs. It protects the query by testing whether the data can be transformed (without losing information) to the hierarchy given in the guard, and transforms the data if needed. A query guard focuses only on the *structure, not the semantics,* of the data because semantic web technologies, *e.g.,* ontologies, already address the orthogonal semantic matching problem.

A query guard allows the query to couple to any hierarchy that can be converted, cast, or coerced to the type (hierarchy) needed by the query. The guard protects the query by checking whether the data can be transformed, without losing information, to the type (hierarchy) needed by the query. Some transformations lose information when the hierarchy is manipulated, but the guard can alert the programmer to lossy transformations. The data could be physically [7] or *virtually* transformed [8].

As an example of querying data with a query guard, assume that we want to extract the book publishers using the XQuery query given below.

```
<data> {
    for $b in doc("x.xml")//book
    return <book>{$b/title} {$b/publisher}</book>
} </data>
```

Suppose that the query is applied to the hierarchy depicted in Fig. 1. The query will *fail* to produce the desired result because the path expression in the query do not match the shape of the data. The failure will not generate an error, rather the query will run to completion and yield an empty or partial answer. On the other hand, if the query is run on the data in Fig. 2 it will produce the desired result.

We developed a language called XMorph to express query guards for plug-and-play queries and data sockets [5,7,10]. A guard for the example XQuery query is given below.

```
MORPH bibilography [
        (GROUP book [title]) [
          title author publisher
        ]
      ]
```

The guard specifies that a `<bibliography>` has as children `<book>`s, and each `<book>` is grouped by `<title>` and has `<title>`, `<author>`, and `<publisher>` children, that is, it is the hierarchy of Fig. 2. With the guard the query can now be run successfully on the data in Figs. 1 and 2, or other book mini-world hierarchies since the socket will transform the data to what is needed for the query to evaluate.

Some transformations potentially lose information. Consequently, it is important for a query guard to identify and report a *lossy* transformation. It is not readily apparent in the aforementioned example whether the guard is "good" in the sense that it protects the query by neither manufacturing nor discarding data. This issue is vital to a user. If the transformation specified by a guard is lossy then the subsequent query evaluation will be similarly lossy and inaccurate. Let's introduce terminology to more precisely describe what we mean by a *good* guard. This terminology is adapted from the vocabulary of type systems in programming languages since a guard plays a role similar to a data type in a programming language, *i.e.*, it defines how the data is structured or encoded. A guard is *narrowing* if it ensures that data is not created, *widening* if it ensures that no data is lost, *strongly-typed* if it both narrowing and widening, *weakly-typed* if it neither narrowing nor widening, or has a *type mismatch* if the guard mentions a type that is absent from the source. A query guard can provide detailed feedback about which part of a guard is lossy. A programmer can use this feedback to add syntax to a query guard to indicate that the loss is acceptable, *e.g.*, most narrowing transformations will be fine, just as a C++ programmer might add a `cast()` to transform the result of an expression to a suitable type.

3 A Temporal Hierarchical Model

A temporal hierarchy can be modeled as a labeled tree.

Definition 1 (Temporal Hierarchy). *Let T be a set of chronons which forms a discrete image of a continuous time-line. A temporal hierarchy is a tuple (V, E, Σ, L, T, S), where*

- *V is a set of nodes,*
- *$E : V \times V$ is a tree edge set of the form (p, c), where p is the parent and c is the child,*
- *Σ is an alphabet of labels and text values,*
- *$L : V \to \Sigma$ is a label/text value function that maps a node to a label/text value,*
- *T is the chronon set, and*

- $S : V \rightarrow 2^T$ *is a timestamp function that maps a node to a timestamp (a set of chronons).*

The hierarchy is said to be temporally-consistent iff $\forall p, c[(p, c) \in E \Rightarrow S(c) \subset S(p)]$.

For simplicity, we discuss a data model with only one time dimension. The temporally-consistent property formally specifies that a child's timestamp has to be included in its parent's timestamp. Note that each edge implicitly has the same timestamp as that of the child node. This is because the two nodes are related only when the child exists. The model ignores some features of XML's DOM such as sibling order, node types, *e.g.*, attribute, processing instruction, comment, element, and text nodes, and labels and values are used for element names and text nodes, respectively. While these aspects could be modeled, the simpler model is sufficient for our purposes.

For this paper, we assume that the labels are unambiguous, *e.g.*, a `<title>` element is the title of a book rather than an author. A method to disambiguate labels is given elsewhere [10].

To support grouping in data transformations we extend the tree model to a partial order by explicitly adding groups as defined below.

Definition 2 (Grouped Temporal Hierarchy). *A grouped, temporal hierarchy is a tuple* $(G, V_G, E_G, \Sigma, L, T, S_G, X_G)$, *constructed from a temporal hierarchy,* (V, E, Σ, L, T, S), *where*

- $G : V \rightarrow V_G$ *is a group identity function, which maps a node to a group node (there is a single group node for each group),*
- V_G*: is a set of nodes,* $V \bigcup \{root\}$,
- $E_G : V_G \times V_G$ *is the edge set where* $E_G = \{(G(v), G(w)) \mid (v, w) \in E\}$,
- $S_G : V_G \rightarrow 2^T$ *is a node timestamp function that maps a group node,* $v \in V_G$, *to a timestamp, which is which is computed as*

$$S_G(g) = \bigcup_{\forall v[G(v)=g]} [S(v)]$$

and

- $X_G : E_G \rightarrow 2^T$ *is an edge timestamp function that maps an edge,* $(v, w) \in E_G$, *to a timestamp, which is computed as*

$$X_G((v, w)) = \bigcup\{S(y) \cap S(z) \mid G(y) = v \ \wedge \ G(z) = w \ \wedge \ (y, z) \in E\}$$

As an example, consider Fig. 4 which is the grouped temporal hierarchy corresponding to the temporal hierarchy in Fig. 1. Each edge in the figure is timestamped. There are groups for the book with title *t1* and author *a1*, for the author `a1`.

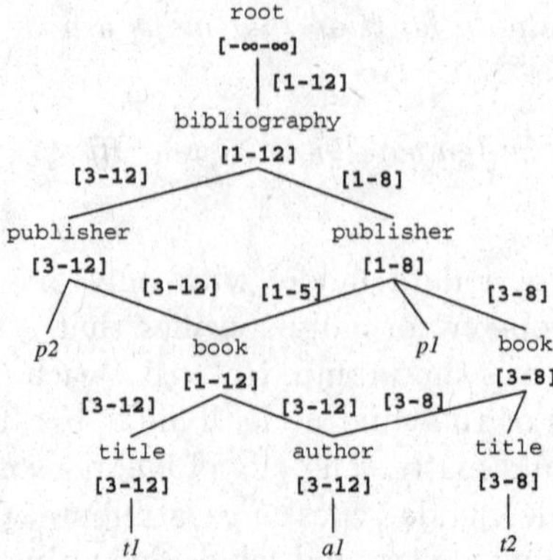

Fig. 4. The grouped, temporal hierarchy for the data of Fig. 1

4 Transforming Temporal Data

A non-temporal transformation transforms data by finding relationships between nodes. Our technique used *closest* relationships, which are nodes connected by a path that is the shortest for all nodes of the node *types* at the start and end of the path. A node type is the concatenation of label on a path from the root to a node. For instance, the type of the `<book>` nodes in Fig. 4 is `bibliography.publisher.book`. Suppose that our XMorph query guard makes `<publisher>`s children of `<book>`s. Then the shortest path between `<publisher>` and `<book>` types has length 1. The `<book>` with title *t2* then is closest to only the `<publisher>` *p1* since the shortest path to that `<publisher>` is of length 1 but the shortest path to `<publisher>` *p2* is 3.

4.1 Closest Lifetimes

Closest relationships have lifetimes.

Definition 3 (Closeness time). *In a grouped, temporal hierarchy,* $(G, V_G, E_G, \Sigma, L, T, S_G, X_G)$*, let* $v, w \in V_G$ *be a pair of closest nodes, and* P *be the set of shortest paths between* v *and* w*. Then* v *is closest to* w *at time* t *where*

$$t = \bigcup_{p \in P} [\bigcap_{e \in p} X_G(e)]$$

The definition says that the lifetime of a closest relationship is the union of the times of the paths between the nodes, where the time of a path is the intersection of the times on the path's edges. Consider the lifetime of the closest relationship between the `<author>` *a1* and `<publisher>` *p1* in Fig. 4. There is one shortest path through each `<book>` node. The leftmost path has a lifetime of [3-12] $\bigcap$ [1-5] = [3-5] while the rightmost path's lifetime is [3-8] $\bigcap$ [3-8] = [3-8]. So the lifetime is [3-5] $\bigcup$ [3-8] = [3-8].

4.2 Computing Closest Lifetimes

We now show how to compute the timestamp as data is transformed. The (non-temporal) transformation determines how to place children beneath parents as described elsewhere [7]. The lifetime of a node in the transformed data can be computed as the child is created. Let $v = \{(v_1, t_1), \ldots, (v_n, t_n)\}$ where t_i is the time of node v_i, and $w = \{(w_1, s_1), \ldots, (w_m, s_m)\}$ be a pair of closest, grouped nodes where v is the parent and w is the child in the transformed data. Then the time for w in the transformed data is

$$\bigcup\{t_i \cap s_k \mid (v_i, t_i) \in v \wedge (w_m, s_m) \in w \wedge v_i \text{ is closest to } w_k\}$$

Because a temporal hierarchy is temporally-consistent (a child's lifetime is a subset of a parent's lifetime), a shortest path always pases through a least common ancestor, and the lifetime along a path is computed by intersection, the lifetimes for every edge in the path are not needed, but can be inferred from the lifetime of the source and sink nodes. As an example, consider the task of placing publisher *p1* beneath the grouped book with title *t1*. There are two book nodes in the group, $\{(b_1$, [3-2]), $(b_2$ [1-5])} and one node in the publisher group $\{(p_1$, [1-8])}. b_1 is not closest to p_1 (it is closer to publisher *p2*) so the lifetime is the intersection of b_2 and p_1, which is [1-5].

To analyze the time cost of the lifetime computation, let N be the number of nodes in a grouped node and c be the cost of determining if a pair is close, then the time cost is $O(cN^2)$.

4.3 Information Loss

We can also compute information loss with low cost. Observe that a transformation may "shrink" the metadata (through temporal intersection) but will never increase it (the lifetime of a grouped node will never be increased, rather the temporal union just pieces together the grouped lifetime from the members of the group). A *reversible* transformation retains information, and the ability to reverse the transformation, while a *narrowing* transformation loses closest relationships present in the data.

Theorem 1. *A temporal transformation is reversible if it is based on a reversible non-temporal transformation, that is, if it preserves all of the non-temporal closest relationships, and if all nodes in the transformed data (modulo grouping) have the same lifetime as the node in the source data (modulo grouping).*

Proof. Assume a temporal hierarchy, (V, E, Σ, L, T, S) which is transformed to temporal hierarchy, $(V', E', \Sigma', L', T', S')$. If the non-temporal part of the transformation is reversible then we know that we can reverse the transformation to obtain the original set of edges, nodes, label function, etc. (this proof is given elsewhere [27]). So we need to show that we can obtain S from S' Assume $v \in S$ and $S(v) = t$. We know that there exists $v \in V'$ because the transformation is (non-temporal) reversible. Assume $S'(v) = t'$. Then there are three cases.

$t \subset t'$ - Information has been added. There exists at least one snapshot in the transformed data that contains v which does not exist in the source. The transformation, therefore, must be *widening* and is not necessarily reversible.

$t' \subset t$ - Information has been lost. There exists at least one snapshot in the source data that contains v which does not exist in the source. The transformation is *narrowing*.

$t' = t$ - The source and transformed data contain the same snapshots, hence no information is lost.

So it is necessary for the lifetimes to be the same to guarantee that the transformation preserves the timestamp function. ■

The temporal information loss can be quantified as follows. For each edge, (p, c), in the transformed data, compute the timestamp shrinkage, $v_I = S(c) - S(p)$. Let $V_I = \bigcup v_I$ for all v in the transformed data and let r be the root of the hierarchy. Then the amount of information loss is how many snapshots are lost vis-a-vis the number of snapshots in the document, $|(S(r) - V_I)|/|S(r)|$.

4.4 Other Temporal Semantics

Other temporal semantics, such as earliest and latest semantics, have been described [13], but as they generalize sequenced semantics, the techniques developed in this paper apply to those semantics.

A more interesting kind of transformation utilizes the metadata in the transformation. In a *version transformation* each combination of children creates a distinct version of a node. A versioned temporal hierarchy would help answer queries such as "select the latest version of each book".

Definition 4 (Versioned temporal hierarchy). *Let* $D = (V, E, \Sigma, L, T, S)$ *be a temporal hierarchy. The versioned hierarchy of* D*, denoted* $D_V = (V_V, E_V, \Sigma, L, T, S_V)$*, is defined as follows.*

- $V_V = V \bigcup \{v_1, \ldots, v_m\}$ *where* v_i *is a* `version` *node, there is one version node for every change in the children of a node.*
- $E_V = E_1 \bigcup E_2$ *where*
  - $E_1 = \{(v, v) \mid (v, c) \in E \;\wedge\; v \text{ is a version node } \wedge\; S_V(v) \subseteq S(v)\}$, *and*
  - $E_2 = \{(v, c) \mid (v, c) \in E \;\wedge\; v \text{ is a version node } \wedge\; S_V(v) \subseteq S(c)\}$
- $S_V = S \bigcup \Upsilon$ *where* Υ *is a function that maps a version node to a timestamp that represents the lifetime of the version (maximal time when the children remain the same).*

As an example, Fig. 5 is the versioned hierarchy for the data in Fig. 1.

Versioning can be computed during a transformation by sorting the children of a transformed node by their timestamps and chopping them into versions. While this increases the runtime cost by $O(N\log N) + O(V)$ where N is the number of transformed nodes and V is the number of versions. Since there can be at most two versions per (interval) timestamp, since only the endpoints represent a change in the existence of a child, $O(V) = O(N)$, the overall worst-case time cost is the cost of the sort.

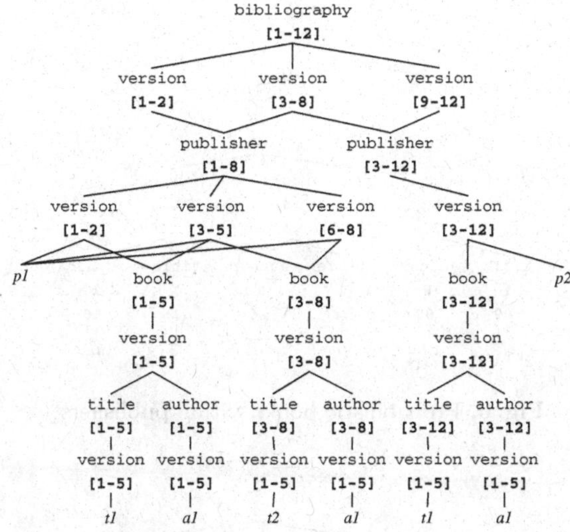

Fig. 5. Versioned books within publishers

4.5 Other Kinds of Metadata

The techniques developed in this paper can be generalized to apply to other kinds of metadata by using different functions to compute the metadata along a path and combine metadata from paths in grouping, which for temporal data are basically intersection and union, respectively. Consider Bayesian probabilistic metadata, and assume probabilistic independence. Figure 6 shows the data of Fig. 1 but with probabilities for metadata. Each node has two probabilities in the figure. The top number is probability that the node is a child of the parent, that is, the probability of the node's existence, which we will call the *existence probability*. The bottom number is the conditional probability that the node exists, computed as the conditional probability of its parent's existence times the probability of its existence. So for example, the `<book>` for `<publisher>` *p2* has an existence probability of .1 (the top number), and a conditional probability of .09 (the bottom number) which is computed as its parent's conditional probability, .9, times its probability, .1. The probability along a path is computed using multiplication. Paths are combined using Bayesian addition (assuming independence). The transformed data, with a Bayesian independence assumption, is shown in Fig. 7. The leftmost `<book>` has as its existence probability the formula "1 - the probability that neither `<book>` in the group exists". The group has two `<book>`s, which exist with probability .09 and .4, respectively (as computed in Fig. 6). So the existence probability of the grouped `<book>` is $1 - (1 - .09) * (1 - .4)$. Other kinds of metadata, security, provenance, etc., will use other operations to enforce a semantics.

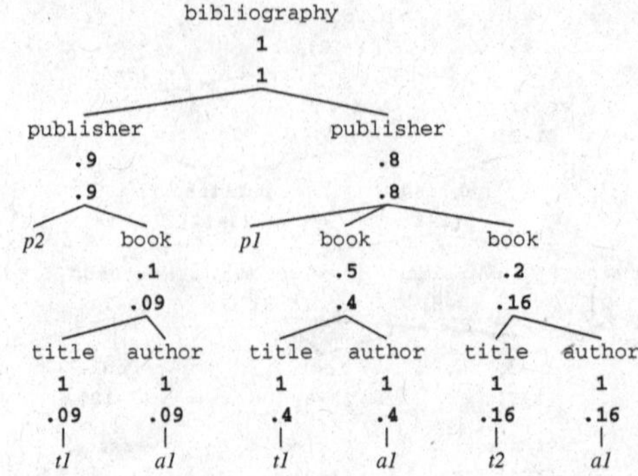

Fig. 6. Probabilistic books within publishers

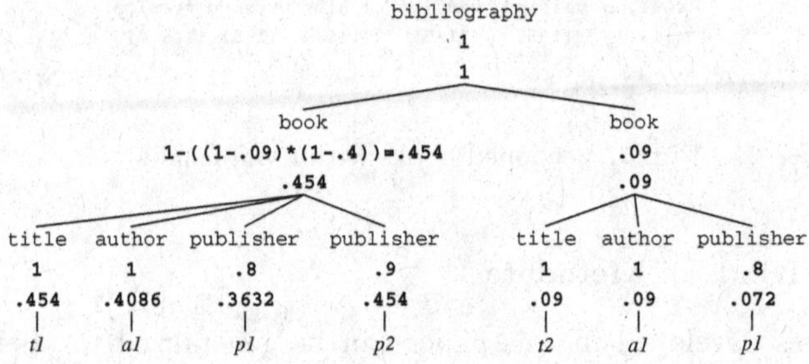

Fig. 7. Transformed probabilistic data

5 Related Work

Previous hierarchy-related research in querying data with the wrong shape can be broadly classified into several categories. **Query relaxation/approximation** techniques loosen the tight coupling of path expressions to the hierarchy of data is to relax the path expressions or approximately match them to the data by exploring a space of hierarchies that are within a given edit distance, *c.f.*, [1]. **Hierarchical search engines** de-couple queries from specific hierarchies, similar to our aims, and can find data in differently-shaped hierarchies, *c.f.*, [20]) **Structure-independent querying** techniques use a least common ancestor to query data independent of its hierarchy, *c.f.*, [18]. Finally, there is research in **declarative transformation languages** [17,23]. We extend the final approach in this paper and describe how to transform data annotated with metadata. There is no previous research on working with data annotated with metadata in any of the above categories.

6 Conclusion

Transforming data is an important part of query evaluation. When data is annotated with metadata, the transformation has to preserve the semantics of the metadata, particularly when the data is grouped. In this paper we investigated the transformation of data annotated with temporal metadata. We presented a sequenced transformation technique, which restructures temporal data while ensuring sequenced semantics. We also presented a versioning transformation technique that reorganizes the data into versions. We are currently implementing the transformation in XMorph. More on the project, including code, a tutorial, and a demo, can be found at http://digital.cs.usu.edu/~cdyreson/XMorph.

References

1. Amer-Yahia, S., Cho, S.R., Srivastava, D.: Tree pattern relaxation. In: Jensen, C.S., Šaltenis, S., Jeffery, K.G., Pokorny, J., Bertino, E., Böhn, K., Jarke, M. (eds.) EDBT 2002. LNCS, vol. 2287, pp. 496–513. Springer, Heidelberg (2002). doi:10.1007/3-540-45876-X_32
2. Böhlen, M.H., Jensen, C.S.: Sequenced semantics. In: Liu, L., Özsu, M.T. (eds.) Encyclopedia of Database Systems, pp. 2619–2621. Springer, Heidelberg (2009)
3. Böhlen, M.H., Jensen, C.S., Snodgrass, R.T.: Temporal statement modifiers. ACM Trans. Database Syst. **25**(4), 407–456 (2000)
4. Currim, F., Currim, S., Dyreson, C.E., Snodgrass, R.T., Thomas, S.W., Zhang, R.: Adding temporal constraints to XML schema. IEEE Trans. Knowl. Data Eng. **24**(8), 1361–1377 (2012)
5. Dyreson, C., Bhowmick, S., Jannu, A., Mallampalli, K., Zhang, S.: XMorph: a shape-polymorphic, domain-specific XML data transformation language. In: ICDE, pp. 844–847 (2010)
6. Dyreson, C., Zhang, S.: The benefits of utilizing closeness in XML. In: DEXA Work, pp. 269–273 (2008)
7. Dyreson, C.E., Bhowmick, S.S.: Querying XML data: as you shape it. In: ICDE, pp. 642–653 (2012)
8. Dyreson, C.E., Bhowmick, S.S., Grapp, R.: Querying virtual hierarchies using virtual prefix-based numbers. In: International Conference on Management of Data (SIGMOD 2014), Snowbird, UT, USA, 22–27 June 2014, pp. 791–802 (2014)
9. Dyreson, C.E., Bhowmick, S.S., Grapp, R.: Virtual eXist-db: liberating hierarchical queries from the shackles of access path dependence. PVLDB **8**(12), 1932–1943 (2015)
10. Dyreson, C.E., Bhowmick, S.S., Mallampalli, K.: Using XMorph to transform XML data. PVLDB **3**(2), 1541–1544 (2010)
11. Dyreson, C.E., Grandi, F.: Temporal XML. In: Liu, L., Özsu, M.T. (eds.) Encyclopedia of Database Systems, pp. 3032–3035. Springer, Heidelberg (2009)
12. Dyreson, C.E., Mekala, K.G.: Prefix-based node numbering for temporal XML. In: Bouguettaya, A., Hauswirth, M., Liu, L. (eds.) WISE 2011. LNCS, vol. 6997, pp. 172–184. Springer, Heidelberg (2011). doi:10.1007/978-3-642-24434-6_13
13. Dyreson, C.E., Rani, V.A., Shatnawi, A.: Unifying sequenced and non-sequenced semantics. In: 22nd International Symposium on Temporal Representation and Reasoning (TIME 2015), Kassel, Germany, 23–25 September 2015, pp. 38–46 (2015)
14. Dyreson, C., Snodgrass, R.T., Currim, F., Currim, S.: Schema-mediated exchange of temporal XML data. In: Embley, D.W., Olivé, A., Ram, S. (eds.) ER 2006. LNCS, vol. 4215, pp. 212–227. Springer, Heidelberg (2006). doi:10.1007/11901181_17

15. Jagadish, H.V., Al-Khalifa, S., Chapman, A., Lakshmanan, L.V.S., Nierman, A., Paparizos, S., Patel, J.M., Srivastava, D., Wiwatwattana, N., Wu, Y., Yu, C.: TIMBER: a native XML database. VLDB J. **11**(4), 274–291 (2002)
16. Jensen, C.S., et al.: The consensus glossary of temporal database concepts — February 1998 version. In: Etzion, O., Jajodia, S., Sripada, S. (eds.) Temporal Databases: Research and Practice. LNCS, vol. 1399, pp. 367–405. Springer, Heidelberg (1998). doi:10.1007/BFb0053710
17. Krishnamurthi, S., Gray, K.E., Graunke, P.T.: Transformation-by-example for XML. In: Pontelli, E., Santos Costa, V. (eds.) PADL 2000. LNCS, vol. 1753, pp. 249–262. Springer, Heidelberg (1999). doi:10.1007/3-540-46584-7_17
18. Li, Y., Yu, C., Jagadish, H.V.: Schema-free XQuery. In: VLDB, pp. 72–83 (2004)
19. Liu, Z.H., Hammerschmidt, B.C., McMahon, D.: JSON data management: supporting schema-less development in RDBMS. In: International Conference on Management of Data (SIGMOD 2014), Snowbird, UT, USA, 22–27 June 2014, pp. 1247–1258 (2014)
20. Liu, Z., Walker, J., Chen, Y.: XSeek: a semantic XML search engine using keywords. In: VLDB, pp. 1330–1333 (2007)
21. McGee, W.C.: The information management system IMS/VS part i: general structure and operation. IBM Syst. J. **16**(2), 84–95 (1977)
22. Melnik, S., Gubarev, A., Long, J.J., Romer, G., Shivakumar, S., Tolton, M., Vassilakis, T.: Dremel: interactive analysis of web-scale datasets. Commun. ACM **54**(6), 114–123 (2011)
23. Pankowski, T.: A high-level language for specifying XML data transformations. In: Benczúr, A., Demetrovics, J., Gottlob, G. (eds.) ADBIS 2004. LNCS, vol. 3255, pp. 159–172. Springer, Heidelberg (2004). doi:10.1007/978-3-540-30204-9_11
24. Snodgrass, R.T.: The temporal query language TQuel. ACM Trans. Database Syst. **12**(2), 247–298 (1987)
25. Snodgrass, R.T. (ed.): The TSQL2 Temporal Query Language. Kluwer, Dordrecht (1995)
26. Tahara, D., Diamond, T., Abadi, D.J.: Sinew: a SQL system for multi-structured data. In: International Conference on Management of Data (SIGMOD 2014), Snowbird, UT, USA, 22–27 June 2014, pp. 815–826 (2014)
27. Zhang, S., Dyreson, C.E.: Symmetrically exploiting XML. In: WWW, pp. 103–111 (2006)

Index Structures for Preference Database Queries

Markus Endres(✉) and Felix Weichmann

Institute for Computer Science,
University of Augsburg, Universitätsstr. 6a, 86159 Augsburg, Germany
endres@informatik.uni-augsburg.de,
felix.weichmann@student.uni-augsburg.de
http://www.dbis.informatik.uni-augsburg.de

Abstract. Preference queries enable satisfying search results by delivering best matches, even when no tuple in a dataset fulfills all preferences perfectly. Several methods were developed for preference query processing, such as window-based, distributed, divide-and-conquer, and index-based algorithms. In particular, all index-based algorithms were designed to evaluate Pareto preferences, where the participating preferences are all equally important. In this paper we present index structures for base preferences. Our comprehensive experiments show how indexing data for preference database queries enable faster access of the data tuples and therefore lead to performance advantages when evaluating preferences.

1 Introduction

Preferences are a well established framework to create personalized information systems. Skyline queries [3] are the most prominent representatives of preference queries. An implementation of preferences in database systems is PreferenceSQL [7] and the commercial product EXASolution [9] as well as a prototype of the Microsoft SQL Server [4]. Preferences in database systems are modeled as strict partial orders and a preference query returns the maximal elements according to this order, i.e., those tuples from the dataset which are not dominated w.r.t. the given preference.

Example 1. Assume the sample dataset in Table 1 and the wish for a car with *highest power* and a *price between 34000 and 37000 USD*, where both preferences should be considered as equally important (a Pareto preference). Then this query would identify the tuples with ID 4 and 5 as best objects. The tuple with ID 4 has a perfect match concerning the price, but the power of the tuple with ID 5 is higher. Therefore, both tuples are indifferent and form the result set.

Search efficiency is the most important performance criteria to preference query processing. In addition, as preference queries have been considered as an analytical tool in some commercial database systems [4,9], and the datasets to be processed in real-world applications are of considerable size, there is definitely the need for improved query performance. Indexing data is one natural

H. Christiansen et al. (Eds.): FQAS 2017, LNAI 10333, pp. 137–149, 2017.
DOI: 10.1007/978-3-319-59692-1_12

Table 1. Sample dataset of cars.

Car	id	Make	Color	Power	Price
	1	BMW	Green	180	35000
	2	Audi	Green	170	32000
	3	Mercedes	Blue	200	38000
	4	BMW	Blue	230	34000
	5	Mercedes	Black	250	20000
	6	Mitsubishi	Black	120	50000
	7	Mitsubishi	Black	140	53000
	8	Audi	Eed	150	37000

choice to achieve this performance improvement. The advantage of index-based algorithms is that they need to access only a portion of the dataset to compute the Skyline, while non-index-based algorithms have to visit the whole dataset at least once. However, index-based algorithms have to incur additional time and space costs for building and maintaining the indexes. In addition, unlike most existing algorithms that require at least one pass over the dataset to return the first interesting point, indexing data for preference queries can be used to progressively return interesting points as they are identified.

For the evaluation of Pareto preference queries as in Example 1 there exist several index structures, see [5] for an overview. However, all these index structures were exclusively designed for Skyline/Pareto queries. In this paper we refer to *indexing techniques* for *base preferences*. We do not consider indexes for Pareto preferences as in previous work, but offer indexing methods based on common index structures for simple preference database queries and show how they perform against state-of-the-art preference computation algorithms. To the best of our knowledge there exist no other index structures for base preferences as described in this paper. Hence, this is the first work on this topic and our comprehensive experiments show the performance advantage in several synthetic and real world use cases.

The rest of the paper is organized as follows: Sect. 2 introduces preferences in database systems and presents common index data structures for database queries. In Sect. 3 we discuss the applicability of the common index structures to preference queries. Section 4 reports our comprehensive experiments, and Sect. 5 concludes with a summary and outlook.

2 Background

2.1 Preferences in Database Systems

Following [6], a *preference* P a *strict partial order* on the attribute list A. The result of a preference is computed by the *preference selection* and is called *Best-Matching-Only* (BMO) set. The BMO-set contains all tuples t from an input relation R which are not dominated w.r.t. the preference P: To specify a database preference, a variety of intuitive constructors have been defined. Preferences on single attributes are called *base preferences.* There are *base preference constructors* for *discrete* (*categorical*) and for *continuous* (*numerical*) domains.

Numerical Preferences. The interval preference BETWEEN$_d(A, [low, up])$ expresses the wish for a value between a *lower* and an *upper* bound. If this is infeasible, values having the smallest distance to $[low, up]$ are preferred, where the distance is discretized by the discretization parameter d. In the case of $d = 0$ the *distance* describes how far the domain value v is away from the optimal value. A d-parameter $d > 0$ represents a discretization of the distance to v, which is used to group ranges of attribute values together. Choosing $d > 0$ effects that attribute values inside d-intervals "left and right" of $[low, up]$ become indifferent, c.f. [6]. Specifying $low = up$ (=: z) in BETWEEN$_d$ we get the AROUND$_d(A, z)$ preference, where the desired value should be z. Furthermore, the constructors LOWEST$_d(A, \inf_A)$ and HIGHEST$_d(A, \sup_A)$ prefer the minimal and maximal values within the distance d, where $\inf_A$ and $\sup_A$ are the infimum and supremum of the attribute values. In the preference ATLEAST$_d(A, z)$ the desired values should be greater or equal to z. If this is infeasible, values within a distance of d are acceptable. ATMOST$_d(A, z)$ is its dual preference.

Categorical Preferences. A LAYERED$_m(A, (L_1, \ldots, L_m))$ preference on a categorical domain expresses that a user has a set of preferred values given by the disjoint sets L_i. Thereby the values in L_1 are the most preferred values, L_2 are the second choice, and so on. There are several sub-constructors of LAYERED$_m$. The positive preference POS(A, *POS-set*) for example is defined as LAYERED$_2$(A, (*POS-set*, dom(A)*POS-set*)) and expresses that a user has a set of preferred values given by the *POS-set.* The negative preference NEG(A, *NEG-set*) is the counterpart to the POS preference. It is possible to combine these preferences to POS/POS or POS/NEG.

Example 2. Consider Table 1. If we specify P_1 := AROUND$_5$(power, 130), the result are the cars with ID 6 and 7, because both have the same distance to the desired value and there does not exists a perfect match. The wish for an Audi or BMW leads to P_2 := POS(make, {Audi, BMW}). The result is ID $\in \{1, 2, 4, 8\}$.

It is possible to combine several base preferences into more complex preferences, where one has to decide the relative importance of the given preferences. Equal importance is modeled by the *Pareto preference*, whereas for ordered importance we use *Prioritization.* Both are not topic of this paper, but are discussed elsewhere.

2.2 Index Data Structures

In this section we recapitulate well-known index structures for databases which also can be applied to preference queries. Note that there are many other indexes, but the mentioned structures are practical for preference queries as well.

Range Trees have been designed to answer range queries efficiently [8]. They are similar to a B^+-trees, where all values in the left child are less than or equal to the value maintained at the node, while all values in the right child are greater. In a range tree all the data is stored in the leaves. Thereby, (1) the leaves of the tree are maintained in a *sorted order*, and (2) the leaves are *linked* to the next and previous nodes. The combined effect is that the data points form a sorted doubly linked list. A range tree is a balanced search tree and hence the search time is in $\mathcal{O}(\log(k) + |S|)$, k the number of values in the tree and $|S|$ the number of tuples in the answer set.

Hash Index uses a *hash function* $h(v)$ that takes a search key v and computes an integer in the range 0 to $B-1$, where B is the number of *buckets* [2]. A *bucket directory* holds the headers of B linked lists, one for each bucket of the array. If a tuple has search key v, then we store the tuple by linking it to the bucket list for the bucket numbered $h(v)$. Hash functions complete searching for *any* key in $\mathcal{O}(1)$ time, since one only has to lookup $h(v)$ for a search key v. Thus, in a database querying context, hash functions are desirable for *exact match queries*, but cannot support range queries well.

Trie Index (from re*trie*val) is used to index strings and to support efficient evaluation of categorical preferences. The root of a trie [2] (also known as Prefix B-tree [1]) represents the empty string. Each edge defines the next character of a string. The last character ends in a leaf node. Hence, every path from a root to a leaf encodes a string. The complexity of a search in a trie is given as $\mathcal{O}(l)$, where l is the length of the search string.

3 Indexes for Preference Queries

When considering indexing for *base preferences*, we have to keep in mind, that until now the fastest method to evaluate such preferences is a *linear scan* over the dataset and always store the temporarily best tuples in a set S. At the end of the scan S contains the BMO objects. The runtime complexity is $\mathcal{O}(n)$, where n is the size of the dataset. This linear scan is a modified version of the well-known BNL algorithm [3], which was developed for Skylines. Keep in mind that the costs for building and maintaining the index structures for preferences are the same as in the original data structures.

3.1 An Index for Numerical Preferences

Since all numerical preferences are sub-constructors of BETWEEN_d, it is enough to present an index structure for this preference and to discuss the search in the special cases for all other preferences.

If the query is a range query like $\text{BETWEEN}_d(A, [low, up])$, index structures like binary search trees, quadtrees, K-d-trees, and Hash index fail. For example, for the range query in a binary search tree, at a node, both branches may need to be traversed. If the query is for all points greater than a value, then the search degenerates to traversing all the branches and nodes of the tree, thereby suffering a performance worse than that of linear scan. If we use hashing, then we get no help for queries with large ranges. For example, if attribute A is restricted to range $a \leq A \leq b$, then we must look in the buckets for every value between a and b for possible values of A. There may easily be more values in this range than there are buckets, meaning that we must look in all, or almost all, the buckets. Hence, we need another data structure which is feasible for range queries.

Extended Range Trees. For numerical preferences we use a modified Range tree. Our extended Range tree (cp. Fig. 1) consists of a B^+-tree, where the leaves build a doubly linked list in a sorted order. Additional references to the first and the last element of the doubly linked list complete our modification.

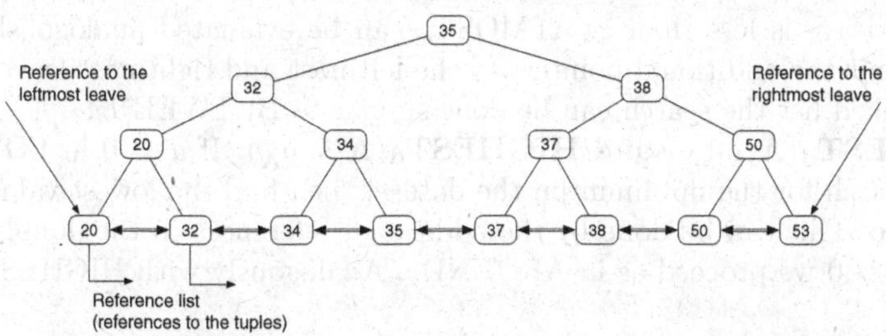

Fig. 1. A one-dimensional Range tree for the price (in thousands) in Table 1.

Thus an evaluation for a BETWEEN$_d$ preference consists of a lookup in the tree, iteration over part of the doubly linked list and the return of the reference list. Additionally the index holds references for the first and last element of the doubly linked list such that a lookup in the index can be skipped for the LOWEST$_d$, HIGHEST$_d$, ATMOST$_d$, and ATLEAST$_d$ preferences.

Index-Based Evaluation of Numerical Preference Queries. We now have to discuss how the search does work in detail. The correctness of the search procedure is guaranteed by the fact that the leaves are sorted.

BETWEEN$_\mathbf{d}$(A, [low; up]): If we want to answer BETWEEN$_d$(A, [low; up]) preference queries, we search for all points that are $\geq low$ and $\leq up$. The query proceeds by first searching for the leaf that has the largest value just less than or equal to low. It then traverses all the leaves using the forward pointers until a leaf that is just greater than up is reached. If no tuple in [low; up] is found, i.e., there is no match in the dataset, two cases may occur:

- **d = 0**: $d = 0$ means that the tuples with the lowest distance to the interval [low; up] are the preferred values. Consider the direct leaves left l and right r of [low; up] and compute their distance $d_l(low, l) = low - l$ and $d_r(up, r) = r - up$. The index with the shortest distance corresponds to the preferred values.

– **d > 0**: the preferred values lie in $[low - c \cdot d; low] \cup [up; up + c \cdot d]$, $c = 1, \ldots$, until $c \cdot d$ reaches the infimum/supremum of the domain of A. The intervals with the lowest c contain the best matches.

AROUND$_\mathbf{d}$(A, z): In AROUND$_d(A, z)$ the desired value should be z. If this is infeasible, values within a distance of d are acceptable. Hence, we first search for an exact match of z in the Range tree and if nothing is found, we continue as with the BETWEEN$_d$ preference.

ATLEAST$_\mathbf{d}$(A, z) and ATMOST$_\mathbf{d}$(A, z): These preferences correspond to a search in $[z; +\infty]$ and $[-\infty; z]$, respectively. For the ATLEAST$_d$ preference the search proceeds by returning all leaves that can be traversed using the backward pointers from the rightmost leave until an index entry $\leq z$ is found. For this we use the additional references to the doubly linked list. If z is not a node in the tree structure, the ATLEAST$_d$ preference returns the values with the lowest distance to z. Hence, we can proceed as above but have first to check if the rightmost leave is less than z. ATMOST$_d$ can be evaluated analogously. Note that without the additional pointers to the leftmost and rightmost leaves in the doubly linked list the search can be done similar to BETWEEN$_d$.

LOWEST$_\mathbf{d}$(A, inf$_\mathbf{A}$) and HIGHEST$_\mathbf{d}$(A, sup$_\mathbf{A}$): If $d = 0$ in LOWEST$_d$ we just search for the minimum in the dataset, i.e., find the lowest value in the Range tree. This can be done by the additional references to the doubly linked list. For $d > 0$ we proceed as in AROUND$_d$. Analogously with HIGHEST$_d$.

3.2 Indexes for Categorical Preferences

For the evaluation of categorical preferences we can use index structures which support *exact match queries*, because we always search for a perfect match in the index. All categorical preferences like POS, POS/NEG, etc., can be modeled using the LAYERED$_m(A, (L_1, \ldots, L_m))$ constructor. Hence, it is sufficient to consider indexing techniques for this preference.

Hash Index. If we want to evaluate a LAYERED$_m(A, (L_1, \ldots, L_m))$ preference, the idea is to search for all objects $t \in L_i$ successively, i.e., we do an exact match query for each t until we find a match. This can be seen in the following example.

Example 3. Consider Table 1 and its attribute *color* which should be indexed. We have 4 distinct colors and map them to the integers 0, 1, 2, 3 as in Fig. 2. The buckets contains linked lists with pointers to the tuples in the dataset. If we want to evaluate the preference $P :=$ LAYERED(color, ($L_1 :=$ {blue, red}, $L_2 :=$ {green})) we do a lookup for *blue* in the bucket directory ($h(blue) = 1$) and follow the pointers to the two objects with ID 3 and 4. Afterwards we search for *red* in the Hash index and find object 8. Since we already have perfect matches we do not have to consider L_2 anymore.

Fig. 2. Hash index. $B = 4$.

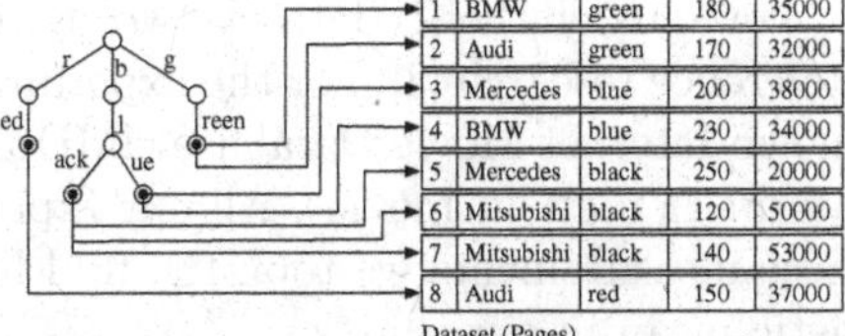

Fig. 3. Compressed Trie index.

Since the evaluation of LAYERED$_m$ is just to search the index for the values in L_1, and if none is found search for values in L_2, and so on, we get a *worst-case search complexity* of $|\bigcup_{i=1}^m L_i| \cdot \mathcal{O}(1)$ (all L_i sets must be searched in the worst-case). Note that in general we have $|\bigcup_{i=1}^m L_i| \ll n$ (n the size of the dataset) and therefore we speed-up the evaluation of a LAYERED$_m$ preference and all its sub-constructors.

Trie Index. The biggest use of tries is in *exact string* retrieval and hence are suitable for indexing data for LAYERED$_m$ preference queries. When a string is queried, the path from the root is traversed by looking up the characters in the query successively. If any character is absent, the query returns no answer. If the search ends in a final node (double circle in Fig. 3), the corresponding string is returned. For a query string of length l, the search finishes in $\mathcal{O}(l)$ time [2].

For a dataset of k distinct strings, a binary search tree requires $\mathcal{O}(\log_2(k))$ time to search a string. For large databases, l is much smaller than $\log_2(k)$ and, therefore, a trie searches more efficiently. The worst-case complexity to search for LAYERED$_m(A, (L_1, \ldots, L_m))$ is given by $|\bigcup_{i=1}^m L_i| \cdot \mathcal{O}(l)$, since we have to lookup each attribute value in all L_i.

Example 4. We construct a trie for the attribute *color* in Table 1. Strings with the same prefix such as "blue" and "black" share the same path up to the common prefix "bl". A space-saving version of the trie is given in Fig. 3, where all the unary nodes of a trie on a path are compressed into a single node. The edges are then labeled by substrings, and not necessarily single characters.

4 Experiments

In this section we show that our index approach outperforms a "linear scan" (**LinScan**) algorithm, which is a modified BNL with linear runtime [3], by far. In all our experiments the data tuples and index structures are held in main memory. This reduction of I/O-operations should favor the LinScan algorithm. Note that to the best of our knowledge our work is the first one on indexing base preferences and therefore there are no other index structures as competitors.

We implemented a Java 7.0 prototype, which is available as open source project on GitHub[1]. The experiments were performed on a common PC running Linux on an Intel Core1 Duo CPU with 3.33 GHz and 4 GB main memory.

[1] https://github.com/endresma/PreferenceIndex.git.

For our synthetic datasets we used the data generator commonly used in preference research [3]. For the experiments on real-world data, we used the well-known Internet Movie Database (IMDb, http://www.imdb.com), which contains information about movies. All our experiments were performed 100 times. From these measurements we took the mid half of the sorted data and use the arithmetic mean in our charts.

4.1 Numerical Index Structures

For numerical base preferences we used the Range tree index implementation as described in Sect. 3.1. All measurements on the Range tree index have been carried out with a BETWEEN_d preference as it can substitute all other numerical preferences. In addition, since our implementation of the Range tree holds references to the first and last element in the tree a lookup can be skipped for LOWEST_d, HIGHEST_d, ATMOST_d, and ATLEAST_d. Hence, we do not benchmark these preferences.

Synthetic Data – Gaussian Distribution. The following experiments use generated data on a Gaussian distribution. This is common in database experiments and allows to carefully explore the behavior of index methods. Each set of data contains a number of values between 0 and 1000 (the *range* of a data set).

Figure 4 shows the measured *execution times* in nanoseconds for BETWEEN_d. We varied the data size (number of tuples) from 10^2 to 10^6, the d parameter ($d = 0, 10$) and the interval borders *low* and *up*. Figure 4a and b model a "real" BETWEEN_d preference, whereas Fig. 4c corresponds to an AROUND_d preference. Note that we use a log scale for the y-axis. It is apparent, that the time used to build the index is multiple times that needed to evaluate the preferences with the LinScan algorithm. However, if the index is constructed, the index based evaluation of the preferences is hardly noteworthy.

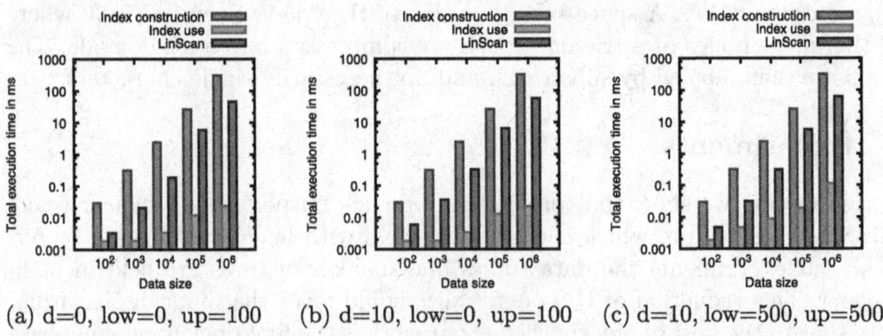

(a) d=0, low=0, up=100 (b) d=10, low=0, up=100 (c) d=10, low=500, up=500

Fig. 4. Execution time (in ms) for the evaluation of $\text{BETWEEN}_d(A; [low, up])$.

Figure 5 shows the maximal relative difference w.r.t. the execution time (exTime) of LinScan and the index-based evaluation of BETWEEN_d preferences with varying intervals [*low*; *up*] on $d = 0$ and $d = 10$. That means, we compute *deltaTime* := *LinScan exTime* - *Index exTime* and plot the ratio

$$\gamma_1 := \text{deltaTime}/\text{LinScan exTime} \tag{1}$$

on the y-axis. This shows that with increasing data size the difference between the LinScan execution time and index execution time increases as well. Our measurements suggest that the index is more than two times faster than the LinScan even on small relations and as expected much faster for large data sets.

In Fig. 6 we present the ratio of the execution time of LinScan and the index-based preference evaluation on different $[low, up]$ intervals, i.e.,

$$\gamma_2 := \text{LinScan exTime}/\text{Index exTime} \tag{2}$$

Thereby, the first three measurements have the same low and up parameters, simulating an AROUND$_d$ preference. It is probable that these sets have been the fastest because of the relatively smaller size of the BMO-set. In summary, the index-based approach is hundreds to thousands of times faster on a dataset with only 10^6 objects.

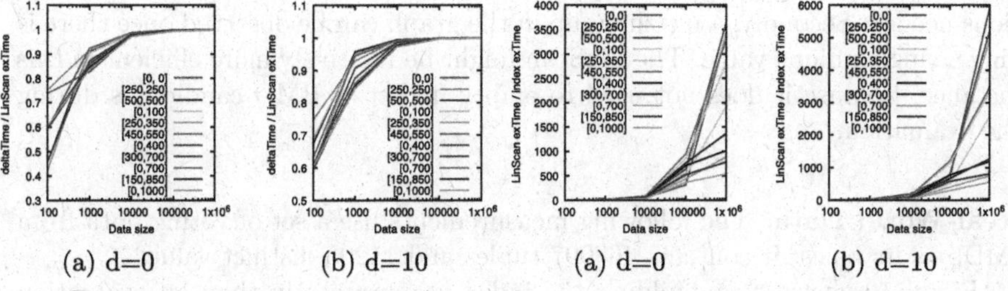

Fig. 5. γ_1 for BETWEEN$_d$. **Fig. 6.** γ_2 for BETWEEN$_d$.

Influence of the Number of Distinct Values. Both the trees height and the size of the doubly linked list are determined by the number of distinct values within the dataset. The ratio between the data size and the number of distinct values is a significant factor for the effectiveness of an index. We use different sets of generated data to measure the behavior of our index techniques. Each set of data contains 10^6 objects with a varying number of distinct values from 1 to 10^6.

As the operation for inserting a value into the Range tree index is costly we expected the index build time to rise proportionally to the number of distinct values in the dataset. This has been measured and can be seen in Fig. 7. The LinScan execution time is nearly constant because of the linear scan over 10^6 tuples each time. The index execution time is much better than LinScan even for 10^6 distinct values. Again, a log scale is used for the y-axis.

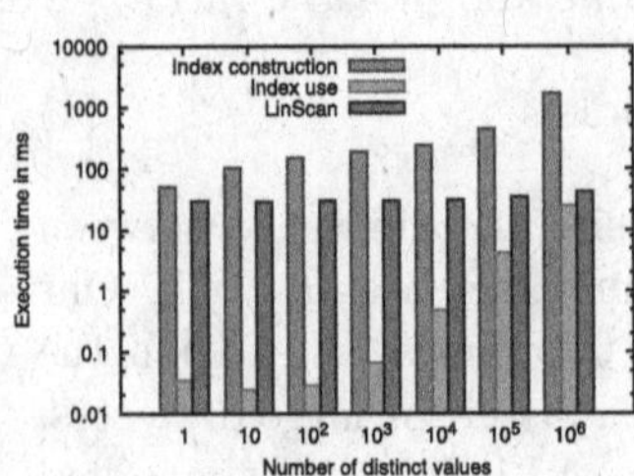

Fig. 7. Runtime for $\text{BETWEEN}_d(A, [0, 10^6])$.

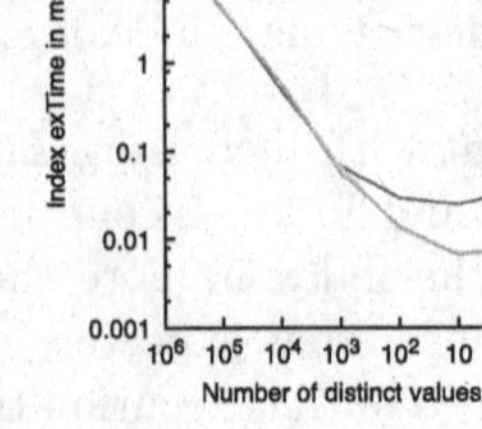

Fig. 8. Execution time.

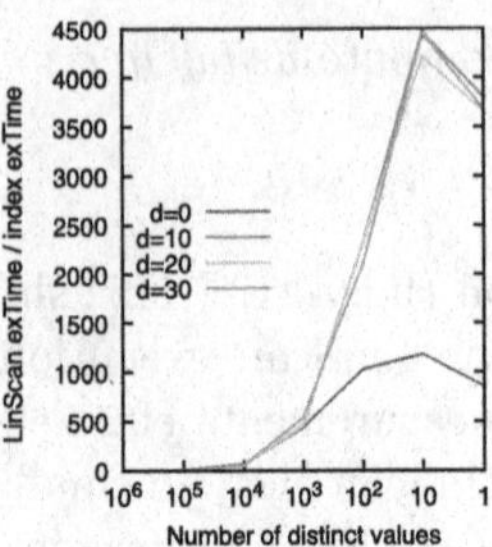

Fig. 9. γ_2

Similarly the index performs worse if there are only distinct values, cp. Fig. 8, where we used 10^6 tuples, varied the d value and the number of distinct values. Nevertheless, the index still performs better than the LinScan algorithm.

Two interesting observations can be made with Fig. 9. Firstly, the evaluation of a BETWEEN_d preference that has a parameter $d > 0$ is more costly than without. Thus the gain when using an index is greater as there are fewer evaluations needed. Secondly, a puzzling dip in the graph can be observed once there is only a single unique value. The LinScan might be relatively more efficient in this instance, because it does not need to empty its list of BMO candidates during the evaluation.

Real-World Data. The following measurements use a set of voting data from IMDb as its basis. It contains 468097 tuples and 11295 distinct values.

Figure 10 shows that building the index is more costly than an evaluation with LinScan. Again, once the index is constructed, the evaluation is much faster than LinScan. In this experiment we used $d = 0, 10, 50$, varied the BETWEEN_d preference, and plotted the *execution time per object* in ns.

Figure 11 presents the γ_1 ratio (Eq. 1) and that the evaluation on the index is much faster than with LinScan. We used different $[low; up]$ intervals for the BETWEEN_d preference and varied the d from 0 to 50.

In Fig. 12 we present γ_2 (Eq. 2) and present the ratio of the LinScan execution time to the index execution time with different $[low; up]$ intervals and d values. Again, the index-based evaluation is more costly for a d parameter $d > 0$, but still better than LinScan.

In all our real world experiments the observations made earlier on synthetic data were confirmed. Hence, our index-based evaluation of numerical base preferences is also applicable for real data sets.

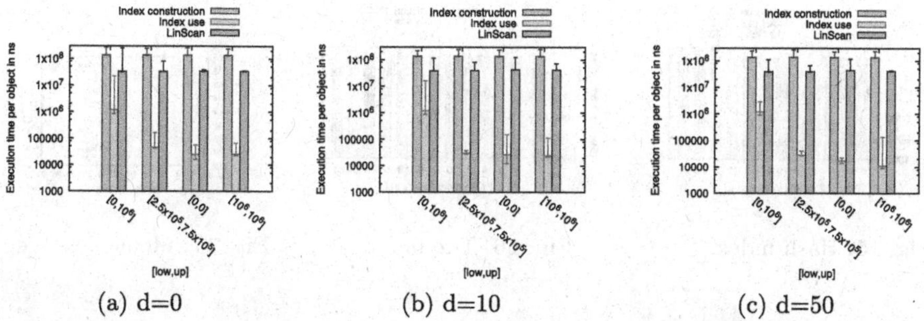

(a) d=0 (b) d=10 (c) d=50

Fig. 10. Execution times on the IMDb real world data set.

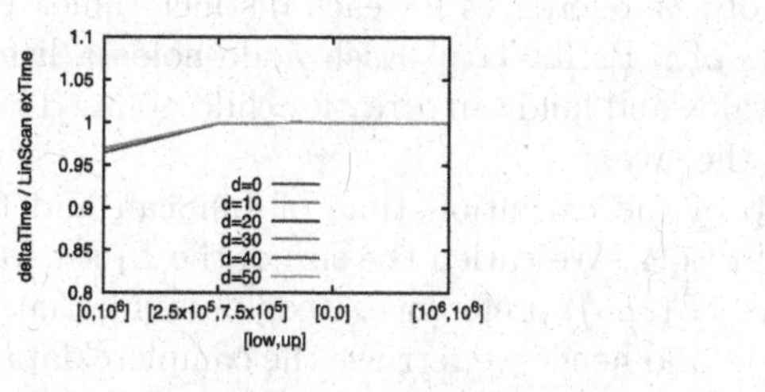

Fig. 11. γ_1

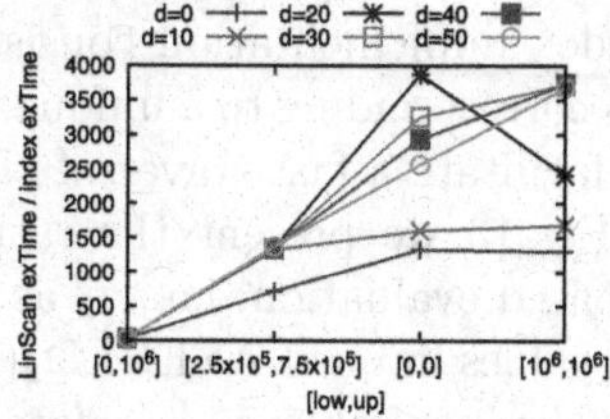

Fig. 12. γ_2

4.2 Categorical Index Structures

Our categorical preference LAYERED$_m$ was analyzed on real-world data only, because there is no useful and reasonable data generator for strings. The following measurements use a set of genre data from IMDb as its basis. It contains 1580880 objects and 31 distinct values. In the measurements we used the preference LAYERED$_2(A, (L_1, L_2))$, which is a POS preference, and varied the L_1 set in its size w.r.t. the distinct values in the data set.

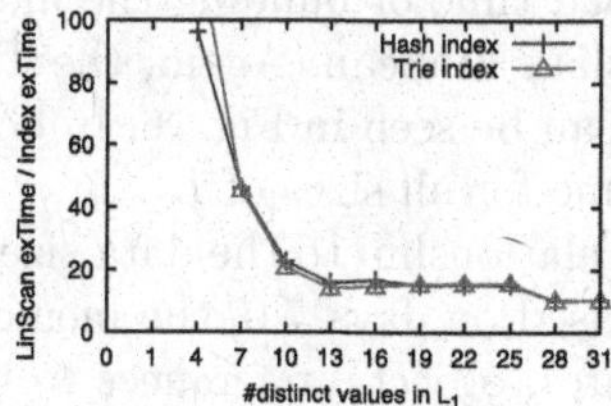

Fig. 13. γ_2 w.r.t. different sizes of L_1.

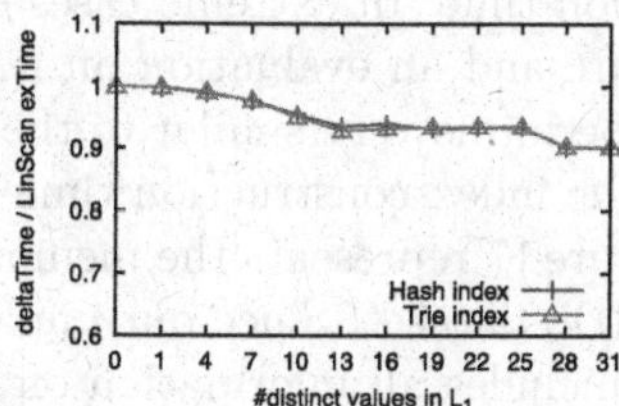

Fig. 14. γ_1 w.r.t. different sizes of L_1.

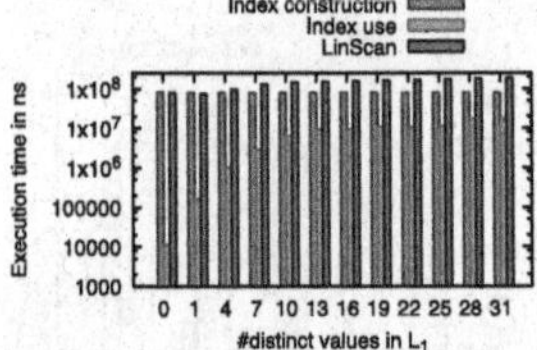

Fig. 15. Hash index.

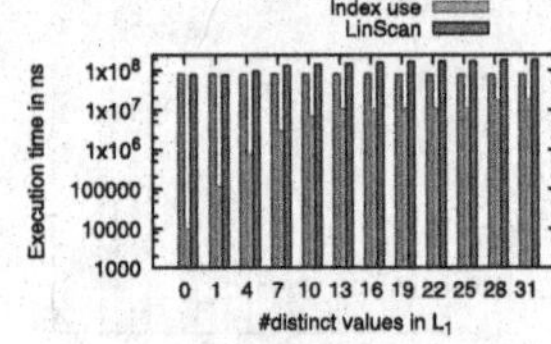

Fig. 16. Trie index.

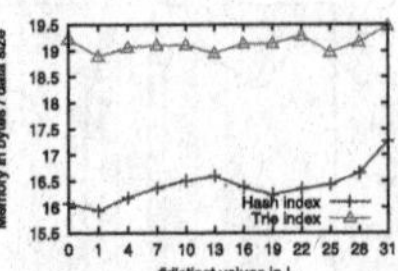

Fig. 17. Memory usage.

We compared the Hash index and the Trie index to LinScan and to each other. The Hash index implementation is based on the standard Java `HashMap` containing a corresponding list of object references for each distinct value. The Trie index implementation consists of a Prefix-Tree. Each node holds a list of objects corresponding to a unique value and holds an array for child nodes. These arrays facilitate a fast traversal of the tree.

In Fig. 13 we present the ratio of the execution time of LinScan and the index-based evaluation, i.e., γ_2 as in Eq. 2. We varied the size of the L_1 set from 0 to 31 values in our LAYERED$_2(A, (L_1, L_2))$ preference. Keep in mind, that we have 31 distinct values in our dataset and hence we retrieve the complete dataset in the case of $|L_1| = 31$ and only a fraction of the set if $|L_1| \rightarrow 0$. We skipped the results for $|L_1| = 0, 1$, because the ratio is too high for a usable presentation (actually it is about 8000). Our figure states that the index is extremely fast for small L_1 sets and still much better than LinScan if we have to check all values.

Figure 14 presents the γ_1 ratio (Eq. 1), i.e., the maximal relative difference in the execution time between LinScan and the index-based approaches. The x-axis denotes how many of the distinct values are contained in layer L_1. It shows that the index performs best for small layers and is much better than LinScan even for a layer containing all distinct values. The two index structures Hash index and Trie index perform very similar.

Something more interesting can be observed for the Hash index in Fig. 15. Depending on the layer L_1 size, the index build time is less than the LinScan execution time. In extreme cases even the combined time of building the index structure and an evaluation on it, can be faster than LinScan. Again, the Trie index performs very similar to the Hash index as can be seen in Fig. 16. In both cases the index construction time is nearly the same for all sizes of L_1.

Figure 17 represents the memory usage in the relationship to the data size of the IMDb dataset. Since our implementation is based on Java 7.0, the memory usage includes all information on all data structures, objects, references to the objects, additional memory requirements for the Java engine, ...[2] As one can see, the Hash index needs much less memory than the Trie index, but both have a similar execution time behavior.

[2] We used the Java Runtime object with the methods `totalMemory()` and `freeMemory()` to determine the total amount of used memory in the JVM.

5 Conclusion and Future Work

In this paper we presented index structures for preference database queries. Our indexing techniques rely on common database indexing approaches and therefore do not require additional adaption of a database back-end engine. One advantage of our approach is that we can provide the BMO points progressively, since index structures support this in a natural way.

Our extensive performance study shows that the proposed index methods provide quick response times compared to a linear scan when the index is build once. Hence, as with all indexes, indexing make sense with quite static data. In addition, since we rely on common index structures, building and maintaining costs for our preference indexes remain unchanged.

For future work we plan to develop indexing methods for ordered importance of preferences, i.e., Prioritization as well as geo-spatial preferences and preferences based on full text.

References

1. Bayer, R., Unterauer, K.: Prefix B-trees. ACM Trans. Database Syst. (TODS) **2**(1), 11–26 (1977)
2. Bhattacharya, A.: Fundamentals of Database Indexing and Searching. CRC Press, Chapman & Hall Book, Boca Raton (2015)
3. Börzsönyi, S., Kossmann, D., Stocker, K.: The skyline operator. In: Proceedings of ICDE 2001, pp. 421–430. IEEE, Washington, DC (2001)
4. Chaudhuri, S., Dalvi, N., Kaushik, R.: Robust cardinality and cost estimation for skyline operator. In: Proceedings of ICDE 2006, p. 64. IEEE Computer Society, Washington, DC (2006)
5. Chomicki, J., Ciaccia, P., Meneghetti, N.: Skyline queries, front and back. In: Proceedings of SIGMOD 2013, vol. 42, no. 3, pp. 6–18 (2013)
6. Kießling, W.: Foundations of preferences in database systems. In: Proceedings of VLDB 2002, pp. 311–322. VLDB, Hong Kong, China (2002)
7. Kießling, W., Endres, M., Wenzel, F.: The preference SQL system - an overview. Bull. Tech. Commitee Data Eng. **34**(2), 11–18 (2011). IEEE Computer Society
8. Lueker, G,S.: A data structure for orthogonal range queries. In: Proceedings of FOCS 1978, SFCS 1978, pp. 28–34. IEEE CS, Washington, DC (1978)
9. Mandl, S., Kozachuk, O., Endres, M., Kießling, W.: Preference analytics in EXASolution. In: Proceedings of BTW 2015 (2015)

Knowledge Discovery and Information/Data Retrieval

Content-Based Meta-Discovery Service of Remote Sensing Images

Bordogna Gloria[1(✉)], Ceresi Andrea[2], and Sterlacchini Simone[2]

[1] IREA CNR, Milan, Italy
bordogna.g@irea.cnr.it
[2] IDPA CNR, Milan, Italy
ceresi.a@irea.cnr.it, simone.sterlacchini@idpa.cnr.it

Abstract. The paper proposes a novel perspective on Web discovery services of remote sensing images and derived products currently available through the Web portals of providers managing big geo-spatial data repositories. Actual discovery services do not provide facilities for ranking images based on queries specifying spatial-content conditions, i.e. asking for images having desired pixels values in a Region Of Interest (ROI). Our objective is to enable such a facility by designing both a query language with linguistic terms to ask for the desired qualitative characteristics of the image content in a ROI, and a retrieval mechanism to evaluate the degrees of satisfaction of the images with respect to the query spatial-content conditions. The retrieval mechanism is implemented as a meta-discovery service, i.e., as a front-end on the discovery service of the image provider, that does not need to access the images, but just their previews, empowering the retrieval with ranking capabilities. It requires a spatial-content inverted index, previously built off-line by processing all image previews so as to achieve scalability and retrieval efficiency.

Keywords: Spatial-content inverted index · Fuzzy sets · Discovery service · Remote sensing images

1 Introduction

Down-stream services of remote sensing images such as those provided by the major international organizations for Earth Observation (namely the ESA Earth Online catalogues for SENTINEL data products, the ASI eGeos catalogue for COSMO-SkyMed Data and products, the NASA catalogue for MODIS data products, and so forth) are becoming more and more used for different purposes spanning from agriculture to risk mapping and ecological studies [1]. With the advent of the Copernicus initiative, in a short time big geo-data time series of remote sensing images and products derived by their processing with high spatial and temporal resolution will be available free of charge. This poses new challenges to the discovery services of such highly dynamic repositories, which need to improve the current search capabilities by exploiting techniques of content based image retrieval based on the indexing of the visual content of images, such as color, texture, shapes [2–4]. In fact, current search facilities for image

H. Christiansen et al. (Eds.): FQAS 2017, LNAI 10333, pp. 153–163, 2017.
DOI: 10.1007/978-3-319-59692-1_13

retrieval offered to final users, the image stakeholders, rely on textual metadata describing ancillary information about the images, such as author (in terms of sensor description), creation date, quality (spatial and thematic resolution), georeference (the coordinates of the Bounding Box (BB) of Earth covered by the image), and keywords (usually about the image semantics, i.e. what the pixel values represent). In the case of raw images, such as the optical multi-spectral ones, the semantics of pixel values can concern the detected reflectance in one or multiple bands of the visible and near-infrared electromagnetic spectrum. In the case of remote sensing image *products* (images derived by processing the raw ones with atmospheric noise filters and projection distortions correction algorithms), pixel values become an indicator of some property of the Earth surface, such as the Normalized Difference Vegetation Index (NDVI) – a proxy of the vegetation vigor – a Normalized Water Index (NWI) – a proxy of the presence of rivers, water basins and wetlands – and many others. In metadata records we usually find very little about the semantics of pixel values of the images, although international standard schemas encompass this possibility. [5].

With no information on the spatial distribution of the pixel values, the ability to answer spatial-content requests is impossible. Nevertheless, often stakeholders of remote sensing images are interested in analyzing a small area of Earth, named "Region Of Interest" (ROI) – appearing as a subpart of the image frame – only if the ROI has, on average, a specific property value.

For example, agronomists need to monitor agronomic parcels in time to forecast and plan agro-practices, such as the most suitable dates for crops' harvesting. To this end they need to compare the NDVI of the ROI in the most recent available image with the long term average maximum NDVI of that same ROI. For each year within a past period of time, they have to retrieve the image in which the ROI had its maximum NDVI during the year to compute the long-term average maximum NDVI of the ROI [7]. For carrying out this activity the current practice is formulating a request for images of NDVI containing the ROI and detected during a past time range, and then visually inspecting all the retrieved image previews to identify those with high NDVI values in the ROI, so as to download and process only the needed images. When considering long periods of time and image time-series with frequent revisiting time, this is a time-consuming activity since one has to inspect hundreds of images, and after a while one can give up or hurry up to finish the job, thus possibly applying inhomogeneous criteria.

Our objective is to automatize such a process by designing a meta-discovery service capable of answering spatial-content-based queries by retrieving only the images satisfying the spatial content conditions, for example a *very high* level of NDVI in a specific ROI. This can help agronomists to save their time when the number of images is huge, and to perform a selection applying a more homogenous criterion than the visual inspection, invariably affected by subjectivity.

By proposing this paper, we aim at empowering the current discovery services of big geo-data archives, without requiring the extension of current standard metadata formats, and by minimizing the number of images to download. The proposed meta-discovery approach needs first to download the images' *previews* – low-sized quicklook images that form part of each raw image's ancillary data – and to analyze their pixel values to generate a spatial-content inverted index. When a user submits a query, it is split into two parts: the selection conditions that can be answered based on metadata are sent to the provider discovery service so for it to identify a first set of images. These images are filtered basing on the satisfaction of the spatial-content conditions, evaluated by exploiting the previously-built spatial-content inverted index. This way, a matching score is computed for each image preview so that only the K-top ranked corresponding images are downloaded. The approach exploits a fuzzy-based compressed representation of image previews content, defined in this paper, by means of terms from a formal language and exploits current scalable techniques of textual information retrieval to both represent and retrieve georeferenced images whose content may match, even partially, a spatial-content-based query [8]. An example of application in a case study using a set of NDVI images derived by MODIS data processing is discussed.

2 The Spatial-Content Representation Indexing Structure

A well-known method to define a fuzzy representation of the visual image content is based on first partitioning the image into several segments (objects), for each segment extracting appropriate features, such as the segment color and texture, and finally classifying them in a fuzzy framework, resulting in a content interpretation closer to the human perception [8, 9].

The First of all we are going to define the spatial-content representation of an image preview, and then we will describe the processes needed to automatically generate the inverted index.

Given a preview of $N \times N$ pixels of a monochromatic image, taking values on a numeric domain D, we represent it by m regular tiles, with $m \ll N \times N$, and set depending on the minimum dimension of a ROI within the image preview that the remote sensing experts deem as necessary to characterize the ROI content. The ROI dimension is defined basing on the use cases of the service. For example, in the agronomic context, the minimum ROI dimension corresponds to the dimension of an agronomic area in the preview. The greater the number of tiles (m), the finer the spatial representation of the content. A preview P is represented by a tuple:

$$R(P) = \left\langle PID, L, \cup_k = 1, \ldots, m\left\{s_k, z - code_k\right\}\right\rangle$$

where:

- PID is a unique identifier of the image associated with preview P;
- L is a string of characters defining the name of the property represented in the image, e.g. NDVI;
- s_k is a string of characters in a set $\{A, B, C, \ldots Z\}$ among which a lexicographic order is defined, $A < B < C < \ldots < Z$; s_k is a term of the formal language that we defined to synthetize the values of the pixels within the tiles as it will be described below; it has a maximum dimension of h characters, where h is the quantization number of the domain D of the pixel values;
- $z\text{-}code_k$ is a natural number uniquely identifying the position of the k tile within the image previews. This means that there is a bi-univocal relationship between a *z-code*

and the pair of coordinates (i, j) of the row and column where the tile is located in the image previews.

In the case of an *RGB* image preview, we have $R(I_R)$, $R(I_G)$, $R(I_B)$, one for each color.

2.1 Generation of the Content String and Content Index

The domain D of pixel values is partitioned into h linguistic values $\{v_1, \ldots, v_h\}$ whose semantic is defined by overlapping triangular-shaped membership functions on D (see Fig. 1) so that the order among their cores, $core\left(\mu_{v_1}\right) < \ldots < core(\mu_{v_h})$, induces an order among the linguistic values $v_1 < \ldots < v_h$ [10]. To encode this order, each linguistic value v_j is uniquely associated with a lexicographically ordered character set $\{A, B, C, \ldots, Z\}$ with cardinality equal to h so that v_1 is associated with A, v_2 with B, and so forth. The value h is chosen as an odd number not greater than 7 in order to allow humans to discern the semantics of the elements. For example, given $h = 7$ linguistic values we can define their membership functions as shown in Fig. 1:

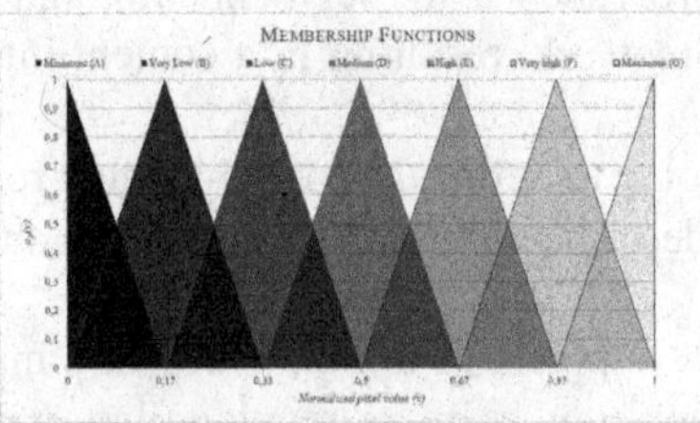

Fig. 1. Membership functions defining the semantics of the linguistic terms that are used to define a fuzzy partition of the domain of pixel values.

Minimum < *VeryLow* < *Low* < *Medium* < *High* < *VeryHigh* < *Maximum* they are encoded by characters $A < B < C < D < E < F < G$ respectively.

For each tile t of an image preview P, a character string s is created so that the order of the characters in s reflects the order among the not null values $F(v_i)$, with $i = 1, \ldots, h$, in which $F(v_i)$ is computed by $F{:}[0, 1]h \rightarrow R$ defined as follows:

$$F\left(v_i\right) = \sum\nolimits_{p \in t} \mu_{vi}(p) \tag{1}$$

where $p \in D$ is the value of a pixel within the tile t of preview P, and $\mu_{vi}(p)$ is the membership degree of p to the fuzzy set defining the meaning of the linguistic term v_i.

Given the linguistic values $v_1, \ldots, v_h$ so that $v_i < v_j \forall i < j$, and the ordered character set $\mathbf{A} = \left\{A_1, A_2, \ldots, A_h | A_i < A_j \forall i < j\right\}$, the string $s = s[1], s[2], \ldots, s[h]$, is generated by concatenating characters $s[1], s[2], \ldots, s[h] \in \mathbf{A}$ so that:

$$s[i] = A_k | F(v_k) = Argmax_i\left\{F\left(v_1\right), F\left(v_2\right), \ldots F\left(v_h\right)\right\} \wedge F(v_k) > 0 \tag{2}$$

where $Argmax_i$ is the function that selects the i-th greatest of its arguments.

Let us make an example. Given the following linguistic values: $\{Low, Medium, High\}$ (so that $n = 3$) labelled by $\{A, B, C\}$ respectively, a tile represented by a *content-string* $s = ABC$ will mostly contain *low* pixel values, some *medium* values and a few *high* values, meaning that it will quite probably represent a woodland or a large crop area with little or no snow or clouds. A tile represented by "*CAB*" will mostly contain *high* pixel values, some *low* pixel values and lastly a few *medium* values: it will be a tile in which white areas interweave with very dark ones – the latter in smaller but noticeable account – forming what is likely to be a portion of a city, or a mountain range during the thawing season. Notice that the number (n) of the linguistic values determines the maximum length of the *content-strings*, so that the more the linguistic values, the finer is the tile representation: having {*None*, *Low*, *Medium*, *High*, *Maximum*} would produce finer descriptions, even not necessarily longer strings though. It is also noticeable that the shorter the *content-string*, the lower the pixels' variability in the tile: still having $n = 3$, a string "*A*" means that the associated tile only contains *low* pixel values: an almost totally dark area, likely to be a water basin. At this stage, it is up to the user to associate a semantic relationship between the linguistic values and the specific real entities she/he is looking for, although an automatic association can be done, as will we see further. As to these examples, a white area (*content-string* "*C*") can be a cloud *or* a snow-covered plain, and it is up to the user to decide that by searching "C" he means searching a cloud. However, as we will show in Sect. 3, lower level of classification can be automatically performed.

We name such strings "*content words*", since they represent the image contents like terms represent contents of textual documents. All content words s of all tiles in all images are organized in a textual *inverted index* data structure [4, 8]: for each entry s in the dictionary, that can be structured as a B-tree, its posting list contains elements of the kind $\langle z - code, [PID_1, PID_2, \ldots] \rangle$. This way, when searching a string s we can know which tiles and images it represents:

$$s \rightarrow \langle z - code_1, [PID_1, PID_2, \ldots] \rangle, \langle z - code_2, [PID_1, PID_2, \ldots] \rangle, \ldots \tag{3}$$

For example, by searching a regular expression "A*" in which "*" is the wildcard we can retrieve all the images mostly containing *low* values in any of their tiles just by a binary search in the dictionary.

2.2 Generation of the *Z-Code* and Spatial Index

If we want to efficiently search the images with a tile containing a desired linguistic value we need a spatial indexing too. This is useful if one is interested in images containing a ROI having desired linguistic value of the pixels. Let us now describe how the *z-code* is generated for a tile. To this end we order the tiles by a *z-order* code [12]. Having $m = 2M$ tiles, even number, the tiles are sequentially numbered by applying the Morton coding: the z-order code of a tile is computed by first associating to each tile the pair of coordinate indices (i,j) with $i,j = 1, \ldots, K$ and $K^2 = m$, representing the tile position along the x and y axis; then to convert these coordinates to a Morton code, *z-code,* we have to convert the decimal values of coordinates to binary and to interleave the bits of each coordinate.

For example given a tile t with the coordinates $(4, 2)$, their binary representation is $\langle 001;010 \rangle$, and the correspondent binary representation of the *z-code* is [001001] which corresponds to represent $(4, 2)$ with the $z - code = 36$.

This allows mapping the bi-dimensional information of the tiles coordinates into one dimension, while preserving information on the spatial proximity between tiles: two tiles with close *z-codes* (close integers) are also spatially close, except for unavoidable jumps. Once tiles are sorted using their *z-codes*, any one-dimensional data structure, such as a B-tree, or hash table, can be used to organize and search them. In fact, the resulting ordering of *z-codes* is equivalent to the order one would get by a spatial access method in a spatial data structure such as a quadtree [12].

Now, we can organize the posting lists in the inverted index so that each entry is ordered with respect to *z-code*.

This way if one searches images that contain mostly "*low*" values in a ROI covered by tile in position [*z-code*], one first seeks "A*" in the dictionary by applying a binary search, then retrieves the posting lists of all entries in the dictionary starting with "A"; finally, in each posting list a binary search of [*z-code*] is performed to retrieve the *PIDs* satisfying the query.

Let us assume to have two image previews, depicted in Fig. 2(b) and (c) as a result of a query to the provider discovery service, and let us assume that the pixel values are discretized into three ($h = 3$) linguistic values $\{A, B, C\}$ and 16 tiles ($m = 16$) as in Fig. 2 (a).

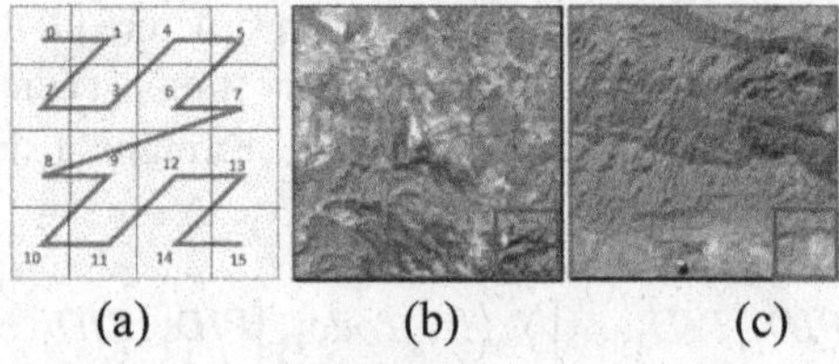

Fig. 2. (a) Z-order codes (*z-code*) of the tiles in image previews $m = 16$. In the image previews (b) and (c) the green color represents *high* NDVI, while the brown color depicts *low* NDVI and light brown *medium* NDVI.

The content strings of the tiles of the two images Fig. 2(b) and (c) and the inverted index are shown in Table 1. It can be observed that the dictionary contains the ordered *content strings s* while the posting file holds their occurrences within the images ordered by tiles as specified by their *z- codes*. The length of the content strings reflect the homogeneity of the pixel values within the tiles with respect to the three values *low, medium, high.*

A query asking images containing the tile with $z - code = 15$ with *high* values (i.e. the query "C*") will be evaluated by searching the string starting with "C" in the dictionary. "C" will be found with 1 access assuming to copy in memory 4 words; then in the correspondent posting list the *z-code* 15 will be searched with a binary search so that finally the image preview (c) will be retrieved.

Notice that we can apply some similarity matching when we do not find in the dictionary the search string: in such cases the string with the greatest Common Subsequence (LCS), with the search string is selected and a score is computed as the LCS. This value is used as Retrieval Status Value (RSV) for the correspondent image. For example, if one searches "BCA" in the dictionary, which is not present, "BC" will be selected since its LCS $= 0,66$.

Table 1. Content-spatial inverted index. Brackets are not part of the original data structure, and are shown here just to help identify the relating image in Fig. 2.

A	7 (c),
AB	11 (b), 12 (b), 14 (b), 15 (b)
ABC	9 (b),
AC	4 (c), 5 (c), 6 (c) 12 (c),
ACB	13 (c)
BA	14 (c)
BC	0 (b), 1 (b), 2 (b), 3 (b), 4 (b), 5 (b), 6 (b), 7 (b), 10 (c), 11 (c)
C	0 (c), 1 (c), 2 (c), 3 (c), 8 (b) (c), 9 (c), 10 (b) 13 (b), 15 (c)

A similarity matching can also be applied to the *z-code* search so as to allow a given tolerance on the position, for example a maximum distance of 1. If one looks for string "BC" within tile 9, the image (c) will be retrieved since in the posting list of "BC" we have tile 10 of image (c) which is at distance 1 from 9.

3 The Spatial-Content-Based Querying

A request to the meta-discovery service is composed of two parts:

- PART I – The first part of the query specifies the selection conditions that can be answered by the provider discovery service on the bases of the metadata. These conditions specify the ROI by a BB or a *geographic-name,* the desired timestamp of the image (or a temporal relationship), the semantic of the image content by a *label,* desired resolution and so on The conditions in Part I are submitted to the provider discovery service, that retrieves the PIDs of those images satisfying all of them.
- PART II – The second part of the query specifies the spatial-content conditions. They are evaluated by accessing the spatial-content index to retrieve the PIDs satisfying each of them. Finally, their RSVs are combined. During query evaluation the *query term* specifying the content-based condition is translated into a linguistic term and further to *content-string* and the pair of coordinates (i, j) is automatically mapped into a *z-order code.* Notice that we can select *query terms* from a controlled dictionary where each term is the name of a real world entity, such as *cloud, meadow, urban area*, that might appear into the images and that can be associated with the linguistic terms previously introduced: for example in an NDVI image database, "*cloud*" is synonymous of "*very high*" NDVI, "*meadow*" is associated with "*medium*" or

"*medium-low*" NDVI depending on the season. The result is a list of images' PIDs, ranked in decreasing order of satisfaction of the query conditions.

- When more pairs ⟨*query term*, *tile coordinates* (i, j)⟩ are specified in the same query, they can be aggregated either by the fuzzy "AND" or by the fuzzy "OR" operators, which are resolved by merging the ranked lists each pair evaluation produces by the *min* or the *max* of the RSVs respectively.

The last part of the query evaluation consists in selecting from the candidate list retrieved by query part 1 only the PIDs that satisfy query part 2, that is PIDs with $RSV > 0$ and in presenting them ranked according to the decreasing values of their RSVs.

4 Experiment

In order to evaluate the feasibility of the approach we simulated a content-based meta-discovery on a sample collection of time series of NDVI image (whose domain is $D = [0, 1]$) computed for the time period between 2010 to 2015 from MODIS multi-spectral remote sensing images with a revisiting period of 7 days. The images have distinct BB and a dimension of 1580 KB each. So conducted the experiment simulates a worse scenario with respect to a real one, where the dimension of the image previews is smaller in size. First of all, in order to test scalability and efficiency several indexing processes have been performed on a PC with 16 MB RAM and Intel i7 4th generation processor, 7200 rpm HD with increasing numbers of tiles and linguistic values with triangular shape. Table 2 reports the dimension of the metadata, the indexing process elapsed time and the compression ratios with respect to the metadata and index. The compression ratio determines the granularity of the ROI that can be specified in a query. Our intention is to provide a discovery service capable to select an ordered list of images that match the query condition on a minimum ROI (a BB) as specified by a stakeholder. This BB dimension determines the number of tiles. The number of linguistic values determines the granularity of the query terms that can be specified. To select the proper number of tiles we specified the minimum ROI (45.459;9.509;45.157;10.078) corresponding to the cultivated plains of Lombardy region, South East of Milano and North West of Cremona, extending for about 20 km^2. This ROI dimension determined the choice of the compression ratio close to 2000 obtained with 64 tiles. Furthermore eight linguistic values have been considered, seven of which with triangular shaped membership functions evenly distributed on [0, 1] as depicted in Fig. 1 and a point-like membership function for no data values defined as follows: $\mu_{NoData}(-1) = 1$ else $\mu_{NoData}(v) = 0$ for $v \neq -1$.

The objective of the query session was to retrieve images in which the specified ROIs, that we know being agronomic districts, thus cultivated with crops or pasture, are in a particular phase of vegetation growth: they can be crops at their apex, or in a rotating phase when distinct crops are in distinct growth phases ion the same ROI, or in the rest season.

Table 2. Indexing performance.

Number of tiles					
Number linguistic terms	Metadata dimension	Index dimension	In dexing time	Images/metadata compression ratio	Images/index compression ratio
4(2 × 2)					
5	7061	82744	30″	61907,5	5282,9
7	7098	82070	36″	61584,8	5326,3
9	8145	85178	36″	53668,3	5131,9
13	9226	88668	38″	47380,1	4929,9
16(4 × 4)					
5	25677	114646	31″	17024,1	3812,9
7	26151	115148	36″	16715,6	3796,2
9	30001	125410	36″	14570,5	3485,6
13	34318	137827	37″	12737,6	3171,6
64(8 × 8)					
5	92485	215680	31″	4726,5	2026,7
7	96234	219511	37″	4542,4	1991,4
9	109464	247301	37″	3993,4	1767,6
13	126414	285835	39″	3457,9	1529,3
256(16 × 16)					
5	338843	575559	31″	1290,1	759,5
7	362619	602552	37″	1205,5	725,5
9	405906	671909	37″	1076,9	650,6
13	466782	785128	39″	936,5	556,8
1024(32 × 32)					
5	3432298	4839002	36″	127,4	90,3
7	3558918	4982012	39″	122,8	87,7
9	3686587	5163856	41″	118,6	84,7
13	3890199	5486662	43″	112,4	79,7
4096(64 × 64)					
5	17728559	24458585	43″	24,7	17,9
7	18319131	25096190	46″	23,9	17,4
9	18646665	25539918	49″	23,4	17,1
13	19299867	26474816	56″	22,6	16,5
16384(128 × 128)					
5	70039113	96485408	1′2″	6,2	4,5
7	72163621	98728312	1′11″	6,1	4,4
9	72804625	99622136	1′16″	6,0	4,4
13	74607471	102105390	1′28″	5,9	4,3

Maximum values are mostly due to the presence of clouds, while, when asking "*crop harvesting time*" associated with *medium* NDVI, we expected in top positions of the retrieved list the images taken during summer time, the period in which the vegetation is at the apex in the agronomic district: thus, in evaluating the precision of the retrieval with respect to such queries we considered that the correct answers are images with timestamp during summertime, when the crops were at the maximum vigorous in the ROI. Conversely, we expected in top positions the images taken in wintertime when asking for "*bare soil*" associated with *minimum-low* NDVI, when meadows are in the resting season, and the images taken either in spring or in autumn when asking for "*rotating crops*" associated with *low-medium NDVI* in the same ROI.

The Recall and Precision obtained for six queries are shown in Table 3 which outlines a greater average precision with respect to recall which is actually more suitable for a discovery service, where one wants to minimize the download of images which are not relevant to the request, while is interested in obtaining one or at most a few relevant images.

Table 3. Recall and Precision for six queries.

	Precision	Recall
q1	1.00	0.36
q2	0.53	0.40
q3	1.00	0.21
q4	0.66	0.93
q5	1.00	0.74
q6	1.00	0.70
Average	0.86	0.56

5 Conclusion

The proposal has been conceived for empowering current discovery services of big geo-data repositories of remote sensing image products with content-based image retrieval capabilities. As far as we know this is a novel feature in the context of remote sensing image provider discovery services. It is based on a simple, effective and original fuzzy content and spatial based representation of the image variable, that exploits current textual information retrieval techniques for achieving scalability. Further work is needed in order to perform a thorough implementation and evaluation of the proposal.

Acknowledgements. The present work was carried out within the SIMULATOR-ADS project funded by Regione Lombardia grant POR FESR 2014-2020 and STRESS project, funded by Fondazione Cariplo 2016.

References

1. Nogueras-Iso, J., Zarazaga-Soria, F.J., Béjar, R., Álvarez, P.J., Muro-Medrano, P.R.: OGC Catalog Services: a key element for the development of Spatial Data Infrastructures. Comput. Geosci. **31**(2), 199–209 (2003)
2. Chang, S.K., Hsu, A.: Image information systems: where do we go from here? IEEE Trans. Knowl. Data Eng. **4**(5), 279–298 (1992)
3. Gudivada, V.N., Raghavan, J.V.: Special issue on content-based image retrieval systems. IEEE Comput. Mag. **28**(9), 18–22 (1995)
4. Bordogna, G., Pagani, M.: A flexible content-based image retrieval model and a customizable system for the retrieval of Shapes. J. Am. Soc. Inform. Sci. Tecnol. **61**(5), 907–926 (2010)

5. The European Parliament and the Council of the European Union. Directive 2007/2/EC of the European Parliament and of the Council of 14 March establishing an Infrastructure for Spatial Information in the European Community (INSPIRE). Official Journal of the European Union, 2007, L 108, 1 (2007). http://eur-lex.europa.eu/legal-content/EN/ALL/?uri=CELEX:32007L0002, Accessed 10 Oct 2014
6. Espinoza, D., Molina, M., Quartulli, M., Datcu M.: Query by example in earth-observation image archives using data. In: IGARSS, 978-1-4673-1159, 5/12, pp. 6035–6038 (2012)
7. Bordogna, G., Kliment, K., Frigerio, L., Boschetti, M., Brivio, P.A., Crema, A., Stroppiana, D.: A spatial data infrastructure integrating multisource heterogeneous geospatial data and time series: a study case in agriculture. ISPRS Int. J. Geo-Inf. **5**(5), 73 (2016)
8. Bloch, I.: Fuzzy sets for image processing and understanding. Fuzzy Sets Syst. **281**, 280–291 (2015)
9. Doulamis, A.D., Doulamis, N.D., Kollia, S.D.: Content-based image retrieval using fuzzy visual representation. In: 10th European Signal Processing Conference, Tampere, Finland, pp. 1–4 (2000)
10. Zadeh, L.A.: The concept of a linguistic variable and its application to approximate reasoning. Inf. Sci. **8**(3), 199–249 (1975)
11. Gennaro, C., Amato, G., Bolettieri, P., Savino, P.: An approach to content-based image retrieval based on the lucene search engine library. In: Lalmas, M., Jose, J., Rauber, A., Sebastiani, F., Frommholz, I. (eds.) ECDL 2010. LNCS, vol. 6273, pp. 55–66. Springer, Heidelberg (2010). doi:10.1007/978-3-642-15464-5_8
12. Rigaux, P., Scholl, M., Voisard, A.: Spatial Databases with Applications to GIS. Morgan Kaufmann Publ., Burlington (2002)

Machine Learning Method for Paraphrase Identification

Oleksandr Marchenko[1(✉)], Anatoly Anisimov[1], Andrii Nykonenko[2], Tetiana Rossada[1], and Egor Melnikov[3]

[1] Taras Shevchenko National University of Kyiv, Kyiv, Ukraine
omarchenko@univ.kiev.ua
[2] International Research and Training Center for IT and Systems, Kyiv, Ukraine
[3] PHASE ONE: KARMA LTD., London, UK

Abstract. A new effective algorithm and a system for paraphrase identification have been developed using a machine learning approach. The system architecture has the form of a multilayer classifier. According to their strategies, sub-classifiers of the lower level make decisions about the presence of paraphrase in sentences, while a super-classifier of the upper level makes the final decision. Conducted experiments demonstrated that the system has the accuracy of the paraphrase detection comparable with the best known analogous systems while being superior to all of them in implementation.

Keywords: Machine learning · SVM · Paraphrase identification

1 Introduction

The paraphrase identification task is one of the primary objectives in computational linguistics. This is due to the close relativeness of the paraphrase detection to the difficult problem of semantic analysis of natural language texts. To date, the development of algorithms for paraphrase detection has attained many significant achievements. Such algorithms use mainly a machine learning approach. As a rule, systems that demonstrate the most accurate results on standard paraphrase corpora use powerful and resource-consuming techniques such as Recursive Neural Networks, Convolutional Neural Networks, and Non-negative Matrix Factorization. In addition to non-triviality and ambiguity in the applications of neural networks, we should also emphasize the algorithmic complexity of Non-negative Matrix Factorization. These methods are too complex to be applied in practical systems operating in real time. This is the main obstacle limiting their practical use.

The authors of this paper set the goal to develop a full-fledged system operating online in real time that should recognize paraphrase and be capable of processing huge flows of information. Therefore, we choose the method of Support Vector Machine as the basic approach along with the development of the original multilevel classification system. The key idea behind this approach is the

H. Christiansen et al. (Eds.): FQAS 2017, LNAI 10333, pp. 164–173, 2017.
DOI: 10.1007/978-3-319-59692-1_14

development of a set of lower level sub-classifiers that are trained to accurately identify certain types of paraphrases. The super-classifier at the upper level analyzes the data provided by the sub-classifiers and decides about the presence of paraphrase.

The system has been developed and tested using the standard Microsoft Research Paraphrase Corpus (MSRP), and it demonstrates the accuracy of paraphrase identification that can be compared to the best up-to-date systems.

2 Related Work

Most of the previous works dedicated to paraphrase identification that use methods of machine learning aimed at creating an optimal set of features also known as effective feature space.

There were determined several types of features including:

- features based on strings and words including n-gram overlap of words and symbols [13], and features based on the assessment of machine translation quality [10];
- features based on the knowledge that use external lexical resources such as WordNet [5];
- features based on evaluating differences of syntax correlations between two sentences [2];
- features being evaluated in corpora based on the distribution models of similarity and Latent Semantic Analysis [6,7].

In modern studies, researchers refrain from the hand-crafted selection of features for distribution modeling and neural network solutions. Hua He, Kevin Gimpel and Jimmy Lin [8] implemented convoluted neural network for calculating multi-perspective similarity of sentences. Their system demonstrates precision at the state-of-the-art level (accuracy = 78.6%, F1 = 84.73% on the MSRP corpus). Cheng and Kartsaklis [1] implemented distributional models together with recursive neural network for syntax-aware multi-sense word embeddings for deep compositional models of meaning, thus completing the task with much better results than the ones demonstrated previously (accuracy = 78.6%, F1 = 85.3% on MSRP). At present, the best results are demonstrated by Ji and Eisenstein [9] who use Non-negative Matrix Factorization and Kullback-Leibler divergence to optimize features space (accuracy = 80.4%, F1 = 85.9% on MSRP).

Nitin Madnani, Joel Tetreault and Martin Chodorow [10] developed the algorithm that consists of 8 machine translation quality metrics for calculating the similarity of sentences and one upper level classifier that makes the final decision based on the assessments of the lower level metrics. Despite the absence of powerful and resource-consuming computations, this algorithm demonstrates the state-of-the-art level results (accuracy = 77.4%, F1 = 84.1% on MSRP), significantly exceeding in simplicity of implementation all the aforementioned methods.

The algorithm presented in this article could be considered as belonging to that class of methods for paraphrase identification.

3 Description of the Method

To detect paraphrases, a two-level classifier was built (Fig. 1). On the lower level, the input data are pairs of sentences. The task is to check whether these sentences constitute paraphrases of each other. It is achieved by selection of prime classifiers, each of them is trained to detect paraphrases of a certain type. These classifiers determine the presence or absence of paraphrase for each incoming pair. On the upper level, the received results are assessed by the main classifier that makes the final decision.

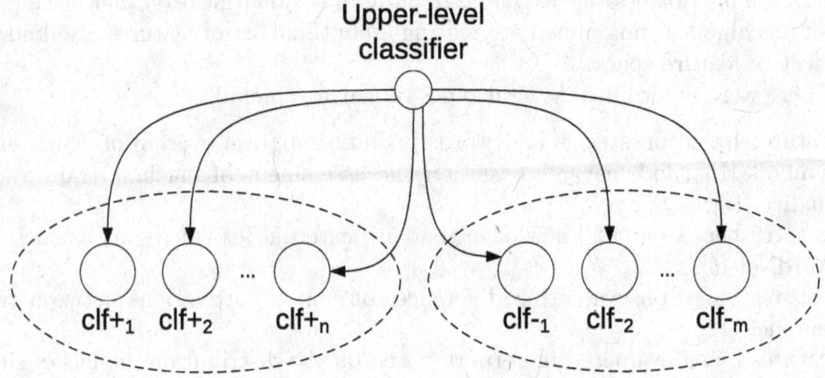

Fig. 1. Architecture of the two-level classifier

For training, a set of tagged pairs of sentences is required for the system (tag 1 – paraphrase/0 – absence of paraphrase).

We denote the first and the second sentences as r and c respectively, $|x|$ - is a count of tokens in a sentence x.

Features used for training are as follows:

1. Sentence Length Difference – comparison of lexeme quantities in sentences.

$$SLD(r,c) = \frac{|r| - |c|}{|r|} \quad (1)$$

$$SLD^{*}(r,c) = \frac{1}{d^{|r|-|c|}} \quad (2)$$

where d - is a constant number (we took $d = 0.8$).

2. N-Grams Comparing – comparison of unigrams, bigrams, and trigrams

$$NGC_N(r,c) = \frac{|NGrams_N(r) \bigcap NGrams_N(c)|}{|NGrams_N(r)|} \quad (3)$$

where $NGrams_N(x)$ – the set of word sequences with length N in a sentence x.

3. Dependencies Similarity – similarity of syntax dependencies

$$DS(r,c) = \frac{\sum\limits_{d \in DT_r} \sum\limits_{i \in r_{dep=d}} \max\limits_{j \in c_{dep=d}} sim(i,j) \cdot BP(|r_{dep=d}|, |c_{dep=d}|)}{|DT_r| \cdot BP(|DT_r|, |DT_c|)} \tag{4}$$

where DT_x – set of all existing syntax dependencies in a sentence x; $x_{dep=d}$ – all lexemes of a sentence x connected with dependency d; $sim(x,y)$ – indicator of similarity for lexemes x and y calculated on the basis of WordNet; $BP(x,y)$ – Brevity Penalty:

$$BP(x,y) = \begin{cases} 1, & if\ y > x \\ e^{1-\frac{x}{y}}, & if\ y \le x \end{cases} \tag{5}$$

4. Dependencies Comparing – comparison of syntax dependencies

$$DC(r,c) = \frac{|dependencies(r) \bigcap dependencies(c)|}{|dependencies(r)|} \tag{6}$$

where $dependencies(x) = \{(i,j,d) : i$ and j are connected with the relation d in a sentence x $\}$

5. Syntactic N-Grams Comparing – comparison of syntax unigrams, bigrams, and trigrams. The calculation is done the same way as for usual N-grams, though here syntax N-grams are sequences of lexemes, which are subgraphs of sentence dependency trees.

Measures of semantic proximity developed in the models of machine translation are also used:

6. BLEU [11]

$$BLEU(r,c) = BP(r,c) \times exp\left[\sum_{n=1}^{L} \frac{1}{L} \times log(p_n(r,c))\right] \tag{7}$$

where L is the maximum n-gram size. The n-gram precision p_n is given as follows:

$$p_n(r,c) = \frac{\sum_{x \in NGrams_n(c)} count(x, NGrams_n(r) \cap NGrams_n(c))}{\sum_{x \in NGrams_n(c)} count(x, NGrams_n(c))} \tag{8}$$

where $count(x, X)$ is the count of an element x in a set X.

7. BLEU, where sequences of meaningful words are used for N-grams, that is:

$$IDF(x, docs) > K \tag{9}$$

where IDF is the abbreviation for the Inverse Document Frequency:

$$IDF(x, docs) = log(\frac{|docs|}{|docs|_{x \in docs}}); \tag{10}$$

$docs$ – corpus of documents; K – a certain threshold depending on the peculiarities of a document corpus.

8. BLEU, where sequences of syntax N-grams are used.
9. NIST [4]

$$NIST(r,c) = \sum_{n=1}^{N} BP(r,c) \times \frac{\sum_{x \in NGrams_n(c)} Info(x)}{count(x, NGrams_n(c))} \tag{11}$$

   where $Info(x)$ is the information weight, we use IDF metric to compute (11): $Info(x) = IDF(x, docs)$.
10. METEOR calculates a lexical similarity score based on a word-to-word alignment between two strings [3]. Words are matched if and only if their surface forms are identical; words are matched if they are both members of a synonym set according to the WordNet database.
11. BADGER is a method based on information theory and data compression. It implements efficient Normalized Compression Distance (NCD) utilizing the Burrows Wheeler Transformation (BWT) [12].

Each measure $M(x,y)$ has two variants of implementation: *precision* $M(x,y)$ is a function as is, and *recall* $M(y,x)$ – the same function is used but the arguments-sentences are given in inverse order. All measures using comparison of lexemes have two variants of implementation: total lexeme coincidence and lexemes synonyms coincidence.

To train the classifiers of the lower level, it is necessary to create training sets for each classifier (Fig. 2). Each of them should be able to determine paraphrases of a certain set of types. Besides, each type of paraphrases could be contained in training sets for several classifiers. Due to this, the coverage of all types of paraphrases and mutual insurance of classifiers are guaranteed while solving a task. Thus, questions arise – what a paraphrase type is, how to model it, and how to determine the type of paraphrases for each pair of sentences. As a working hypothesis the following assumption is used: two pairs of sentences belong to the set of paraphrases of the same type, if after processing these two pairs of sentences they have a certain subset of features with close values.

During the *first stage* of the algorithm training, for set of pairs of sentences from the training sub-corpus of the Microsoft Research Paraphrase Corpus (MSRP) a training matrix is being calculated for values of features f_i.

During the *second stage*, with the use of clustering algorithms the training matrix is partitioned into the set of matrices: $training_1^+$, $training_2^+$, ..., $training_N^+$ and $training_1^-$, $training_2^-$,..., $training_M^-$:

$$training^+ = \bigcup_{i=1}^{N} training_i^+, training^- = \bigcup_{i=1}^{M} training_i^- \tag{12}$$

$$training^+ \cup training^- = training \tag{13}$$

where $training^+$ and $training^-$ are the sets of vectors formed by feature values for all pairs of sentences tagged as paraphrase or non-paraphrase correspondingly.

To make classifiers be able to "support" each other when making decisions in each particular case, a training set should consist of several different types of paraphrases so that the sets can intensively overlap. For this, the following condition should be met for $training^+$ and $training^-$:

$$\forall i \exists j : training_i^+ \cap training_j^+ \neq \varnothing \quad (14)$$

$$\forall i \exists j : training_i^- \cap training_j^- \neq \varnothing. \quad (15)$$

The *third stage.* Based on the matrices received at the second stage, training sets are formed by creating $n = \binom{N}{k}$ combinations with sets of $\{training_i^+\}$ and adding to each combination the full $training^-$ set, where k is a number of merged sets. All the corresponding pairs of sentences with vectors of feature values being included into a certain obtained combination form a training set for a classifier of lower level clf_i^+. Thus, we obtain training sets for $n = \binom{N}{k}$ classifiers clf_i^+. Training sets for $m = \binom{M}{k}$ classifiers clf_i^- are formed the same way.

The *fourth stage.* Training the set of classifiers clf_1, clf_2, ..., clf_{n+m} is performed on the basis of the obtained sets. After the training, all classifiers process the whole MSRP training set. Matrix of classifiers decisions for all pairs of sentences that belong to the training corpus together with "paraphrase"/"non-paraphrase" tags serve as the training set for the super-classifier.

During the *fifth stage*, the training of the upper-level classifier is performed.

To build the classifiers for the upper and the lower levels, the method of Support Vector Machine is used.

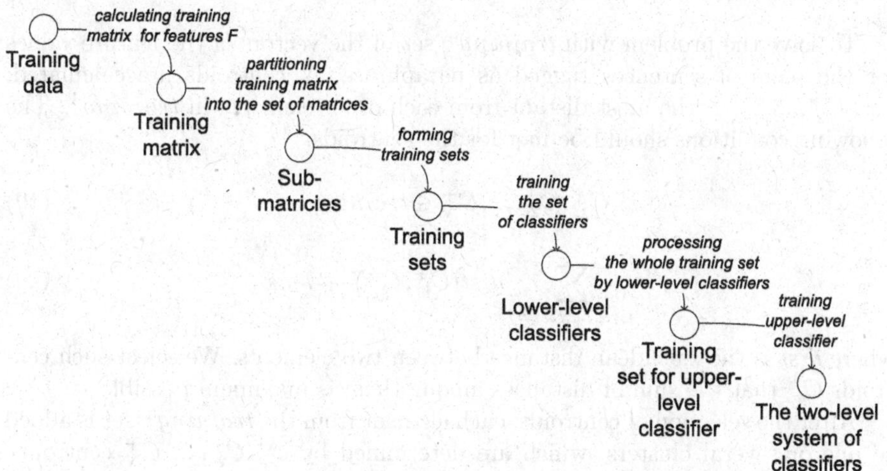

Fig. 2. Steps of algorithm for building system of classifiers

4 Algorithm for Building System of Classifiers

Step 1. Automated partitioning of *training*$^+$ into classes according to the types of paraphrases.

Pairs of paraphrase that belong to the same type should correlate according to the values of calculated features. Thus, the values should be *close.* Some of the features can be irrelevant for the paraphrase of a certain type. That is why it is necessary to determine C^+ set of such typical sub-sets of paraphrase $\{c\}$ that include any two elements with the similar set of values for a certain set of features. The following conditions should be met:

$$\bigcup_{c \subseteq C^+} c = training^+ \tag{16}$$

$$\forall c_1 \subseteq C^+ \, \exists c_2 \subseteq C^+ : c_1 \cap c_2 \neq \varnothing \tag{17}$$

$$\forall c \subseteq C^+ \, \forall x, y \in c : x \simeq^l y \tag{18}$$

where:

- C^+ is the set of the received typical sub-sets;
- $x \simeq^l y \Leftrightarrow \exists X \subseteq F : \|X\| = l \& \forall f \in X : |f(x) - f(y)| < \varepsilon$ for selected l and ε;
- F is the set of the implemented features;
- l is a number of features having close values for pairs of sentences that belong to one type of paraphrases; ε is the maximum value of differences for such features. Optimal values for l and ε were selected during conducted experiments.

To solve the problem with *training*$^+$ set of the vectors of the feature values for the pairs of sentences tagged as paraphrase, N centroids are calculated: C_1^+, C_2^+,..., C_N^+ – the most distant from each other elements in *training*$^+$. The following conditions should be met for the centroids:

$$C_1^+, C_2^+, ..., C_N^+ \in training^+ \tag{19}$$

$$\sum_{i,j \in 1..N \& i \neq j} dist(C_i^+, C_j^+) \to max \tag{20}$$

where *dist* is the Euclidean distance between two elements. We select such centroids C_i^+ that the sum of distances among them is maximum possible.

After the selection of centroids, each element from the *training*$^+$ set is added to one or several clusters, which are determined by C_1^+,C_2^+,..., C_N^+ centroids. Condition that element x gets to the cluster c_i^+ determined by the centroid C_i^+ if the $x \simeq^l C_i^+$ holds. This way, N clusters are built: c_1^+, c_2^+, ..., c_N^+.

For the elements that haven't been selected to any class, Step 1 is repeated recursively, though with modified N, l and ε parameters. As a result, N' clusters are built, each of them consists of pairs of paraphrase sentences taken from the training set, which together form the *training*$^{+}$ set. Besides, they should not have an empty intersection. The intensity of intersections is determined by parameters N, l and ε.

Step 2. From c_1^+, c_2^+, .., $c_{N'}^+$ we form $n = \binom{N'}{k}$ of all possible combinations of k clusters. To each of combinations, a *training*$^{-}$ set is added. After selecting the corresponding pairs of sentences from the **training** corpus, the training sets T_1^+, T_2^+, ..., T_n^+ are received.

Step 3. Using standard methods from library http://scikit-learn.org/stable/modules/feature_selection.html for each training set T_1^+, T_2^+, ..., T_n^+ for SVM method, the optimal set of features $\{f_1, f_2, ..., f_k\}$ is formed using the initial set of the implemented features F.

Step 4. Classifiers of the lower level clf_1^+, clf_2^+, ..., clf_n^+ train based on T_1^+, T_2^+, ...,T_n^+ using the corresponding optimal sets of features.

Step 5. The same way the classifiers clf_1^-, clf_2^-, ..., clf_m^- are generated. Together with clf_1^+, clf_2^+, ..., clf_n^+ they constitute the classifiers of the lower level clf_1, clf_2, ..., clf_{n+m}.

Step 6. When the training is completed, all the classifiers process the whole training set. The matrix of solutions made by classifiers clf_1, clf_2, ..., clf_{n+m} for all pairs of sentences from the training corpus together with the pairs tags serve as a training set for super-classifier of the upper level. The training of the classifier of the upper level is performed.

Step 7. The trained system processes the test corpus of the pairs of sentences.

5 Results of Experiments

Training and testing were performed using the Microsoft Research Paraphrase Corpus set. The corpus consists of 5,800 sentences taken from different sources with tags signaling whether a certain pair constitutes paraphrase or not. Besides, the corpus is divided into the training set with 4,076 pairs of sentences (2,753 positive: 67,5%) and a the testing set with 1,725 pairs of sentences (1,147 positive: 66,5%).

Tables 1 and 2 demonstrate the results of experiments on the Microsoft Research Paraphrase Corpus set.

As seen, the chosen method has demonstrated the results that can be compared with the best existing algorithms (Table 1, www.aclweb.org/aclwiki/index.php?title=Paraphrase_Identification_(State_of_the_art)) with–out additional implementation of powerful methods such as neural networks, Latent Semantic Analysis, and Non-negative Matrix Factorization. To some extent, the

Table 1. Comparisons of our system results (the last line) with the existing state-of-the-art systems

Algorithm	Description	Accuracy	F1
MTMETRICS [10]	Combination of eight machine translation metrics	77.4%	84.1%
Multi-Perspective CNN [8]	Multi-perspective Convolutional NNs and structured similarity layer	78.6%	84.7%
SAMS-RecNN [1]	Recursive NNs using syntax-aware multi-sense word embeddings	78.6%	85.3%
TF-KLD [9]	Matrix factorization with supervised reweighting	80.4%	85.9%
Two-level classifier	Multilayer classifier	77.86%	85.16%

Table 2. Experiment results

Algorithm	Precision	Recall	Accuracy	F1
Single classifier based on SVM	76.29%	89.19%	74.38%	82.23%
Two-level classifier ($N = 5$, $l = 7$, $\varepsilon = 1.3e - 3$, $k = 3$)	75.02%	95.03%	75.65%	83.84%
Two-level classifier ($N = 5$, $l = 8$, $\varepsilon = 1.3e - 3$, $k = 2$)	76.76%	95.64%	77.86%	85.16%

developed method could be considered as a generalization of the algorithm [10]. From this point of view our algorithm gives better precision results compared to its predecessor. The main improvement of implementation has been achieved by optimization of training sets for lower level classifiers in such a way that each of them should be able to determine paraphrases of a certain set of types and each type of paraphrases could be contained in training sets for several classifiers. Hence, the coverage of all types of paraphrases and mutual insurance of classifiers are guaranteed.

The proposed two-level system demonstrates accuracy of paraphrase identification and evaluation of F1 almost as good as the best existing state-of-the-art systems. At the same time it has advantages that are the ease of implementation and less required computing resources.

To evaluate the efficiency of the developed two-level architecture we have built a single system of paraphrase identification based on SVM algorithm implemented with the use of the abovementioned features 1–11. Standard methods of http://scikit-learn.org/stable/modules/feature_selection.html library have been used to optimize the set of features. As we can see from the results of Table 2, the two-level system developed in both implemented configurations (the second and the third lines) overcomes the single system based on the SVM method (the first line).

6 Conclusions

The research paper describes a new effective algorithm for the paraphrase identification task using machine learning. The experiments demonstrated high accuracy in paraphrase identification that can be compared to the results achieved by the existing state-of-the-art systems while being superior to all of them in implementation.

Acknowledgments. The authors of the article are grateful to PHASE ONE: KARMA LTD. company, especially to the Unplag team for the support in research and considerable assistance in the development, testing and implementation of the paraphrase identification method.

References

1. Cheng, J., Kartsaklis, D.: Syntax-aware multi-sense word embeddings for deep compositional models of meaning. In: Proceedings of EMNLP 2015, pp. 1531–1542 (2015)
2. Das, D., Smith, N.A.: Paraphrase identification as probabilistic quasi-synchronous recognition. In: Proceedings of the Joint Conference of the 47th Annual Meeting of the Association for Computational Linguistics, pp. 468–476 (2009)
3. Denkowski, M., Lavie, A.: Extending the meteor machine translation metric to the phrase level. In: Proceedings of NAACL (2010)
4. Doddington, G.: Automatic evaluation of machine translation quality using n-gram co-occurrence statistics. In: Proceedings of HLT, pp. 138–145 (2002)
5. Fellbaum, C.: WordNet: An Electronic Lexical Database. MIT Press, Cambridge (1998)
6. Guo, W., Diab, M.: Modeling sentences in the latent space. In: Proceedings of the 50th Annual Meeting of the Association for Computational Linguistics, pp. 864–872 (2012)
7. Hassan, S.: Measuring semantic relatedness using salient encyclopedic concepts. Ph.D. thesis. University of North Texas (2011)
8. He, H., Gimpel, K., Lin, J.: Multi-perspective sentence similarity modeling with convolutional neural networks. In: Proceedings of EMNLP 2015, pp. 1576–1586 (2015)
9. Ji, Y., Eisenstein, J.: Discriminative improvements to distributional sentence similarity. In: Proceedings of Empirical Methods in Natural Language Processing (EMNLP 2013), pp. 891–896 (2013)
10. Madnani, N., Tetreault, J., Chodorow, M.: Re-examining machine translation metrics for paraphrase identification. In: Proceedings of the 2012 Conference of the North American Chapter of the Association for Computational Linguistics: Human Language Technologies, pp. 182–190 (2012)
11. Papineni, K., Roukos, S., Ward, T., Zhu, W.-J.: BLEU: a method for automatic evaluation of machine translation. In: Proceedings of ACL (2002)
12. Parker, S.: BADGER: a new machine translation metric. In: Proceedings of the Workshop on Metrics for Machine Translation at AMTA (2008)
13. Wan, S., Dras, M., Dale, R., Paris, C.: Using dependency-based features to take the "para-farce" out of paraphrase. In: Australasian Language Technology, Workshop, pp. 131–138 (2006)

DRIMS: A Software Tool to Incrementally Maintain Previous Discovered Rules

Alain Pérez-Alonso[1(✉)], Ignacio J. Blanco[2], Jose M. Serrano[3], and Luisa M. González-González[1]

[1] University "Marta Abreu" of Las Villas, 54830 Santa Clara, Villa Clara, Cuba
{apa,luisagon}@uclv.edu.cu
[2] University of Granada, 18071 Granada, Spain
iblanco@decsai.ugr.es
[3] University of Jaén, 23071 Jaén, Spain
jschica@ujaen.es

Abstract. A wide spectrum of methods for knowledge extraction have been proposed up to date. These expensive algorithms become inexact when new transactions are made into business data, an usual problem in real-world applications. The incremental maintenance methods arise to avoid reruns of those algorithms from scratch by reusing information that is systematically maintained. This paper introduces a software tool: Data Rules Incremental Maintenance System (DRIMS) which is a free tool written in Java for incrementally maintain three types of rules: association rules, approximate dependencies and fuzzy association rules. Several algorithms have been implemented in this tool for relational databases using their active resources. These algorithms are inspired in efficient computation of changes and do not include any mining technique. We operate on discovered rules in their final form and sustain measures of rules up-to-date, ready for real-time decision support. Algorithms are applied over a generic form of measures allowing the maintenance of a wide rules' metrics in an efficient way. DRIMS software tool do not discover new knowledge, it has been designed to efficiently maintain interesting information previously extracted.

Keywords: Association rules · Approximate dependencies · Incremental maintenance · Active databases

1 Introduction

Association Rules (ARs), Approximate Dependencies (ADs) and Fuzzy Association Rules (FARs) are ones of the best studied models for knowledge discovery in the data mining research field. They represent associations or dependencies among attributes' values in a data repository [1]. Many algorithms have been proposed to improve the mining process and create more efficient methods [4,22,35]. However, these proposed algorithms could become expensive when dealing with

H. Christiansen et al. (Eds.): FQAS 2017, LNAI 10333, pp. 174–185, 2017.
DOI: 10.1007/978-3-319-59692-1_15

huge amounts of data, commonly stored in data warehouses or very large and big databases.

The knowledge discovered by these methods is specific for the current stage of the repository in which they were run. In real-world applications, a data repository is not static and records are commonly inserted, updated or deleted, following real activities in the universe of discourse. These continuous changes can render the measures of rules inexact and eventually invalid [16]. The incremental rule mining method arise to avoid re-run algorithms from scratch and re-scan the whole data. This is specifically useful when real-time data information is required. Example applications can be found in the field of data streams like web click stream data, sensor networks data, and network traffic data [19,20,32]. Emerging research in big data offers similar issues in association with velocity and volume [27,34]. At this time, many research efforts are being made to improve the performance [14,16,18].

In this work we describe a Data Rules Incremental Maintenance System (DRIMS) tool that formally implements incremental maintenance algorithms into relational databases using their active resources [24]. DRIMS is a free and open-source tool completely written in Java available from the GitHub platform [25]. There are two main applications of the tool: (1) the tool safety manages a repository of rules such as creating new rules, and (2) the tool can generate an SQL script to maintain the rules measures up-to-date in an efficient way. We also present the algorithms implemented in DRIMS, and the experimental results obtained from active relational database with real educational data and repository datasets. A common characteristic of algorithms implemented is the efficient maintenance of existing rules, keeping their measures just-in-time available for real-time decision support [29].

The remainder of this paper is organized as follows. Some related works are reviewed in Sect. 2. The algorithms implemented in DRIMS are described in Sect. 3. In Sect. 4 we briefly present the graphical user interface. Section 5 presents the experimental results of the proposed methods for the performance evaluation. Finally, Sect. 6 concludes this paper summarizing the results of our work.

2 Related Work

Association rules can formally be represented as an implication of itemsets (sets of items) in transactional databases [1]. Let $It = \{It_1, It_2, \ldots, It_m\}$ be a non-empty set of m distinct attributes. Let T be the transaction scheme that contains a set of items such that $It \subseteq T$. An AR is an implication of the form $X \Rightarrow Y$ where $X, Y \subset It$ such that $X \neq \emptyset$, $Y \neq \emptyset$ and $X \cap Y = \emptyset$. In this statement X and Y are called rule itemsets and they are the antecedent and consequent of the rule, respectively. The ADs and FARs can be represented through an AR perspective. We follow our research group's results in ADs [28] and FARs [9].

Numerous algorithms for mining ARs have been proposed at this time based on Apriori approach [1]. These Apriori-like algorithms generate the candidate itemsets level-by-level, which might cause multiple scans of the database and high computational costs. In order to avoid re-scanning the whole data and breaking Apriori bottlenecks, many algorithms have been proposed by using tree-structures [14,30]. The frequent-pattern tree (FP-tree) proposed by [12] is a milestone for the development of ARs based upon this method. The FP-tree is used to compress a database into a tree structure which stores only large items. After the FP-tree is constructed, a mining algorithm called FP-growth derives all large itemsets in a second step [12].

In real-world applications, data repository is not static. Generally, data will increase with time. Traditional batch mining algorithms solve this problem by re-scanning the whole data when new transactions are inserted, deleted or modified. This is clearly inefficient because all previous mined information is wasted. The incremental mining defines this issue as an update problem and reduces it to find the new set of large itemsets incrementally. Algorithm FUP (Fast UPdate) [8], is the first algorithm for incremental mining of ARs when new data transactions are added to a database.

Although the FUP approach improves a mining performance in dynamic environments, the original database is still required to be re-scanned. Extended tree structures are being designed for FP-tree to handle efficiently this problem [14,16,18]. These proposals improve the pioneer tree-structure in different ways but maintain the execution of FP-growth algorithm in a second step. Some related researches are still in progress.

Unlike incremental mining methods, DRIMS handles the update problem by maintaining the measures of previous discovered rules, just like we explain in detail for ARs and ADs [26]. That does not lead to maintain itemsets information, instead, existing rules measures are directly updated in an incremental way. After the rules discovering process, DRIMS keeps only the extracted rules. In Fig. 1 three scenarios are illustrated when a system decision-maker needs the

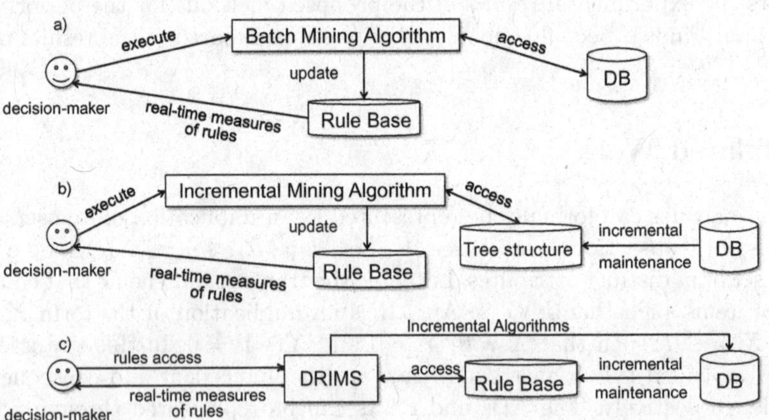

Fig. 1. (a) Real-time measures by batch mining method, (b) incremental mining method, and (c) DRIMS incremental maintenance proposal.

real-time measures of previously discovered rules. That includes the batch mining method, the incremental mining method, and DRIMS algorithms.

3 Data Rules Maintenance Proposals

ARs, ADs and FARs are different data relationships that share some similarities [21]. These data dependencies are referred to as Data Rules (DRs) in the remainder of this paper for a common reference. Many research activities propose measures of rules with different properties such as the certainty factor [3], and their number is overwhelming [10,15]. Existing measures for DRs are usually defined by counting a total number of records that satisfy some condition. These conditions are generally associated with the antecedent, consequent, rule examples, and counterexamples among others [10,15].

In DRIMS algorithms, each DR measure value is considered a set of k distinct data rule measure-parts $DRM = \{Mp_1, Mp_2, \ldots, Mp_k\}$ in which each item represents a different part of the measure formula. Measure-parts must be atomic, it means that they cannot be divided into smaller items and still bring the same measure value. For example, confidence can be split into two parts: count of antecedent and count of (antecedent ∪ consequent). On the other hand, the certainty factor needs three parts: count of antecedent, count of consequent and count of (antecedent ∪ consequent). In this way, it is possible to maintain efficiently several metrics at the same time because metrics shares some measure-parts. For example, following [15] it is viable with only five distinct measure-parts to maintain 20 interestingness measures simultaneously. The final data rule measure value is a formula over DRM parts.

3.1 Immediate Incremental Maintenance Algorithm

An immediate approach in DRIMS is oriented to update the rule base immediately after the event takes place, in an active fashion. The primitive event type, called a primitive structural event (PSE), is a single low-level event. A composite type is a combination of multiple primitive or composite structural events (CSE). This immediate approach verifies the specific rules that must be updated only with the changes made by a PSE. It means that only one record can be checked at a time. Incremental view maintenance algorithms offer multiple solutions. Specifically, a counting algorithm for view maintenance [11] provides an interesting perspective. The following Algorithm 1 presents the proposed immediate incremental maintenance where rule measures are updated for data operations.

The measure-parts Mp_k are constantly updated in the proposed algorithm. However, the incrementing of measure-parts are quite different depending on the DR type. For example, to obtain an AD measure each measure-part $Mp_k \in ADM$ is calculated by aggregating the *catt* attribute in AE_k [26]. For this immediate proposal, rule base refreshing is made without access to the base relation.

Algorithm 1. Immediate incremental maintenance for a DR

Input: A composite structural event *CSE* that modifies the attributes related in list L, and measure-parts *DRM* of $X \Rightarrow Y$ data rule.
Output: An updated measure-parts *DRM*.
Method:

```
foreach PSE ∈ CSE do
    if (PSE = Δ t⁻⁺) then                                   /* update event */
        if (L ∩ {X ∪ Y} ≠ ∅) then
            foreach Mp_k ∈ DRM do
                if (L ∩ {involved attributes in Mp_k} ≠ ∅) then
                    update Mp_k, increment with t_0⁻⁺;
                    update Mp_k, decrement with t_1⁻⁺;
    else if (PSE = Δ t⁺) then                               /* insert event */
        foreach Mp_k ∈ DRM do
            update Mp_k, increment with t⁺;
    else                                        /* delete event (PSE = Δt⁻) */
        foreach Mp_k ∈ DRM do
            update Mp_k, decrement with t⁻;
return DRM
```

3.2 Deferred Incremental Maintenance Method

A deferred approach efficiently maintains a fuzzy rule base up-to-date but not for each data operation. This method computes modified instances in a data transition and updates fuzzy rule base for these relevant instances. Principal differences of immediate and deferred maintenance approaches are illustrated in Fig. 1.

The deferred proposal is divided into two subproblems. The first subproblem consists of computing the relevant affected instances of a database transition. In this step, we build a relevant operations set at real-time, after each primitive structural event takes place. A different approach would be to scan the original operation set to reduce their number. The second one is related to incrementally update the rule base with those relevant instances.

Affected transition instances computation must consider the relationships among primitive events. These interactions are controlled by net effect policies [6,7,24]. For example, if a record is inserted and next deleted in the same database transition, then these events do not provoke any variation to the final database state and its measures of rules. In this approach, each database relation related with any rule has two auxiliary relations: insert relation (I) and delete relation (D). The insert and delete auxiliary relations register the insert, update, and delete events ($t^{+} \cup t_1^{-+}$ and $t^{-} \cup t_0^{-+}$ respectively) according to net effect considerations [26]. These relevant structural events are computed over relations in real-time by the active Algorithm 2.

Algorithm 2. Compute relevant instances that may modify DRs

Input: A composite structural event *CSE*, I and D the auxiliary relations of base relation.

Output: Auxiliary relations I and D updated for a *CSE*.

Method:

```
foreach PSE ∈ CSE do
    if (PSE = Δ t⁻⁺) then                                /* update event */
        if ({t_0⁻⁺ ∩ I} = ∅) then
            insert into I values t_1⁻⁺;
            insert into D values t_0⁻⁺;
        else
            update u∈I set u=t_1⁻⁺ where u=t_0⁻⁺;
    else if (PSE = Δ t⁺) then                            /* insert event */
        insert into I values t⁺;
    else                                      /* delete event (PSE = Δt⁻) */
        if ({t⁻ ∩ I}= ∅) then
            insert into D values t⁻;
        else
            delete u∈I where u = t⁻;
return I, D
```

This active process adds a minimum activity over regular data operations, just the necessary ones to store relevant instances and to apply net effect policies. The behavior of the algorithm is similar when considering only insertion and deletion events, but note the benefits of using update occurrences when a record is already inserted or modified. The rule base is updated only with these instances, by incrementing previous rules information. These rule base updates could be made automatically with a decision-maker's rule base access or scheduled. In this step, Algorithm 3 is presented in order to update *DRM*.

Algorithm 3. Deferred incremental maintenance for relevant instances

Input: I, D auxiliary relations of Algorithm 2 output, and measure-parts *DRM*.

Output: An updated measure-parts *DRM*.

Method:

```
foreach Mp_k ∈ DRM do
    update Mp_k, increment with I;
    update Mp_k, decrement with D;
empty I;
empty D;
return DRM
```

This deferred proposal, like the immediate one, updates the rule base without access to the base relation. This is an important feature in a huge amount of data where the access to complete information is highly inefficient. Also, it entails the benefits of having only two auxiliary relations against more.

4 A Graphical User Interface

To increase the usability of our algorithms, we have designed DRIMS, a simple and friendly user interface Fig. 2 (left). It has a wizard-based interface, where through a few steps, users can create their own rules. The tool has two main possible applications: manage a repository of rules (such as create new rules, delete old rules or modify the existing ones) and the implementation of algorithms to maintain rules measures up-to-date in an efficient way.

The tool has three main menus, two of them are intended for rule's repository management and a third for the implementation of those rules into a business database. Creating rules in the repository is done through a multi-step wizard where the antecedent and consequent are defined as shown in Fig. 2 (right).

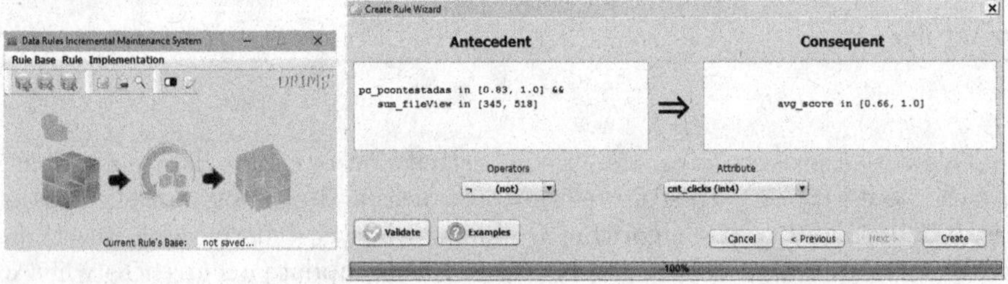

Fig. 2. The graphical user interface of DRIMS at start-up (left) and rule creation (right).

4.1 Prerequisites

As previously presented in the introduction, compilation and execution of DRIMS requires an installed and configured Java environment. The Java Runtime Environment (JRE) is a free software and may be obtained from ORACLE's web pages[1]. In the current version, DRIMS can implement algorithms in two of the main opensource database managements systems: PostgreSQL[2] and MySQL[3]. However, the tool also allows to create rules without maintaining a connection to the database.

---

1 Java Runtime Environment, https://www.java.com/en/download/.

2 PostgreSQL Global Development Group, http://www.postgresql.org.

3 MySQL Community Server, http://dev.mysql.com/downloads/mysql/.

4.2 Rules Implementation

The data rules are stored through an XML repository. The tool validates that repository using an XSD schema. For each rule, regardless of its type, the common attributes are stored. That includes the antecedent and consequent of the rule, the type to which it belongs and the relationship to which it refers. Note that in the case of FARs their linguistic labels are also stored for each existing attribute in the rule. In the case of ARs the tool processes quantitative rules' [31] as well as other more complex types of rules such as negative association rules [33].

Finally, the rules stored in the repository can be implemented directly in the business database as shown in Fig. 3 (left). The antecedent and consequent of the rules are grammatically parsed by a small translator made with ANTLR v4 [23] grammar parser. With the use of ANTLR/StringTemplates the SQL script that implements the incremental maintenance of the rule measure is generated.

The SQL script generated is composed primarily of active database resources [24] such as triggers. Besides the triggers, DRIMS tool can creates in business database catalog other objects such as views, functions and tables. These resources are created according to the chosen method and the rule's type to be implemented. In the graphical interface as shown by Fig. 3 (right) we can to list all resources of the generated script. This window also allows to run this script in the business database and save it as a plain text.

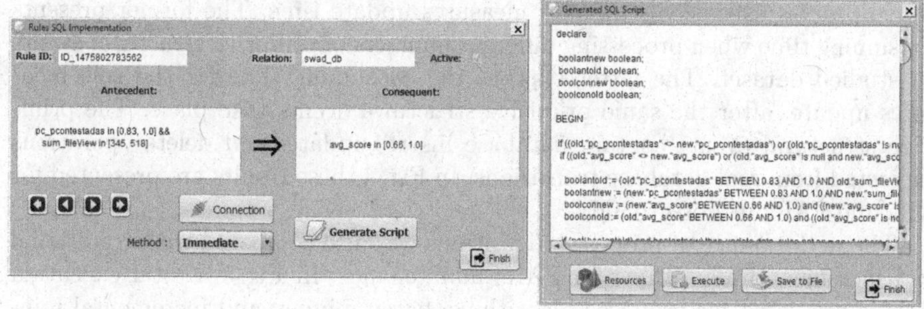

Fig. 3. The graphical user interface for rule's implementation (left) and script's manipulation (right).

5 Experimental Results

The experiments over DRIMS algorithms have been designed to observe the different behaviors of the proposed methods in order to consider their implementation in real applications. The experiments also compare the proposed algorithms with those reported in the literature. These are being performed on real data and real structural events obtained from SWAD, a web system for education support at the University of Granada [5].

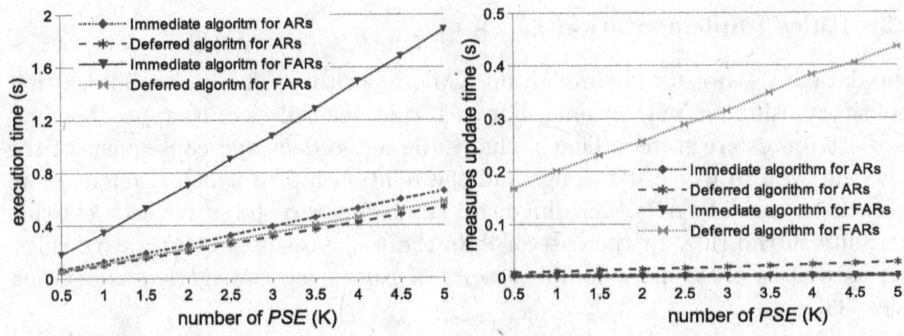

Fig. 4. Proposals comparison for ARs and FARs maintenance on execution times (left) and measures update times (right) in PostgreSQL.

Results illustrate the performance of proposed algorithms in order to maintain seven ARs, seven ADs and seven FARs. These rules were discovered using the KEEL data mining software tool [2]. Maintenance is implemented using the certainty factor metric from two open source database management systems: PostgreSQL Server version 9.2.2 and MySQL Server version 5.6.13. Both management systems show similar results. The experiments were carried out on a dedicated GNU/Linux server with eight processors i7-2600 at 3.4 GHz and 15 GB of main memory.

The experiments have been designed to observe two approaches' behavior: active process execution time and measures update time. The former presents consuming time when processing different numbers of primitive structural events on studied dataset. The latter exposes the consuming time for the rule measures update, after the same primitive structural events take place. The primitive structural events contain database insert, update, and delete operations extracted from real database transitions. In Fig. 4 these results are presented for ARs and FARs in PotsgreSQL.

The performance of proposed algorithms was also compared with traditional and incremental algorithms for FARs maintenance. In Fig. 5 a total execution time is presented for proposed algorithms, batch mining, and incremental mining methods for different datasets. These datasets were obtained from the UCI Machine Learning Repository [17]: the Diabetes 130-US hospitals for years 1999–2008 (diabetes), the Color Texture and the Color Moments parts of Corel Image Features. Details about these datasets can be found on the UCI Machine Learning website. For diabetes datasets nine attributes were selected. Seven FARs were extracted using KEEL data mining software tool from each dataset in order to be incrementally maintained by proposed algorithms.

Our proposal reflects the total time of executing 5 K data operations plus updates measures of rules in order to maintain the fuzzy rule base up-to-date. Batch and incremental mining methods reflect the mining execution time for the same goal. The fuzzy Apriori algorithm stands for batch mining methods. For incremental mining methods we only consider the fuzzy FP-growth [13] execution

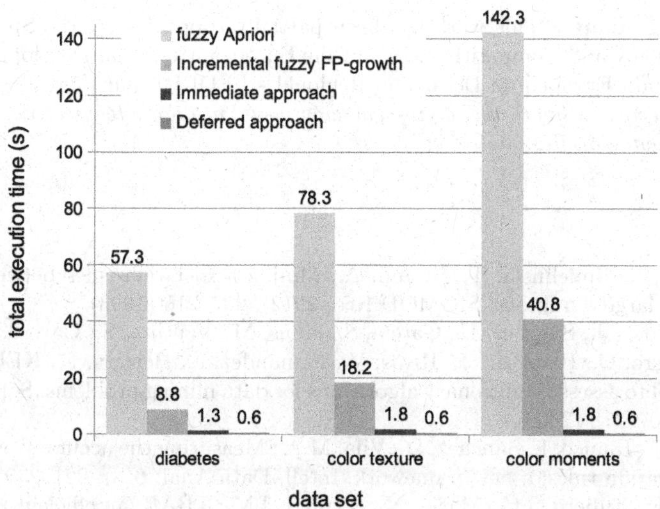

Fig. 5. Related and proposed algorithm comparison of total execution time for FARs maintenance in different datasets.

time and depreciate the fuzzy FP-tree build time, assuming it was incrementally maintained. This approach is referred to as incremental fuzzy FP-growth. For fuzzy Apriori and fuzzy FP-growth algorithms, three fuzzy regions were defined for numeric attributes. The minimum support threshold was set at 10% and minimum confidence threshold at 80%. Both mining algorithm experiments were developed using the KEEL data mining software tool.

6 Conclusion

In real-world applications, records are commonly inserted, updated or deleted outdating the previous extracted knowledge as inexact and invalid. In some scenarios, it is necessary to re-run traditional mining or incremental mining algorithms only for updating previous discovered rules. It is possible, from another perspective, to maintain the known rules incrementally by computing data changes efficiently.

In this paper, DRIMS is presented as the free and open-source software tool for incrementally maintaining previous discovered rules. It has a wizard-based interface, where through a few steps users can create and manage their own rules. This tool implements two algorithms for maintenance purpose of association rules, approximate dependencies and fuzzy association rules. Experimental results on real data and operations show that DRIMS maintenance proposals achieve a better performance against the batch mining and incremental mining approach. We believe this work represents a powerful enhancement to the incremental maintenance of previous discovered data rules and their implementation in business relational databases for real-time decision support.

Acknowledgements. This work has been partially supported by the Spanish Ministry of Economy and Competitiveness and the European Regional Development Fund - ERDF (Fondo Europeo de Desarrollo Regional - FEDER) under project TIN2014-58227-P *Descripción lingüística de información visual mediante técnicas de minería de datos y computación flexible.*

References

1. Agrawal, R., Imieliński, T., Swami, A.: Mining association rules between sets of items in large databases. SIGMOD Rec. **22**(2), 207–216 (1993)
2. Alcalá-Fdez, J., Sánchez, L., García, S., Jesus, M., Ventura, S., Garrell, J., Otero, J., Romero, C., Bacardit, J., Rivas, V., Fernández, J., Herrera, F.: KEEL: a software tool to assess evolutionary algorithms for data mining problems. Soft Comput. **13**(3), 307–318 (2009)
3. Berzal, F., Blanco, I., Sánchez, D., Vila, M.A.: Measuring the accuracy and interest of association rules: a new framework. Intell. Data Anal. **6**(3), 221–235 (2002)
4. Berzal, F., Cubero, J.C., Marín, N., Serrano, J.M.: TBAR: an efficient method for association rule mining in relational databases. Data Knowl. Eng. **37**(1), 47–64 (2001)
5. Cañas, A., Calandria, D., Ortigosa, E., Ros, E., Díaz, A.: Swad: web system for education support. In: Fernández-Manjón, B., Sánchez-Pérez, J.M., Gómez-Pulido, J.A., Vega-Rodriguez, M.A., Bravo-Rodriguez, J. (eds.) Computers and Education: E-Learning, From Theory to Practice, pp. 133–142. Springer, Dordrecht (2007)
6. Cabot, J., Teniente, E.: Computing the relevant instances that may violate an OCL constraint. In: Pastor, O., Falcão e Cunha, J. (eds.) CAiSE 2005. LNCS, vol. 3520, pp. 48–62. Springer, Heidelberg (2005). doi:10.1007/11431855_5
7. Ceri, S., Widom, J.: Deriving production rules for incremental view maintenance. In: Proceedings of the 17th International Conference on Very Large Data Bases, pp. 577–589 (1991)
8. Cheung, D., Han, J., Ng, V., Wong, C.Y.: Maintenance of discovered association rules in large databases: an incremental updating technique. In: Proceedings of the Twelfth International Conference on Data Engineering, pp. 106–114 (1996)
9. Delgado, M., Marin, N., Sánchez, D., Vila, M.A.: Fuzzy association rules: general model and applications. IEEE Trans. Fuzzy Syst. **11**(2), 214–225 (2003)
10. Greco, S., Słowiński, R., Szczęch, I.: Properties of rule interestingness measures and alternative approaches to normalization of measures. Inf. Sci. **216**, 1–16 (2012)
11. Gupta, A., Mumick, I.S., et al.: Maintenance of materialized views: problems, techniques, and applications. IEEE Data Eng. Bull. **18**(2), 3–18 (1995)
12. Han, J., Pei, J., Yin, Y.: Mining frequent patterns without candidate generation. SIGMOD Rec. **29**(2), 1–12 (2000)
13. Hong, T.P., Lin, T.C., Lin, T.C.: Mining complete fuzzy frequent itemsets by tree structures. In: 2010 IEEE International Conference on Systems Man and Cybernetics (SMC), pp. 563–567 (2010)
14. Lee, Y.S., Yen, S.J.: Incrementally mining frequent patterns from large database. In: Pedrycz, W., Chen, S.-M. (eds.) Information Granularity, Big Data, and Computational Intelligence. Studies in Big Data, vol. 8, pp. 121–140. Springer, Heidelberg (2015)
15. Lenca, P., Meyer, P., Vaillant, B., Lallich, S.: On selecting interestingness measures for association rules: user oriented description and multiple criteria decision aid. Eur. J. Oper. Res. **184**(2), 610–626 (2008)

16. Li, X., Deng, Z.-H., Tang, S.: A fast algorithm for maintenance of association rules in incremental databases. In: Li, X., Zaïane, O.R., Li, Z. (eds.) ADMA 2006. LNCS, vol. 4093, pp. 56–63. Springer, Heidelberg (2006). doi:10.1007/11811305_5
17. Lichman, M.: UCI machine learning repository (2013)
18. Lin, C.W., Hong, T.P.: Maintenance of pre large trees for data mining with modified records. Inform. Sci. **278**, 88–103 (2014)
19. Liu, C.-Y., Tseng, C.-Y., Chen, M.-S.: Incremental mining of significant URLs in real-time and large-scale social streams. In: Pei, J., Tseng, V.S., Cao, L., Motoda, H., Xu, G. (eds.) PAKDD 2013. LNCS, vol. 7819, pp. 473–484. Springer, Heidelberg (2013). doi:10.1007/978-3-642-37456-2_40
20. Liu, H., Lin, Y., Han, J.: Methods for mining frequent items in data streams: an overview. Knowl. Inf. Syst. **26**(1), 1–30 (2011)
21. Medina, R., Nourine, L.: A unified hierarchy for functional dependencies, conditional functional dependencies and association rules. In: Ferré, S., Rudolph, S. (eds.) ICFCA 2009. LNCS, vol. 5548, pp. 98–113. Springer, Heidelberg (2009). doi:10.1007/978-3-642-01815-2_9
22. Nakayama, H., Hoshino, A., Ito, C., Kanno, K.: Formalization and discovery of approximate conditional functional dependencies. In: Decker, H., Lhotská, L., Link, S., Basl, J., Tjoa, A.M. (eds.) DEXA 2013. LNCS, vol. 8055, pp. 118–128. Springer, Heidelberg (2013). doi:10.1007/978-3-642-40285-2_12
23. Parr, T.: The Definitive ANTLR 4 Reference, 2nd edn. Pragmatic Bookshelf, Dallas (2013)
24. Paton, N.W., Díaz, O.: Active database systems. ACM Comput. Surv. **31**(1), 63–103 (1999)
25. Pérez-Alonso, A., Blanco, I., Serrano, J.M., González-González, L.M.: Drims: data rules incremental maintenance system (2016). https://github.com/AlainPerez/DRIMS-Repository
26. Pérez-Alonso, A., Medina, I.J.B., González-González, L.M., Serrano Chica, J.M.: Incremental maintenance of discovered association rules and approximate dependencies. Intell. Data Anal. **21**(1), 117–133 (2017)
27. Qin, S.J.: Process data analytics in the era of big data. AIChE J. **60**(9), 3092–3100 (2014)
28. Sánchez, D., Serrano, J.M., Blanco, I., Martín-Bautista, M.J., Vila, M.A.: Using association rules to mine for strong approximate dependencies. Data Min. Knowl. Disc. **16**(3), 313–348 (2008)
29. Sauter, V.: Decision Support Systems for Business Intelligence. Wiley, Hoboken (2014)
30. Shah, S., Chauhan, N., Bhanderi, S.: Incremental mining of association rules: a survey. Int. J. Comput. Sci. Inf. Technol. **3**(3), 4071–4074 (2012)
31. Srikant, R., Agrawal, R.: Mining quantitative association rules in large relational tables. ACM SIGMOD Rec. **25**, 1–12 (1996)
32. Tan, J., Bu, Y., Zhao, H.: Incremental maintenance of association rules over data streams. In: 2nd International Conference on Networking and Digital Society (ICNDS), vol. 2, pp. 444–447 (2010)
33. Wu, X., Zhang, C., Zhang, S.: Efficient mining of both positive and negative association rules. ACM Trans. Inf. Syst. **22**(3), 381–405 (2004)
34. Wu, X., Zhu, X., Wu, G.Q., Ding, W.: Data mining with big data. IEEE Trans. Knowl. Data Eng. **26**(1), 97–107 (2014)
35. Zia, Z.K., Tipu, S.K., Khan, M.I.: Research on association rule mining. Adv. Comput. Math. Appl. **2**(1), 226–236 (2012)

Querying Streams of Alerts for Knowledge-Based Detection of Long-Lived Network Intrusions

Miguel-Angel Sicilia(✉), Javier Bermejo-Higuera, Elena García-Barriocanal, Salvador Sánchez-Alonso, Daniel Domínguez-Álvarez, and Miguel Monzón-Fernández

University of Alcalá, Polytechnic Building, Ctra. Barcelona Km. 33.6, 28871 Alcalá de Henares, Madrid, Spain
{msicilia,javier.bermejo,elena.garciab,salvador.sanchez}@uah.es,
{d.domingueza,miguel.monzon}@edu.uah.es

Abstract. Intrusion detection relies on the analysis of flows of network and system events that are checked against signatures or models of normality to raise alerts. However, these alerts are often the result of having detected a single step in the unfolding sequence of activities of an attacker, and techniques relying on simple alerting fall short in recognizing or preventing subsequent actions. Here we present the design and prototype implementation of a novel intrusion detection approach based on agents that are triggered in reaction to alerts that use *attack patterns* as working hypotheses. Those agents query the real-time stream of alerts, matching them with a particular attack pattern and a graph model of the network being monitored. The architecture for that system scales using the distributed streaming framework of Apache Kafka and a lightweight agent container, allowing for long-lived monitoring of attack hypotheses, each of them embodied in a single agent. The approach is tested against synthetic flows of data representing single-node and multi-step "island hopping" scenarios.

Keywords: Intrusion detection · Attack patterns · Stream queries · Asynchronous agents

1 Introduction

Current *Intrusion Detection Systems* (IDS) work on real-time streams of data. A stream can be considered an infinite sequence of append-only `(info, timestamp)` pairs, where the tuple represents a piece of data about an event, be it at the system, network or application level. Considering this, the fundamental task of an IDS (as for example Snort [15]) deployed in a single network node (or in a subnetwork in the case of other kind of detection systems [11]) is that of contrasting the stream of raw events with a set of rules or models with the purpose of detecting suspicious or anomalous evidence and deliver alerts from

H. Christiansen et al. (Eds.): FQAS 2017, LNAI 10333, pp. 186–197, 2017.
DOI: 10.1007/978-3-319-59692-1_16

them. This also in general applies to more complex systems that aggregate and correlate events, e.g. *Log Managers* (LM) as GrayLog[1] or Splunk[2], or *Security Event and Information Management* (SIEM) systems as OSSIM[3].

Alert data produced by these systems can also be considered a stream, a derived one in which events are yet qualified (and usually enriched or combined) by some other component. Typically, IDS, LM or SIEM systems classify the alerts they produce using some form of taxonomy or tagging, a priority indicator, and provide some additional references to external information that refers to the knowledge used to craft the rule or filter. This is the base information on which decision-making and response is currently supported. Existing research has proposed the use of ontologies for a better description of the alerts and their context [19], but they are not widely deployed to date.

Significant progress on intrusion detection has resulted in a variety of detection techniques. However, many of them rely on an approach that use rules or filters that require seeing one or a number of event simultaneously, due to the rule firing paradigm as in e.g. [16]. This does not fit well with the detection of convoluted, multi-step attack patterns, that may span days or even months. Concretely, the emergence of Advanced Persistent Threats (APT) requires new approaches [4] in which detection becomes a long-term process and uses some form of adversarial knowledge, that is currently only available via descriptions of attack patterns in semi-structured form.

In this paper, we present the model, design and prototype implementation of an approach to long-term intrusion detection that combines three sources of information: an adversarial knowledge model extracted from known attack patterns, a model of the network structure and status, and a semantically homogeneous stream of data. Decision processes on what is an intrusion take place along an undefined time span, instead of as an instantaneous rule firing event. The main element of the approach is that of agents that hypothesize that a given attack pattern is unfolding, and query the continuous stream of data in search for evidence, that is matched against the representation of the attack pattern itself. As a result of using a network model that conveys data on network paths and vulnerability scores, it is also able to produce predictions on estimated highly likely adverse events. This is achieved by the ability to integrate models similar to those of the `Cauldron` system [9].

The model scales by relying on state-of-the-art SIEM or LM for the aggregation of real-time events, and then uses message brokering systems and independent agents instead of a monolithic knowledge-based approach, allowing for scalability and flexibility in updating the set of adversarial models.

The rest of this paper is structured as follows. Section 2 briefly surveys previous related work on intrusion detection models. Then, the agent and query model is described in Sect. 3. Section 4 reports the prototype implementation of

[1] https://www.graylog.org/.
[2] https://www.splunk.com.
[3] https://www.alienvault.com/products/ossim.

that model on scalable technologies and a setup for experimentation and testing. Finally, conclusions and outlook are provided in Sect. 5.

2 Related Work

In this section we first briefly revise existing surveys on intrusion detection techniques, and then succinctly discuss the two main features of the presented approach: using a knowledge-based agent model and scalability.

2.1 Existing Surveys and Approaches to Pattern Detection

There are many surveys related to intrusion detection, reflecting the volume and variety of the literature in the topic. Some of them are restricted to some particular technique of machine intelligence or type of network, but only a few adopt a more general scope. Among them, in the report [1] we can find a broader taxonomy. Following that, our approach can be considered a higher level approach based on *programmed signatures*, and using state-modeling and in some sense *expert-system* based as it combines different models. But it is also *compound* in the sense that the events produced by any other computational technique [24] can be used as input. The work of Cuppens and Miege [6] approach alert correlation using abduction on scenarios, and are thus similar to the graph based method described here, but they do not tackle with the monitoring and querying aspects of the stream of alerts.

2.2 Agent-Based Systems and Intrusion Detection

The idea of using multi-agent systems for intrusion detection has been around for more than two decades. Early ideas on that topic focused on the autonomous capacity of agents to monitor hosts and then interchange information among them using transceiver architectures [2,18]. However, the role of those agents has been largely taken over by IDS software that is now widely deployed across networks. This is the reason why we aim at complementing IDS software as in many other more recent approaches that add some agent-based collaboration [12] rather than implementing the IDS using agents [7]. In other direction, the aggregation and correlation of events is now the role of also widely used SIEM or LM systems [25]. For that reason, we use a narrower approach to agents, as a way of decoupling query and reasoning, complementing the deployment of the just mentioned software pieces for the particular purpose of long-term monitoring, similarly as for example in [5].

2.3 Scalability of Intrusion Detection

IDS are optimized to cope with high volumes of network packets, and there have been proposals to use specialized hardware-software architectures as GPUs for the task [22]. As our approach complements the IDS and SIEM deployment, it focuses on scalability at another point in the architecture, after the aggregation of events done by LM or SIEM [20]. It is thus a sort of analytic task that could be scaled in clusters with approaches as those described in [21].

3 Proposed Model

The model proposed is based on a functional architecture as depicted in Fig. 1. The model is based on assuming that alerting and logs are centrally managed in a LM or similar system. Then, an event queue (EQ) is used as a buffer for the agents that query the incoming flow of alerts. In other direction, a network model is gathered from the network, represented as a labeled graph. That graph may incorporate information from routers and firewalls along with vulnerability status of nodes, similarly to the models used in [9]. All that different models are used by three kind of agents with a clear separation of concerns. These are described in the following subsections, together with a third source of knowledge, that of attack hypotheses (i.e. representations of attack patterns).

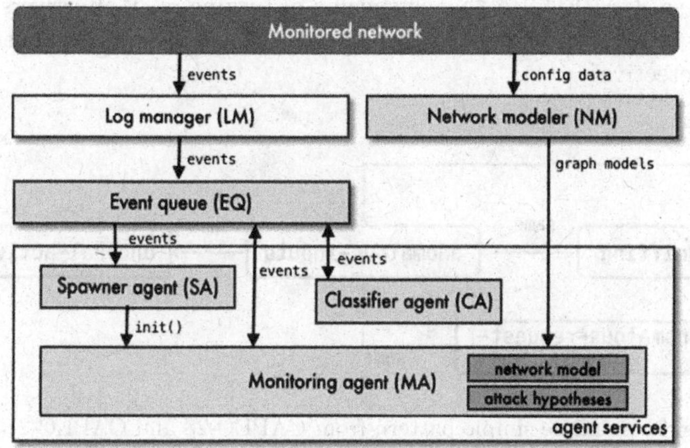

Fig. 1. Functional architecture of the proposed solution

3.1 Attack Patterns

The key characteristic of the approach presented here is that it is knowledge-based in the sense that it queries events, network models and the current provisional hypothesis driven by an attack pattern. This requires that the steps in that attack pattern are expressed in the same vocabulary. The *Common Attack Pattern Enumeration and Classification* (CAPEC) taxonomy provides a sort of ontology for describing attack steps [13], but requires some additional formalization. Most of the patterns found in CAPEC are actually basic, single step, but some can serve as a basis for a more complete language, possibly adapting also other patterns that can be found in the literature, for example, those typical in worm infection [14]. The *Malware Attribute Enumeration and Characterization* (MAEC) framework links malware description to patterns making use of CAPEC for describing the relevant behaviour with a high-level malware taxonomy [10].

The pattern itself can be represented as a directed acyclic graph (DAG) of steps, each of which correspond to a directly or indirectly observable event, with one or several start states. Formally, we will consider for each pattern i a graph $\Phi_i = (S, T)$ where S is the set of nodes representing steps and T the set of arcs that represent possible following events and are tagged with ontology properties, e.g. $type(t_k)$ with $t_k \in T$ may be `same` guarding the transition so that it constrains it to an event in the same node as the previous, or `other` to represent that the attack unfolds to a different node (or other possible relations). Each node $s_j \in S$ is tagged with $kind(s_j)$ that represents a term in the taxonomy or ontology of alert types. Initial steps are explicitly labeled as $init(s_j)$. For example, CAPEC-28 "fuzzing" pattern can be represented as a simple sequence of detection events. However, the current description of attack patterns is mainly described from the attacker's perspective. This makes that for example other fuzzing patterns are also in CAPEC are not formally cross-referenced, e.g. CAPEC-215 that is specific of fuzzing on Web servers. Figure 2 provides an integrated view of both patterns using the security controls referenced as "detective".

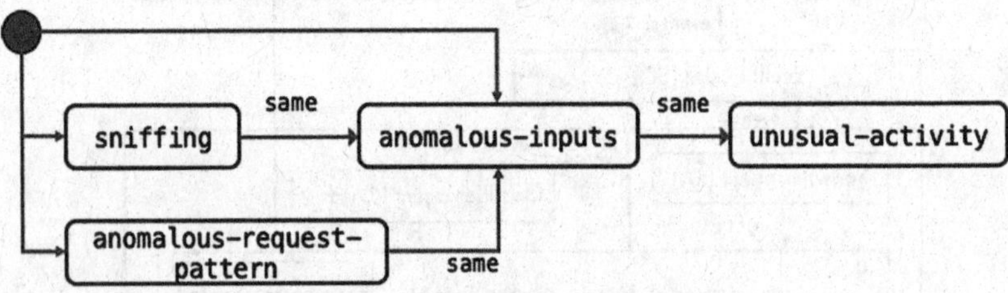

Fig. 2. Example simple pattern from CAPEC-28 and CAPEC-215

In CAPEC, it is possible to extract relationships among detectable events also indirectly via `CanFollow` relationships, but these are still used rather sparsely in the database.

It should be noted that the patterns represented in the kind of models described impose some constraints on the modeling of attacker behaviour. They could be extended for example to probabilistic graphs to incorporate more information, or allow for relating patterns among them as variants or clusters of typical co-occurring attacker behaviour. However, here we stick to the basic graph model as the first proof of concept of the architecture.

3.2 Stream Queues and Classification

It is assumed that events across the network are gathered in a sort of log management (LM) system or a SIEM, which may do some sort of initial processing or interpretation of events produced by independent systems as IDSs.

All the interesting events considered by the LM are then sent to a stream queue that serves as a single source of events for the rest of the system. Events in the sequence of events E are in the form $e_i = (info, timestamp)$. The required fields in $info$ are only the *location* of the event (typically, the address of the host affected), and the *kind* of the event.

Different intrusion detection systems use different vocabularies for reporting the types of alerts in *kind*. The first task is thus that of classifying events according to some sort of ontology, so that other agents use a single, consistent terminology. That ontology is the same as that used in attack pattern graphs Φ to label the nodes, e.g. $kind(s_j)$. The use of an ontology language in formal logics allows for the application of subsumption and reasoning in general when deciding graph traversal, but flat hierarchies can also be used for simplicity.

As an example, the following Snort rule fragment detects a particular kind of sniffing activity.

```
alert icmp $EXTERNAL_NET any -> $HOME_NET any
(msg:"PROTOCOL-ICMP PING Sniffer Pro/NetXRay network scan";
itype:8; content:"Cinco Network, Inc.";
...classtype:misc-activity; ...)
```

However, the `classtype` is in this case non informative. The ontology would mediate in transforming an event triggered by this alert into a *kind* `sniffing` (or a subclass of it), so that it can be matched against graphs as depicted in Fig. 2. This will be the main task of classifier agents, as described below.

3.3 Spawning Monitoring Agents

A first agent spawner takes the database of attack patterns $[\Phi]$ and attempts to match the current event in the stream with the start states of attack patterns. Each pair (Φ_i, a) is an hypothesis that an attacker is starting his activity based on the evidence given by event a with the intention captured in Φ_i.

It should be noted that eventually different agents under different hypotheses may be working on the same stream of events. This requires the scalability of the system with a worst case complexity of $O(init([\Phi]) \times |E|)$ with $init([\Phi])$ the amount of start states in the pattern database. It is difficult to estimate the actual average workload needed as some agents may live for long periods of time. This requires a lightweight approach with small overhead to the concurrent activity of monitoring agents.

3.4 Long-Lived Queries Using Attack Graphs

Each monitoring agent takes the current network graph G as the baseline, initially annotating the node with the triggering event.

The graph $G = (N, A)$ is a network model of nodes n_i and their connectivity that may be of a complex nature[4]. In general, it is required that it is capable of answering two basic questions described in Table 1, in order for the algorithm to decide on the progress in the pattern.

Table 1. Primitives for the graph model G

Verb	Result
reachable(n_i, n_j)	Node is reachable from other node
vulnerable(n_i, m_j)	Node is vulnerable to given attack mechanism m_j

It should be noted that vulnerability can be implemented in flexible terms. An option may be that of using some global scoring as CVSS that has been used as a belief elsewhere [8], or a more informed combination of such with some measure or estimation of weakness to the given mechanism of attack category. Reachability can be interpreted in a crisp sense as network reachability, but it can also be combined with some score measuring the attack surface of the node.

The process of querying the stream of data can then be seen as a graph matching algorithm. Given an attack pattern Φ taken as working hypothesis, the process is that of taking the next event from the stream of alerts and consider if the alert represents a possible event under the current annotated network graph G. Algorithm 1 describes the main elements of the algorithmic approach.

Algorithm 1. Match alert stream under hypothesis ϕ

```
procedure MATCH-ALERT(a, G, Φ)                  ▷ Match next alert to current state
    loc, kind ← info(a)
    next ← targets(G, kind)                     ▷ Potential nodes for given alert
    if loc ∈ next ∧ matches(a, Φ) then          ▷ Match with attack graph
        G, n ← annotate(G, a)
    end if
    if istarget(G, n, Φ) ∨ curtime() > LIMIT then    ▷ Check finalization
        alert(self)
        selfdestruct()
    end if
end procedure
```

[4] It should be noted that this graph in general has 'self loops' as in general the same node is accessible to an attacker in an unfolding situation.

The *targets* function queries the network graph G for nodes that are *reachable* and *vulnerable* for the current state of the unfolding attack. Reachability is checked against the network restrictions (subnetworks, firewalls), and vulnerability is relative to the attack mechanism *kind*. Then, if the node affected by the event is in that potential set of targets, the attack graph is used to check if the inclusion of the event in the graph conforms to the pattern. Eventually, the graph model is annotated for upcoming iterations. Termination is considered after some timeout or when a leave in the attack graph is reached.

The process can be seen as a continuous query to the stream of events followed by queries that match the attack graph and the network graph. Finally, prediction can be done by querying the next steps in the pattern graph, then matching with the current state of the network graph.

4 Implementation and Experimental Evaluation

4.1 Prototype Architecture

The prototype has been deployed using Apache Kafka[5], a fault-tolerant and scalable queue system as the stream back-end of the alert system. This serves as the source of alerts (*records* in Kafka) and simulates the infrastructure that in practice will be provided by a SIEM or LM system.

The agent system was implemented using the `aiomas` framework in Python, that abstracts RPC (remote procedure call) and network messaging together with concurrent programming using `asyncio` standard libraries, providing light coroutine primitives and scalability to thousands of agents in one or several containers. Classifiers and triggerers are grouped as Kafka consumers thus providing effective load balancing, while monitoring are not, as all the events need to be broadcasted to them.

The network graph G is handled using `networkx`, after querying a `Neo4j` graph database. Attack pattern graphs Φ are also handled with `networkx` but in this case, using `graphviz` text files as input just as a convenience format, as they are typically very small in size, and the ones extracted from CAPEC are uncomplicated.

The `ClassifierAgent` uses a mapping of the following alert type classifications with a terminology extracted from the indicators in CAPEC patterns:

- Snort 2.9.9 default classifications[6].
- Suricata 3.2.1. classification metadata[7].

A total of 28 terms were extracted from the three sources of information. This may seem a rather small amount, but it should be noted that some indicators are not considered alerts as they have also legitimate uses, and the descriptions of the patterns are not complete in many cases. There are alert types that

[5] https://kafka.apache.org/.
[6] http://manual-snort-org.s3-website-us-east-1.amazonaws.com/.
[7] https://github.com/inliniac/suricata/blob/master/classification.config.

require additional context-specific information as Suricata's `policy-violation` that refers to corporate security policies (and are thus unspecific in nature), and others generic as `misc-activity` that have not been included.

The classifier agent simply inspects the **raw** source Kafka *topic* (a topic is a category of records), substitutes the *kind* field of the events and then submits the alert to the **processed** queue, that is used by the `TriggererAgent`. That agent matches the next event to initial states of attack graphs and eventually spawns new `MonitoringAgents` under the hypothesis of a particular graph Φ_i with the network graph annotated in the *location* node of that event with the given *kind* term.

Finally, `MonitoringAgents` subscribe to the processed stream of events and follows the above-described algorithm looking for potential unfolding attacks. These agents inspect the same topic as the triggerer agent, so that it is possible that the same event is used both for starting and hypothesis check and also as evidence for an intermediate step in an existing check.

4.2 Evaluation with Graph Models from CAPEC

Evaluating intrusion detection for high-level attack patterns is challenging due to a complete lack of datasets. There are datasets and proposals for datasets synthesis [17] for particular classes of scenarios, but not in the case of multi-step patterns that are the focus of our proposal. It is thus impractical to attempt to evaluate the approach using the usual performance indicators as precision, recall or false negatives or positives.

As a consequence, the evaluation of the approach has been done in two steps. The first step was that of assessing the modeling approach using meta and standard CAPEC patterns. The second was that of generating synthetic traffic from hypothetical attackers simulated using agent-based modeling.

The analysis of CAPEC 2.9 descriptions (using its downloadable XML serialization) found only 202 occurrences of the `type=''Detective''` attribute for `capec:Security_Control` elements, with many of them repeated. Most of them did not have a direct mapping to the taxonomy of alerts extracted from IDS classifications, and many of them were sitting at the application level, including indicators related to anomalous SQL or Web traffic. In any case, information for building the complete graphs was incomplete, as detective indicators rarely covered all the `capec:Attack_Step` phases in the attack but were generic or related only to its inception.

The implementation used the `miniKanren` embedded *Domain Specific Language* (DSL) for logic programming [3], available for many languages (here we have used the `logpy`[8] implementation of `miniKanren`). The language is expressive enough for the above-presented simple queries that match the annotated state of the network graph with the attack pattern, and provides a declarative environment for its augmentation.

[8] https://github.com/logpy/logpy.

The core query needed is that of locating the next network nodes that are affected by k in the current (h_{curr}, k) pair representing the host and alert type of the next stream alert. The following code shows the basic two parallel goals accounting for events expected on the *same* or *other* host, according to the pattern hypothesis (h and $k2$ are fresh variables).

```
res = run(0, h,
          conde(
              [hosts(h, True), vulnerable(h, k),
              affected(h, k2), same(k2, k)],

              [(hosts, h, True), (vulnerable, h, k),
              (affected, h2, k2), (other, k2, k),
              (equalo, (h, h2), False)] ))
```

That basic query entails that the actual h_{curr} is among the responses, the event has to be annotated. Further, other elements in h can be considered predicted or at-risk nodes (the query for a given bound k can be driven by the most critical vulnerabilities, for instance). An interesting consequence of the progressive graph traversal is that each agent does not need to have its own copy of the full network model, but only of those nodes that are *reachable* from the set of nodes already involved, so that graph is built stepwise.

The most interesting patterns are those that are informally called "island hopping" attacks, in which an attacker breaks into a host then uses that host as a platform to break into others. This has been simulated using the `mesa`[9] agent-based modeling (ABM) framework. ABM libraries allow for the explicit modeling of adversarial behaviour, which is key in experimenting with attack pattern detection.

5 Conclusions and Outlook

As security threats in cyberspace become more pervasive and complex, there is a need for knowledge-based approaches to intrusion detection. The adversarial and persistent nature of complex attacks requires the capability of long-term monitoring under adversarial hypotheses.

In this paper, we have reported a model and implementation of an agent-based system that combines a knowledge model based on known attack patterns with querying and matching a semantically homogeneous stream of events with a graph model representing the network and its constraints. The model has the following relevant features: (a) it integrates with current state of the art technology that combines IDS events into LM or SIEM systems, (b) it scales to larger networks and net flows by using queuing systems and decentralizing the monitoring process, and (c) it is able to operate with different hypotheses in parallel and along long time spans, becoming a promising approach to convoluted and persistent attacks. The main limitation of the approach presented is that of

[9] https://github.com/projectmesa/mesa.

the current lack of elaboration of attack patterns, which are described in semi-structured form and have different degrees of elaboration, which makes difficult in practice its translation to graph models. Also, matching event classifications from IDS to a common vocabulary is challenging, so more work is needed in establishing a complete and consistent language for querying investigative events.

The approach presented here can be extended in a number of ways. There are a number of elements in the architecture that could be used as additional information for the decision-making process. These may include considering vulnerability scores as probabilities, a priori probabilities for attack pattern graphs and vagueness in priority scores in alert events. However, the lack of empirical datasets for convoluted patterns constrains the possible contrast of such approaches to date. In other direction, the interaction of the approach presented with a feedback cycle as that implemented for single-step detection in the AI^2 system [23] has the potential of overcoming the limitations of encoding attack patterns manually.

Acknowledgements. This research has been conducted in the frame of the project "*Sistema de Analítica Predictiva para Defensa en el Ciberespacio basada en escenarios reproducibles*" (PREDECIBLE), programme "DN8644-COINCIDENTE", funded by the National Armaments Directorate of the Ministry of Defence of Spain (PREDECIBLE, project number 10032/15/005600, DN8644-COINCIDENTE).

References

1. Axelsson, S.: A survey and taxonomy, vol. 99. Chalmers University of Technology, Technical report (2000)
2. Balasubramaniyan, J.S., García-Fernandez, J.O., Isacoff, D., Spafford, E., Zamboni, D.: An architecture for intrusion detection using autonomous agents. In: Proceeding of the 14th Annual Computer Security Applications Conference, pp. 13–24. IEEE (1998)
3. Byrd, W.E.: Techniques, applications, and implementations (Doctoral dissertation, Department of Computer Science, Indiana University) (2009)
4. Chen, P., Desmet, L., Huygens, C.: A study on advanced persistent threats. In: Decker, B., Zúquete, A. (eds.) CMS 2014. LNCS, vol. 8735, pp. 63–72. Springer, Heidelberg (2014). doi:10.1007/978-3-662-44885-4_5
5. Coppolino, L., D'Antonio, S., Formicola, V., Romano, L.: Integration of a system for critical infrastructure protection with the OSSIM SIEM platform: a dam case study. In: Flammini, F., Bologna, S., Vittorini, V. (eds.) SAFECOMP 2011. LNCS, vol. 6894, pp. 199–212. Springer, Heidelberg (2011). doi:10.1007/978-3-642-24270-0_15
6. Cuppens, F., Miege, A.: Alert correlation in a cooperative intrusion detection framework. In: Proceeding of the IEEE Symposium on Security and Privacy, pp. 202–215. IEEE (2002)
7. Helmer, G., Wong, J.S., Honavar, V., Miller, L., Wang, Y.: Lightweight agents for intrusion detection. J. Syst. Softw. **67**(2), 109–122 (2003)
8. Houmb, S.H., Franqueira, V.N., Engum, E.A.: Quantifying security risk level from CVSS estimates of frequency and impact. J. Syst. Softw. **83**(9), 1622–1634 (2010)

9. Jajodia, S., Noel, S., Kalapa, P., Albanese, M., Williams, J.: mission-centric cyber situational awareness with defense in depth. In: Military Communications Conference, 2011-MILCOM, pp. 1339–1344. IEEE (2011)
10. Lee, A., Varadharajan, V., Tupakula, U.: On malware characterization and attack classification. In Proceedings of the First Australasian Web Conference, vol. 144, pp. 43–47. Australian Computer Society (2013)
11. Liao, H.J., Lin, C.H.R., Lin, Y.C., Tung, K.Y.: Intrusion detection system: a comprehensive review. J. Network Comput. Appl. **36**(1), 16–24 (2013)
12. Mishra, A., Nadkarni, K., Patcha, A.: Intrusion detection in wireless ad hoc networks. IEEE Wirel. Commun. **11**(1), 48–60 (2004)
13. Pauli, J., Engebretson, P.H.: Towards a specification prototype for hierarchy-driven attack patterns. In: Fifth International Conference on Information Technology: New Generations, ITNG 2008, pp. 1168-1169. IEEE (2011)
14. Robiah, Y., Rahayu, S.S., Sahib, S., Zaki, M.M., Faizal, M.A., Marliza, R.: An improved traditional worm attack pattern. In: International Symposium in Information Technology (ITSim), vol. 2, pp. 1067–1072. IEEE (2010)
15. Roesch, M.: Lightweight intrusion detection for networks. In: Lisa, vol. 99, no. 1, pp. 229–238 (1999)
16. Sadighian, A., Fernandez, J.M., Lemay, A., Zargar, S.T.: ONTIDS: a highly flexible context-aware and ontology-based alert correlation framework. In: Danger, J.-L., Debbabi, M., Marion, J.-Y., Garcia-Alfaro, J., Zincir Heywood, N. (eds.) FPS 2013. LNCS, vol. 8352, pp. 161–177. Springer, Cham (2014). doi:10.1007/978-3-319-05302-8_10
17. Shiravi, A., Shiravi, H., Tavallaee, M., Ghorbani, A.A.: Toward developing a systematic approach to generate benchmark datasets for intrusion detection. Comput. Secur. **31**(3), 357–374 (2012)
18. Spafford, E.H., Zamboni, D.: Intrusion detection using autonomous agents. Comput. Networks **34**(4), 547–570 (2000)
19. Undercoffer, J., Joshi, A., Pinkston, J.: Modeling computer attacks: an ontology for intrusion detection. In: Vigna, G., Kruegel, C., Jonsson, E. (eds.) RAID 2003. LNCS, vol. 2820, pp. 113–135. Springer, Heidelberg (2003). doi:10.1007/978-3-540-45248-5_7
20. Vaarandi, R., Niziski, P.: Comparative analysis of open-source log management solutions for security monitoring and network forensics. In: Proceedings of the 2013 European Conference on Information Warfare and Security, pp. 278–287 (2013)
21. Vallentin, M., Sommer, R., Lee, J., Leres, C., Paxson, V., Tierney, B.: The NIDS cluster: scalable, stateful network intrusion detection on commodity hardware. In: Kruegel, C., Lippmann, R., Clark, A. (eds.) RAID 2007. LNCS, vol. 4637, pp. 107–126. Springer, Heidelberg (2007). doi:10.1007/978-3-540-74320-0_6
22. Vasiliadis, G., Antonatos, S., Polychronakis, M., Markatos, E.P., Ioannidis, S.: Gnort: high performance network intrusion detection using graphics processors. In: Lippmann, R., Kirda, E., Trachtenberg, A. (eds.) RAID 2008. LNCS, vol. 5230, pp. 116–134. Springer, Heidelberg (2008). doi:10.1007/978-3-540-87403-4_7
23. Veeramachaneni, K., Arnaldo, I., Korrapati, V., Bassias, C., Li, K.: AI^2 training a big data machine to defend. In: IEEE International Conference on Intelligent Data and Security (IDS), pp. 49–54 (2016)
24. Wu, S.X., Banzhaf, W.: The use of computational intelligence in intrusion detection systems: a review. Appl. Soft Comput. **10**(1), 1–35 (2010)
25. Zuech, R., Khoshgoftaar, T.M., Wald, R.: Intrusion detection and big heterogeneous data: a survey. J. Big Data **2**(1), 3 (2015)

Intuitionistic Sets

Multiplicative Type of Operations over Intuitionistic Fuzzy Pairs

Krassimir Atanassov[1,2(✉)], Eulalia Szmidt[3,4(✉)], and Janusz Kacprzyk[3,4(✉)]

[1] Department of Bioinformatics and Mathematical Modelling,
Institute of Biophysics and Biomedical Engineering,
Bulgarian Academy of Sciences,
105 Acad. G. Bonchev Str., 1113 Sofia, Bulgaria
krat@bas.bg

[2] Intelligent Systems Laboratory Prof. Asen Zlatarov University,
8010 Burgas, Bulgaria

[3] Systems Research Institute, Polish Academy of Sciences,
ul. Newelska 6, 01-447 Warsaw, Poland
{szmidt,kacprzyk}@ibspan.waw.pl

[4] Warsaw School of Information Technology,
ul. Newelska 6, 01-447 Warsaw, Poland

Abstract. Intuitionistic Fuzzy Sets (IFSs) are an extension of fuzzy sets. Each element x of the IFS A has degrees of a membership $(\mu_A(x))$ and of a non-membership $(\nu_A(x))$ so that $0 \leq \mu_A(x) + \nu_A(x) \leq 1$. The pair $\langle \mu_A(x), \nu_A(x) \rangle$ is called an Intuitionistic Fuzzy Pair (IFP). A lot of operations, relations and operators are defined over IFPs. In the paper, novel operations over IFPs are introduced and some of their basic properties are studied. Geometrical interpretations of these operations are given. Open problems are formulated.

Keywords: Intuitionistic fuzzy conjunction · Intuitionistic fuzzy disjunction · Intuitionistic fuzzy pair · Multiplication · Intuitionistic fuzzy negation

1 Introduction

In [2], the authors introduced the concept of Intuitionistic Fuzzy Pair (IFP), defined some operations, relations and operators over it and properties of their properties. Here, some new operations from multiplicative type are introduced and some of their algebraic properties are studied.

The IFP is an object in the form $\langle a, b \rangle$, where $a, b \in [0, 1]$ and $a + b \leq 1$, that is used for evaluation of objects or processes and which components (a and b) are interpreted as degrees of membership and non-membership, or degrees of validity and non-validity, or degree of correctness and non-correctness, etc. The geometrical interpretations of the IFPs are the same as those of the IFSs. The most popular of them is shown in Fig. 1.

H. Christiansen et al. (Eds.): FQAS 2017, LNAI 10333, pp. 201–208, 2017.
DOI: 10.1007/978-3-319-59692-1_17

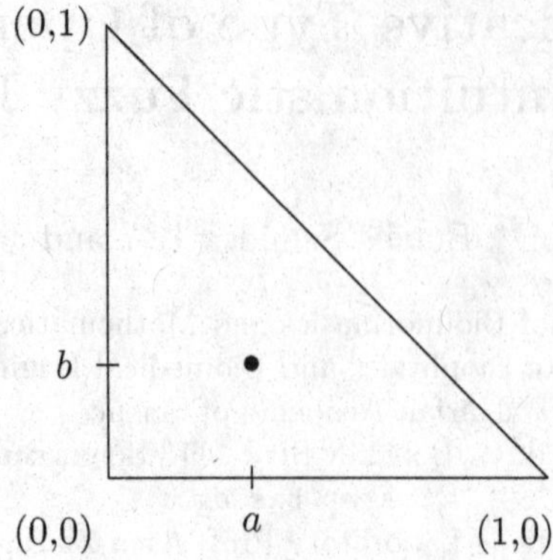

Fig. 1. The most popular geometrical interpretations of the IFPs

For the needs of the discussion below, by analogy with, e.g., [1], we define the notion of Intuitionistic Fuzzy Tautological Pair (IFTP) by:

"x is an IFTP if and only if $a \geq b$",

while p is a Tautological Pair (TP) iff $a = 1$ and $b = 0$.

Let us have two IFPs $x = \langle a, b\rangle$ and $y = \langle c, d\rangle$. In [2], a lot of relations are defined over IFPs. The most important from them are

$$\begin{array}{l} x < y \ \text{ iff } \ a < c \text{ and } b > d, \\ x \leq y \ \text{ iff } \ a \leq c \text{ and } b \geq d, \\ x > y \ \text{ iff } \ a > c \text{ and } b < d, \\ x \geq y \ \text{ iff } \ a \geq c \text{ and } b \leq d, \\ x = y \ \text{ iff } \ a = c \text{ and } b = d. \end{array}$$

Also, the following analogues of operations "conjunction" and "disjunction" are introduced in [2]:

$$\begin{array}{l} x \wedge_1 y = x \cap y = \langle \min(a, c), \max(b, d)\rangle, \\ x \vee_1 y = x \cup y = \langle \max(a, c), \min(b, d)\rangle, \\ x \wedge_2 y = x.y = \langle a.c, b + d - b.d\rangle, \\ x \vee_2 y = x + y = \langle a + c - a.c, b.d\rangle. \end{array}$$

Let, as above, $x = \langle a, b\rangle$ be an IFP and let $\alpha, \beta \in [0, 1]$. In [2], the basic modal type of operators are defined. Here, we give definition of only some of them, that will be used in the discussion below:

$$\begin{array}{l} G_{\alpha,\beta}(x) = \langle \alpha.a, \beta.b\rangle \\ H_{\alpha,\beta}(x) = \langle \alpha.a, b + \beta.(1 - a - b)\rangle \\ J_{\alpha,\beta}(x) = \langle a + \alpha.(1 - a - b), \beta.b\rangle, \end{array}$$

where for the last two operators, $\alpha + \beta \leq 1$.

2 Main Results

Now, for two IFPs $x = \langle a, b\rangle$ and $y = \langle c, d\rangle$, we introduce the following novel operations from multiplicative type:

$$\begin{aligned} x \times_1 y &= \langle \max(a,c), bd\rangle, \\ x \times_2 y &= \langle \min(a,c), bd\rangle, \\ x \times_3 y &= \langle ac, bd\rangle, \\ x \times_4 y &= \langle ac, \min(b,d)\rangle, \\ x \times_5 y &= \langle ac, \max(b,d)\rangle. \end{aligned}$$

First, we must mention that for every two IFPs x and y: $x \times_i y$ is an IFP for each $1 \le i \le 5$ and

$$x \times_5 y \le x \times_4 y \le x \times_3 y \le x \times_2 y \le x \times_1 y.$$

Moreover, the inequalities are valid:

$$\begin{aligned} & x \wedge_2 y \le x \times_5 y \le x \times_1 y \le x \vee_2 y, \\ & x \times_5 y \le x \wedge_1 y \le x \times_2 y, \\ & x \times_4 y \le x \vee_1 y \le x \times_1 y. \end{aligned}$$

Second, we see that for $a, b, \alpha, \beta \in [0,1]$ so that $a + b \le 1$ and $\alpha + \beta \le 1$:

$$\langle \alpha, \beta\rangle \times_3 \langle a, b\rangle = G_{\alpha,\beta}(\langle a, b\rangle).$$

On the other hand, operator $G_{\alpha,\beta}$ is applicable for values of α and β for which $1 < \alpha + \beta \le 2$, while the pair $\langle \alpha, \beta\rangle$ is not an IFP. Operations $\times_1$ and $\times_2$ are to some extent analogues of operator $J_{\alpha,\beta}$, while operations $\times_4$ and $\times_5$ are analogues of operator $H_{\alpha,\beta}$.

Third, let x and y have the above forms and let $z = \langle e, f\rangle$. Then, we check directly the validity of the following equalities for $1 \le i \le 5$:

$$\begin{aligned} x \times_i y &= y \times_i x, \\ (x \times_i y) \times_i z &= x \times_i (y \times_i z). \end{aligned}$$

Fourth, for each IFP x:

$$\begin{aligned} \langle 0,1\rangle \times_1 x &= x = x \times_1 \langle 0,1\rangle, \\ \langle 1,0\rangle \times_5 x &= x = x \times_5 \langle 1,0\rangle, \\ \langle 1,0\rangle \times_1 x &= \langle 1,0\rangle = x \times_1 \langle 1,0\rangle, \\ \langle 0,1\rangle \times_5 x &= \langle 0,1\rangle = x \times_5 \langle 0,1\rangle, \end{aligned}$$

while the rest operations do not satisfy similar equalities.

Let

$$\mathcal{L} = \{\langle a, b\rangle | a, b \in [0, 1] \ \&\ a + b \leq 1\}$$

be the set of all IFPs. The following assertions follow from above results

Theorem 1. $\langle \mathcal{L}, \times_1, \langle 0, 1\rangle\rangle$ and $\langle \mathcal{L}, \times_5, \langle 1, 0\rangle\rangle$ are commutative monoids.

Theorem 2. $\langle \mathcal{L}, \times_2\rangle$, $\langle \mathcal{L}, \times_3\rangle$ and $\langle \mathcal{L}, \times_4\rangle$ are commutative semigroups.

None of these five objects is a group.

Theorem 3. If x and y are IFTPs, then $x \times_1 y, x \times_2 y$ and $x \times_3 y$ are IFTPs.

Theorem 4. If x and y are TPs, then $x \times_1 y, x \times_2 y$, ..., $x \times_5 y$ are TPs.

Fifth, in intuitionistic fuzzy propositional logic there are already definitions of 53 different intuitionistic fuzzy negations, only one from which is a classical one, as defined by

$$\neg\langle a, b\rangle = \langle b, a\rangle.$$

Now, we see that for every two IFPs x and y:

$$\begin{aligned} \neg(\neg x \times_1 \neg y) &= \neg(\neg\langle a, b\rangle \times_1 \neg\langle c, d\rangle) \\ \neg(\langle b, a\rangle \times_1 \langle d, c\rangle) &= \neg\langle \max(b, d), ac\rangle \\ \langle ac, \max(b, d)\rangle &= x \times_5 y \end{aligned}$$

and

$$\begin{aligned} \neg(\neg x \times_5 \neg y) &= \neg(\neg\langle a, b\rangle \times_5 \neg\langle c, d\rangle) \\ \neg(\langle b, a\rangle \times_5 \langle d, c\rangle) &= \neg\langle bd, \max(a, c)\rangle \\ \langle \max(a, c), bd\rangle &= x \times_1 y; \\ \neg(\neg x \times_2 \neg y) &= \neg(\neg\langle a, b\rangle \times_2 \neg\langle c, d\rangle) \\ \neg(\langle b, a\rangle \times_2 \langle d, c\rangle) &= \neg\langle \min(b, d), ac\rangle \\ \langle ac, \min(b, d)\rangle &= x \times_4 y \end{aligned}$$

and

$$\begin{aligned} \neg(\neg x \times_4 \neg y) &= \neg(\neg\langle a, b\rangle \times_4 \neg\langle c, d\rangle) \\ \neg(\langle b, a\rangle \times_4 \langle d, c\rangle) &= \neg\langle bd, \min(a, c)\rangle \\ \langle \max(a, c), bd\rangle &= x \times_2 y. \end{aligned}$$

Therefore, operations $\times_1$ and $\times_2$ have the behaviour of operation disjunction, while operations $\times_4$ and $\times_5$ have the behaviour of operation conjunction.

On the other hand,

$$\begin{aligned}\neg(\neg x \times_3 \neg y) &= \neg(\neg\langle a,b\rangle \times_3 \neg\langle c,d\rangle)\\ \neg(\langle b,a\rangle \times_3 \langle d,c\rangle) &= \neg\langle bd, ac\rangle\\ \langle ac, bd\rangle &= x \times_3 y.\end{aligned}$$

Therefore, operation $\times_3$ has the behaviour of Toader Buhaescu operation (see [3]):

$$\langle a,b\rangle @ \langle c,d\rangle = \langle \frac{a+c}{2}, \frac{b+d}{2}\rangle.$$

Obviously, it can be interpreted as a conjunction, as well as a disjunction.

Therefore, we can extend the list of existing operations intuitionistic fuzzy conjunctions and disjunctions with the new 3 conjunctions ($\times_3, \times_4, \times_5$) and 3 new disjunctions ($\times_1, \times_2, \times_3$).

Having in mind that a lot of intuitionistic fuzzy conjunctions and disjunctions do not satisfy the standard De Morgan's Laws and satisfy their modified forms about the different intuitionistic fuzzy negations (see [1]), an interesting **Open Problem** is the following: which form will have De Morgan's Laws for the other 52 negations and the above five operations.

Sixth, if we have IFPs x and y, defined above and if they have the geometrical interpretation from Fig. 2, then the geometrical interpretations of IFPs $x \times_1 y$, ..., $x \times_5 y$ are shown on Figs. 3, 4, 5, 6 and 7.

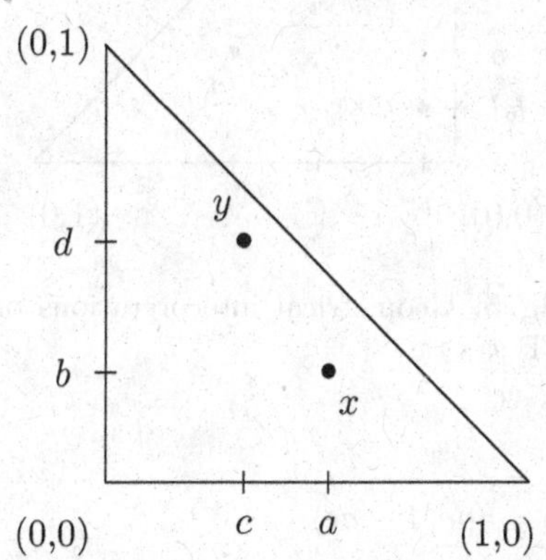

Fig. 2. Geometrical interpretation of IFP x and y

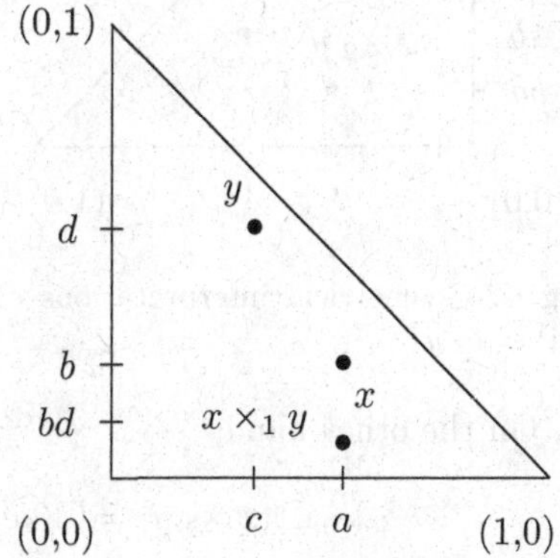

Fig. 3. Geometrical interpretations of IFP $x \times_1 y$

Seventh, for each IFP x with the form $\langle a, b\rangle$, the following two modal type operators are defined, e.g., in [1]:

$$\Box x = \langle a, 1 - a\rangle,$$
$$\Diamond x = \langle 1 - b, b\rangle.$$

Now, we can check the validity of the following inequalities for each i ($1 \le i \le 5$):

$$\Box x \times_i \Box y \ge \Box(x \times_i y),$$
$$\Diamond x \times_i \Diamond y \le \Diamond(x \times_i y).$$

Really, for example for $i = 4$, we obtain:

$$\begin{aligned}\Box x \times_4 \Box y &= \Box\langle a, b\rangle \times_4 \Box\langle c, d\rangle\\ &= \langle a, 1 - a\rangle \times_4 \langle c, 1 - c\rangle\\ &= \langle ac, \min(1 - a, 1 - c)\rangle\\ &= \langle ac, 1 - \max(a, c)\rangle\\ &\ge \langle ac, 1 - ac\rangle.\end{aligned}$$

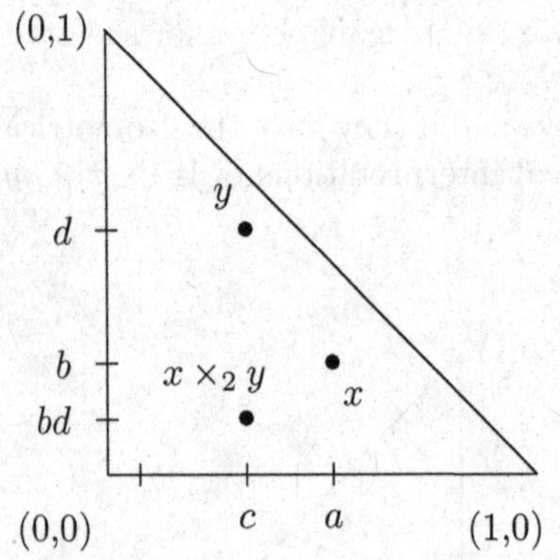

Fig. 4. Geometrical interpretations of IFP $x \times_2 y$

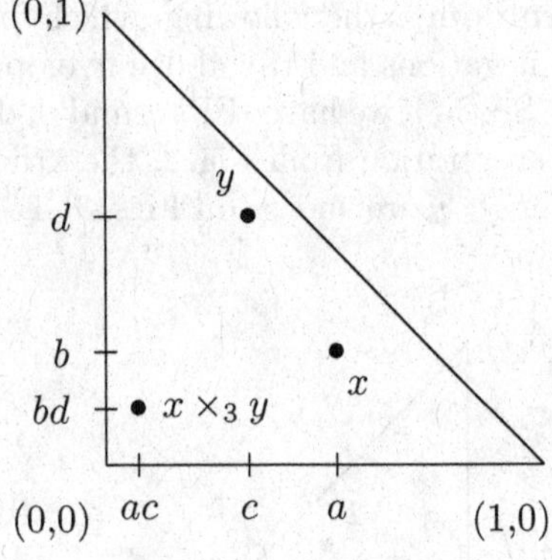

Fig. 5. Geometrical interpretations of IFP $x \times_3 y$

On the other hand,

$$\Box(x \times_4 y) = \Box\langle ac, \min(b, d)\rangle = \langle ac, 1 - ac\rangle.$$

Therefore, the assertion is proved.

Eight, let as above, $x = \langle a, b\rangle$ be an IFP and let $\alpha, \beta \in [0, 1]$. In [2], the two basic level of operators are defined by:

$$P_{\alpha,\beta}(x) = \langle \max(\alpha, a), \min(\beta, b)\rangle$$
$$Q_{\alpha,\beta}(x) = \langle \min(\alpha, a), \max(\beta, b)\rangle,$$

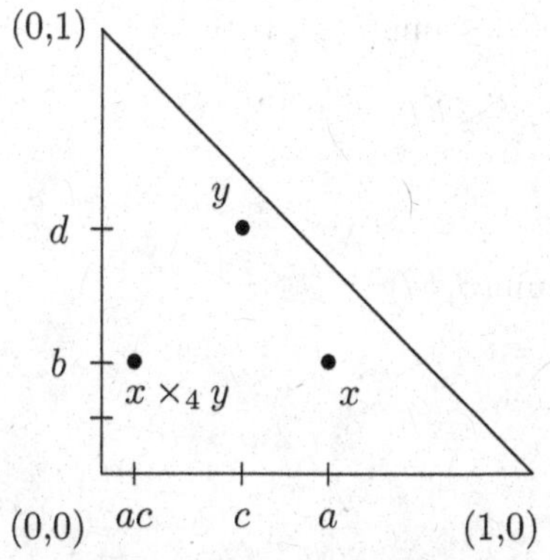

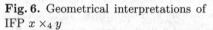

Fig. 6. Geometrical interpretations of IFP $x \times_4 y$

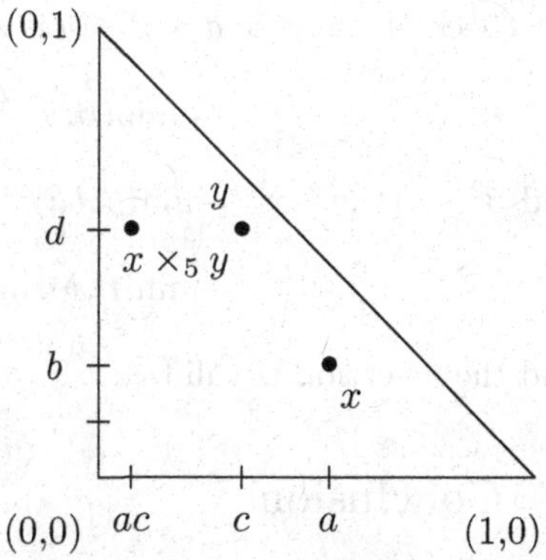

Fig. 7. Geometrical interpretations of IFP $x \times_5 y$

where $\alpha + \beta \leq 1$. Then the following inequalities for each i $(1 \leq i \leq 5)$ hold:

$$P_{\alpha,\beta}(x) \times_i P_{\alpha,\beta}(y) \geq P_{\alpha,\beta}(x \times_i y),$$
$$Q_{\alpha,\beta}(x) \times_i Q_{\alpha,\beta}(y) \leq Q_{\alpha,\beta}(x \times_i y).$$

Really, for example for $i = 1$ we obtain:

$$\begin{aligned} P_{\alpha,\beta}(x) \times_1 P_{\alpha,\beta}(y) &= P_{\alpha,\beta}(\langle a, b\rangle) \times_1 P_{\alpha,\beta}(\langle c, d\rangle) \\ &= \langle \max(\alpha, a), \min(\beta, b)\rangle \times_1 \langle \max(\alpha, c), \min(\beta, d)\rangle \\ &= \langle \max(\max(\alpha, a), \max(\alpha, c)), \min(\beta, b).\min(\beta, d)\rangle \\ &= \langle \max(\alpha, a, c), \min(\beta, b).\min(\beta, d)\rangle. \end{aligned}$$

On the other hand,

$$\begin{aligned} P_{\alpha,\beta}(x \times_1 y) &= P_{\alpha,\beta}(\langle a, b\rangle \times_1 \langle c, d\rangle) \\ &= P_{\alpha,\beta}(\langle \max(a, c), bd\rangle) \\ &= \langle \max(\alpha, \max(a, c)), \min(\beta, bd)\rangle \\ &= \langle \max(\alpha, a, c), \min(\beta, bd)\rangle. \end{aligned}$$

The inequality

$$\min(\beta, b).\min(\beta, d) \leq \min(\beta, bd)$$

is always valid, because, if $\beta \geq \max(b, d)$, then $\beta \geq bd$ and

$$\min(\beta, b).\min(\beta, d) = bd = \min(\beta, bd);$$

if $b \leq \beta \leq d$, then $bd \leq b \leq \beta$ and

$$\min(\beta, b).\min(\beta, d) = b.\beta \leq bd = \min(\beta, bd);$$

the check of the case $d \leq \beta \leq b$ is analogous; if $\beta \leq \min(b, d)$, then

$$\min(\beta, b).\min(\beta, d) = \beta^2 \leq bd$$

and $\beta^2 \leq \beta$, i.e., $\beta^2 \leq \min(\beta, bd)$. Therefore,

$$\min(\beta, b).\min(\beta, d) \leq \min(\beta, bd)$$

and the assertion is valid.

3 Conclusion

In the present paper, we introduce some novel operations, that in future will be used as a basis of defining of consequent operations and operators. More specifically, operation $\times_1$ can be used for introducing of a new operation implication, while operations $\times_1$, $\times_2$, $\times_4$ and $\times_5$ – for definitions of novel modal type of operators. An **Open Problem** is: which forms will have the possible intuitionistic fuzzy implications and generated by them intuitionistic fuzzy negations? Can they be basis for generating of new intuitionistic fuzzy conjunctions and disjunctions?

Acknowledgments. The first author is thankful for the support provided by the Bulgarian National Science Fund under Grant Ref. No. DFNI-I-02-5.

References

1. Atanassov, K.: Intuitionistic Fuzzy Logics. Springer, Cham (2017)
2. Atanassov, K., Szmidt, E., Kacprzyk, J.: On intuitionistic fuzzy pairs. Notes Intuitionistic Fuzzy Sets **19**(3), 1–13 (2013)
3. Buhaescu, T.: Some observations on intuitionistic fuzzy relations. Itinerant Seminar on Functional Equations, Approximation and Convexity, Cluj- Napoca, pp. 111- 118 (1989)

New Modified Level Operator N_γ Over Intuitionistic Fuzzy Sets

Vassia Atanassova(✉)

Bioinformatics and Mathematical Modelling Department,
Institute of Biophysics and Biomedical Engineering,
Bulgarian Academy of Sciences,
105 Acad. Georgi Bonchev Street, 1113 Sofia, Bulgaria
vassia.atanassova@gmail.com

Abstract. The present paper takes the idea of the level operator $N_{\alpha,\beta}$ and proposes a modification called N_γ. The aim of the original level operator is to generate a subset of an intuitionistic fuzzy set A, called (α, β)-set, whose degrees of membership are above a given level (threshold) α and degrees of non-membership are below a given level β, where both α, β are fixed numbers in the [0, 1] interval and $\alpha + \beta \leq 1$. In the modification proposed here, we introduce the operator N_γ that also generates a subset of an intuitionistic fuzzy set A, where the elements of the subset are those elements of A, for which the ratio of their degrees of membership to their degrees of non-membership, respectively, is greater or equal to a given number $\gamma > 0$.

Keywords: Intuitionistic fuzzy sets · Level operator · InterCriteria analysis

1 Introduction

Following the idea of a fuzzy sets of level α, in [5] K. Atanassov introduced the concept of (α, β)-set, generated by an intuitionistic fuzzy sets A in a universe E, where $\alpha, \beta \in [0, 1]$, $\alpha + \beta \leq 1$, are fixed numbers. The formal notation of the operator producing this subset of A is the following:

$$N_{\alpha,\beta}(A) = \{\langle x, \mu_A(x), \nu_A(x)\rangle | x \in E \;\&\; \mu_A(x) \geq \alpha \;\&\; \mu_A(x) \leq \beta\}.$$

Obviously, this level operator decreases the number of elements, preserving only those elements whose degrees of membership are above a given level (threshold) α and their degrees of non-membership are below a given level β. A series of properties of the operator $N_{\alpha,\beta}$ are checked, involving the set-theoretic operations "negation", "union", "intersection" and the relation "inclusion". Several trivial modifications have also been introduced.

Although $N_{\alpha,\beta}$ as such has not been referred to in the context of the recently proposed method of InterCriteria Analysis (ICA, first defined in [8]), the idea embodied in this level operator has already been heavily used. In ICA, a dataset of evaluations or measurements of m different objects against n different criteria is processed in order to calculate the pairwise correlations between the n criteria in the form of intuitionistic

H. Christiansen et al. (Eds.): FQAS 2017, LNAI 10333, pp. 209–214, 2017.
DOI: 10.1007/978-3-319-59692-1_18

fuzzy pairs, [8]. Determining the top correlating pairs of criteria from the set of $n(n-1)/2$ requires the definition of reasonably chosen thresholds for both the membership and the non-membership parts of the intuitionistic fuzzy pairs. The methods of determining these thresholds have been the subject of an extensive multistep research since 2015, [10, 16], which is still a matter of further improvement and tuning. For a part of the research community, investigating the ICA method in both theoretical and applied aspect, including the author, this very question of defining the thresholds against which the calculated intercriteria evaluations are "sifted through", represents the most challenging and distinctive leg of the ICA research (see [10]) and one most crucial for the utilization of the ICA method to practical applications.

In this paper, we propose a new input to the theory of intuitionistic fuzzy sets by showing how the level operator $N_{\alpha,\beta}$ can be modified to the new operator N_γ, considering its potential to further advance the methodology of defining ICA thresholds.

The reader may find it interesting that the idea about this new operator comes from an area as distant from mathematical logic as marital counselling. It is inspired by the theory of the American psychologist John M. Gottman that marital relationships are likely to be stable if they exhibit the "magic ratio" of 5:1 of positive to negative interactions between the partners (see [11]).

2 Main Results

Let us remind the reader of the definitions of the most basic modal and topological operators over intuitionistic fuzzy sets (IFSs).

Definition 1 ([3]). Let E be a fixed universe and $A \subset E$ be a given IFS. Let the functions $\mu_A, \nu_A : E \to [0, 1]$ determine its degrees of membership and non-membership. Then, the modal operators called, respectively, *Necessity* and *Possibility*, are defined by:

$$\square A = \{\langle x, \mu_A(x), 1-\mu_A(x)\rangle \mid x \in E\},$$

$$\lozenge A = \{\langle x, 1-\nu_A(x), \nu_A(x)\rangle \mid x \in E\}.$$

Based on this definition, it is easily proved the basic property that when A is a proper IFS, i.e., there exists an element $x \in E$, for which $\pi_A(x) > 0$, then $\square A \subset A \subset \lozenge A$ and $\square A \neq A \neq \lozenge A$, [3]. More properties and relations between the standard set operations and these modal operators were proven in details in [4].

Definition 2 ([4]). Let E be a fixed universe and $A \subset E$ be a given IFS. Then the topological operators *Closure* and *Interior*, denoted respectively by $\mathcal{C}(A)$ and $\mathcal{I}(A)$, are defined, as follows:

$$\mathcal{C}(A) = \{\langle x, \sup_{y \in E} \mu_A(y), \inf_{y \in E} \nu_A(y)\rangle \mid x \in E\},$$

$$\mathcal{I}(A) = \{\langle x, \inf_{y \in E} \mu_A(y), \sup_{y \in E} \nu_A(y)\rangle \mid x \in E\}.$$

Before [4], both operators were defined by K. Atanassov in October 1983 (according to [6]) and their basic properties were studied. In [4], the relations between the standard set operations and these topological operators, as well as between the modal and the topological operators over IFSs were studied.

For the needs of the present study, we introduce here the following working definition.

Definition 3. Let us call an IFS A *ν-positive*, if for each IFS A we have $(\forall x \in E)$ $(\nu_A(x) > 0)$. Let us define for each ν-positive IFS A the following operator

$$N_\gamma(A) = \{\langle x, \mu_A(x), \nu_A(x)\rangle | x \in E \ \& \ \frac{\mu_A(x)}{\nu_A(x)} \geq \gamma\},$$

where γ is an arbitrary non-negative real number.

We are ready to formulate the following statements for the properties of the newly defined operator.

Theorem 1. For every two ν-positive IFSs A and B:

(a) $N_\gamma(A \cap B) \subset N_\gamma(A) \cap N_\gamma(B)$,
(b) $N_\gamma(A \cup B) \supset N_\gamma(A) \cup N_\gamma(B)$.

Proof. For both statements, we will use the consideration that from $\mu_A \geq \gamma.\nu_A$ and $\mu_B \geq \gamma.\nu_B$ it follows that $\max(\mu_A, \mu_B) \geq \gamma.\min(\nu_A, \nu_B)$.

(a)
$$\begin{aligned} N_\gamma(A \cup B) &= \{\langle x | \frac{\min(\mu_A(x), \mu_B(x))}{\max(\nu_A(x), \nu_B(x))} \geq \gamma\} \subset \{\langle x | \frac{\mu_A(x)}{\nu_A(x)} \geq \gamma \ \& \ \frac{\mu_B(x)}{\nu_B(x)} \geq \gamma\} \\ &= \{\langle x | \frac{\mu_A(x)}{\nu_A(x)} \geq \gamma\} \cap \{\langle x | \frac{\mu_B(x)}{\nu_B(x)} \geq \gamma\} = N_\gamma(A) \cap N_\gamma(B). \end{aligned}$$

(b)
$$\begin{aligned} N_\gamma A \cup N_\gamma B &= \{\langle x | \frac{\mu_A(x)}{\nu_A(x)} \geq \gamma\} \cup \{\langle x | \frac{\mu_B(x)}{\nu_B(x)} \geq \gamma\} \\ &= \{\langle x | \frac{\mu_A(x)}{\nu_A(x)} \geq \gamma \cup \frac{\mu_B(x)}{\nu_B(x)} \geq \gamma\} \subset \{\langle x | \frac{\max(\mu_A(x), \mu_B(x))}{\min(\nu_A(x), \nu_B(x))} \geq \gamma\} \\ &= N_\gamma\left(\{\langle x, \max(\mu_A(x), \mu_B(x)), \min(\nu_A(x), \nu_B(x)) | x \in E\}\right) = (N_\gamma A \cup B). \end{aligned}$$

This completes the proof. □

Theorem 2. For every ν-positive IFS A, $N_\gamma(\mathcal{I}(A)) \subset N_\gamma(A) \subset N_\gamma(\mathcal{C}(A))$.

Proof. Let for the IFS A, it holds that $\frac{\inf_y(\mu_A(y))}{\sup_y(\nu_A(y))} \geq \gamma$. Then, from

$$\sup_y(\mu_A(y)) \geq \mu_A(x) \geq \inf_y(\mu_A(y)) \geq \gamma.\sup_y(\nu_A(y)) \geq \gamma.\nu_A(x) \geq \gamma.\inf_y(\nu_A(y)),$$

it follows that $N_\gamma(\mathcal{I}(A)) \subset N_\gamma(A) \subset N_\gamma(\mathcal{C}(A))$. This completes the proof. □

Theorem 3. For every ν-positive IFS A, $N_\gamma(\Box A) \subset A \subset N_\gamma(\Diamond A)$.

Proof. For the ν-positive IFS A, it follows that $1 - \mu_A(x) \geq \nu_A(x) > 0$. Hence, if $x \in N_\gamma(A)$, then $\frac{\mu_A(x)}{1-\mu_A(x)} \geq \gamma$. Therefore, $\frac{1-\nu_A(x)}{\nu_A(x)} \geq \frac{\mu_A(x)}{\nu_A(x)} \geq \frac{\mu_A(x)}{1-\mu_A(x)} \geq \gamma$ and, hence, $N_\gamma(\Box A) = \{\langle x \mid \frac{\mu_A(x)}{1-\mu_A(x)} \geq \gamma\} \subset \{\langle x \mid \frac{\mu_A(x)}{\nu_A(x)} \geq \gamma\} = A \subset \{\langle x \mid \frac{1-\nu_A(x)}{\nu_A(x)} \geq \gamma\} = N_\gamma(\Diamond A)$. This completes the proof. □

Theorem 4. $N_\gamma(N_\delta(A)) = N_\delta(N_\gamma(A)) = N_{\max(\gamma,\delta)}(A)$.

Proof. For the ν-positive IFS A, it follows that

$$\begin{aligned} N_\gamma(N_\delta(A)) &= N_\gamma(\{\langle x, \mu_A(x), \nu_A(x)\rangle | x \in E \;\&\; \frac{\mu_A(x)}{\nu_A(x)} \geq \delta\}) \\ &= \{\langle x, \mu_A(x), \nu_A(x)\rangle | x \in E \;\&\; \frac{\mu_A(x)}{\nu_A(x)} \geq \gamma \;\&\; \frac{\mu_A(x)}{\nu_A(x)} \geq \delta\} \\ &= \{\langle x, \mu_A(x), \nu_A(x)\rangle | x \in E \;\&\; \frac{\mu_A(x)}{\nu_A(x)} \geq \max(\gamma, \delta)\} = N_{\max(\gamma,\delta)}(A). \end{aligned}$$

This completes the proof. □

Finally, we will note the graphical interpretation of the new operator N_γ onto the intuitionistic fuzzy interpretational triangle, given on the Fig. 1 below.

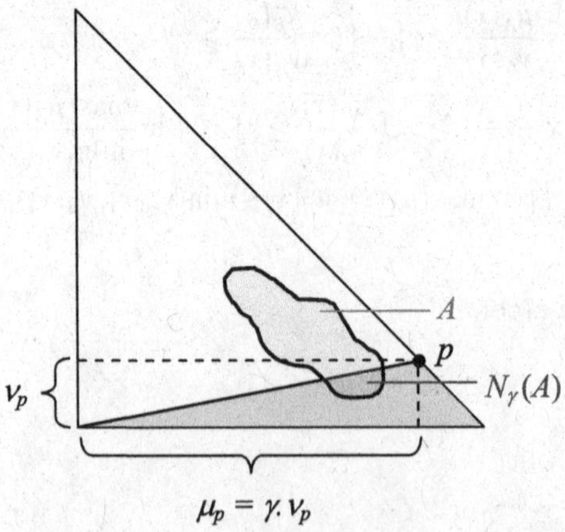

Fig. 1. Graphical visualization of the operator N_γ onto the IF triangle

3 Conclusion

In the modification proposed here, we introduce the operator N_γ which for a given intuitionistic fuzzy set A produces a subset of $N_\gamma(A)$, where the elements of the subset are those elements of A, for which the ratio of their degrees of membership to their degrees of non-membership, respectively, is greater or equal to a given number $\gamma > 0$. Several basic properties are checked for the so proposed operator of level type.

The idea about this modification was inspired by an application of the intuitionistic fuzzy sets-based method of InterCriteria Analysis, where defining and finely tuning of the thresholds of evaluation of the results of ICA analysis has been the core subject of an extensive recent investigation in both theoretical (e.g. [1, 7, 9, 14, 15]) and applied aspect (e.g. [2, 12, 13]). The idea to determine the best correlating ICA pairs (and IFS elements), based on a factor with which their membership exceeds their non-membership parts, is a novel idea, which is in line with the recent development of the ICA threshold analysis, which aims at rendering account on both the intercriteria membership and non-membership degrees together in parallel, rather than using them in isolation or consecutively [10].

Practical applicability of the operator N_γ in ICA or in any other relevant, IFS-based decision making method, has been so far an unexplored, yet perspective direction of research, which requires approbation and analysis with concrete datasets from diverse application areas.

Acknowledgements. The author is grateful for the support provided under Grant Ref. No. DFNI-I-02-5/2014 “Intercriteria Analysis: A New Method for Decision Making” funded by the National Science Fund of Bulgaria.

References

1. Angelova, N., Atanassov, K., Riecan, B.: Intercriteria analysis of the intuitionistic fuzzy implication properties. Notes on Intuitionistic Fuzzy Sets **21**(5), 20–23 (2015)
2. Angelova, M., Roeva, O., Pencheva, T.: Intercriteria analysis of crossover and mutation rates relations in simple genetic algorithm. Ann. Comput. Sci. Inf. Syst. **5**, 419–424 (2015)
3. Atanassov, K.T.: Intuitionistic Fuzzy Sets, VII ITKR Session, Sofia, 20–23 June 1983 (1983). (Deposed in Centr. Sci.-Techn. Library of the Bulg. Acad. of Sci., 1697/84) (in Bulgarian). Reprinted: Int. J. Bioautomation **20**(S1), S1–S6 (2016)
4. Atanassov, K.T.: Intuitionistic fuzzy sets. Fuzzy Sets Syst. **20**(1), 87–96 (1986)
5. Atanassov, K.T.: Intuitionistic Fuzzy Sets. Springer Physica-Verlag, Heidelberg (1999)
6. Atanassov, K.: On Intuitionistic Fuzzy Sets. Springer, Berlin (2012)
7. Atanassov, K., Atanassova, V., Gluhchev, G.: Intercriteria analysis: ideas and problems. Notes on Intuitionistic Fuzzy Sets **21**(1), 81–88 (2015)
8. Atanassov, K., Mavrov, D., Atanassova, V.: Intercriteria decision making: a new approach for multicriteria decision making, based on index matrices and intuitionistic fuzzy sets. Issues in Intuitionistic Fuzzy Sets and Generalized Nets **11**, 1–8 (2014)
9. Atanassova, V., Doukovska, L., Michalikova, A., Radeva, I.: Intercriteria analysis: from pairs to triples. Notes on Intuitionistic Fuzzy Sets **22**(5), 98–110 (2016)

10. Doukovska, L., Atanassova, V., Sotirova, E., Vardeva, I., Radeva, I.: Defining Consonance Thresholds in InterCriteria Analysis: Overview (submitted)
11. Gottman, J.: Why marriages succeed or fail: and how you can make yours last. Simon and Schuster (1995)
12. Pencheva, T., Angelova, M., Vassilev, P., Roeva, O.: Intercriteria analysis approach to parameter identification of a fermentation process model. In: Atanassov, K.T., Castillo, O., Kacprzyk, J., Krawczak, M., Melin, P., Sotirov, S., Sotirova, E., Szmidt, E., Tré, G.D., Zadrożny, S. (eds.) Novel Developments in Uncertainty Representation and Processing. AISC, vol. 401, pp. 385–397. Springer, Cham (2016). doi:10.1007/978-3-319-26211-6_33
13. Roeva, O., Vassilev, P.: Intercriteria analysis of generation gap influence on genetic algorithms performance. In: Atanassov, K.T., Castillo, O., Kacprzyk, J., Krawczak, M., Melin, P., Sotirov, S., Sotirova, E., Szmidt, E., Tré, G.D., Zadrożny, S. (eds.) Novel Developments in Uncertainty Representation and Processing. AISC, vol. 401, pp. 301–313. Springer, Cham (2016). doi:10.1007/978-3-319-26211-6_26
14. Todorova, L., Vassilev, P., Surchev, J.: Using phi coefficient to interpret results obtained by intercriteria analysis. In: Atanassov, K.T., Castillo, O., Kacprzyk, J., Krawczak, M., Melin, P., Sotirov, S., Sotirova, E., Szmidt, E., Tré, G.D., Zadrożny, S. (eds.) Novel Developments in Uncertainty Representation and Processing. AISC, vol. 401, pp. 231–239. Springer, Cham (2016). doi:10.1007/978-3-319-26211-6_20
15. Vassilev, P., Todorova, L., Andonov, V.: An auxiliary technique for intercriteria analysis via a three dimensional index matrix. Notes on Intuitionistic Fuzzy Sets **21**(2), 71–76 (2015)
16. Project publications, Intercriteria.net. http://intercriteria.net/publications/

Application of Topological Operators over Data from InterCriteria Analysis

Olympia Roeva[1(✉)], Peter Vassilev[1], and Panagiotis Chountas[2]

[1] Institute of Biophysics and Biomedical Engineering, Bulgarian Academy of Science, Sofia, Bulgaria
olympia@biomed.bas.bg, peter.vassilev@gmail.com
[2] Department of Computer Science, Faculty of Science and Technology (FST), University of Westminster, 115 New Cavendish Street, London W1W 6UW, UK
P.I.Chountas@westminster.ac.uk

Abstract. In this paper, two topological operators T and U over intuitionistic fuzzy sets are considered and applied. As a case study a parameter identification problem of *E. coli* fed-batch cultivation process model using genetic algorithms is investigated. A new result regarding T and U is established. The results obtained by the application of the topological operators over data processed by InterCriteria Analysis are discussed.

Keywords: InterCriteria Analysis · Topological operators · Intuitionistic fuzzy sets · Genetic Algorithms

1 Introduction

The InterCriteria Analysis (ICrA) – is developed with the aim to more profoundly understand the nature of the criteria involved and discover on this basis existing correlations between the criteria themselves [2]. ICrA implements the apparatuses of index matrices (IM) [5] and intuitionistic fuzzy sets (IFS) [8] in order to compare some criteria reflecting the behaviour of considered objects [18,21]. The ICrA approach has been found different problem applications in science and practice – neural networks [19], properties of the crude oils [20], e-learning [14], algorithms performance [15], ecology [13], economics [10], etc.

The notion IFS was introduced by K. Atanassov (see [6]) as a natural generalization of the fuzzy sets. There are several topological operators defined over IFS [4,7,9] some with possible concrete applications for solving of different problems [3,11].

In the present paper we consider the operators T [3] and U [4] as an instrument for knowledge discovery in the case of insufficient or partial data sets. As a test problem the application of ICrA approach to modelling of an *E. coli* fed-batch cultivation process is studied. For the purpose of model parameter identification Genetic Algorithms (GAs) are applied. These algorithms are known to offer good solutions, even global optima, within reasonable computing time [12].

H. Christiansen et al. (Eds.): FQAS 2017, LNAI 10333, pp. 215–225, 2017.
DOI: 10.1007/978-3-319-59692-1_19

2 Topological Operators *T* and *U* over IFSs

We will briefly remind the most important basic definitions and notions.

Let X be a universe set, $A \subset X$. An IFS is defined with the help of two mappings $\mu_A : X \to [0,1]$ (membership function or degree of "agreement") and $\nu_A : X \to [0,1]$ (non-membership function or degree of "disagreement") such that for all $x \in X$,

$$\mu_A(x) + \nu_A(x) \leq 1 \tag{1}$$

Definition 1. *Following [8], we call the set of ordered triples*

$$A^* \stackrel{\text{def}}{=} \{\langle x, \mu_A(x), \nu_A(x)\rangle | x \in X\}$$

an IFS and the mapping π_A, which is given for all $x \in X$ by

$$\pi_A(x) \stackrel{\text{def}}{=} 1 - \mu_A(x) - \nu_A(x), \tag{2}$$

a degree of "uncertainty".

Further, we will be interested in two topological operators defined over IFSs. The first one was introduced in [3] and is the following:

$$T(A) = \left\{ \left\langle x, \frac{\mu_A(x)}{\sup\limits_{y \in X}(\mu_A(y) + \nu_A(y))}, \frac{\nu_A(x)}{\sup\limits_{y \in X}(\mu_A(y) + \nu_A(y))} \right\rangle | x \in X \right\}. \tag{3}$$

The second operator $U(A)$ is the following [4].

$$U(A) = \left\{ \left\langle x, \frac{\mu_A(x) - \inf\limits_{y \in X} \mu_A(y)}{u_{\inf}(A)}, \frac{\nu_A(x) - \inf\limits_{y \in X} \nu_A(y)}{u_{\inf}(A)} \right\rangle | x \in X \right\}, \tag{4}$$

where $u_{\inf}(A) = 1 - \inf\limits_{y \in X} \mu_A(y) - \inf\limits_{y \in X} \nu_A(y) - \inf\limits_{y \in X} \pi_A(y)$.

Here, we will establish an interesting relation between these two operators:

Theorem 1. *For any IFS A, it is fulfilled:*

$$U(A) = U(T(A)) \tag{5}$$

Proof. We have

$$U(T(A)) = U\left\langle x, \frac{\mu}{\sup\limits_{y\in X}(\mu+\nu)}, \frac{\nu}{\sup\limits_{y\in X}(\mu+\nu)}\right\rangle$$

$$= \left\langle x, \frac{\frac{\mu}{\sup(\mu+\nu)} - \frac{\inf\mu}{\sup(\mu+\nu)}}{1-\inf\frac{\mu}{\sup(\mu+\nu)} - \inf\frac{\nu}{\sup(\mu+\nu)} - \inf(1-\frac{\mu+\nu}{\sup(\mu+\nu)})},\right.$$

$$\left.\frac{\frac{\nu}{\sup(\mu+\nu)} - \frac{\inf\nu}{\sup(\mu+\nu)}}{1-\inf\frac{\mu}{\sup(\mu+\nu)} - \inf\frac{\nu}{\sup(\mu+\nu)} - \inf(1-\frac{\mu+\nu}{\sup(\mu+\nu)})}\right\rangle$$

$$= \left\langle x, \frac{\mu-\inf\mu}{\sup(\mu+\nu)-\inf\mu-\inf\nu-\inf(\sup(\mu+\nu)-\mu-\nu)},\right.$$

$$\left.\frac{\nu-\inf\nu}{\sup(\mu+\nu)-\inf\mu-\inf\nu-\inf(\sup(\mu+\nu)-\mu-\nu)}\right\rangle$$

Using (2) *we rewrite this as:*

$$U(T(A)) = \left\langle x, \frac{\mu-\inf\mu}{-\inf\mu-\inf\nu-\inf(-(1-\pi))},\right.$$

$$\left.\frac{\nu-\inf\nu}{-\inf\mu-\inf\nu-\inf(-(1-\pi))}\right\rangle$$

Since $\inf(-x) = -\sup(x)$ *and* $\sup(1-x) = 1-\inf(x)$, *we may rewrite the last as:*

$$U(T(A)) = \left\langle x, \frac{\mu-\inf\mu}{-\inf\mu-\inf\nu+\sup(1-\pi)},\right.$$

$$\left.\frac{\nu-\inf\nu}{-\inf\mu-\inf\nu+\sup(1-\pi)}\right\rangle$$

$$= \left\langle x, \frac{\mu-\inf\mu}{1-\inf\mu-\inf\nu-\inf\pi},\right.$$

$$\left.\frac{\nu-\inf\nu}{1-\inf\mu-\inf\nu-\inf\pi}\right\rangle$$

$$= U(A),$$

which establishes the validity of (5).

3 InterCriteria Analysis

In what follows, we briefly remind the basic notions related to the ICrA.

Given an IM [5] of real numbers whose index sets consist of the names of the criteria (for rows) and objects (for columns), ICrA generates an IM with index sets consisting of the names of the criteria (for rows and for columns) with elements Intuitionistic Fuzzy Pairs (IFPs). An IFP $\langle \mu_{C,C'}, \nu_{C,C'} \rangle$ denotes the degrees of "agreement" and "disagreement" between two criteria applied on different objects [2].

Further O is the set of all objects $O_1, O_2, \ldots, O_n$ being evaluated, and $C(O)$ – the set of values assigned by a given criteria C to the objects, i.e.

$$O \overset{\text{def}}{=} \{O_1, O_2, \ldots, O_n\}, C(O) \overset{\text{def}}{=} \{C(O_1), C(O_2), \ldots, C(O_n)\}.$$

Let $x_i = C(O_i)$. Then the following set can be defined

$$C^*(O) \overset{\text{def}}{=} \{\langle x_i, x_j \rangle | i \neq j \,\&\, \langle x_i, x_j \rangle \in C(O) \times C(O)\}.$$

In order to compare two criteria we must construct the vector of all internal comparisons of each criteria, which fulfil exactly one of three relations R, $\overline{R}$ and $\tilde{R}$. We require that for a fixed criterion C and any ordered pair $\langle x, y \rangle \in C^*(O)$ it is true:

$$\langle x, y \rangle \in R \Leftrightarrow \langle y, x \rangle \in \overline{R}, \tag{6}$$

$$\langle x, y \rangle \in \tilde{R} \Leftrightarrow \langle x, y \rangle \notin (R \cup \overline{R}), \tag{7}$$

$$R \cup \overline{R} \cup \tilde{R} = C^*(O). \tag{8}$$

We will only consider lexicographically ordered pairs $\langle x, y \rangle$. Let, for brevity

$$C_{i,j} = \langle C(O_i), C(O_j) \rangle.$$

Then for a fixed criterion C we construct the vector

$$V(C) = \{C_{1,2}, C_{1,3}, \ldots, C_{1,n}, C_{2,3}, C_{2,4}, \ldots, C_{2,n}, C_{3,4}, \ldots, C_{3,n}, \ldots, C_{n-1,n}\}.$$

Further, to simplify our considerations, we replace the vector $V(C)$ with $\hat{V}(C)$, where for each $1 \leq k \leq \frac{n(n-1)}{2}$ for the k-th component it is true:

$$\hat{V}_k(C) = \begin{cases} 1 \text{ iff } V_k(C) \in R, \\ -1 \text{ iff } V_k(C) \in \overline{R}, \\ 0 \text{ otherwise.} \end{cases}$$

Then when comparing two criteria we determine $\mu_{C,C'}$ between the two as the number of matching components. The number of components of opposing signs in the two vectors is $\nu_{C,C'}$.

4 Case Study

We applied consistently 14 differently tuned GA to estimate the parameters μ_{max}, k_S and $Y_{S/X}$ in the non-linear model of an *E. coli* fed-batch cultivation process [17]:

$$\frac{dX}{dt} = \mu_{max}\frac{S}{k_S + S}X - \frac{F_{in}}{V}X, \tag{9}$$

$$\frac{dS}{dt} = -\frac{1}{Y_{S/X}}\mu_{max}\frac{S}{k_S + S}X + \frac{F_{in}}{V}(S_{in} - S), \tag{10}$$

$$\frac{dV}{dt} = F_{in}, \tag{11}$$

where

- X is the biomass concentration, [g/l];
- S – substrate concentration, [g/l];
- F_{in} – the feeding rate, [l/h];
- V – the bioreactor volume, [l];
- S_{in} – the substrate concentration in the feeding solution, [g/l];
- μ_{max} – the maximum value of the specific growth rate, [1/h];
- k_S – the saturation constant, [g/l];
- $Y_{S/X}$ – the yield coefficient, [-].

We define the objective function as:

$$J = \|Z\|^2 \to \min, \tag{12}$$

where $\|\|$ denotes the ℓ^2-vector norm, $Z_{\text{mod}} \stackrel{\text{def}}{=} [X_{\text{mod}}\ S_{\text{mod}}]$ (model predictions) and $Z_{\text{exp}} \stackrel{\text{def}}{=} [X_{\text{exp}}\ S_{\text{exp}}]$ (known experimental data) and $Z = Z_{\text{mod}} - Z_{\text{exp}}$.

For the model identification we use real experimental data for biomass and glucose concentrations of an *E. coli* MC4110 fed-batch fermentation process [16].

We use 14 GA with various population sizes – from 5 to 200 chromosomes in the population. The number of generations is fixed to 200. The detailed description of identification procedure is given in [16].

5 Results and Discussion

We apply 14 different GA – GA_5, GA_{10}, GA_{20}, GA_{30}, GA_{40}, GA_{50}, GA_{60}, GA_{70}, GA_{80}, GA_{90}, GA_{100}, GA_{110}, GA_{150} and GA_{200}, where the index shows the number of chromosomes in the population, to the parameters identification of the model (9)–(11). Because of the stochastic nature of the applied algorithms we perform series of 30 runs for each GA. Computer specification to run all identification procedures are Intel Core i5-2329 3.0 GHz, 8 GB Memory, Windows 8 operating system.

We use the obtained results – estimates of the model parameters μ_{max}, k_S and $Y_{S/X}$ – to compare the performance of 14 differently tuned GA. We apply ICrA over the three IMs constructed for each model parameter [18]. The IMs contain the obtained 30 parameters estimates (Run_i, $i = 1, 2, ..., 30$) applying the 14 GA. For example, the IM for μ_{max}-estimates has the following form:

$$IM_{\mu_{max}} = \begin{array}{c|cccccc} & Run_1 & Run_2 & Run_3 & ... & Run_{29} & Run_{30} \\ \hline GA_5 & 0.56 & 0.53 & 0.55 & ... & 0.48 & 0.52 \\ GA_{10} & 0.52 & 0.50 & 0.55 & ... & 0.48 & 0.52 \\ GA_{20} & 0.50 & 0.49 & 0.52 & ... & 0.53 & 0.49 \\ ... & ... & ... & ... & ... & ... & \\ GA_{150} & 0.49 & 0.49 & 0.49 & ... & 0.49 & 0.49 \\ GA_{200} & 0.49 & 0.49 & 0.49 & ... & 0.49 & 0.49 \end{array} \qquad (13)$$

The IM_{k_S} and $IM_{Y_{X/S}}$ are constructed in a similar way to (13). The complete IMs are available at http://intercriteria.net/wp-content/uploads/2017/03/GA_model_estim.xlsx.

As can be seen from (13) the numerical values of the model estimates are rounded up to the second decimal place. Since the concrete physical meaning of the three model parameters an estimate of $\mu_{max} = 0.489655$ g/l should be actually taken as $\mu_{max} = 0.49$ g/l. As a result, many equal parameters estimates are obtained. This is especially true in the case of $Y_{X/S}$-estimates, where 70% of the estimates are equal. This is a good example for application of ICrA.

After ICrA implementation we obtain three IMs that determine $\mu_{C,C'}$ and $\nu_{C,C'}$ between criteria, i.e. between 14 differently tuned GA, according to the estimates of μ_{max}, k_S and $Y_{S/X}$. On Fig. 1 the obtained ICrA results are visualized in the intuitionistic fuzzy interpretation triangle. The complete numerical results of ICrA application are available at http://intercriteria.net/wp-content/uploads/2017/03/GA_model_estim_ICrA_results.xlsx.

ICrA shows to the relations between the performance of the considered 14 GA are in clear dissonance according to [1]. This is so, because we search for correlations on the basis of the results taken individually for each model parameter. When the correlations between differently tuned GA are sought considering estimates of all parameters together in one IM, then there are many pairs in positive consonance [17].

Due to a lot of equal estimates, in all three cases, the resulting values of degree of "uncertainty" $\pi_{C,C'}$ are very high. There are results with $\pi_{C,C'} = 0.60$ in case of μ_{max}- and $Y_{X/S}$-estimates, and $\pi_{C,C'} = 0.67$ in case of k_S-estimates. Such high values of $\pi_{C,C'}$ make the analysis difficult. In such cases application of some topological operators could be useful. Here, the considered above two topological operators – T and U are applied over the obtained ICrA results. Using the intuitionistic fuzzy interpretation triangle the results after application of the T and U operators are presented in Figs. 2 and 3, respectively.

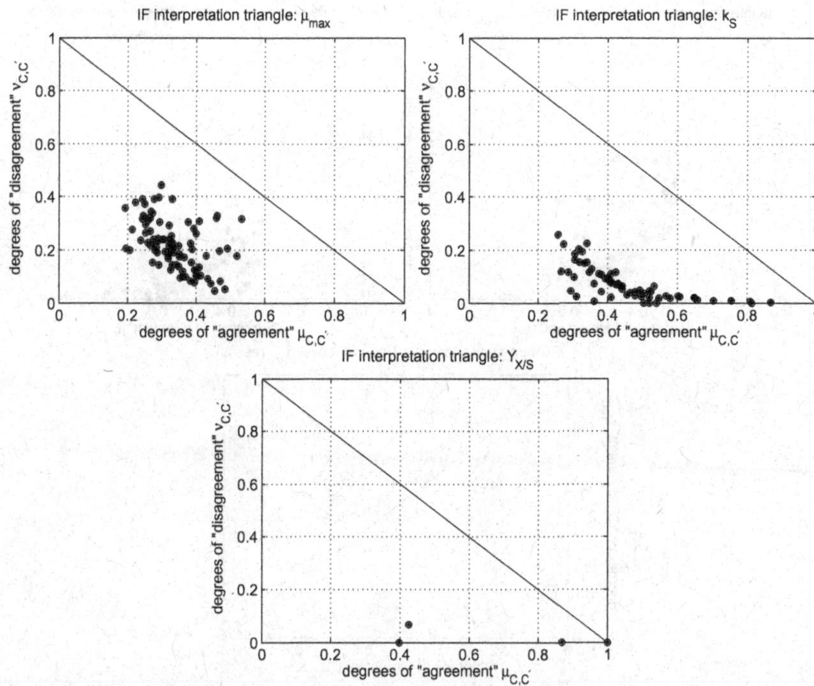

Fig. 1. Presentation of ICrA the intuitionistic fuzzy interpretation triangle: based on μ_{max}-, k_S- and $Y_{S/X}$-estimates, respectively

It can be seen that using T is appropriate when all $\pi_{C,C'}$ are non-zero, in which case it enhances the elements which are closest to the line passing through points $(0,1)$,$(1,0)$, i.e. these with lesser value of uncertainty. On the other hand, the presence of zero $\pi_{C,C'}$ values means that there are already elements which are completely defined, hence, no further enhancement is possible. This is precisely the case of T operator application over $Y_{X/S}$ results.

The uniformly expanding operator U pushes the points in all directions but with emphasis on diminishing $\mu_{C,C'}, \nu_{C,C'}$ values which are close to $(0,0)$.

Considering data for k_S estimates, operator T reveals the following correlations, scaled according to [1]:

- weak positive consonance for criteria pairs:
  $GA_{150} - GA_{80}, GA_{200} - GA_{80}, GA_{100} - GA_{90}, GA_{150} - GA_{90}$,
  $GA_{200} - GA_{90}, GA_{100} - GA_{70}, GA_{150} - GA_{70}, GA_{200} - GA_{70}$;
- positive consonance for criteria pairs:
  $GA_{100}-GA_{80}, GA_{110}-GA_{100}, GA_{150}-GA_{110}, GA_{200}-GA_{110}, GA_{110}-GA_{90}$;
- strong positive consonance for criteria pairs:
  $GA_{150} - GA_{100}, GA_{200} - GA_{100}, GA_{200} - GA_{150}$.

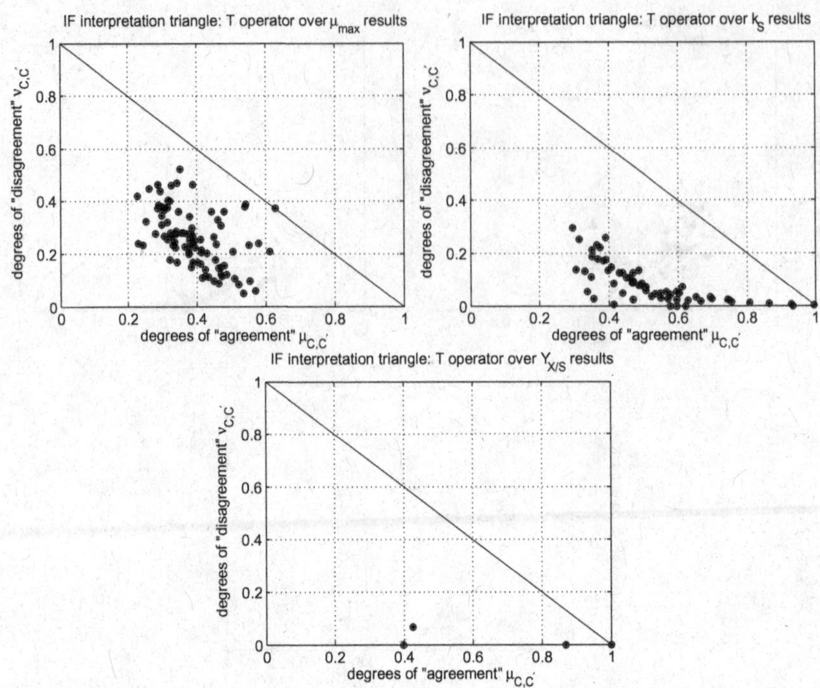

Fig. 2. Presentation of ICrA the intuitionistic fuzzy interpretation triangle: T operator over μ_{max}-, k_S- and $Y_{S/X}$-estimates, respectively

Considering data for k_S estimates, operator U reveals the following correlations:

- weak positive consonance for criteria pair: $GA_{110} - GA_{90}$;
- strong positive consonance for criteria pairs: $GA_{150} - GA_{100}, GA_{200} - GA_{100}, GA_{200} - GA_{150}$;
- positive consonance for criteria pairs: $GA_{100} - GA_{80}, GA_{110} - GA_{100}, GA_{150} - GA_{110}, GA_{200} - GA_{110}$.

The above shows that U discriminates more than T, as the exhibited consonance is the same or weaker for the criteria pairs – the differently tuned GA. The resulting pairs in consonance, are in agreement with the findings from [17].

The discussed results show the applicability of the topological operators T and U to exploring existing intercriterial correlation even based on only one aspect of the whole problem.

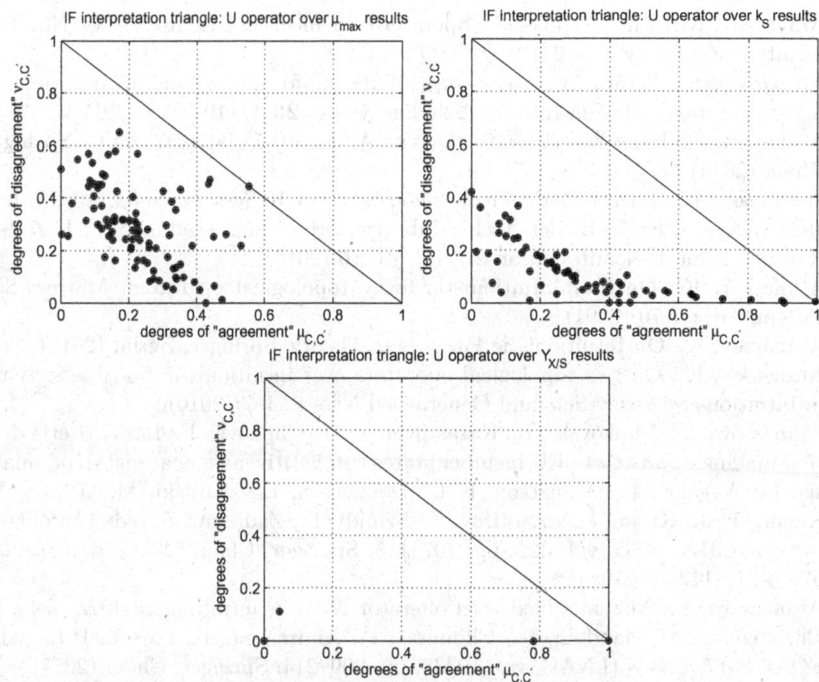

Fig. 3. Presentation of ICrA the intuitionistic fuzzy interpretation triangle: U operator over μ_{max}-, k_S- and $Y_{S/X}$-estimates, respectively

6 Conclusion

In this paper two topological operators, namely T and U, are studied and a new result regarding an interesting property of the operators is established. The performance of GA is investigated based on a parameter identification problem of *E. coli* fed-batch cultivation process model with the application of ICrA. The topological operators are then successfully applied over the data processed by ICrA in order to reveal indistinguishable correlations in the stated here problem.

Acknowledgment. The work is partially supported by the Bulgarian National Scientific Fund under the grant DFNI-I02/5 "InterCriteria Analysis. A New Approach to Decision Making".

References

1. Atanassov, K., Atanassova, V., Gluhchev, G.: InterCriteria analysis: ideas and problems. Notes Intuitionistic Fuzzy Sets **21**(1), 81–88 (2015)
2. Atanassov, K., Mavrov, D., Atanassova, V.: Intercriteria decision making: a new approach for multicriteria decision making, based on index matrices and intuitionistic fuzzy sets. Issues IFSs GNs **11**, 1–8 (2014)

3. Atanassov, K.: A new topological operator over intuitionistic fuzzy sets. Notes on Intuitionistic Fuzzy Sets **21**(3), 90–92 (2015)
4. Atanassov, K.: Errata, or a new form of the uniformly expanding intuitionistic fuzzy operator. Notes on Intuitionistic Fuzzy Sets **23**(1), 100–104 (2017)
5. Atanassov, K.: Index Matrices: Towards an Augmented Matrix Calculus. Springer, Cham (2014)
6. Atanassov, K.: Intuitionistic Fuzzy Sets, VII ITKR Session, Sofia, 20–23 June 1983 (Deposed in Centr. Sci.-Techn. Library of the Bulg. Acad. of Sci., 1697/84). Reprinted: Int J Bioautomation **20**(S1), S1–S6 (2016)
7. Atanassov, K.: On four intuitionistic fuzzy topological operators. Mathw. Soft Comput. **8**, 65–70 (2001)
8. Atanassov, K.: On Intuitionistic Fuzzy Sets Theory. Springer, Berlin (2012)
9. Atanassov, K.: On two topological operators over intuitionistic fuzzy sets. Issues in Intuitionistic Fuzzy Sets and Generalized Nets **8**, 1–7 (2010)
10. Atanassova, V., Doukovska, L., Karastoyanov, D., Čapkovič, F.: InterCriteria decision making approach to EU member states competitiveness analysis: trend analysis. In: Angelov, P., Atanassov, K.T., Doukovska, L., Hadjiski, M., Jotsov, V., Kacprzyk, J., Kasabov, N., Sotirov, S., Szmidt, E., Zadrożny, S. (eds.) Intelligent Systems'2014. AISC, vol. 322, pp. 107–115. Springer, Cham (2015). doi:10.1007/978-3-319-11313-5_10
11. Atanassova, V.: New modified level operator N_γ over intuitionistic fuzzy sets. In: Christiansen, H., Jaudoin, H., Chountas, P., Andreasen, T., Larsen, H.L. (eds.) FQAS 2017. LNCS (LNAI), vol. 10333, pp. 209–214. Springer, Cham (2017)
12. Fidanova, S., Paprzycki, M., Roeva, O.: Hybrid GA-ACO algorithm for a model parameters identification problem. In: IEEE Proceedings of the Federated Conference on Computer Science and Information Systems, pp. 413–420 (2014)
13. Ilkova, T., Petrov, M.: InterCriteria analysis for evaluation of the pollution of the Struma river in the Bulgarian section. Notes on Intuitionistic Fuzzy Sets **22**(3), 120–130 (2016)
14. Krawczak, M., Bureva, V., Sotirova, E., Szmidt, E.: Application of the intercriteria decision making method to universities ranking. In: Atanassov, K.T., et al. (eds.) Novel Developments in Uncertainty Representation and Processing. AISC, vol. 401, pp. 365–372. Springer, Cham (2016). doi:10.1007/978-3-319-26211-6_31
15. Pencheva, T., Angelova, M.: InterCriteria analysis of simple genetic algorithms performance. In: Georgiev, K., Todorov, M., Georgiev, I. (eds.) Advanced Computing in Industrial Mathematics. Studies in Computational Intelligence, vol. 681, pp. 147–159. Springer, Cham (2017)
16. Roeva, O., Fidanova, S., Paprzycki, M.: Influence of the population size on the genetic algorithm performance in case of cultivation process modelling. In: IEEE Proceedings of the Federated Conference on Computer Science and Information Systems, pp. 371–376 (2013)
17. Roeva, O., Vassilev, P., Fidanova, S., Paprzycki, M.: InterCriteria analysis of genetic algorithms performance. In: Fidanova, S. (ed.) Recent Advances in Computational Optimization. Studies in Computational Intelligence, vol. 655, pp. 235–260. Springer, Cham (2016)
18. Roeva, O., Fidanova, S., Vassilev, P., Gepner, P.: InterCriteria analysis of a model parameters identification using genetic algorithm. In: IEEE Proceedings of the Federated Conference on Computer Science and Information Systems, pp. 501–506 (2015)

19. Sotirov, S., Sotirova, E., Melin, P., Castilo, O., Atanassov, K.: Modular neural network preprocessing procedure with intuitionistic fuzzy intercriteria analysis method. In: Andreasen, T., et al. (eds.) Flexible Query Answering Systems. AISC, vol. 400, pp. 175–186. Springer, Cham (2016)
20. Stratiev, D., Sotirov, S., Shishkova, I., Nedelchev, A., Sharafutdinov, I., Veli, A., Mitkova, M., Yordanov, D., Sotirova, E., Atanassova, V., Atanassov, K., Stratiev, D., Rudnev, N., Ribagin, S.: Investigation of relationships between bulk properties and fraction properties of crude oils by application of the intercriteria analysis. Pet. Sci. Technol. **34**(13), 1113–1120 (2016)
21. Todinova, S., Mavrov, D., Krumova, S., Marinov, P., Atanassova, V., Atanassov, K., Taneva, S.: Blood plasma thermograms dataset analysisby means of intercriteria and correlation analyses for the case of colorectal cancer. Int. J. Bioautomation **20**(1), 115–124 (2016)

Application of the InterCriteria Analysis Over Air Quality Data

Evdokia Sotirova[1(✉)], Veselina Bureva[1], Irena Markovska[2], Sotir Sotirov[1], and Desislava Vankova[3(✉)]

[1] Intelligent Systems Laboratory, University "Prof. Dr. Assen Zlatarov", Burgas, Bulgaria
{esotirova, vbureva, ssotirov}@btu.bg

[2] Department of Silicate Technology, University "Prof. Dr. Assen Zlatarov", Burgas, Bulgaria
imarkovska@btu.bg

[3] Medical University-Varna "Prof. Dr. P. Stoyanov", Varna, Bulgaria
vanko07@gmail.com

Abstract. In the paper application of the InterCriteria analysis approach to real dataset with instances of hourly averaged responses from an array of 5 metal oxide chemical sensors embedded in an air quality chemical multisensor device [29, 30] is represented. The InterCriteria analysis is a new method that can be used for multicriteria decision making. The aim is to analyze the correlations between 12 indicators representing the recordings of on field deployed air quality chemical sensor devices responses.

Keywords: Air quality · InterCriteria analysis · Intuitionistic fuzzy sets · Index matrix · Multicriteria decision making

1 Introduction

By InterCriteria analysis (ICA) method the so-called tasks of multicriteria decision making can be solved. Not only the criteria themselves, but also the available data, obtained by measurement or evaluation of the objects with respect to the criteria, may be varying and heterogeneous in nature. Sometimes the measurement or evaluation according to some of the criteria may prove time-consuming, cost-ineffective, resource-demanding, etc. In such cases, for the decision maker it will be of significance advantage to ignore in future decision making all or part of these "unfavourable" criteria without this having an adverse effect on the accuracy of the decision. For this aim, it would be beneficial to detect sufficiently high and predictable correlations between the given "unfavourable" criteria and others among the set of criteria which are faster, cheaper and easier to measure or evaluate.

The purpose of this development is to identify the most correlated criteria in a real dataset with measurements of hourly averaged responses from an array of 5 metal oxide chemical sensors embedded in an air quality chemical multisensor device [30, 31]. By applying the ICA approach over extracted data for air quality, we can find the criteria that have the highest dependencies. In this way we can observe the behavior of them in

H. Christiansen et al. (Eds.): FQAS 2017, LNAI 10333, pp. 226–235, 2017.
DOI: 10.1007/978-3-319-59692-1_20

time (several years). Analogously we can receive the opposite indicators or indicators that frequently are independent from each other. In the current observation the dataset with 6934 measurements on hourly averaged concentrations for CO, Non Metanic Hydrocarbons, Benzene, Total Nitrogen Oxides (NOx) and Nitrogen Dioxide (NO_2) recorded in over a year [30, 31] were analyzed.

2 The InterCriteria Analysis

The ICA method was introduced by K. Atanassov, D. Mavrov and V. Atanassova in [3]. Several applications of the method have already been published [1, 2, 8–29, 34]. The method was employed to study the relations between the petroleum properties [32], and between bulk properties and fraction properties of crude oils [33].

The method is based on the theory of intuitionistic fuzzy sets and index matrices. Intuitionistic fuzzy sets were first defined by Atanassov [4, 6] as an extension of the concept of fuzzy sets defined by Zadeh [35]. The theory of index matrices was introduced in [5].

The objects can be estimated on the basis of several criteria. The number of criteria can be reduced by calculating the correlations in each pair of criteria in the form of intuitionistic fuzzy pairs of values [4]. The intuitionistic fuzzy pairs of values are the intuitionistic fuzzy evaluations in the interval [0, 1]. The relations can be established between any two groups of indicators C_w and C_t.

Let us have a number of C_q criteria, $q = 1, \ldots, n$, and a number of O_p measurements, $p = 1, \ldots, m$; that is, we use the following sets: a set of group of criteria $C_q = \{C_1, \ldots, C_n\}$ and a set of measurements $O_p = \{O_1, \ldots, O_m\}$.

We obtain an index matrix M that contains two sets of indices, one for rows and another for columns. For every p, q $(1 \leq p \leq m, 1 \leq q \leq n)$, O_p in an evaluated object, C_q is an evaluation criterion, and $a_{Op,Cq}$ is the evaluation of the p-th object against the q-th criterion, defined as a real number or another object that is comparable according to a relation R with all the other elements of the index matrix M.

$$M = \begin{array}{c|ccccccc} & C_1 & \ldots & C_k & \ldots & C_l & \ldots & C_n \\ \hline O_1 & a_{O_1,C_1} & \ldots & a_{O_1,C_k} & \ldots & a_{O_1,C_l} & \ldots & a_{O_1,C_n} \\ \ldots & \ldots & \ldots & \ldots & \ldots & \ldots & \ldots & \ldots \\ O_i & a_{O_i,C_1} & \ldots & a_{O_i,C_k} & \ldots & a_{O_i,C_l} & \ldots & a_{O_i,C_n} \\ \ldots & \ldots & \ldots & \ldots & \ldots & \ldots & \ldots & \ldots \\ O_j & a_{O_j,C_1} & \ldots & a_{O_j,C_k} & \ldots & a_{O_j,C_l} & \ldots & a_{O_j,C_n} \\ \ldots & \ldots & \ldots & \ldots & \ldots & \ldots & \ldots & \ldots \\ O_m & a_{O_m,C_1} & & a_{O_m,C_k} & & a_{O_m,C_l} & \ldots & a_{O_m,C_n} \end{array}.$$

The next step is to apply the InterCriteria Analysis for calculating the evaluations. The result is a new index matrix M^* with intuitionistic fuzzy pairs $\langle \mu_{C_k,C_l}, \nu_{C_k,C_l} \rangle$ that represents an intuitionistic fuzzy evaluation of the relations between every pair of criteria C_k and C_l. In this way the index matrix M that relates the evaluated objects with the evaluating criteria can be transformed to another index matrix $M*$ that gives the relations among the criteria:

$$M* = \begin{array}{c|ccc} & C_1 & \ldots & C_n \\ \hline C_1 & \langle \mu_{C_1,C_1}, \nu_{C_1,C_1} \rangle & \ldots & \langle \mu_{C_1,C_n}, \nu_{C_1,C_n} \rangle \\ \ldots & \ldots & \ldots & \ldots \\ C_n & \langle \mu_{C_q,C_1}, \nu_{C_q,C_1} \rangle & \ldots & \langle \mu_{C_n,C_n}, \nu_{C_n,C_n} \rangle \end{array}$$

The last step of the algorithm is to determine the degrees of correlation between groups of indicators depending of the chosen threshold for μ and ν from the user. The correlations between the criteria are called "positive consonance", "negative consonance" or "dissonance". Here we use the scale used in previous studies that is shown in Table 1 [7].

Table 1. Scale for determination of the relative values the correlations between the criteria

Type of correlations between the criteria
strong positive consonance [0,95; 1]
positive consonance [0,85; 0,95)
weak positive consonance [0,75; 0,85)
weak dissonance [0,67; 0,75)
dissonance [0,57; 0,67)
strong dissonance [0,43; 0,57)
dissonance [0,33; 0,43)
weak dissonance [0,25; 0,33)
weak negative consonance [0,15; 0,25)
negative consonance [0,05; 0,15)
strong negative consonance [0; 0,05]

3 Application of the ICA Over Air Quality Data

We explore real data extracted from UCI Machine Learning Repository i.e., from a site which provide free access to data [30, 31]. Using InterCriteria Analysis approach the behavior of the objects or criteria can be monitoring and optimized.

The ICA method was applied to the 6934 measurements on hourly averaged concentrations. Twelve criteria representing the recordings of on field deployed air quality chemical sensor devices responses are used [30, 31]:

(1) True hourly averaged concentration CO in mg/m^3 – CO(GT);
(2) PT08.S1 (tin oxide) hourly averaged sensor response – PT08.S1(CO);
(3) True hourly averaged Benzene concentration in microg/m^3 – C6H6(GT);
(4) PT08.S2 (titania) hourly averaged sensor response – PT08.S2(NMHC);
(5) True hourly averaged NOx concentration in ppb – NOx(GT);

(6) PT08.S3 (tungsten oxide) hourly averaged sensor response – PT08.S3(NOx);
(7) True hourly averaged NO_2 concentration in microg/m^3 – NO_2(GT);
(8) PT08.S4 (tungsten oxide) hourly averaged sensor response – PT08.S4(NO_2);
(9) PT08.S5 (indium oxide) hourly averaged sensor response – PT08.S5(O3);
1(0) Temperature in °C – T;
(11) Relative Humidity (%) – RH;
(12) Absolute Humidity – AH.

The testing matrices which containμ μ-values and ν-values from the air quality chemical sensor devices are presented in the Tables 2 and 3. The values in the matrices are colored in shades of gray for the varying degrees of consonance and dissonance from darkest gray (highest values) to white.

Table 2. Membership part of the intuitionistic fuzzy pairs

μ	CO (GT)	PT08.S1 (CO)	C6H6 (GT)	PT08.S2 (NMHC)	NOx (GT)	PT08.S3 (NOx)	NO2 (GT)	PT08.S4 (NO2)	PT08.S5 (O3)	T	RH	AH
CO (GT)	1,000	0,844	0,895	0,895	0,865	0,128	0,815	0,810	0,824	0,582	0,460	0,543
PT08.S1 (CO)	0,844	1,000	0,883	0,883	0,837	0,095	0,785	0,881	0,871	0,610	0,519	0,629
C6H6 (GT)	0,895	0,883	1,000	1,000	0,887	0,098	0,836	0,850	0,865	0,613	0,463	0,558
PT08.S2 (NMHC)	0,895	0,883	1,000	1,000	0,887	0,098	0,836	0,850	0,865	0,613	0,463	0,558
NOx (GT)	0,865	0,837	0,887	0,887	1,000	0,157	0,857	0,793	0,845	0,561	0,480	0,528
PT08.S3 (NOx)	0,128	0,095	0,098	0,098	0,157	1,000	0,214	0,116	0,130	0,398	0,481	0,379
NO2 (GT)	0,815	0,785	0,836	0,836	0,857	0,214	1,000	0,733	0,788	0,589	0,411	0,489
PT08.S4 (NO2)	0,810	0,881	0,850	0,850	0,793	0,116	0,733	1,000	0,825	0,615	0,566	0,700
PT08.S5 (O3)	0,824	0,871	0,865	0,865	0,845	0,130	0,788	0,825	1,000	0,556	0,521	0,581
T	0,582	0,610	0,613	0,613	0,561	0,398	0,589	0,615	0,556	1,000	0,290	0,586
RH	0,460	0,519	0,463	0,463	0,480	0,481	0,411	0,566	0,521	0,290	1,000	0,704
AH	0,543	0,629	0,558	0,558	0,528	0,379	0,489	0,700	0,581	0,586	0,704	1,000

The representation of the IF pairs as points into the intuitionistic fuzzy triangle is shown in Fig. 1. In Figs. 2, 3 and 4 the dependences between criteria during the year are shown.

Table 3. Non-membership part of the intuitionistic fuzzy pairs

ν	CO (GT)	PT08.S1 (CO)	C6H6 (GT)	PT08.S2 (NMHC)	NOx (GT)	PT08.S3 (NOx)	NO2 (GT)	PT08.S4 (NO2)	PT08.S5 (O3)	T	RH	AH
CO (GT)	0,000	0,131	0,080	0,080	0,108	0,846	0,155	0,164	0,151	0,392	0,515	0,431
PT08.S1 (CO)	0,131	0,000	0,117	0,117	0,161	0,904	0,209	0,118	0,128	0,389	0,481	0,371
C6H6 (GT)	0,080	0,117	0,000	0,000	0,110	0,901	0,159	0,150	0,134	0,386	0,537	0,441
PT08.S2 (NMHC)	0,080	0,117	0,000	0,000	0,110	0,901	0,159	0,150	0,134	0,386	0,537	0,441
NOx (GT)	0,108	0,161	0,110	0,110	0,000	0,840	0,135	0,205	0,152	0,436	0,517	0,469
PT08.S3 (NOx)	0,846	0,904	0,901	0,901	0,840	0,000	0,781	0,884	0,870	0,601	0,518	0,621
NO2 (GT)	0,155	0,209	0,159	0,159	0,135	0,781	0,000	0,261	0,206	0,405	0,583	0,506
PT08.S4 (NO2)	0,164	0,118	0,150	0,150	0,205	0,884	0,261	0,000	0,175	0,384	0,433	0,300
PT08.S5 (O3)	0,151	0,128	0,134	0,134	0,152	0,870	0,206	0,175	0,000	0,443	0,478	0,418
T	0,392	0,389	0,386	0,386	0,436	0,601	0,405	0,384	0,443	0,000	0,709	0,413
RH	0,515	0,481	0,537	0,537	0,517	0,518	0,583	0,433	0,478	0,709	0,000	0,295
AH	0,431	0,371	0,441	0,441	0,469	0,621	0,506	0,300	0,418	0,413	0,295	0,000

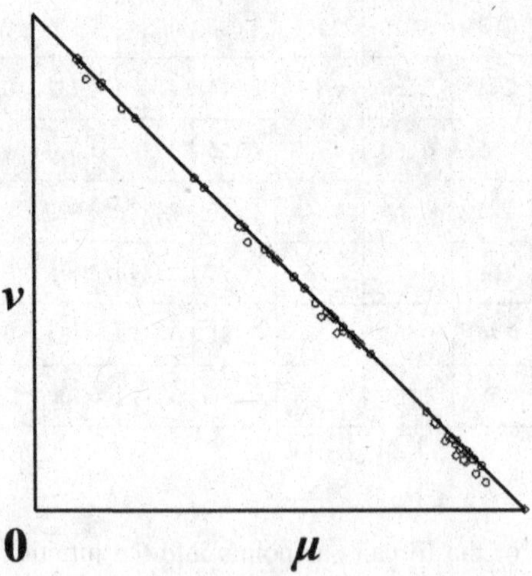

Fig. 1. IF pairs in the intuitionistic fuzzy triangle

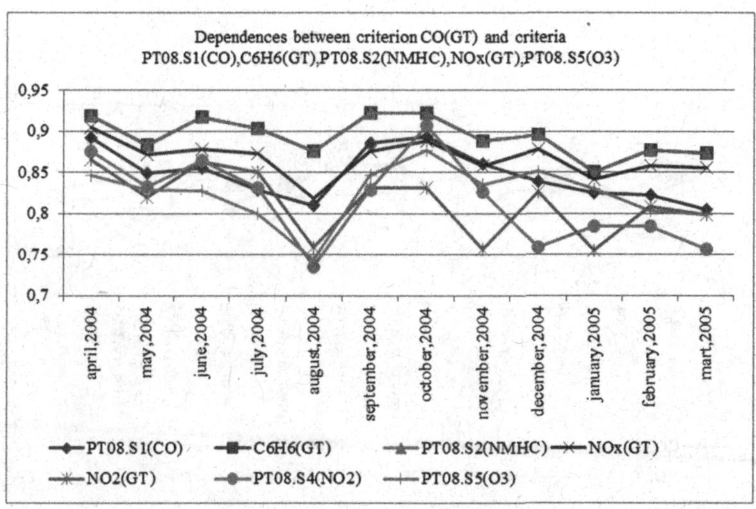

Fig. 2. Dependences between criterion CO(GT) and criteria PT08.S1(CO), C6H6(GT), PT08.S2 (NMHC), NOx(GT), PT08.S5(O3)

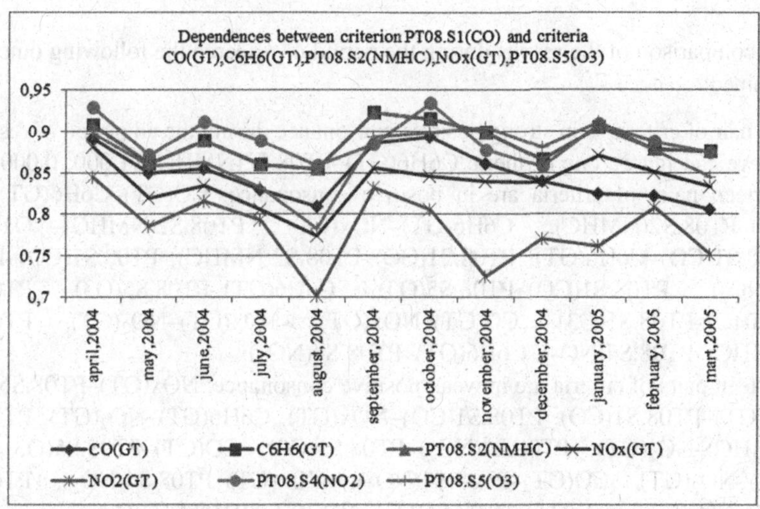

Fig. 3. Dependences between criterion PT08.S1(CO) and criteria CO(GT), C6H6(GT), PT08.S2 (NMHC), NOx(GT), PT08.S5(O3)

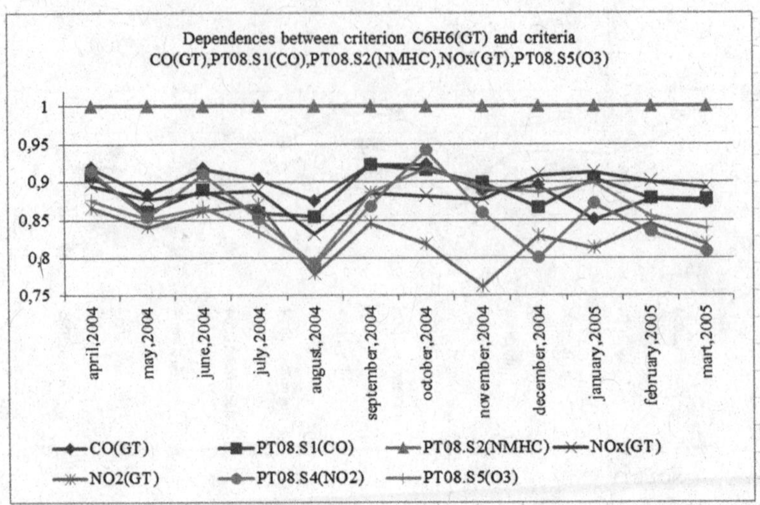

Fig. 4. Dependences between criterion C6H6(GT) and criteria CO(GT), PT08.S1(CO), PT08.S2 (NMHC), NOx(GT), PT08.S5(O3)

4 Analysis of the Results

Via the comparison of the results during the period of research the following outcomes are obtained:

- One pair of criteria is in strong positive consonance during the all period of research and we can ignore one of them: C6H6(GT)–PT08.S2(NMHC) ⟨1,000; 0,000⟩;
- Fourteen pairs of criteria are in positive consonance: CO(GT)–C6H6(GT), CO (GT)–PT08.S2(NMHC), C6H6(GT)–NOx(GT), PT08.S2(NMHC)–NOx(GT), PT08.S1(CO)–C6H6(GT), PT08.S1(CO)–PT08.S2(NMHC), PT08.S1(CO)–PT08. S4(NO_2), PT08.S1(CO)–PT08.S5(O3), C6H6(GT)–PT08.S5(O3), PT08.S2 (NMHC)–PT08.S5(O3), CO(GT)–NOx(GT), NOx(GT)–NO_2(GT), PT08.S2 (NMHC)–PT08.S4(NO_2), C6H6(GT)–PT08.S4(NO_2);
- Thirteen pairs of criteria are in weak positive consonance: NOx(GT)–PT08.S5(O3), CO(GT)–PT08.S1(CO), PT08.S1(CO)–NOx(GT), C6H6(GT)–NO_2(GT), PT08.S2 (NMHC)–NO_2(GT), PT08.S4(NO_2)–PT08.S5(O3), CO(GT)–PT08.S5(O3), CO (GT)–NO_2(GT), CO(GT)–PT08.S4(NO_2), NOx(GT)–PT08.S4(NO_2), PT08.S1 (CO)–NO_2(GT), NO_2(GT)–PT08.S5(O3), NO_2(GT)–PT08.S4(NO_2);
- The rest thirty-eight criteria are in weak dissonance, dissonance or in negative consonance;
- The correlation between criteria appears periodically;
- The dependences between criteria are relatively constant, but there is a very slight decrease over the time.

5 Conclusion

In the research reported here the authors have applied the ICA method to the data of the real dataset with measurements of hourly averaged responses from an array of 5 metal oxide chemical sensors embedded in an air quality chemical multisensor device. There is reasonable consistency across the criteria for period of the research. This would seem to indicate that the criteria and their measurements are reasonably reliable. The observations can thus help to determine the behavior of the criteria and relations among them over time.

In order to determine the behavior of each criteria over time we should observe the results of the application of ICA method for several years. If this criterion has a strong correlation, again, in the next step we can try to ignore it in future decision making without this having an adverse effect on the accuracy of the decision.

Acknowledgments. The authors are thankful for the support provided by the Bulgarian National Science Fund under Grant Ref. No. DFNI-I-02-5 "*InterCriteria Analysis: A New Approach to Decision Making*".

References

1. Angelova, M., Roeva, O., Pencheva, T.: InterCriteria analysis of a cultivation process model based on the genetic algorithm population size influence. Notes Intuitionistic Fuzzy Sets **21**(4), 90–103 (2015)
2. Angelova, M., Roeva, O., Pencheva, T.: InterCriteria analysis of crossover and mutation rates relations in simple genetic algorithm. In: Proceedings of the 2015 Federated Conference on Computer Science and Information Systems (FedCSIS 2015), pp. 419–424 (2015)
3. Atanassov, K., Mavrov, D., Atanassova, V.: InterCriteria decision making: a new approach for multicriteria decision making, based on index matrices and intuitionistic fuzzy sets. Issues Intuitionistic Fuzzy Sets Gen. Nets **11**, 1–8 (2014)
4. Atanassov, K., Szmidt, E., Kacprzyk, J.: On intuitionistic fuzzy pairs. Notes Intuitionistic Fuzzy Sets **19**(3), 1–13 (2013)
5. Atanassov, K.: Index Matrices: Towards an Augmented Matrix Calculus. Studies in Computational Intelligence Series, vol. 573. Springer, Cham (2014)
6. Atanassov, K.: On Intuitionistic Fuzzy Sets Theory. Springer, Berlin (2012)
7. Atanassov, K., Atanassova, V., Gluhchev, G.: InterCriteria analysis: ideas and problems. Notes Intuitionistic Fuzzy Sets **21**(1), 81–88 (2015)
8. Atanassova, V., Doukovska, L., Atanassov, K., Mavrov, D.: InterCriteria decision making approach to EU member states competitiveness analysis. In: Proceedings of the International Symposium on Business Modeling and Software Design (BMSD 2014), pp. 289–294 (2014)
9. Atanassova, V., Doukovska, L., Karastoyanov, D., Čapkovič, F.: InterCriteria decision making approach to EU member states competitiveness analysis: trend analysis. In: Angelov, P., et al. (eds.) Intelligent Systems 2014. AISC, vol. 322, pp. 107–115. Springer, Cham (2015). doi:10.1007/978-3-319-11313-5_10

10. Atanassova, V., Doukovska, L., Mavrov, D., Atanassov, K.: InterCriteria decision making approach to EU member states competitiveness analysis: temporal and threshold analysis. In: Angelov, P., et al. (eds.) Intelligent Systems'2014. AISC, vol. 322, pp. 95–106. Springer, Cham (2015). doi:10.1007/978-3-319-11313-5_9
11. Bureva, V., Sotirova, E., Sotirov, S., Mavrov, D.: Application of the InterCriteria decision making method to Bulgarian universities ranking. Notes Intuitionistic Fuzzy Sets **21**(2), 111–117 (2015)
12. Doukovska, L., Karastoyanov, D., Stoymenov, N., Kalaykov, I.: Intercriteria decision making approach for iron powder briquetting. In: Proceedings of the Fifth International Symposium on Business Modeling and Software Design (BMSD 2015), pp. 292–296 (2015)
13. Doukovska, L., Atanassova, V., Shahpazov, G., Capkovic, F.: InterCriteria analysis applied to EU micro, small, medium and large enterprises. In: Proceedings of the Fifth International Symposium on Business Modeling and Software Design (BMSD 2015), pp. 284–291 (2015)
14. Doukovska, L., Shahpazov, G., Atanassova, V.: Intercriteria analysis of the creditworthiness of SMEs. A case study. Notes Intuitionistic Fuzzy Sets **22**(2), 108–118 (2016)
15. Fidanova, S., Roeva, O., Paprzycki, M.: InterCriteria analysis of ant colony optimization application to GPS surveying problems. Issues Intuitionistic Fuzzy Sets and Gen. Nets **12**, 20–38 (2015)
16. Fidanova, S., Roeva, O.: InterCriteria analysis of different metaheuristics applied to *E. coli* cultivation process. In: Numerical Methods for Scientific Computations and Advanced Applications, pp. 21–25 (2016)
17. Fidanova, S., Roeva, O., Gepner, P., Paprzycki, M.: InterCriteria analysis of ACO start strategies. In: Proceedings of the 2016 Federated Conference on Computer Science and Information Systems (FedCSIS 2016), pp. 547–550 (2016)
18. Fidanova, S., Roeva, O., Mucherino, A., Kapanova, K.: InterCriteria analysis of ant algorithm with environment change for GPS surveying problem. In: Dichev, C., Agre, G. (eds.) AIMSA 2016. LNCS, vol. 9883, pp. 271–278. Springer, Cham (2016). doi:10.1007/978-3-319-44748-3_26
19. Ilkova, T., Petrov, M.: Intercriteria analysis for identification of Escherichia coli fed-batch mathematical model. Mat. Methods Technol. **9**, 598–608 (2015)
20. Ilkova, T., Roeva, O., Vassilev, P., Petrov, M.: InterCriteria analysis in structural and parameter identification of L-lysine production model. Issues Intuitionistic Fuzzy Sets Gen. Nets **12**, 39–52 (2015)
21. Karastoyanov, D., Doukovska, L., Gyoshev, S., Kalaykov, I.: Intercriteria decision making approach for metal chips briquetting. In: Proceedings of the Fifth International Symposium on Business Modeling and Software Design (BMSD 2015), pp. 297–301 (2015)
22. Kostadinov, T., Petkov, T.: An example of intercriteria analysis application to weather parameters. Notes Intuitionistic Fuzzy Sets **21**(2), 126–133 (2015)
23. Krawczak, M., Bureva, V., Sotirova, E., Szmidt, E.: Application of the InterCriteria decision making method to universities ranking. In: Atanassov, K.T., et al. (eds.) Novel Developments in Uncertainty Representation and Processing. AISC, vol. 401, pp. 365–372. Springer, Cham (2016). doi:10.1007/978-3-319-26211-6_31
24. Pencheva, T., Angelova, M., Vassilev, P., Roeva, O.: InterCriteria analysis approach to parameter identification of a fermentation process model. In: Atanassov, K.T., et al. (eds.) Novel Developments in Uncertainty Representation and Processing. AISC, vol. 401, pp. 385–397. Springer, Cham (2016). doi:10.1007/978-3-319-26211-6_33
25. Pencheva, T., Angelova, M., Atanassova, V., Roeva, O.: InterCriteria analysis of genetic algorithm parameters in parameter identification. Notes Intuitionistic Fuzzy Sets **21**(2), 99–110 (2015)

26. Roeva, O., Vassilev, P.: InterCriteria analysis of generation gap influence on genetic algorithms performance. In: Atanassov, K.T., et al. (eds.) Novel Developments in Uncertainty Representation and Processing. AISC, vol. 401, pp. 301–313. Springer, Cham (2016). doi:10.1007/978-3-319-26211-6_26
27. Roeva, O., Fidanova, S., Paprzycki, M.: InterCriteria Analysis of ACO and GA Hybrid Algorithms. Studies in Computational Intelligence, vol. 610, pp. 107–126. Springer, Cham (2016)
28. Roeva, O., Fidanova, S., Vassilev, P., Gepner, P.: InterCriteria analysis of a model parameters identification using genetic algorithm. In: Proceedings of the 2015 Federated Conference on Computer Science and Information Systems, pp. 501–506 (2015)
29. Ribagin, S., Shannon, A., Atanassov, K.: Intuitionistic fuzzy evaluations of the elbow joint range of motion. In: Atanassov, K.T., et al. (eds.) Novel Developments in Uncertainty Representation and Processing. AISC, vol. 401, pp. 225–230. Springer, Cham (2016). doi:10.1007/978-3-319-26211-6_19
30. Saverio, D.V.: ENEA - National Agency for New Technologies, Energy and Sustainable Economic Development. Air Quality Data Set. https://archive.ics.uci.edu/ml/datasets/Air+Quality
31. Saverio, D.V., Massera, E., Piga, M., Martinotto, L., Francia, G.D.: On field calibration of an electronic nose for benzene estimation in an urban pollution monitoring scenario. Sens. Actuators B Chem. **129**(2), 750–757 (2008)
32. Stratiev, D., Shishkova, I., Nedelchev, A., Kirilov, K., Nikolaychuk, E., Ivanov, A., Sharafutdinov, I., Veli, A., Mitkova, M., Tsaneva, T., Petkova, N., Sharpe, R., Yordanov, D., Belchev, Z., Nenov, S., Rudnev, N., Atanassova, V., Sotirova, E., Sotirov, S., Atanassov, K.: Investigation of relationships between petroleum properties and their impact on crude oil compatibility. Energy Fuels **29**(12), 7836–7854 (2015)
33. Stratiev, D., Sotirov, S., Shishkova, I., Nedelchev, A., Sharafutdinov, I., Veli, A., Mitkova, M., Yordanov, D., Sotirova, E., Atanassova, V., Atanassov, K., Stratiev, D., Rudnev, N., Ribagin, S.: Investigation of relationships between bulk properties and fraction properties of crude oils by application of the intercriteria analysis. Pet. Sci. Technol. **34**(13), 1113–1120 (2016)
34. Vankova D., Sotirova, E., Bureva, V.: An application of the InterCriteria analysis approach to health-related quality of life. In: 11th International Workshop on IFSs, Banská Bystrica, Slovakia, 30 October 2015, vol. 21, no. 5, pp. 40–48 (2015). Notes on Intuitionistic Fuzzy Sets
35. Zadeh, L.: Fuzzy sets. Inf. Control **8**, 333–353 (1965)

Generalized Net Model

Generalized Net of Cluster Analysis Process Using STING: A Statistical Information Grid Approach to Spatial Data Mining

Veselina Bureva(✉), Evdokia Sotirova, Stanislav Popov, Deyan Mavrov, and Velichka Traneva

Intelligent Systems Laboratory, University "Prof. Dr. Assen Zlatarov" Burgas, Burgas, Bulgaria
{vbureva,esotirova}@btu.bg, stani_popov@yahoo.com, dg@mavrov.eu, veleka13@gmail.com

Abstract. Cluster analysis is one of the main topics in data mining. It helps to group elements with similar behavior in one group. Therefore, a good clustering method will produce high quality clusters containing objects similar to one another within the same group and dissimilar to the objects in other clusters. In the current research work one of the basic grid-based methods for clustering is modelled using Generalized nets.

Keywords: Cluster analysis · Generalized nets · Grid-Based cluster analysis · Spatial data mining

1 Introduction

Cluster analysis groups data points in clusters using a specified similarity or distance measure. Depending on the type of the clustering procedure and the input data the cluster analysis can be applied using different approaches: partitioning methods, hierarchical methods, density-based methods, grid-based methods, model-based methods and several hybrid approaches. It is applied in different areas for performing tasks such as data summarization, compression and reduction; collaborative filtering, customer segmentation and recommender systems; dynamic trend detection; social network analysis, biological data analysis and multimedia data analysis; or as an intermediate step of other data mining tasks. In some applications, we are interested in discovering outliers, not clusters (outlier analysis). The discussion in the current paper is focused on *grid-based cluster analysis*. It is performed using a multiresolution grid data structure. The space is quantized into a finite number of cells and the clustering procedure is executed over them. Typical examples of grid-based approaches include STING, WaveCluster and CLIQUE. STING explores statistical information stored in grid cells, WaveCluster clusters objects using a wavelet transform method and CLIQUE represents a grid- and density-based approach for clustering in a high-dimensional data space [1, 2, 10]. In this paper the STING: Statistical Information Grid-based Algorithm, which is introduced in [14], is modelled using Generalized nets [4, 5]. The STING algorithm contains the following steps [14]:

H. Christiansen et al. (Eds.): FQAS 2017, LNAI 10333, pp. 239–248, 2017.
DOI: 10.1007/978-3-319-59692-1_21

(1) Determine a layer to start from.
(2) For each cell of this layer, calculate the confidence interval (or estimated range) of probability that this cell is relevant to the query.
(3) From the interval calculated above, we label each cell as *relevant* or *not relevant*.
(4) If this layer is the bottom layer, go to Step 6; otherwise, go to Step 5.
(5) Go down the hierarchy structure by one level. Go to Step 2 for those cells that form the *relevant* cells of the higher-level layer.
(6) If the specification of the query is met, go to Step 8; otherwise, go to Step 7.
(7) Retrieve the data that is located in the *relevant* cells and do further processing. Return the result that meets the requirement of the query. Go to Step 9.
(8) Find the regions of *relevant* cells. Return those regions that meet the requirement of the query. Go to Step 9.
(9) Stop.

2 Generalized Net of the Cluster Analysis Process Using STING: A Statistical Information Grid Approach to Spatial Data Mining

Generalized nets are used for describing and modelling real processes as well as to simulate and control them [4, 5]. There are several methods and algorithms for knowledge discovery that are already modeled with generalized nets. Some of them are presented in [3, 6, 7, 9, 11–13]. A Hierarchical generalized net model of the process of clustering and its subnet presenting a Hierarchical generalized net model of the process of selecting a method for clustering are explored in [6, 7]. The present Generalized net model can be also utilized as a replacement for the transition Z_4 of the Hierarchical generalized net model of the process of selecting a method for clustering introduced in [6], but in order to describe the process more clearly, the authors have constructed it as a separate model. The Intuitionistic fuzzy histograms of grid-based clustering are explained in [8].

The presented generalized net models the process of applying cluster analysis to spatial data using the grid-based method STING. The GN-model (Fig. 1) contains 6 transitions and 29 places. The transitions represent the following processes:

- Z_1 – "Activities with spatial queries";
- Z_2 – "Activities with spatial database";
- Z_3 – "Divide the spatial area into rectangle cells, constructing the hierarchical structure and determining a layer to start from";
- Z_4 – "Determine attribute-dependent and attribute-independent parameters for each cell";
- Z_5 – "Calculate the confidence interval of probability for each cell that it is relevant to the query";
- Z_6 – "Retrieve the data that is located in the relevant cells and do further processing".

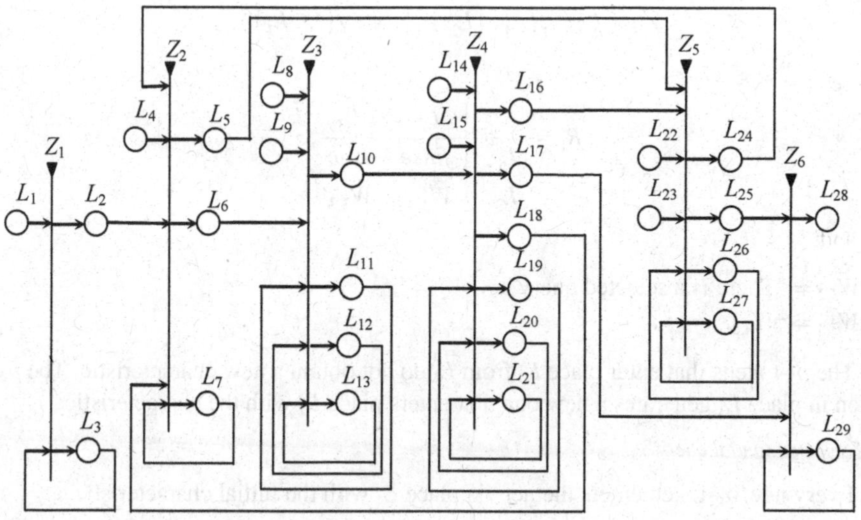

Fig. 1. Generalized net of the cluster analysis process using STING: A Statistical Information Grid Approach to Spatial Data Mining

Initially in the place L_3 there is one β_1-token. It will be in its own place during the entire time the GN is functioning. It has the following characteristic:

"*Current status of spatial queries*".

The β_1-token in place L_3 generates new β-tokens at certain points in time which can move to place L_2 with the characteristic:

"*Selected spatial query*".

At the start of the GN's operation there is also one α_1-token that is located in place L_7 with the initial characteristic

"*Spatial database*".

The α_1-token in place L_7 generates new α-tokens that at certain points in time which will move to places L_5 and L_6, respectively with characteristics:

"*Selected spatial information for further processing*"

in place L_5 and

"*Selected spatial data*"

in place L_6.

β_2-tokens will enter the net via place L_1 at some points in time. These points will be determined stochastically, when the model is simulated, or they will correspond to real events in cases when the GN is used for observation of real processes. These tokens have the initial characteristic "*Spatial query*". These β_2-tokens will merge with the β_1-token in place L_3.

Transition Z_1 has the form:

$$Z_1 = \langle \{L_1, L_3\}, \{L_2, L_3\}, R_1, \vee(L_1, L_3) \rangle,$$

where

$$R_1 = \begin{array}{c|cc} & L_2 & L_3 \\ \hline L_1 & false & true \\ L_3 & W_{3,2} & W_{3,3} \end{array},$$

and:

- $W_{3,2}$ = "There is a selected query";
- $W_{3,3} = \neg W_{3,2}$.

The β_2-tokens that enter place L_3 from L_1 do not obtain a new characteristic. The β-token in place L_3 generates a new one that enters place L_2 with the characteristic:

"*Selected spatial query*".

Every new α_2-token enters the net via place L_4 with the initial characteristic

"*Spatial data*".

The transition Z_2 has the form:

$$Z_2 = \langle \{L_2, L_4, L_7, L_{18}, L_{24}\}, \{L_5, L_6, L_7\}, R_2, \vee(\wedge(L_4, L_2), L_7, L_{18}, L_{24}) \rangle,$$

where

$$R_2 = \begin{array}{c|ccc} & L_5 & L_6 & L_7 \\ \hline L_2 & false & false & true \\ L_4 & false & false & true \\ L_7 & W_{7,5} & W_{7,6} & W_{7,7} \\ L_{18} & false & false & true \\ L_{24} & false & false & true \end{array},$$

and:

- $W_{7,5}$ = "There is selected spatial data for further processing";
- $W_{7,6}$ = "There is selected data for spatial query";
- $W_{7,7} = \neg(W_{7,5} \wedge W_{7,6})$.

The α_2-tokens, entering in place L_7 from L_4, do not obtain a new characteristic. The α_1-token in place L_7 generates new tokens that enter in places L_5 and L_6 with the characteristics:

"*Selected spatial data for further processing*"

in place L_5 and

"*Selected spatial data*"

in place L_6.

Tokens β_3 and β_4 enter the net via places L_8 and L_9, respectively. These tokens have the initial characteristics:

"Threshold t"

in place L_8 and

"Layer to start from"

in place L_9.

The transition Z_3 has the form:

$$Z_3 = \langle \{L_6, L_8, L_9, L_{11}, L_{12}, L_{13}\}, \{L_{10}, L_{11}, L_{12}, L_{13}\}, R_3, \vee(L_6, \wedge(L_8, L_9, L_{12}), L_{11}, L_{13})\rangle,$$

where

$R_3 =$

	L_{10}	L_{11}	L_{12}	L_{13}
L_6	*false*	*false*	*false*	*true*
L_8	*false*	*true*	*false*	*false*
L_9	*false*	*true*	*false*	*false*
L_{11}	$W_{11,10}$	$W_{11,11}$	*false*	*false*
L_{12}	*false*	$W_{12,11}$	$W_{12,12}$	*false*
L_{13}	*false*	*false*	$W_{13,12}$	$W_{13,13}$

,

and:

- $W_{13,12}$ = "The spatial area has been divided into rectangular cells";
- $W_{13,13} = \neg W_{13,12}$;
- $W_{12,11}$ = "A hierarchical structure has been assigned";
- $W_{12,12} = \neg W_{12,11}$;
- $W_{11,10}$ = "A level to start from has been determined, along with a threshold t";
- $W_{11,11} = \neg W_{11,10}$.

The α-tokens, entering in place L_{13} from L_6, do not obtain a new characteristic. The α- and β-tokens in place L_{13} generate a new one that enters in place L_{12} with the characteristic:

"Spatial area, divided into rectangular cells".

At the second activation of the transition the α-token from place L_{12} generates a new token that enters in place L_{11} with the characteristic:

"Assigned hierarchical structure".

At the third activation of the transition the α- and β-tokens from place L_{11} generate a new α-token that enters in place L_{10} with the characteristic:

"A hierarchical structure with a determined level to start the procedure from and a chosen threshold t"

in place L_{10}.

Constructing the hierarchical structure for the selected spatial data per the query is the first main step of the STING algorithm. The input spatial area is divided into rectangular cells. Each cell of the current layer is split to several child cells. The procedure is repeated until the bottom layer is determined. The root level 1 corresponds to the entire spatial area. The threshold t, which is used to determine the distribution for a parent cell, is chosen [14].

Tokens β_5 and β_6 enter the net via places L_{14} and L_{15} respectively. These tokens have the initial characteristics

"Parameters"

in place L_{14} and

"Distribution"

in place L_{15}.

The transition Z_4 has the form:

$$Z_4 = \langle \{L_{10}, L_{14}, L_{15}, L_{19}, L_{20}, L_{21}\}, \{L_{16}, L_{17}, L_{18}, L_{19}, L_{20}, L_{21}\}, R_4, \vee(\wedge(\wedge(L_{10}, L_{14}), L_{15}), L_{19}, L_{20}, L_{21})\rangle,$$

where

$R_4 =$

	L_{16}	L_{17}	L_{18}	L_{19}	L_{20}	L_{21}
L_{10}	*false*	*false*	*false*	*false*	*false*	*true*
L_{14}	*false*	*false*	*false*	*false*	*false*	*true*
L_{15}	*false*	*false*	*false*	*false*	*true*	*false*
L_{19}	$W_{19,16}$	$W_{19,17}$	$W_{19,18}$	$W_{19,19}$	*false*	$W_{19,21}$
L_{20}	*false*	*false*	*false*	$W_{20,19}$	$W_{20,20}$	*false*
L_{21}	*false*	*false*	*false*	*false*	$W_{21,20}$	$W_{21,21}$

and:

- $W_{21,20} =$ "There are calculated parameters for each cell";
- $W_{21,21} = \neg W_{21,20}$;
- $W_{20,19} =$ "Distributions for each cell have been set or determined";
- $W_{20,20} = \neg W_{20,19}$;
- $W_{19,16} =$ "There are relevant cells for further processing";
- $W_{19,17} =$ "There are relevant cells";
- $W_{19,18} =$ "There are non-relevant cells";
- $W_{19,21} =$ "There is a need for processing on the bottom layer";
- $W_{19,19} = \neg(W_{19,18} \wedge W_{19,17} \wedge W_{19,16} \wedge W_{19,21})$.

The α- and β-tokens that enter the place L_{21} (from places L_{10} and L_{14}) do not obtain new characteristics. They generate a new α-token that enters in place L_{20}, with the characteristic:

"Calculated parameters for each cell".

At the second activation of the transition the α-token from place L_{20} generates a new token that enters in place L_{19} with the characteristic:

"Determined distribution for each cell".

At the third activation of the transition the α-token from place L_{19} generates a new token that enters in place L_{16}, L_{17} or L_{18}, respectively with the characteristics:

"Non-relevant cells"

in place L_{18},

"Relevant cells"

in place L_{17} and

"Relevant cells for further processing".

in place L_{16}.

At the fourth activation of the transition the α-token from place L_{19} generates a new α-token that enters in place L_{21} with the characteristic:

"Need of parameter calculation for the bottom layer".

The transition is activated as many times as there are levels available in the hierarchical structure. For each cell, attribute-dependent and attribute-independent parameters are calculated. The attribute-independent parameter is "number of the objects in the cell". The attribute-independent parameters are "mean of all values in the cell", "standard deviation of all values of the attribute in this cell", "maximum value of the attribute in this cell", "minimum value of the attribute in this cell" and "type of distribution that the attribute value in the cell follows". Distribution types can be normal, uniform etc., and NONE which means that the distribution is unknown. The distribution can be known beforehand, obtained through hypothesis testing, or calculated by distribution-free techniques in the case when the distribution type is NONE. In the next step a confidence interval is obtained and the cells are labeled as relevant or non-relevant, depending on the specified confidence level. Thereafter the processing of the procedure continues with the examination of the children of relevant cells in lower levels. The result contains all regions that are constructed by relevant cells. If the information is not enough to answer the spatial query, further processing needs to be performed [14].

Tokens β_7 and β_8 enter the net via places L_{22} and L_{23}, respectively. These tokens have as initial characteristics

"Distance measure"

in place L_{22} and

"Density specified"

in place L_{23}.

The transition Z_5 has the form:

$$Z_5 = \langle \{L_5, L_{16}, L_{22}, L_{23}, L_{26}, L_{27}\}, \{L_{24}, L_{25}, L_{26}, L_{27}\}, R_5, \\ \vee(\wedge(\wedge(L_5, L_{16}, L_{22}), L_{23}), L_{26}, L_{27}) \rangle,$$

where

$$R_5 = \begin{array}{c|cccc} & L_{24} & L_{25} & L_{26} & L_{27} \\ \hline L_5 & false & false & false & true \\ L_{16} & false & false & false & true \\ L_{22} & false & false & false & true \\ L_{23} & false & false & true & false \\ L_{26} & W_{26,24} & W_{26,25} & W_{26,26} & W_{26,27} \\ L_{27} & false & false & W_{27,26} & W_{27,27} \end{array},$$

and:

- $W_{27,26}$ = "There are calculated distances";
- $W_{27,27} = \neg W_{27,26}$;
- $W_{26,24}$ = "There are non-relevant cells after further processing";
- $W_{26,25}$ = "There are relevant cells after further processing";
- $W_{26,27}$ = "There are bottom levels that need further processing";
- $W_{26,26} = \neg(W_{26,24} \wedge W_{26,25} \wedge W_{26,27})$.

When the α- and β-tokens enter place L_{27} (from places L_5, L_{16} and L_{22}) they do not obtain new characteristics. They generate a new α-token that enters in place L_{26} with the characteristic:

"Calculated distance measured for each cell".

At the second activation of the transition the α- and β-tokens from place L_{26} generate new α-tokens that enter in place L_{24} and L_{25} with the characteristics:

"Non-relevant cells after further processing"

in place L_{24},

"Relevant cells after further processing"

in place L_{25}.

At the third activation of the transition the α-token from place L_{26} generates a new α-token that enters in place L_{27} with the characteristic:

"Need of further processing of the bottom layer".

Further processing finds all the regions from the hierarchical structure of the relevant cells that satisfy the specified density by performing breadth-first search. For each relevant cell the distance from the center is calculated. Thereafter the distance is compared with the specified density. The algorithm finds regions that are formed by connected cells [14].

The transition Z_6 has the form:

$$Z_6 = \langle \{L_{25}, L_{17}, L_{29}\}, \{L_{28}, L_{29}\}, R_6, \vee(L_{25}, L_{17}, L_{29}) \rangle,$$

where

$$R_6 = \begin{array}{c|cc} & L_{28} & L_{29} \\ \hline L_{25} & false & true \\ L_{17} & false & true \\ L_{29} & W_{29,28} & W_{29,29} \end{array},$$

The α-tokens that enter the places L_{29} do not obtain new characteristics. They generate a new α-token that enter in place L_{28} with the characteristic:

"Result from the spatial query".

3 Conclusion

Grid-based clustering is one of the principal clustering methods applied in spatial data mining. STING presents a statistically based approach for exploring spatial datasets. It constructs a hierarchical structure of cells and mines them for clusters. The constructed Generalized Net model can be used to analyze and monitor the clustering process of the STING algorithm.

Acknowledgment. The authors are grateful for the support provided by the National Science Fund of Bulgaria under grant DN 02/10 New Instruments for Knowledge Discovery from Data and their Modelling.

References

1. Aggarwal, C.C.: Data Mining: The Textbook. Springer, Cham (2015)
2. Aggarwal, C.C., Reddy, C.K.: Data Clustering: Algorithms and Applications. Chapman and Hall/CRC, Boca Raton (2013)
3. Atanassov, K.: Generalized nets as a tool for the modelling of data mining processes. In: Sgurev, V., Yager, R.R., Kacprzyk, J., Jotsov, V. (eds.) Innovative Issues in Intelligent Systems. Series Studies in Computational Intelligence, vol. 623, pp. 161–215. Springer, Heidelberg (2016)
4. Atanassov, K.: Generalized Nets. World Scientific, Singapore (1991)
5. Atanassov, K.: On Generalized Nets Theory. Prof. M. Drinov Academic Publishing House, Sofia (2007)
6. Bureva, V., Sotirova, E., Atanassov, K.: Hierarchical generalized net model of the process of selecting a method for clustering. In: 15th International Workshop on Generalized Nets Burgas, 16 October 2014, pp. 39–48 (2014)
7. Bureva, V., Sotirova, E., Atanassov, K.: Hierarchical generalized net model of the process of clustering. In: Issues in Intuitionistic Fuzzy Sets and Generalized Nets, vol. 1, pp. 73–80. Warsaw School of Information Technology (2014)
8. Bureva, V.: Intuitionistic fuzzy histograms in grid-based clustering. Notes Intuitionistic Fuzzy Sets **20**(1), 55–62 (2014)
9. Dimitrov, D., Roeva, O.: Development of generalized net for testing of different mathematical models of E. coli cultivation process. In: Angelov, P., et al. (eds.) Intelligent Systems'2014. AISC, vol. 322, pp. 657–668. Springer, Cham (2015). doi:10.1007/978-3-319-11313-5_58
10. Han, J., Kamber, M.: Data Mining: Concepts and Techniques, 2nd edn. Morgan Kaufmann Publishers, Elsevier, San Francisco (2006)

11. Roeva, O., Pencheva, T., Atanassov, K., Shannon, A.: Generalized net model of selection operator of genetic algorithms. In: Proceedings of the IEEE International Conference on Intelligent Systems, pp. 286–289 (2010)
12. Roeva, O., Shannon, A., Pencheva, T.: Description of simple genetic algorithm modifications using generalized nets. In: Proceedings of the 6th IEEE International Conference Intelligent Systems, pp. 178–183 (2012)
13. Sotirova, E., Orozova, D.: Generalized net model of the phases of the data mining process. In: Developments in Fuzzy Sets, Intuitionistic Fuzzy Sets, Generalized Nets and Related Topics, vol. II: Applications, Warsaw, Poland, pp. 247–260 (2010)
14. Wang, W., Yang, J., Muntz, R.: STING: a statistical information grid approach to spatial data mining. In: Proceedings of the 23rd International Conference on Very Large Data Bases, Morgan Kaufmann Publishers Inc., pp. 186–195 (1997)

A Generalized Net Model of the Neocognitron Neural Network

Todor Petkov, Plamena Jovcheva, Zhivko Tomov, Stanislav Simeonov, and Sotir Sotirov(✉)

Intelligent Systems Laboratory, University "Prof. Dr. Assen Zlatarov" Burgas, Burgas, Bulgaria
{todor_petkov,ssotirov}@btu.bg, plamena.iovcheva@abv.bg, zhivko57@yandex.ru, st_sim@yahoo.com

Abstract. In this paper a generalized net model of the Neocognitron neural network is presented. A Network Neocognitron is a self-organizing network with the ability to recognize patterns based on the difference of their form. A neocognitron is able to correctly identify an image, even if there is a violation or movement into position. Self-organization in the neocognitron is also realized uncontrollably - training for self-organizing neocognitron takes only a collection of recurring patterns in the recognizable image and does not need the information for categories that include templates. The output producing process is presented by a Generalized net model.

Keywords: Generalized nets · Neural networks · Visual pattern recognition · Unsupervised learning neural network model · Visual nervous system modeling

1 Introduction

Neural Networks [12] are an information processing paradigm that is inspired from the biological nervous systems, such as the human brain. It is composed of a large number of highly interconnected processing elements (neurons) working in symbiosis to solve many kinds of problems. Neural networks are learnt by example. Neural networks are proper to a specific application, such as pattern recognition or data classification, through a learning process. The learning process in these systems involves adjustments to the synaptic connections that exist between the artificial neurons.

Neural networks are one of the useful tools for data mining. There are many types of neural networks [12]. Most of them are represented by generalized nets. One of the neural networks that use different type of architectures is Neocognitron neural network. This type is inspired by the visual nervous system.

2 Neocognitron Neural Network

Network, referred to as "Neocognitron" [10], is a self-organizing network and has the ability to recognize patterns based on the difference of their form. Each template

H. Christiansen et al. (Eds.): FQAS 2017, LNAI 10333, pp. 249–259, 2017.
DOI: 10.1007/978-3-319-59692-1_22

estimated as belonging to a particular category is determined most accurately by neocognitron in the same category.

A neocognitron is able to correctly identify the image, even if there is a violation or movement into position. Self-organization in the neocognitron is also realized uncontrollably - training for self-organization neocognitron takes only a collection of recurring patterns in the recognizable image and does not need the information for categories that include templates. The neocognitron acquires the ability to classify and recognize these structures on their own right, based on differences in shapes. The neocognitron properly recognizes images without the influence of shifts and even in serious shape distortion of the object.

The neocognitron has a hierarchical structure. Recognizable image information that falls in the input layer of the neocognitron is processed step by step, at every stage of the multi-layer network. Cells at a deeper stage usually tend to react selectively with the complex function and at the same time there are susceptible areas and they are sensitive to changes in position of the image. Thus, each cell in a deeper layer is responsible only for a particular model.

According to [10, 11], *C*-cells, which resemble complex cells in the visual cortex, are inserted into the network to allow for positional errors in the features of the stimulus. The input connections of *C*-cells, which come from *S*-cells of the preceding layer, are fixed and invariable. Each *C*-cell receives excitatory input connections from a group of S-cells that extract the same feature but from slightly different positions. The *C*-cell responds if at least one of these *S*-cells yields an output. Even if the stimulus feature shifts in position and another *S*-cell comes to respond instead of the first one, the same *C*-cell keeps responding. Thus, the *C*-cell's response is less sensitive to shift in position of the input pattern. We can also express that *C*-cells make a blurring operation, because the response of a layer of *S*-cells is spatially blurred in the response of the succeeding layer of *C*-cells (Fig. 1).

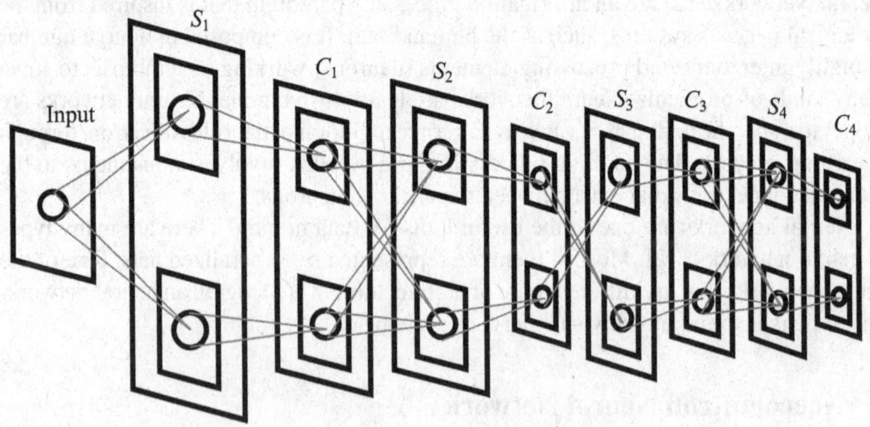

Fig. 1. Architecture of neocognitron [10].

Each unit in the arrays receives signals from a small group of units in the previous layer. The units within a specific array are designated by subscripts; a typical unit in the first array (in the first *S*-layer) is *SIL*. Depending on whether the unit is in a *C*-layer or an *S*-layer, it will receive signals from the designated units in one or more of the arrays in the previous layer.

The output signal of a unit in an *S*-type cell (a cell in any of the *S*-layers) is a function of the excitatory signals it receives from units in the previous layer and the inhibitory signals it receives from those same units. The mechanism is described in terms of an intermediate, or auxiliary, unit (denoted here as a *V* unit) whose signal to the *S* unit is proportional to the (weighted) Euclidean norm of the signal sent by the input units, where

- C_i - output from *C* unit;
- S_i - output from *S* unit;
- v - output from *V* unit;
- W_i - adjustable weight from *C* unit to *S* unit;
- W_o - weight from *V* unit to *S* unit;
- I_i - fixed weight from *C* unit to *V* unit;
- u_i - fixed weight from *S* unit to *C* unit.

The signal sent by the inhibitory unit *V* is

$$v = \sqrt{\sum t_i c_i^2},$$

where the summations are over all units that are connected to V in any array and over all arrays. The input layer is treated as the CO level. Thus, a typical S unit forms its scaled input,

$$x = \frac{1+e}{1+vw_0} - 1,$$

where

$$e = \sum_i c_i w_i$$

is the net excitatory input from *C* units, and vw_0 is the net input from the *V* unit. The output signal is

$$S = \begin{cases} x, & x \geq 0 \\ 0, & x < 0 \end{cases}$$

The inhibitory signal serves to normalize the response of the S unit in a manner somewhat similar to that used in ART2. The output of a *C* layer unit is a function of the net input it receives from all units of the *S* arrays, that feed into it. As was shown in the description of the architecture, that input is typically from 9 or 25 units in each one of three *S* arrays. The net input is

$$c\_in = \sum_i s_i u_i.$$

The output is

$$S = \begin{cases} \dfrac{c\_in}{a + c\_in}, & c\_in > 0 \\ 0, & otherwise \end{cases}.$$

The parameter a depends on the level and is 0.25 for Level 1, 2, and 3 and 1.0 for Level 4.

3 Generalized Nets

Generalized nets (GNs) [2, 3] are defined in a way that is principally different from the ways of defining the other types of Petri nets. The first basic difference between GNs and ordinary Petri nets is the "place – transition" relation. Here the transitions are objects of a more complex nature. A transition may contain m input places and n output places where $m, n \geq 1$.

Formally, every transition is described by a seven-tuple (Fig. 2):

$$Z = \langle L', L'', t_1, t_2, r, M, \square \rangle,$$

where:

(a) L' and L'' are finite, non-empty sets of places (the transition's input and output places, respectively). For the transition in Fig. 2 these are

$$L' = \{l'_1, l'_2, \ldots, l'_m\}$$

and

$$L'' = \{l''_1, l''_2, \ldots, l''_m\};$$

(b) t_1 is the current time-moment of the transition's firing;
(c) t_2 is the current value of the duration of its active state;
(d) r is the *condition* of the transition to determine which tokens will pass (or *transfer)* from the inputs to the outputs of the transition; it has the form of an Index Matrix:

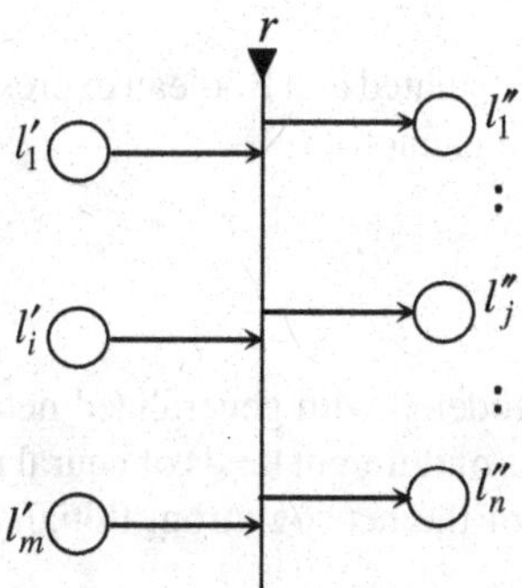

Fig. 2. A GN-transition

$$r = \begin{array}{c|ccccc} & l''_1 & \dots & l''_j & \dots & l''_n \\ \hline l'_1 & & & & & \\ \vdots & & & r_{i,j} & & \\ l'_i & & & (r_{i,j} - \text{predicate}) & & \\ \vdots & & & (1 \le i \le m,\ 1 \le j \le n) & & \\ l'_m & & & & & \end{array},$$

$r_{i,j}$ is the predicate that corresponds to the i-th input and j-th output place. When its truth value is "*true*", a token from the i-th input place transfers to the j-th output place; otherwise, this is not possible;

(e) M is an IM of the capacities of transition's arcs:

$$M = \begin{array}{c|ccccc} & l''_1 & \dots & l''_j & \dots & l''_n \\ \hline l'_1 & & & & & \\ \vdots & & & m_{i,j} & & \\ l'_i & & & (m_{i,j} \ge 0 - \text{natural number}) & & \\ \vdots & & & (1 \le i \le m,\ 1 \le j \le n) & & \\ l'_m & & & & & \end{array};$$

(f) ⇨ is an object of a form similar to a Boolean expression. It may contain as variables the symbols that serve as labels for a transition's input places, and ⇨ is an expression built up from variables and the Boolean connectives ∧ and ∨ and the semantics of which is defined as follows:

$\wedge(l_{i_1}, l_{i_2}, \dots, l_{i_u})$ - every place $(l_{i_1}, l_{i_2}, \dots, l_{i_u})$ must contain at least one token,

$\vee(l_{i_1}, l_{i_2}, \dots, l_{i_u})$ - there must be at least one token in all places $(l_{i_1}, l_{i_2}, \dots, l_{i_u})$, where $\{l_{i_1}, l_{i_2}, \ldots, l_{i_u}\} \subset L'$.

When the value of a type (calculated as a Boolean expression) is "*true*", the transition can become active, otherwise it cannot.

4 GN Model

Many data mining tools are modeled with generalized nets [1, 4–9, 13–24]. There are many papers describing models of different kinds of neural networks. Here we introduce a generalized net description of the neocognitron. Initially the following tokens enter the Generalized Net (GN) [2].

In place L_1 one token with initial characteristic

$$x_0^{a} = \text{}\}\text{Input pattern for Neocognitron''}$$

In place L_{14} one token with initial characteristic

$$x_0^{\beta} = \text{}\}\text{Structure of the neural network''}.$$

The GN – (Fig. 3) is introduced by the following set of transitions:

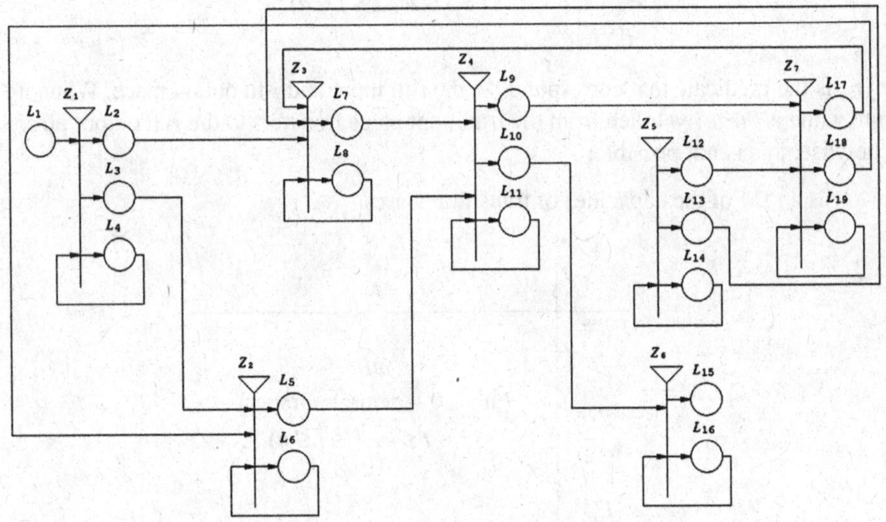

Fig. 3. GN model of neocognitron neural network

$$A = \{Z_1, Z_2, Z_3, Z_4, Z_5, Z_6, Z_7\},$$

Z_1 = Division of the input pattern;
Z_2 = Calculation of the output of V units;
Z_3 = Calculating the e parameter for S units;
Z_4 = Forming of the scaled input of S units;

Z_5 = Initializing of the weights for S and C layers;
Z_6 = Recognition from the network;
Z_7 = Calculating the values from the C units

The GN consists of seven transitions with the following description:

$$Z_1 = \langle \{L_1, L_4\}, \{L_2, L_3, L_4\}, R_1, \vee(L_1, L_4) \rangle,$$

$$R_1 = \begin{array}{c|ccc} & L_2 & L_3 & L_4 \\ \hline L_1 & false & false & true, \\ L_4 & W_{4,2} & W_{4,3} & true \end{array}$$

$W_{4,2} = W_{4,3}$ = "There is an α token in place L_1".

Token α from place L_1 that enters place L_4 does not obtain new characteristic. Token α from place L_4 splits in two tokens and obtains characteristic

$$x_{cu}^{\alpha'} = \}\}\text{Input pattern for training''}$$

Token α from place L_4 that enters place L_4 does not obtain new characteristic. Tokens α' from place L_4 that enter places L_2 and L_3 do not obtain new characteristic.

$$Z_2 = \langle \{L_3, L_6, L_{18}\}, \{L_5, L_6\}, R_2, \vee(L_3 \wedge (L_6, L_{18})) \rangle,$$

$$R_2 = \begin{array}{c|cc} & L_5 & L_6 \\ \hline L_3 & false & true \\ L_6 & W_{6,5} & true' \\ L_{18} & false & true \end{array}$$

$W_{6,5}$ = "The values of V units are calculated".

Token α' from place L_3 that enters place L_6 does not obtain new characteristic. Token η from place L_{18} that enters place L_6 does not obtain new characteristic. Token from place L_6 that enters place L_6 obtains characteristic

$$x_{cu}^{\delta} = \sqrt{\sum t_i c_i^2}$$

Token δ from place L_6 that enters place L_5 does not obtain new characteristic.

$$Z_3 = \langle \{L_2, L_8, L_{13}, L_{17}\}, \{L_7, L_8\}, R_3, \vee(L_2 \wedge (L_8, L_{13}, L_{17})) \rangle,$$

$$R_3 = \begin{array}{c|cc} & L_7 & L_8 \\ \hline L_2 & false & true \\ L_8 & W_{8,7} & true, \\ L_{13} & false & true \\ L_{17} & false & true \end{array}$$

$W_{8,7}$ = "The values for e parameter are calculated"

Token α' from place L_2 that enters place L_8 does not obtain new characteristic. Token η from place L_{17} that enters place L_8 does not obtain new characteristic. Token β'' from place L_{13} unites with tokens α' and η in place L_8 and obtains characteristic

$$x_{cu}^{\varepsilon} = \sum_i c_i w_i$$

Token ε from place L_8 that enters place L_7 does not obtain new characteristic.

$$Z_4 = \langle \{L_5, L_7, L_{11}\}, \{L_9, L_{10}, L_{11}\}, R_4, \vee(L_{11} \wedge (L_5, L_7)) \rangle,$$

$$R_4 = \begin{array}{c|ccc} & L_9 & L_{10} & L_{11} \\ \hline L_5 & false & false & true \\ L_7 & false & false & true' \\ L_{11} & W_{11,9} & W_{11,10} & true \end{array}$$

$W_{11,9}$ = "The values for S units are calculated";
$W_{11,10}$ = "The values for S_3 units are calculated".
Tokens δ and ε from places L_5 and L_7 that enter place L_{11} unite and obtain characteristic

$$x_{cu}^{\varphi} = \frac{1 + pr_1 x_{cu}^{\varepsilon}}{1 + pr_1 x_{cu}^{\delta} w_0}$$

Token ϕ from place L_{11} that enters place L_9 does not obtain new characteristic.
Token that enters place L_{10} from place L_{11} obtains the characteristic

$$x_{cu}^{\varphi'} = \}\}\text{Values for } S_3 \text{ units''}.$$

Tokens ε and δ that enter place L_{11} from place L_{11} do not obtain new characteristic.

$$Z_5 = \langle \{L_{14}\}, \{L_{12}, L_{13}, L_{14}\}, R_5, \vee(L_{14}) \rangle,$$

$$R_5 = \begin{array}{c|ccc} & L_{12} & L_{13} & L_{14} \\ \hline L_{14} & W_{14,12} & W_{14,13} & true' \end{array}$$

$W_{14,12}$ = "The weights for C units are initialized";
$W_{14,13}$ = "The weights for S units are initialized".
Token β from place L_{14} that enters place L_{12} obtains characteristic

$$x_{cu}^{\beta'} = \frac{1}{1 + |k| + |h|}$$

Token β from place L_{14} that enters place L_{13} obtains characteristic

$$x_{cu}^{\beta''} = \}\}\langle w_0, w_i \rangle''$$

Token β from place L_{14} that enters place L_{14} does not obtain new characteristic.

$$Z_6 = \langle \{L_{10}, L_{16}\}, \{L_{15}, L_{16}\}, R_6, \vee(L_{10}, L_{16}) \rangle,$$

$$R_6 = \begin{array}{c|cc} & L_{15} & L_{16} \\ \hline L_{10} & false & true, \\ L_{16} & W_{16,15} & true \end{array}$$

$W_{16,15}$ = "Pattern is recognized".

Token ϕ' from place L_{10} that enters place L_{16} does not obtain new characteristic. Token ϕ' from place L_{16} that enters place L_{15} obtains the characteristic

$$x_{cu}^{\varphi''} = \}\}\text{Recognized pattern''}.$$

$$Z_7 = \langle \{L_9, L_{12}, L_{19}\}, \{L_{17}, L_{18}, L_{19}\}, R_7, \vee(L_{12} \wedge (L_9, L_{19}))\rangle,$$

$$R_7 = \begin{array}{c|ccc} & L_{17} & L_{18} & L_{19} \\ \hline L_9 & false & false & true \\ L_{12} & false & false & true' \\ L_{19} & W_{19,17} & W_{19,18} & true \end{array}$$

$W_{19,17}$ = "The values for S units are calculated";
$W_{19,18}$ = "The values for V units are calculated".

Token ϕ from place L_{12} unites with token β' from place L_{19} and obtains the characteristic

$$x_{cu}^{\eta} = \sum_i s_i u_i$$

Token η from place L_{19} splits into two tokens that enter place L_{17} and L_{18} where they do not obtain new characteristic.

5 Conclusions

The Generalized nets model presented in the paper corresponds to the Neocognitron neural network as a visual nervous system. Self-organization with unsupervised learning using repetitive patterns is a necessary element of the network and eliminates the need for information about the class to which the image belongs. It should also be noted that the neocognitron correctly recognizes images with displacement and curvature of the mold. The algorithm used on this structure is formed as a multilayer network called "Neocognitron" and is modeled with generalized nets.

Acknowledgment. The authors are grateful for the support provided by the project DN-02/10 - "New Instruments for Knowledge Discovery from Data, and their Modelling", funded by the National Science Fund, Bulgarian Ministry of Education, Youth and Science.

References

1. Atanassov, K.: Generalized nets as a tool for the modelling of data mining processes. In: Sgurev, V., Yager, Ronald R., Kacprzyk, J., Jotsov, V. (eds.) Innovative Issues in Intelligent Systems. SCI, vol. 623, pp. 161–215. Springer, Cham (2016). doi: 10.1007/978-3-319-27267-2_6
2. Atanassov, K.: Generalized Nets. World Scientific, Singapore (1991)
3. Atanassov, K.: On Generalized Nets Theory. "Prof. Marin Drinov"Academic Publishing House, Sofia (2007)
4. Atanassov, K., Sotirov, S. Antonov, A.: Generalized net model for parallel optimization of feed-forward neural network. Adv. Stud. Contemp. Math. **15**(1), 109–119 (2007)
5. Atanassov, K., Sotirov S.: Optimization of a neural network of self-organizing maps type with time-limits by a generalized net. Adv. Stud. Contemp. Math. **13**(2), 213–220 (2006)
6. Bureva, V., Sotirova, E., Atanassov, K.: Hierarchical generalized net model of the process of selecting a method for clustering. In: 15th International Workshop on Generalized Nets Burgas, 16 October 2014, pp. 39–48 (2006)
7. Bureva, V., Sotirova, E., Atanassov, K.: Hierarchical generalized net model of the process of clustering, Issues in Intuitionistic Fuzzy Sets and Generalized Nets, vol. 1, Warsaw School of Information Technology, pp. 73–80 (2014)
8. Bureva, V.: Intuitionistic fuzzy histograms in grid-based clustering. Notes Intuitionistic Fuzzy Sets **20O**(1), 55–62 (2014)
9. Bureva, V., Sotirova, E., Chountas, P.: Generalized net of the process of sequential pattern mining by generalized sequential pattern algorithm (GSP). In: Filev, D., et al. (eds.) Intelligent Systems'2014. AISC, vol. 323, pp. 831–838. Springer, Cham (2015). doi: 10.1007/978-3-319-11310-4_72
10. Fukushima, K.: Neocognitron: a self-organizing neural network model for a mechanism of pattern recognition unaffected by shift in position. Biol. Cybern. **36**(4), 193–202 (1980)
11. Fukushima, K.: Restoring partly occluded patterns: a neural network model. Neural Netw. **18**(1), 33–43 (2005)
12. Hagan, M., Demuth, H., Beale, M.: Neural Network Toolbox 7 (2010)
13. Krawczak, M.: Generalized Net Models of Systems, Bulletin of Polish Academy of Science (2003)
14. Sotirov, S.: Generalized net model of the Time Delay Neural Network, Issues in Intuitionistic Fuzzy Sets and Generalized nets, Warsaw, 2010, pp. 125–131 (2010)
15. Sotirov, S.: Modeling the algorithm Backpropagation for training of neural networks with generalized nets – part 1. In: Proceedings of the Fourth International Workshop on Generalized Nets, Sofia, 23 September 2003, pp. 61–67 (2003)
16. Sotirov, S.: Generalized net model of the accelerating backpropagation algorithm. Jangjeon Math. Soc. **2006**, 217–225 (2006)
17. Sotirov, S., Krawczak, M.: Modeling the algorithm Backpropagation for learning of neural networks with generalized nets – part 2. Issues in Intuitionistic Fuzzy Sets Generalized Nets, Warszawa, pp. 65–70 (2007)
18. Pencheva, T., Roeva, O., Shannon, A.: Generalized net models of basic genetic algorithm operators. In: Angelov, P., Sotirov, S. (eds.) Imprecision and Uncertainty in Information Representation and Processing. SFSC, vol. 332, pp. 305–325. Springer, Cham (2016). doi: 10.1007/978-3-319-26302-1_19
19. Roeva, O., Atanassova, V.: Generalized net model of Cuckoo search algorithm. In: 2016 IEEE 8th International Conference on Intelligent Systems, IS 2016 - Proceedings, 2016, pp. 589–592 (2016)

20. Roeva, O., Shannon, A., Pencheva, T., Description of simple genetic algorithm modifications using Generalized Nets. In: IS 2012 - 2012 6th IEEE International Conference Intelligent Systems, Proceedings, pp. 178–183 (2012)
21. Ribagin, S., Chakarov, V., Atanassov, K.: Generalized net model of the scapulohumeral rhythm. In: Sgurev, V., Yager, Ronald R., Kacprzyk, J., Atanassov, Krassimir T. (eds.) Recent Contributions in Intelligent Systems. SCI, vol. 657, pp. 229–247. Springer, Cham (2017). doi: 10.1007/978-3-319-41438-6_13
22. Ribagin, S., Roeva, O., Pencheva, T.: Generalized Net model of asymptomatic osteoporosis diagnosing. In: 2016 IEEE 8th International Conference on Intelligent Systems, IS 2016 – Proceedings, 7 November 2016, pp. 604–608 (2016)
23. Ribagin, S.: Generalized net model of age-associated changes in the upper limb musculoskeletal structures. Comptes Rendus de L'Academie Bulgare des Sciences **67**(11), 1503–1512 (2014)
24. Ribagin, S., Chakarov, V., Atanassov, K.: Generalized net model of the upper limb vascular system. In: IS 2012 - 2012 6th IEEE International Conference Intelligent Systems, Proceedings, pp. 229–232 (2012)

Comparison of Conceptual Models of Overall Telecommunication Systems with QoS Guarantees

Stoyan Poryazov[1], Velin Andonov[1(✉)], and Emiliya Saranova[1,2]

[1] Institute of Mathematics and Informatics, Bulgarian Academy of Sciences, Acad. G. Bonchev Str., bl. 8, 1113 Sofia, Bulgaria
stoyan@cc.bas.bg, velin_andonov@yahoo.com
[2] University of Telecommunications and Post, 1 Acad. S. Mladenov Str., 1700 Sofia, Bulgaria
emiliya@cc.bas.bg

Abstract. Different approaches to conceptual modeling of overall telecommunication systems with QoS guarantees are discussed. Generalized Nets (GNs) are used as an alternative to the already existing conceptual models based on the Service Networks Theory. Two GN representations of a part of the Switching stage are proposed and their advantages and disadvantages are discussed.

Keywords: Overall telecommunication system · Generalized nets · Conceptual model · QoS guarantees

1 Introduction and Related Work

The field of our research includes complex overall telecommunication systems with Quality of Service (QoS) guarantees, taking into consideration: human factors; technical characteristics of the telecom network; the techno-socio-economic environment; QoS indicators, as a base for Quality of Experience (QoE) estimation. The characterization and estimation of QoE, especially in the context of multimedia (voice, video streaming) and Web services has been subject to increasing research interest in the last years. Characterization, estimation and management of the QoE are functions of many factors, but always are based on QoS indicators' values and are still open questions. The two main objectives of our work are creation of verified and validated computer models of:

- QoS prediction, in case of known other parameters;
- QoS guarantying (determination of the volume of necessary network resources, in case of known other parameters and target QoS).

We are fully agreed with the best available book in the field [5]: "A creation of a good conceptual model lays a strong foundation for successful simulation modeling and analysis" and "The state-of-the-art is such that we are not yet in

H. Christiansen et al. (Eds.): FQAS 2017, LNAI 10333, pp. 260–268, 2017.
DOI: 10.1007/978-3-319-59692-1_23

a position to propose a unified definition of a conceptual model or a unified approach to conceptual modeling." The aim of this paper is to present some results of our conceptual modeling practice towards proposition of unified definition of a conceptual model. We use the conceptual modeling for the determination and explication of:

- The concept used in modeling. The telecommunication systems are very complex artefacts and many concepts are used in their investigation, e.g. belonging to mathematics, informatics, economics, sociology, psychology. Each concept may introduce its own terminology and conceptual models.
- The modelled structure (functional, temporal, spatial, financial etc.) of the system of interest. This includes Reference Points, in which the real system's and model's values of the parameters are objects of comparison in the models' validation.
- The assumptions and simplifications of the modelled system used in the model;
- The model specifications, used in discussions among modelers, model users, mathematicians and programmers (model implementers).
- A common base for modelling, verification and validation. Our conceptual model is used for parallel analytical and Informatical modelling, as well as for comparison of the results received from computer simulation (mutual verification of analytical and Informatical models) and measurements in the real system (model validation).
- A common base for forward and inverse modelling and simulation. A conceptual model is used for QoS prediction, and QoS guarantying tasks. This allows mutual verification of the forward and inverse models.

The three conceptual models, presented in this paper, are of one and the same telecommunication system. The first one (in Sect. 2), based on Service Networks Theory concepts including Queuing Theory devices, is briefly described. It is used for the creation of mathematical models of forward (QoS prediction) and inverse (QoS guarantying) tasks [6]. In Sect. 3, ordinary Generalized Net (GN) concepts are used. In Sect. 4 – an extension of the GNs. As a conclusion, the three conceptual models are discussed in Sect. 5.

2 Conceptual Model of Overall Telecommunication System Based on Service Networks Theory

The conceptual model includes user's behavior, a limited number of homogenous terminals; losses due to abandoned and interrupted dialing, blocked and interrupted switching, unavailable intent terminal, blocked and abandoned ringing and abandoned communication. The network traffic for the calling (denoted by A) and the called (denoted by B) terminals and user's traffic are considered seperately in their interrelationship. Two types of virtual devices are used: basic and comprising.

The basic virtual devices types, their names and graphic representation are shown in Fig. 1. There are six different types of basic virtual devices: Generator, Terminator, Modifier, Server, Enter Switch, Switch and Graphic conncetor. Every basic virtual device, except the Switch, has no more than one entrance and/or one exit. Switches have one or two entrances and one or two exits.

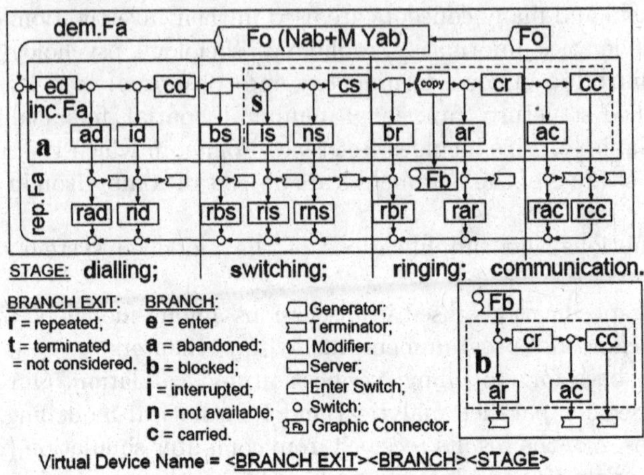

Fig. 1. Conceptual model of a telecommunication system.

Each of the basic devices is characterized by the following parameters: F - intensity (frequency, rate) of the flow [calls/sec]; P - probability of directing the calls of the external flow to the device considered; T - service time in the device of a call [seconds]; Y - intensity of the device traffic [Erlangs]; N - number of service places (lines, servers) in the virtual device (capacity of the device).

Three comprising virtual devices are considered in the conceptual model: **a** – virtual device that comprises all the A-terminals (calling) in the system. It is represented by a continuous line box in Fig. 1; **b** - virtual device that comprises all the B-terminals (called) in the system. It is represented by a dashed line box in Fig. 1; **s** - virtual device corresponding to the switching subsystem. Represented by a dashed line box in the **a**-device in Fig. 1.

3 Generalized Net Model of a Part of the Switching Stage

The theory of GNs [2] and their applications [3] provide alternative approach to the conceptual modeling of telecommunication systems. In this section an ordinary GN is used. The GN in Fig. 2 represents a part of the Switching stage from the conceptual model.

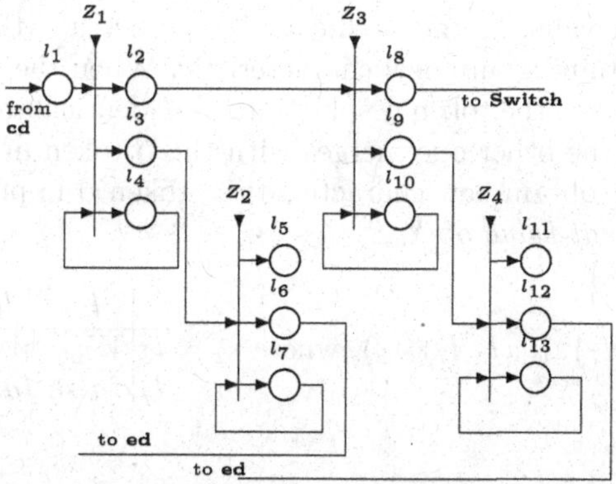

Fig. 2. Generalized net model of a part of the Switching stage.

The places in the GN model correspond to basic devices in the conceptual model as follows: l_1 corresponds to the Enter Switch deivice before the comprising virtual device s; l_2 corresponds to the Switch device at the beginning of the comprising virtual device s; l_3 corresponds to Switch device after the bs device; l_4 corresponds to bs; l_5 corresponds to the Terminator after bs; l_6 corresponds to the Switch after rbs; l_7 corresponds to rbs; l_8 corresponds to the Switch before the cs device; l_9 corresponds to the Switch after is; l_{10} corresponds to is; l_{11} corresponds to the Terminator after is; l_{12} corresponds to the Switch after ris; l_{13} corresponds to ris.

Five different types of tokens are used in the model. Tokens of type α represent the call attempts. They enter the net in place l_1 with characteristic *"volume, duration of service, call destination"*. Token of type β stays in place l_4 in the initial moment. It is used to accumulate data about the bs device. Token of type γ stays in place l_7 in the initial moment. It is used to accumulate data about the rbs device. Token of type δ stays in place l_{10} in the initial moment. It is used to accumulate data about the is device. Token of type ϵ stays in place l_{13} in the initial moment. It is used to accumulate data about the ris device.

All tokens except the tokens of type α have initial characteristic: *"initial values of $Y_{dn}, P_{dn}, F_{dn}, T_{dn}$"*, where dn denotes the corresponding device name. What follows is a description of the transitions.

$$Z_1 = \langle\{l_1, l_4\}, \{l_2, l_3, l_4\}, r_1\rangle, \text{ where } r_1 = \begin{array}{c|ccc} & l_2 & l_3 & l_4 \\ \hline l_1 & W_{1,2} & W_{1,3} & W_{1,4} \\ l_4 & false & false & true \end{array}$$

and

- $W_{1,2} =$ "$Y_{is} + Y_{ns} + Y_{cs} < N_s$";
- $W_{1,3} = \neg W_{1,2}$;
- $W_{1,4} = W_{1,3}$.

When the truth value of the predicate $W_{1,2}$ is "true" the token α enters place l_2 without obtaining any new characteristic. When the truth value of the predicate $W_{1,3}$ is "true" the token α splits into two identical tokens one of which enters place l_3 and the other one merges with the β token in place l_4. In place l_3 the tokens do not obtain new characteristics. Token β in place l_4 obtains the characteristic *"current value of* Y_{bs}".

$$Z_2 = \langle \{l_3, l_7\}, \{l_5, l_6, l_7\}, r_2 \rangle, \text{ where } r_2 = \begin{array}{c|ccc} & l_5 & l_6 & l_7 \\ \hline l_3 & W_{3,5} & W_{3,6} & W_{3,7} \\ l_7 & false & false & true \end{array}$$

and

- $W_{3,5}$ = "the current call is terminated (with a given probability)";
- $W_{3,6}$ = "the current call is repeated (with a given probability)";
- $W_{3,7} = W_{3,6}$.

When the truth value of the predicate $W_{3,5}$ is "true" the current token α enters place l_5 without obtaining any new characteristic. When the truth value of the predicate $W_{3,6}$ is "true" the current token α splits into two identical tokens one of which enters place l_6 and the other one enters place l_7 where it merges with the γ token. In place l_6 the tokens do not obtain new characteristics. Token γ in place l_7 obtains the characteristic *"current value of* Y_{rbs}".

$$Z_3 = \langle \{l_2, l_{10}\}, \{l_8, l_9, l_{10}\}, r_3 \rangle, \text{ where } r_3 = \begin{array}{c|ccc} & l_8 & l_9 & l_{10} \\ \hline l_2 & W_{2,8} & W_{2,9} & W_{2,10} \\ l_{10} & false & false & true \end{array}$$

and

- $W_{2,8}$ = "the current call is carried (with a given probability)";
- $W_{2,9}$ = "the current call is interrupted (with a given probability)";
- $W_{2,10} = W_{2,9}$.

When the truth value of the predicate $W_{2,8}$ is "true" the current α token enters place l_8 without obtaining any new characteristic. When the truth value of the predicate $W_{2,9}$ is "true" the current token α splits into two identical tokens one of which enters place l_9 and the other one enters place l_{10} where it merges with the δ token. In place l_9 the tokens do not obtain new characteristics. Token δ in place l_{10} obtains the characteristic *"current value of* Y_{is}".

$$Z_4 = \langle \{l_9, l_{13}\}, \{l_{11}, l_{12}, l_{13}\}, r_4 \rangle, \text{ where } r_4 = \begin{array}{c|ccc} & l_{11} & l_{12} & l_{13} \\ \hline l_9 & W_{9,11} & W_{9,12} & W_{9,13} \\ l_{13} & false & false & true \end{array}$$

and

- $W_{9,11}$ = "the current call is terminated (with a given probability)";
- $W_{9,12}$ = "the current call is repeated (with a given probability)";
- $W_{9,13} = W_{9,12}$.

When the truth value of the predicate $W_{9,11}$ is "true" the current token α enters place l_{11} without obtaining any new characteristic. When the truth value of the predicate $W_{9,12}$ is "true" the current token α splits into two identical tokens one of which enters place l_{12} and the other one enters place l_{13} where it merges with the ϵ token. In place l_{12} the tokens do not obtain new characteristics. Token δ in place l_{13} obtains the characteristic: *"current value of Y_{ris}"*.

4 Representation of a Part of the Switching Stage with Generalized Nets with Characteristics of the Places

The model proposed in the previous section uses ordinary GNs. In one of the most recent extensions of the GNs – Generalized Nets with Characteristics of the Places (GNCP, [1]) – the places can also obtain characteristics. Here we propose a GNCP model of the same part of the Switching stage as the one in Sect. 3. For the sake of brevity, we use a reduced GNCP. The graphical representaion of the net is shown in Fig. 3.

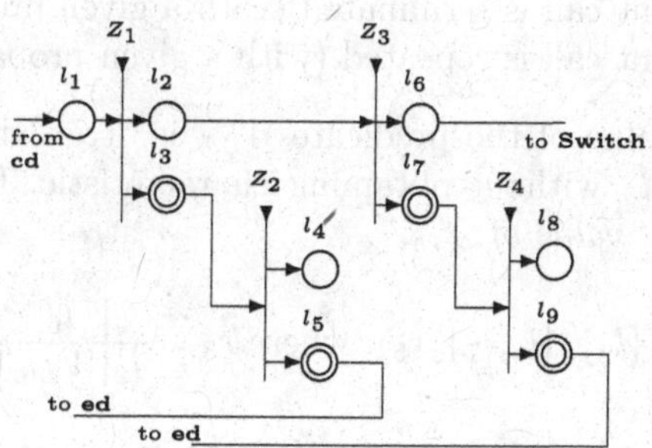

Fig. 3. GNCP model of a part of the Switching stage.

In the GNCP model only one type of tokens is used. The meaning of the places is the following: l_1 corresponds to the Enter Switch deivice before the comprising device S; l_2 corresponds to the Switch at the beginning of the comprising device S; l_3 corresponds bs; l_4 corresponds to the Terminator after bs; l_5 corresponds to rbs; l_6 corresponds to the Switch before the cs device; l_7 corresponds to is; l_8 corresponds to the Terminator after is; l_9 corresponds to ris. The places denoted by two concentric circles obtain characteristics when tokens enter them. These characteristics allow for accumulation of data related to the corresponding virtual device.

Tokens representing the call attempts enter the net through place l_1. They have the same characteristics as in the ordinary GN model. Places l_3, l_5, l_7, l_9 have initial characteristic in the form *"initial values of* Y_{dn}, F_{dn}, P_{dn}, T_{dn}*"* where dn denotes the device corresponding to the place as described above. In places l_2, l_4, l_6, l_8 the tokens do not obtain characteristics.

For completeness we give the formal description of the transitions.

$$Z_1 = \langle \{l_1\}, \{l_2, l_3\}, r_1 \rangle, \text{ where } r_1 = \begin{array}{c|cc} & l_2 & l_3 \\ \hline l_1 & W_{1,2} & W_{1,3} \end{array}$$

and

- $W_{1,2} =$ "$Y_{is} + Y_{ns} + Y_{cs} < N_s$";
- $W_{1,3} = \neg W_{1,2}$.

When the truth value of the predicate $W_{1,3}$ is "true" the current token enters place l_3 without obtaining new characteristic. Place l_3 obtains the characteristic *"current value of* Y_{bs}*"*.

$$Z_2 = \langle \{l_3\}, \{l_4, l_5\}, r_2 \rangle, \text{ where } r_2 = \begin{array}{c|cc} & l_4 & l_5 \\ \hline l_3 & W_{3,4} & W_{3,5} \end{array}$$

and

- $W_{3,4} =$ "The current call is terminated (with a given probability)";
- $W_{3,5} =$ "The current call is repeated (with a given probability)".

When the truth value of the predicate $W_{3,5}$ is "true" the current token in place l_3 enters place l_5 without obtaining characteristic. Place l_5 obtains the characteristic *"current value of* Y_{rbs}*"*.

$$Z_3 = \langle \{l_2\}, \{l_6, l_7\}, r_3 \rangle, \text{ where } r_3 = \begin{array}{c|cc} & l_6 & l_7 \\ \hline l_2 & W_{2,6} & W_{2,7} \end{array}$$

and

- $W_{2,6} =$ "The current call is carried (with a given probability)";
- $W_{2,7} =$ "The current call is interrupted (with a given probability)".

When the truth value of the predicate $W_{2,7}$ is "true" the current token α enters place l_7 without new characteristic. Place l_7 obtains the characteristic *"current value of* Y_{is}*"*.

$$Z_4 = \langle \{l_7\}, \{l_8, l_9\}, r_4 \rangle, \text{ where } r_4 = \begin{array}{c|cc} & l_8 & l_9 \\ \hline l_7 & W_{7,8} & W_{7,9} \end{array}$$

and

- $W_{7,8} =$ "The current call is terminated (with a given probability)";
- $W_{7,9} =$ "The current call is repeated (with a given probability)".

When the truth value of the predicate $W_{7,9}$ is "true" the current token α enters place l_9 without new characteristic. Place l_9 obtains the characteristic *"current value of* Y_{ris}*"*.

5 Comparison of the Approaches and Conclusions

The conceptual model presented in Fig. 1 gives a clearer connection between the functions of the real system and their visual representations. It allows for easy understanding of the connections between the virtual devices and their functions. A downside of this approach is that it uses 7 different virtual devices. It shows the paths of the calls in the system but the calls are not presented in the model.

On the other hand, the GN models use less different components to describe the devices and the paths of the calls: places, arcs, transitions in the ordinary GN model in Fig. 2 and arcs, transitions and two types of places in the GNCP model in Fig. 3. That is why the GN representations are, in a sense, graphically simpler. However, users need special training in order to understand the paths of the calls and the connections between the analogues of the virtual devices in the net. The GNCP model has the simplest graphic representation. It has 4 places less than the GN model in Sect. 3, less arcs and, also, only one type of tokens is used while in the GN model in Sect. 3 we have five types of tokens.

In the telecommunication systems with virtual channel switching one call occupies all devices through which it has passed. With regard to this, it will be interesting to study a GN representation using one of the recently proposed extensions of the GNs – Generalized Nets with Volumetric Tokens – defined in [4]. In our future work, we intend to propose and study different GN analogues to the devices from the Service Networks Theory that would make the GN models more user-friendly.

The presented models of one aspect of a telecommunication system lead to the conclusion that a conceptual model may be invariant to the modeling sub-concepts and tasks, in contrast with considerations in [5]. This have to be taken into account in QoS related tasks.

Acknowledgements. This work is coordinated under EU COST Action IC 1304. The work was partially funded by Bulgarian NSF Project DCOST 01/9 (work of S. Poryazov), and Project DCOST 01/20 (work of E. Saranova).

References

1. Andonov, V., Atanassov, K.: Generalized nets with characteristics of the places. Compt. Rend. Acad. Bulg. Sci. **66**(12), 1673–1680 (2013)
2. Atanassov, K.: On Generalized Nets Theory. Prof. M. Drinov Academic Publ. House, Sofia (2007)
3. Atanassov, K.: Applications of Generalized Nets. World Scientific Publ. Co., Singapore (1993)
4. Atanassova, V.: Generalized nets with volumetric tokens. Compt. rend. Acad. bulg. Sci. **65**(11), 1489–1498 (2012)

5. Robinson, S., Brooks, B., Kotiadis, K., Van Der Zee, D.: Conceptual Modeling for Discrete-Event Simulation, 527 pages. Taylor and Francis Group, LLC, CRC Press (2011). ISBN-13: 978-1-4398-1038-5 (Ebook-PDF)
6. Poryazov, S., Saranova, T.: Some general terminal and network teletraffic equations in virtual circuit switching systems. In: Nejat Ince, A., Topuz, E. (eds.) Modeling and Simulation Tools for Emerging Telecommunications Networks., pp. 471–505. Springer Sciences+Business Media, LLC, Boston (2006). ISBN-10: 0–387-32921-8 (HB)

Generalized Net Model of Muscle Pain Diagnosing

Simeon Ribagin[1(✉)], Panagiotis Chountas[2], and Tania Pencheva[1]

[1] Institute of Biophysics and Biomedical Engineering, Bulgarian Academy of Sciences, Sofia, Bulgaria
sim_ribagin@mail.bg, tania.pencheva@biomed.bas.bg

[2] Department of Computer Science, Faculty of Science and Technology (FST), University of Westminster, 115 New Cavendish Street, London W1W 6UW, UK
P.I.Chountas@westminster.ac.uk

Abstract. Pain is the most common symptom of the many musculoskeletal pathologies. Musculoskeletal pain affects the muscles, ligaments, tendons, nerves and bones and might be caused by diverse factors. Musculoskeletal pain ranges from mild to severe. It can be local or diffuse, and acute or chronic. Due to the wide range of conditions that may cause such a symptom, diagnosing process is challenging and a systematic approach is necessary. In this investigation we present a successful example of generalized nets application in medical diagnosing and propose a novel approach leading to the appropriate diagnostic considerations. The method proposed in this investigation accurately identifies the various steps during the muscle pain diagnosing process and significantly improves the health care level. Obtained so far results could be used to assist in the decision making in the diagnostic processes.

Keywords: Musculoskeletel pain · Generalized nets

1 Introduction

The diagnosis of musculoskeletal pain is made on the basis of the medical history, clinical examinations, diagnostic imaging techniques and simple laboratory investigations. The basic issue associated with muscle pain diagnosing is to find the early pointers to a likely diagnosis. Then as part of the assessment, it is essential to establish a logical step-by-step approach to the medical history as well as a series of screening investigations. Muscle pain may arise due to injury or overexertion, infections, inflammatory or systemic conditions. A number of conditions can be associated with muscle pain, such as viral infections, fibromyalgia, autoimmune disorders, drug-induced disorders, metabolic disorders, etc. The purpose of the present study is to give an example how the apparatus of generalized nets might be successfully applied to medical diagnosing and as such to be proposed as a novel mathematical approach for diagnosing the causes of the muscle pain. Generalized nets (GNs) (see [1,2]) are an apparatus for modeling of parallel and

H. Christiansen et al. (Eds.): FQAS 2017, LNAI 10333, pp. 269–275, 2017.
DOI: 10.1007/978-3-319-59692-1_24

concurrent processes, developed as an extension of the concept of Petri nets and some of their modifications. In general, the GNs may or may not have some of the components in their definition. GNs without some of their components form special classes called reduced GNs [2]. The presented GN-model shows similar features with previous models for medical diagnosing [3–5] but this is the first one highlighting the diagnostic algorithm for patients with muscle pain.

2 Generalized Net Model of Muscle Pain Diagnosing

A reduced GN-model which represents the plan for muscle pain diagnosing is developed here. The proposed GN-model is shown in Fig. 1.

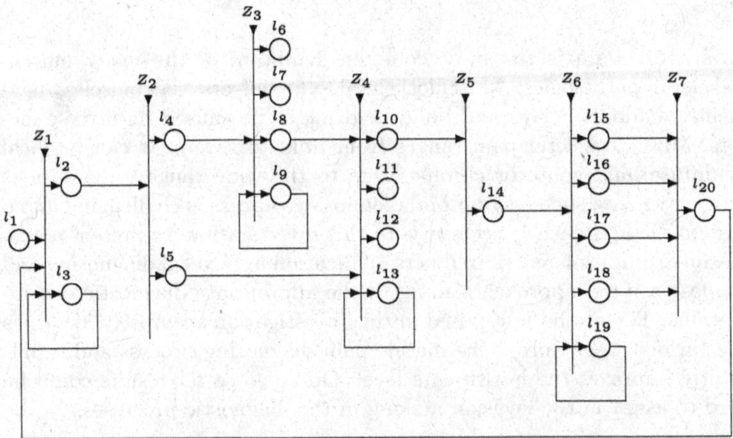

Fig. 1. GN-model of muscle pain diagnosing

The GN-model has 7 transitions and 20 places with the following meanings:

- Z_1 represents the personal data of the patient;
- Z_2 – the current localization of the symptoms;
- Z_3 – the results from the medical history;
- Z_4 – the results from the physical examination;
- Z_5 – the set of laboratory tests;
- Z_6 – the results from the laboratory tests and possible diagnosis;
- Z_7 – the final diagnosis.

The GN-model contains 5 types of tokens: α, β, μ, ν and π. Some of the model transitions contain the so called "special place" where a token stays and collects information about the specific parts of the diagnosing process which are represented as follows:

- place l_3 collects the overall information obtained from the diagnostics steps in the personal record (personal data);

- place l_9 – information obtained from the history of the patient;
- place l_{13} – information about the results from physical examinations;
- place l_{19} – information about the results from the laboratory tests.

During the GM-model functioning, the α-tokens will unite with the tokens from the other types: β, μ, ν and π. After that, some of these tokens can split in order to generate new α-tokens obtaining corresponding characteristics. When there are some α-tokens (α_1, α_2, α_3 and, eventually, α_4), on the next time-moment all they will unite with a token from another type.

The token α enters the net in place l_1 with an initial characteristic:

"*patient with muscle pain*".

The transition Z_1 has the following form:

$$Z_1 = \langle \{l_1, l_3, l_{20}\}, \{l_2, l_3\}, r_1 \rangle$$

where

$$r_1 = \begin{array}{c|cc} & l_2 & l_3 \\ \hline l_1 & false & true \\ l_3 & W_{3,2} & true \\ l_{20} & false & true \end{array}$$

- $W_{3,2}$ = "*information about the current symptoms, medical history and physical examination is necessary*".

The tokens from the three input places of transition Z_1 enter place l_3 and unite with token β with the above mentioned characteristic. On the next time-moment, token β splits to two tokens – the same token β and token α_1. When predicate $W_{3,2}$ is true, the token α_1 enters place l_2 and there it obtains a characteristic:

"*obtain information about the current symptoms, medical history and physical examination*".

The transition Z_2 has the following form:

$$Z_2 = \langle \{l_2\}, \{l_4, l_5\}, r_2 \rangle$$

where

$$r_2 = \begin{array}{c|cc} & l_4 & l_5 \\ \hline l_2 & W_{2,4} & W_{2,5} \end{array}$$

and

- $W_{2,4}$ = "*the muscle pain is local*";
- $W_{2,5}$ = "*the muscle pain is diffuse with no history of trauma, overuse and stress*".

When the predicate $W_{2,4}$ is true, token α_1 enters place l_4 and there it obtains a characteristic:

"obtain information from the medical hystory of the patient".

When the predicate $W_{2,5}$ is true, token α_1 enters place l_5 and there it obtains a characteristic:

"perform physical examination".

The transition Z_3 has the following form:

$$Z_3 = \langle \{l_4, l_9\}, \{l_6, l_7, l_8, l_9\}, r_3 \rangle$$

where

$$r_3 = \begin{array}{c|cccc} & l_6 & l_7 & l_8 & l_9 \\ \hline l_4 & false & false & false & true \\ l_9 & W_{9,6} & W_{9,7} & W_{9,8} & true \end{array}$$

and

- $W_{9,6}$ = *"there is a history of trauma"*;
- $W_{9,7}$ = *"there is a history of recent overexertion and stress"*;
- $W_{9,8} = \neg W_{9,6} \vee \neg W_{9,7}$.

The tokens from all input places of transition Z_3 enter place l_9 and unite with token μ with the characteristic as mentioned above. On the next time-moment, token μ splits to two tokens – the same token μ that stays permanently in the place l_9, and token α_1. When the predicate $W_{9,6}$ is true, token α_1 enters place l_6 and there it obtains a characteristic:

"consider: muscle contusion, muscle strain, muscle rupture, ligament sprain; send patient to X-ray and/or MRI to determine the extent of the injury or to identify possible additional injuries".

When the predicate $W_{9,7}$ is true, token α_1 enters place l_7 and there it obtains a characteristic:

"consider: muscle cramps or delayed onset muscle soreness".

When the predicate $W_{9,8}$ is true, token α_1 enters place l_8 and there it obtains a characteristic:

"perform physical examination".

The transition Z_4 has the following form:

$$Z_4 = \langle \{l_5, l_8, l_{13}\}, \{l_{10}, l_{11}, l_{12}, l_{13}\}, r_4 \rangle$$

where

$$r_4 = \begin{array}{c|cccc} & l_{10} & l_{11} & l_{12} & l_{13} \\ \hline l_5 & false & false & false & true \\ l_8 & false & false & false & true \\ l_{13} & W_{13,10} & W_{13,11} & W_{13,12} & true \end{array}$$

and

- $W_{13,10}$ = "*there is muscle weakness without loss of muscle mass*";
- $W_{13,11}$ = "*there is muscle weakness and loss of muscle mass*";
- $W_{13,12} = \neg W_{13,10}$.

The tokens from all input places of transition Z_4 enter place l_{13} and unite with token ν with the characteristic as mentioned above. On the next time-moment, token ν splits to two tokens – the same token ν that stays permanently in the place l_{12}, and token α_1. When the predicate $W_{13,10}$ is true, token α_1 enters place l_{10} and there it obtains a characteristic:

> "*perform a laboratory tests to rule in potential pathologies associated with muscle pain and weakness*".

When the predicate $W_{13,11}$ is true, token α_1 enters place l_{11} and there it obtains a characteristic:

> "*consider: muscular dystrophy; perform: muscle biopsy, aldolase test, creatine phosphokinase test*".

When the predicate $W_{13,12}$ is true, token α_1 enters place l_{12} and there it obtains a characteristic:

> "*consider: fibromyalgia, psyhological disorders, spinal disorders, endocrine disorders, polymyalgia rheumatica*".

The transition Z_5 has the following form:

$$Z_5 = \langle \{l_{10}\}, \{l_{14}\}, r_5 \rangle$$

where

$$r_5 = \begin{array}{c|c} & l_{14} \\ \hline l_{10} & true \end{array}$$

The token from place l_{10} of transition Z_5 enter place l_{13} and there it obtains a characteristic:

> "*perform: erythrocyte sedimentation rate (ESR) test, serum alkaline phosphatase (SAP) test, creatine phosphokinase (CPT) test*".

The transition Z_6 has the following form:

$$Z_6 = \langle \{l_{14}, l_{19}\}, \{l_{15}, l_{16}, l_{17}, l_{18}, l_{19}\}, r_6 \rangle$$

where

$$r_6 = \begin{array}{c|ccccc} & l_{15} & l_{16} & l_{17} & l_{18} & l_{19} \\ \hline l_{14} & false & false & false & fals & true \\ l_{19} & W_{19,15} & W_{19,16} & W_{19,17} & W_{19,18} & true \end{array}$$

and

- $W_{19,15}$ = "*erythrocyte sedimentation rate (ESR) is high*";
- $W_{19,16}$ = "*serum alkaline phosphatase (SAP) is high*";
- $W_{19,17}$ = "*creatine phosphokinase (CPT) is high*";
- $W_{19,18} = \neg W_{19,15} \vee \neg W_{19,16}$.

The tokens from all input places of transition Z_6 enter place l_{19} and unite with token π with the characteristic as mentioned above. On the next time-moment, token π splits to two tokens – the same token π that stays permanently in the place l_{19}, and token α_1. When the predicate $W_{19,15}$ is true, token α_1 enters place l_{15} and there it obtains a characteristic:

"*consider: polymyalgia rheumatica, systemic lupus erythematosus, myositis or secondary carcinomatosis*".

When the predicate $W_{19,16}$ is true, token α_2 enters place l_{16} and there it obtains a characteristic:

"*consider: liver diseases, osteoporosis, osteomalacia, viral infections, Paget's disease and hyperparathyroidism*".

When the predicate $W_{19,17}$ is true, token α_3 enters place l_{17} and there it obtains a characteristic:

"*consider: drug-induced disorders, inflammatory myopathies*".

When the predicate $W_{19,18}$ is true, token α_4 enters place l_{18} and there it obtains a characteristic:

"*consider: hypothyroidism, fibromyalgia, psyhogenic causes, myofascial pain syndrome*".

The transition Z_7 has the following form:

$$Z_7 = \langle \{l_{15}, l_{16}, l_{17}, l_{18}\}, \{l_{20}\}, r_7 \rangle$$

where

$$r_7 = \begin{array}{c|c} & l_{20} \\ \hline l_{15} & true \\ l_{16} & true \\ l_{17} & true \\ l_{18} & true \end{array}$$

The tokens from the input places of transition Z_7 enter place l_{20} and unite in one token β_1 with some of the characteristics obtained from the previous time-step. The token β_1 returns to transition Z_1 and enters to place l_3 to extend the personal record of the current patient.

3 Conclusions

The so described GN-model may provide a framework that can be used by primary care practitioners to guide diagnostic processes for patients with muscle pain, enabling more accurate and efficient identification of conditions that may lead to pain in the muscles and would assist in optimizing patient outcomes and more effective treatment. The presented in this paper GN-model of diagnostic algorithm for patient with muscle pain is a part of a series of studies for diagnosing through GN-modeling assistance and can be improved in multiple ways to yield better results. This model significantly improves the accuracy of the primary diagnosis and the reliability of the proposed algorithm.

Acknowledgements. Work presented here is partially supported by the Grants: DFNP-142/2016 "Program for career development of young scientists, BAS" and DN02/10 "New Instruments for Knowledge Discovery from Data, and Their Modelling"

References

1. Atanassov, K.: Generalized Nets. World Scientific, Singapore (1991)
2. Atanassov, K.: On Generalized Nets Theory. Prof. M. Drinov Academic Publishing House, Sofia (2007)
3. Ribagin, S., Atanassov, K., Shannon, A.: Generalized net model of shoulder pain diagnosis. Issues Intuitionistic Fuzzy Sets Generalized Nets **11**, 55–62 (2014)
4. Ribagin, S., Roeva, O., Pencheva, T.: Generalized net model of asymptomatic osteoporosis diagnosing. In: Proceeding of 2016 IEEE 8th International Conference on Intelligent Systems (IS), Sofia, pp. 604–608 (2016)
5. Shannon, A., Sorsich, J., Atanassov, K., Nikolov, N., Georgiev, P.: Generalized Nets in General and Internal Medicine, vol. 1. Prof. M. Drinov Academic Publishing House, Sofia (1998)

Generalized Nets as a Tool for Modelling of the Urban Bus Transport

Ivan Valkov[1], Krassimir Atanassov[2,3](✉), and Lyubka Doukovska[4]

[1] National Assembly of the Republic of Bulgaria, 31, Angel Dimitrov Street, Sarafovo, Burgas, Bulgaria
ivalkovv@abv.bg

[2] Department of Bioinformatics and Mathematical Modelling Institute of Biophysics and Biomedical Engineering, Bulgarian Academy of Sciences, Acad. G. Bonchev Street, Bl. 105, 1113 Sofia, Bulgaria
krat@bas.bg

[3] Intelligent Systems Laboratory, Prof. Asen Zlatarov University, 8000 Burgas, Bulgaria

[4] Institute of Information and Communication Technologies, Bulgarian Academy of Sciences, Acad. G. Bonchev Street, Bl. 2, 1113 Sofia, Bulgaria
doukovska@iit.bas.bg

Abstract. It is shown that generalized nets can be used as a tool for modelling of the urban bus transport. An example of a generalized net of a part of the urban bus transport in town Burgas (Bulgaria), is given.

Keywords: Generalized nets · Model · Urban transport

1 Introduction

Generalized Nets (GNs, [1–3]) are a tool for modelling of parallel processes, including as partial cases the standard Petri nets and all their modifications and extensions (as Time Petri nets, E-nets, Colour Petri nets, Predicative-Transition Petri nets, Fuzzy Petri nets, etc.). The apparatus of the GNs is used for modelling of different processes in the areas of Artificial Intelligence, medicine and biology, economics, industry, and many others. Here, GNs are used as a tool for modelling of processes in the urban bus transport.

2 Short Remarks of the Theory of the Generalized Nets

The GNs are defined in a way that is different in principle from the ways of defining the other types of PNs (see [2,3]).

The first basic difference between GNs and the ordinary PNs is the "place – transition" relation. Here, the transitions are objects of more complex nature. A transition may contain m input places and n output places, where the integers $m, n \geq 1$.

H. Christiansen et al. (Eds.): FQAS 2017, LNAI 10333, pp. 276–285, 2017.
DOI: 10.1007/978-3-319-59692-1_25

Formally, every transition is described by a seven-tuple (Fig. 1):

$$Z = \langle L', L'', t_1, t_2, r, M, \square \rangle,$$

where:

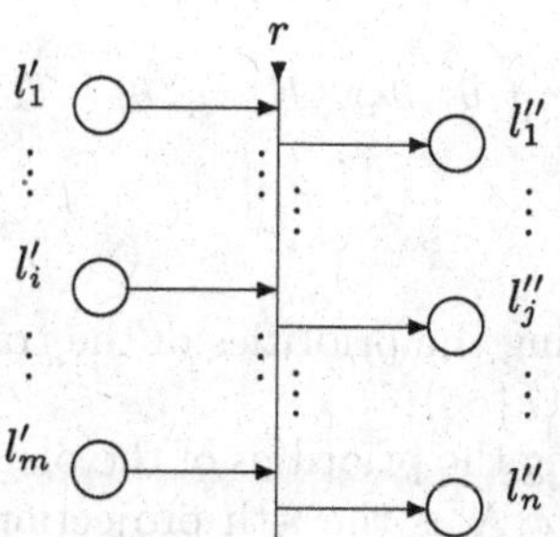

Fig. 1. The form of transition

(a) L' and L'' are finite, non-empty sets of places (the transition's input and output places, respectively); for the transition in Fig. 1 these are $L' = \{l'_1, l'_2, \ldots, l'_m\}$ and $L'' = \{l''_1, l''_2, \ldots, l''_n\}$;
(b) t_1 is the current time-moment of the transition's firing;
(c) t_2 is the current value of the duration of its active state;
(d) r is the transition's *condition* determining which tokens will pass (or *transfer*) from the transition's inputs to its outputs; it has the form of an Index Matrix (IM; see [4]):

$$r = \begin{array}{c|ccccc} & l''_1 & \ldots & l''_j & \ldots & l''_n \\ \hline l'_1 & & & & & \\ \vdots & & & r_{i,j} & & \\ l'_m & & & & & \end{array};$$

$r_{i,j}$ is the predicate that corresponds to the i-th input and j-th output place $(1 \le i \le m, 1 \le j \le n)$. When its truth value is "*true*", a token from the i-th input place transfers to the j-th output place; otherwise, this is not possible;
(e) M is an IM of the capacities $m_{i,j}$ of transition's arcs, where $m_{i,j} \ge 0$ is a natural number:

$$M = \begin{array}{c|ccccc} & l''_1 & \ldots & l''_j & \ldots & l''_n \\ \hline l'_1 & & & & & \\ \vdots & & & m_{i,j} & & \\ l'_m & & & & & \end{array};$$

(f) $\square$ is an object of a form similar to a Boolean expression. It contains as variables the symbols that serve as labels for a transition's input places, and $\square$ is an expression built up from variables and the Boolean connectives $\wedge$ and $\vee$. When the value of a type (calculated as a Boolean expression) is "*true*", the transition can become active, otherwise it cannot.

The ordered four-tuple

$$E = \langle\langle A, \pi_A, \pi_L, c, f, \theta_1, \theta_2\rangle, \langle K, \pi_K, \theta_K\rangle, \langle T, t^o, t^*\rangle, \langle X, \Phi, b\rangle\rangle$$

is called a GN if:

(a) A is a set of transitions;
(b) π_A is a function giving the priorities of the transitions, i.e., $\pi_A : A \rightarrow N$, where $N = \{0, 1, 2, \dots\} \cup \{\infty\}$;
(c) π_L is a function giving the priorities of the places, i.e., $\pi_L : L \rightarrow N$, where $L = pr_1 A \cup pr_2 A$, and $pr_i X$ is the i-th projection of the n-dimensional set, where $n \in N, n \geq 1$ and $1 \leq k \leq n$ (obviously, L is the set of all GN - places);
(d) c is a function giving the capacities of the places, i.e., $c : L \rightarrow N$;
(e) f is a function that calculates the truth values of the predicates of the transition's conditions (for the GN described here, let the function f have the value "*false*" or "*true*", that is, a value from the set $\{0, 1\}$;
(f) θ_1 is a function which indicates the next time-moment when a certain transition Z can be activated, that is, $\theta_1(t) = t'$, where $pr_3 Z = t, t' \in [T, T + t^*]$ and $t \leq t'$. The value of this function is calculated at the moment when the transition ceases to function;
(g) θ_2 is a function which gives the duration of the active state of a certain transition Z, i.e., $\theta_2(t) = t'$, where $pr_4 Z = t \in [T, T + t^*]$ and $t' \geq 0$. The value of this function is calculated at the moment when the transition starts to function;
(h) K is the set of the GN's tokens.
(i) π_K is a function which gives the priorities of the tokens, that is, $\pi_K : K \rightarrow N$;
(j) θ_K is a function which gives the time-moment when a given token can enter the net, that is, $\theta_K(\alpha) = t$, where $\alpha \in K$ and $t \in [T, T + t^*]$;
(k) T is the time-moment when the GN starts to function. This moment is determined with respect to a fixed (global) time-scale;
(l) t^o is an elementary time-step, related to the fixed (global) time-scale;
(m) t^* is the duration of the functioning of the GN;
(n) X is the set of all initial characteristics which the tokens can obtain on entering the net;
(o) Φ is the characteristic function that assigns new characteristics to every token when it makes the transfer from an input to an output place of a given transition.
(p) b is a function which gives the maximum number of characteristics a given token can obtain, that is, $b : K \rightarrow N$.

A given GN may not have some of the above components. In these cases, any redundant component will be omitted. The GNs of this kind form a special class of GNs called *"reduced GNs"*.

3 Generalized Net Models of Some Components of the Urban Bus Transport

Having in mind that the urban bus transport network of any town has the form of a (non-oriented) graph, we can represent it by a GN. Each bus station is represented by a transition with the form of Fig. 2.

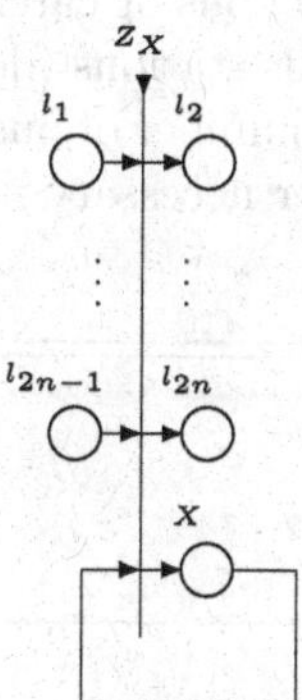

Fig. 2. Sample GN transition, presenting a bus station.

In it, the bus station X has direct connections with n other stations and let us denote them by $Y_1, ..., Y_n$. Here, places l_{2i-1} and l_{2i} correspond to bus lines from and to station Y_i for $i = 1, 2, ..., n$. The IM of the transition conditions has the form

	l_2	l_4	$\dots$	l_{2n}	X
l_1	*false*	*false*	$\dots$	*false*	*true*
l_3	*false*	*false*	$\dots$	*false*	*true*
$\vdots$	$\vdots$	$\vdots$	$\ddots$	$\vdots$	$\vdots$
l_{2n-1}	*false*	*false*	$\dots$	*false*	*true*
X	$W_{X,2}$	$W_{X,4}$	$\dots$	$W_{X,2n}$	$W_{X,X}$

,

where
$W_{X,2}$ = "the bus is directed to bus station Y_1",
$W_{X,4}$ = "the bus is directed to bus station Y_2", ...,
$W_{X,2n}$ = "the bus is directed to bus station Y_n",
$W_{X,X}$ = "the bus must shunt in bus station X".

In the next section, we illustrate the possibility to represent the urban bus transport network of a given town by a GN, using as an example, the urban bus transport network in town Burgas. In the model that follows, we describe only the most important bus stations.

4 Simplified Generalized Net Model of the Urban Bus Transport Network in Burgas

The GN-model contains 8 transitions and 28 places (see Fig. 3). Its tokens represent separate buses that will move from one bus station to the next one.

Each token, entering a place, obtains as a current characteristic information about the time for accomplishment of its previous activity and the number of passengers who leave the respective bus or catch it. The transition input-output places represent initial and final bus stations (depos). There, initially, the tokens obtain as initial characteristic the number of bus line, list of bus stations through which the bus must pass and other necessary information.

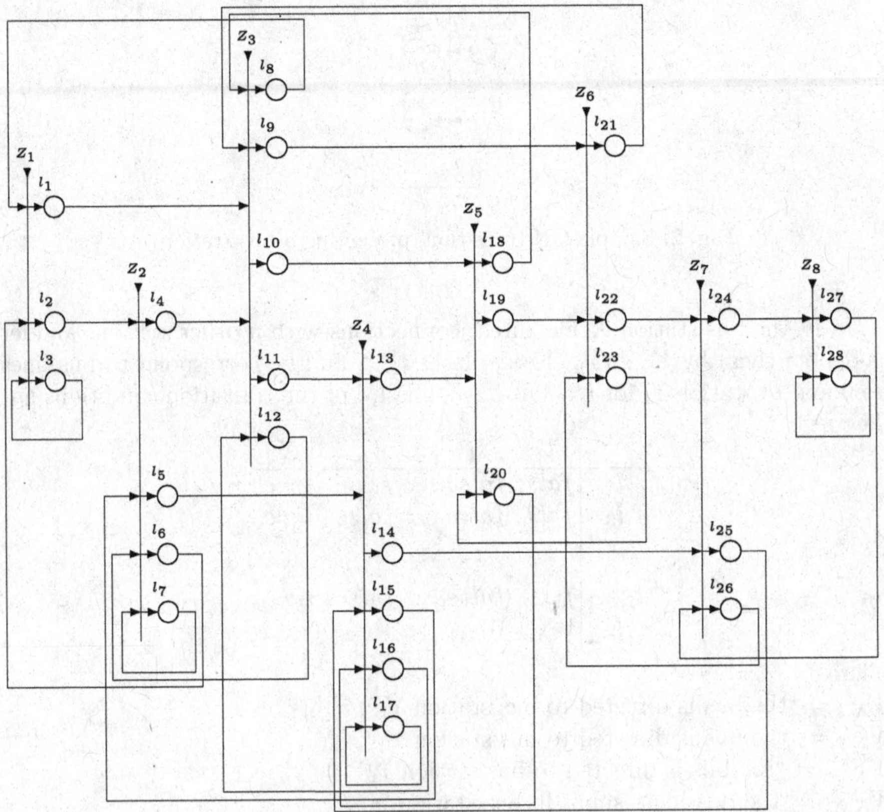

Fig. 3. Simplified Generalized Net Model of the Urban Bus Transport Network in Burgas

The GN-transitions are the following.

$$Z_1 = \langle \{l_3, l_6, l_8\}, \{l_1, l_2, l_3\}, r_1 \rangle$$

where

$$r_1 = \begin{array}{c|ccc} & l_1 & l_2 & l_3 \\ \hline l_3 & W_{3,1} & W_{3,2} & W_{3,3} \\ l_6 & false & false & true \\ l_8 & false & false & true \end{array}$$

where
$W_{3,1} =$ "The next bus station is l_1",
$W_{3,2} =$ "The next bus station is l_2",
$W_{3,3} =$ "The bus must continue stay in station l_3".

$$Z_2 = \langle \{l_2, l_7, l_{12}, l_{15}\}, \{l_4, l_5, l_6, l_7\}, r_2 \rangle$$

where

$$r_2 = \begin{array}{c|cccc} & l_4 & l_5 & l_6 & l_7 \\ \hline l_2 & W_{2,4} & false & false & true \\ l_7 & W_{7,4} & W_{7,5} & W_{7,6} & W_{7,7} \\ l_{12} & false & false & W_{12,6} & true \\ l_{15} & false & false & false & true \end{array}$$

where
$W_{7,4} =$ "The next bus station is l_4",
$W_{7,5} =$ "The next bus station is l_5",
$W_{7,6} = W_{12,6} =$ "The next bus station is l_6",
$W_{7,7} =$ "The bus must continue stay in station l_7".

$$Z_3 = \langle \{l_1, l_4, l_{16}, l_{18}, l_{21}\}, \{l_8, l_9, l_{10}, l_{11}, l_{12}\}, r_3 \rangle$$

where

$$r_3 = \begin{array}{c|ccccc} & l_8 & l_9 & l_{10} & l_{11} & l_{12} \\ \hline l_1 & false & W_{1,9} & W_{1,10} & W_{1,11} & W_{1,12} \\ l_4 & W_{4,8} & W_{4,9} & W_{4,10} & W_{4,11} & false \\ l_{16} & W_{16,8} & W_{16,9} & W_{16,10} & false & W_{16,12} \\ l_{18} & W_{18,8} & false & false & false & W_{18,12} \\ l_{21} & W_{21,8} & false & false & false & W_{21,12} \end{array}$$

where
$W_{1,9} = W_{4,9} = W_{16,9} =$ "The next bus station is l_9",
$W_{1,10} = W_{4,10} = W_{16,10} =$ "The next bus station is l_{10}",
$W_{1,11} = W_{4,11} =$ "The next bus station is l_{11}",
$W_{1,12} = W_{16,12} = W_{18,12} = W_{21,12} =$ "The next bus station is l_{12}",
$W_{4,8} = W_{16,8} = W_{18,8} = W_{21,8} =$ "The next bus station is l_8".

$$Z_4 = \langle \{l_5, l_{11}, l_{17}, l_{20}, l_{25}\}, \{l_{13}, l_{14}, l_{15}, l_{16}, l_{17}\}, r_4 \rangle$$

where

$$r_4 = \begin{array}{c|ccccc} & l_{13} & l_{14} & l_{15} & l_{16} & l_{17} \\ \hline l_5 & W_{5,13} & W_{5,14} & false & false & W_{5,17} \\ l_{11} & W_{11,13} & W_{11,14} & false & W_{11,16} & W_{11,17} \\ l_{17} & W_{17,13} & W_{17,14} & W_{17,15} & W_{17,16} & W_{17,17} \\ l_{20} & false & false & W_{20,15} & W_{20,16} & W_{20,17} \\ l_{25} & false & false & W_{25,15} & W_{25,16} & W_{25,17} \end{array}$$

where
$W_{5,13} = W_{11,13} = W_{17,13} =$ "The next bus station is l_{13}",
$W_{5,14} = W_{11,14} = W_{17,14} =$ "The next bus station is l_{14}",
$W_{17,15} = W_{20,15} = W_{25,15} =$ "The next bus station is l_{15}",
$W_{11,16} = W_{17,16} = W_{20,16} = W_{25,16} =$ "The next bus station is l_{16}",
$W_{5,17} = W_{11,17} = W_{20,17} = W_{25,17} =$ "The bus station l_{17} is final for the bus",
$W_{17,17} =$ "The bus must continue stay in station l_{17}".

$$Z_5 = \langle \{l_{10}, l_{13}, l_{23}\}, \{l_{18}, l_{19}, l_{20}\}, r_5 \rangle$$

where

$$r_5 = \begin{array}{c|ccc} & l_{18} & l_{19} & l_{20} \\ \hline l_{10} & false & W_{10,19} & W_{10,20} \\ l_{13} & W_{13,18} & W_{13,19} & W_{13,20} \\ l_{23} & W_{23,18} & false & W_{23,20} \end{array}$$

where
$W_{10,19} = W_{13,19} =$ "The next bus station is l_{19}",
$W_{10,20} = W_{13,20} = W_{23,20} =$ "The next bus station is l_{20}",
$W_{13,18} = W_{23,18} =$ "The next bus station is l_{23}".

$$Z_6 = \langle \{l_9, l_{19}, l_{26}\}, \{l_{21}, l_{22}, l_{23}\}, r_6 \rangle$$

where

$$r_6 = \begin{array}{c|ccc} & l_{21} & l_{22} & l_{23} \\ \hline l_9 & false & W_{9,22} & W_{9,23} \\ l_{19} & W_{19,21} & W_{19,22} & false \\ l_{26} & W_{26,21} & false & W_{26,23} \end{array}$$

where
$W_{9,22} = W_{19,22} =$ "The next bus station is l_{22}",
$W_{9,23} = W_{9,23} = W_{26,23} =$ "The next bus station is l_{23}",
$W_{19,21} = W_{26,21} =$ "The next bus station is l_{21}".

$$Z_7 = \langle \{l_{14}, l_{22}, l_{27}\}, \{l_{24}, l_{25}, l_{26}\}, r_7 \rangle$$

where

$$r_7 = \begin{array}{c|ccc} & l_{24} & l_{25} & l_{26} \\ \hline l_{14} & true & false & false \\ l_{22} & true & false & false \\ l_{27} & false & W_{27,25} & W_{27,26} \end{array}$$

where
$W_{27,25}$ = "The next bus station is l_{25}",
$W_{27,26}$ = "The next bus station is l_{26}".

$$Z_8 = \langle \{l_{24}, l_{28}\}, \{l_{27}, l_{28}\}, r_8 \rangle$$

where

$$r_8 = \begin{array}{c|cc} & l_{27} & l_{28} \\ \hline l_{24} & false & true \\ l_{28} & W_{28,27} & W_{28,28} \end{array}$$

where
$W_{28,27}$ = "The next bus station is l_{27}",
$W_{28,28}$ = "The bus must continue stay in station l_{28}".

In the present model, we represent a small, but important part of the bus stations of Burgas. Some of them are initial-final bus stations (represented by transitions Z_1, Z_8 and their places l_3, l_{28}, respetively), some of them are intermediate bus stations (represented by transitions Z_3, Z_5, Z_6, Z_7), and some of them are simultaneously as initial-final, as well as intermediate bus stations (represented by transitions Z_2, Z_4 and their places l_7, l_{17}, respetively). In the model, we omit all intermediate bus stations between the given, to/from which there are not lines from/to other directions.

The so constructed GN-model can be used for simulation of different situations that can occur between the buses in real-time. As a result, we can obtain ideas e.g., for keeping or changing the schedule of concrete bus(es) in the current moment.

5 Ideas for Further Research

The present model raises different ideas for future research. One of these ideas is related to the novel multicriteria decision making method called "Intercriteria Analysis" [4,5], based on index matrices [4] that gives possibility for detecting existing relations between pairs of criteria from the set of evaluating criteria based on comparisons of the evaluations of the set of objects being evaluated. The first attempt to use Intercriteria Analysis for searching such patterns in urban bus transport network is described in [6].

Now, in the role of objects there can be the separate buses and of the criteria – the separate bus stations in the network. So, we can construct two IMs with the forms

$$A_e = \begin{array}{c|ccccccc} & O_1 & \cdots & O_i & \cdots & O_j & \cdots & O_n \\ \hline C_1 & e_{C_1,O_1} & \cdots & e_{C_1,O_i} & \cdots & e_{C_1,O_j} & \cdots & e_{C_1,O_n} \\ \vdots & \vdots & \ddots & \vdots & \ddots & \vdots & \ddots & \vdots \\ C_k & e_{C_k,O_1} & \cdots & e_{C_k,O_i} & \cdots & e_{C_k,O_j} & \cdots & e_{C_k,O_n} \\ \vdots & \vdots & \ddots & \vdots & \ddots & \vdots & \ddots & \vdots \\ C_l & e_{C_l,O_1} & \cdots & e_{C_l,O_i} & \cdots & e_{C_l,O_j} & \cdots & e_{C_l,O_n} \\ \vdots & \vdots & \ddots & \vdots & \ddots & \vdots & \ddots & \vdots \\ C_m & e_{C_m,O_1} & \cdots & e_{C_m,O_i} & \cdots & e_{C_m,O_j} & \cdots & e_{C_m,O_n} \end{array}$$

and

$$A_l = \begin{array}{c|ccccccc} & O_1 & \cdots & O_i & \cdots & O_j & \cdots & O_n \\ \hline C_1 & l_{C_1,O_1} & \cdots & l_{C_1,O_i} & \cdots & l_{C_1,O_j} & \cdots & l_{C_1,O_n} \\ \vdots & \vdots & \ddots & \vdots & \ddots & \vdots & \ddots & \vdots \\ C_k & l_{C_k,O_1} & \cdots & l_{C_k,O_i} & \cdots & l_{C_k,O_j} & \cdots & l_{C_k,O_n} \\ \vdots & \vdots & \ddots & \vdots & \ddots & \vdots & \ddots & \vdots \\ C_l & l_{C_l,O_1} & \cdots & l_{C_l,O_i} & \cdots & l_{C_l,O_j} & \cdots & l_{C_l,O_n} \\ \vdots & \vdots & \ddots & \vdots & \ddots & \vdots & \ddots & \vdots \\ C_m & l_{C_m,O_1} & \cdots & l_{C_m,O_i} & \cdots & l_{C_m,O_j} & \cdots & l_{C_m,O_n} \end{array},$$

where the evaluations e_{C_p,O_q} and l_{C_p,O_q} (for $1 \le p \le m, 1 \le q \le n$) represent the number of passengers who, respectively, enter or leave the q-th bus on p-th station. Given the collected data about the parameters e_{C_p,O_q} and l_{C_p,O_q}, the two IMs may give information not only about the passenger stream, but also about the relationships between the intensity of usage of separate bus lines.

On the other hand, if we construct the IM

$$A_t = \begin{array}{c|ccccccc} & O_1 & \cdots & O_i & \cdots & O_j & \cdots & O_n \\ \hline C_1 & t_{C_1,O_1} & \cdots & t_{C_1,O_i} & \cdots & t_{C_1,O_j} & \cdots & t_{C_1,O_n} \\ \vdots & \vdots & \ddots & \vdots & \ddots & \vdots & \ddots & \vdots \\ C_k & t_{C_k,O_1} & \cdots & t_{C_k,O_i} & \cdots & t_{C_k,O_j} & \cdots & t_{C_k,O_n} \\ \vdots & \vdots & \ddots & \vdots & \ddots & \vdots & \ddots & \vdots \\ C_l & t_{C_l,O_1} & \cdots & t_{C_l,O_i} & \cdots & t_{C_l,O_j} & \cdots & t_{C_l,O_n} \\ \vdots & \vdots & \ddots & \vdots & \ddots & \vdots & \ddots & \vdots \\ C_m & t_{C_m,O_1} & \cdots & t_{C_m,O_i} & \cdots & t_{C_m,O_j} & \cdots & t_{C_m,O_n} \end{array},$$

where parameters t_{C_p,O_q} represent the lag times of the buses arriving to the respective stations, we can search possibility to change the bus trafics with aim to minimize these lags.

Acknowledgments. The second and third authors are thankful for the support provided by the Bulgarian National Science Fund under Grant Ref. No. DFNI-I-02-5.

References

1. Alexieva, J., Choy, E., Koycheva, E.: Review, bibliography on generalized nets theory, applications. In: Choy, E., Krawczak, M., Shannon, A., Szmidt, E. (eds.) A Survey of Generalized Nets, Raffles KvB Monograph No. 10, pp. 207–301 (2007)
2. Atanassov, K.: Generalized Nets. World Scientific, Singapore (1991)
3. Atanassov, K.: On Generalized Nets Theory. Prof. M. Drinov Academic Publ. House, Sofia (2007)
4. Atanassov, K.: Index Matrices: Towards an Augmented Matrix Calculus. Springer, Cham (2014)
5. Atanassov, K., Mavrov, D., Atanassova, V.: Intercriteria decision making: a new approach for multicriteria decision making, based on index matrices and intuitionistic fuzzy sets. Issues Intuitionistic Fuzzy Sets Generalized Nets **11**, 1–8 (2014)
6. Valkov, I., Mavrov, D., Sotirova, E.: InterCriteria analysis over public transport system data. In: Proceedings of the IEEE 8th International Conference on Intelligent Systems, Sofia, pp. 560–563, September 2016

Author Index

Printed in the United States
By Bookmasters